AF413210

Dempsey
Bob

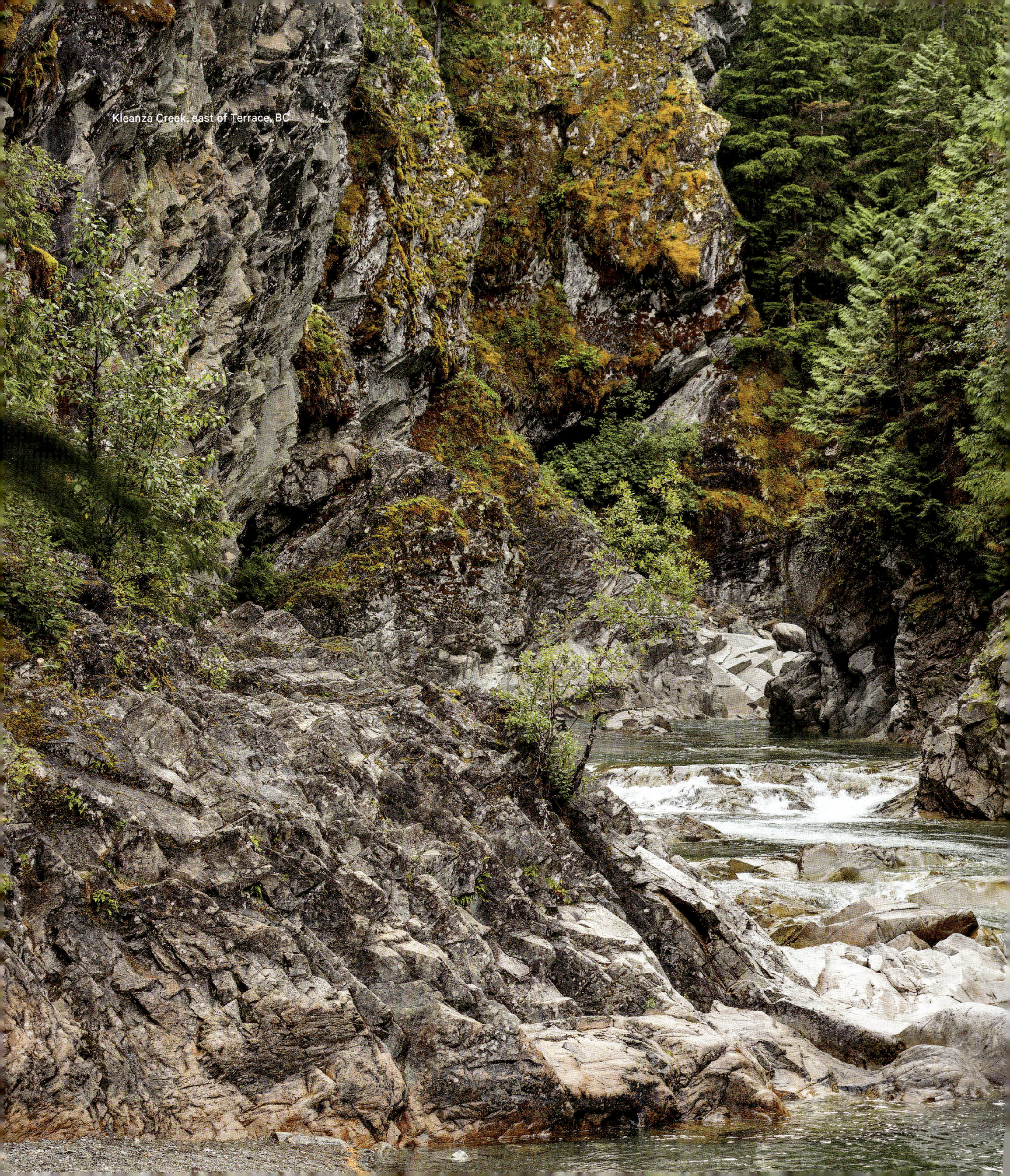
Kleanza Creek, east of Terrace, BC

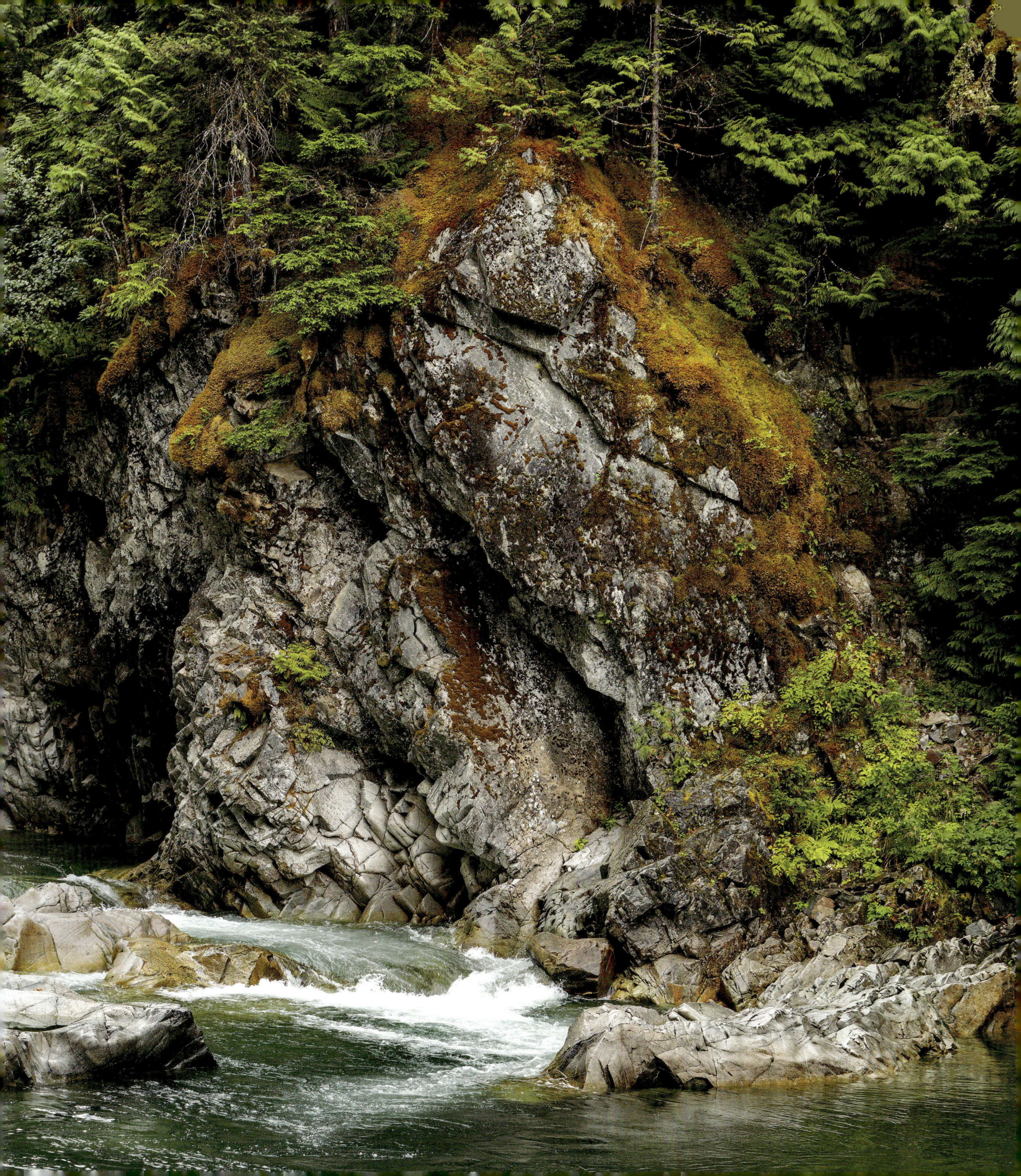

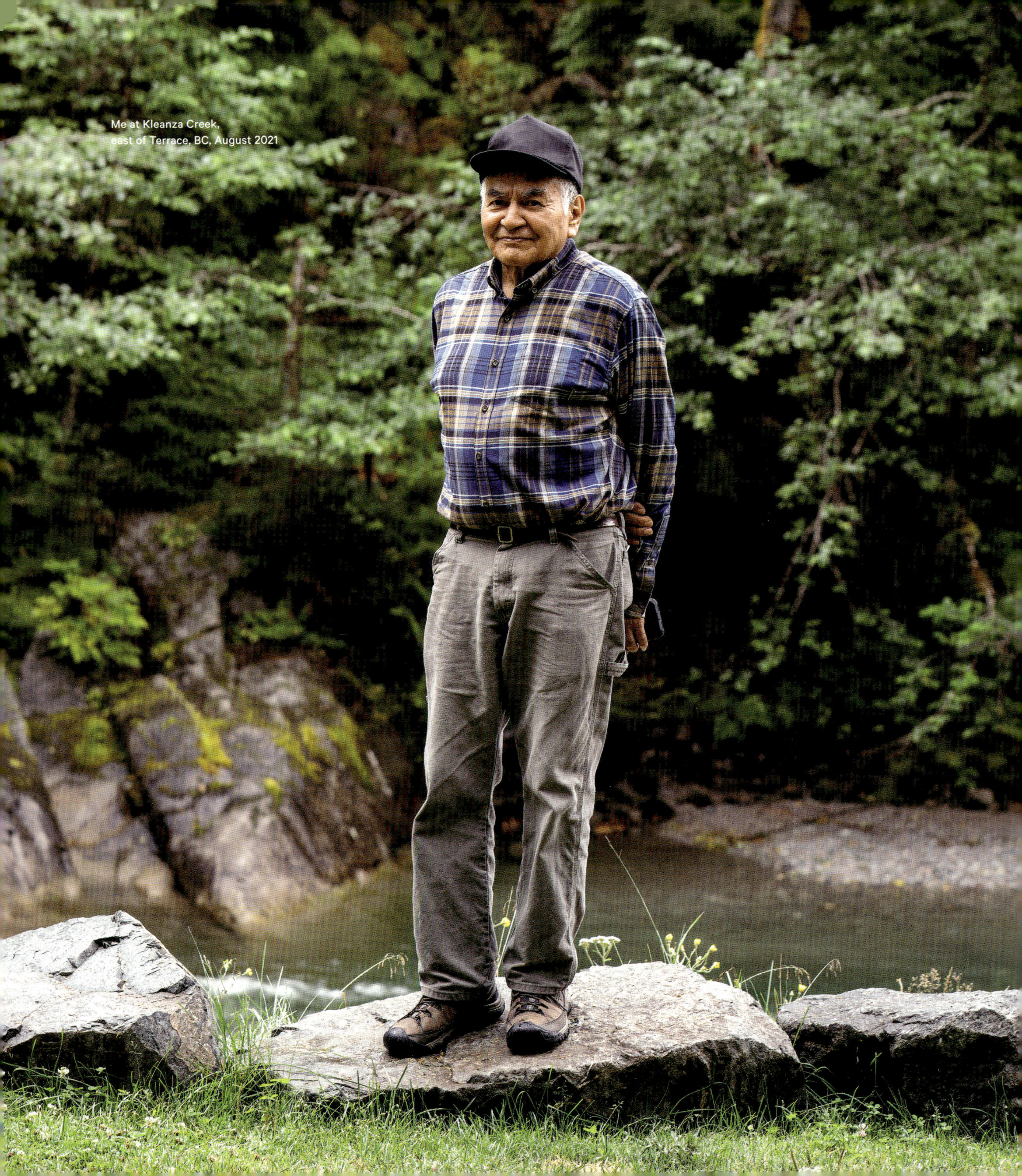
Me at Kleanza Creek,
east of Terrace, BC, August 2021

Dempsey Bob

In His Own Voice

EDITED BY SARAH MILROY

AUDAIN ART MUSEUM · McMichael Canadian Art Collection d'art canadien · Figure.1

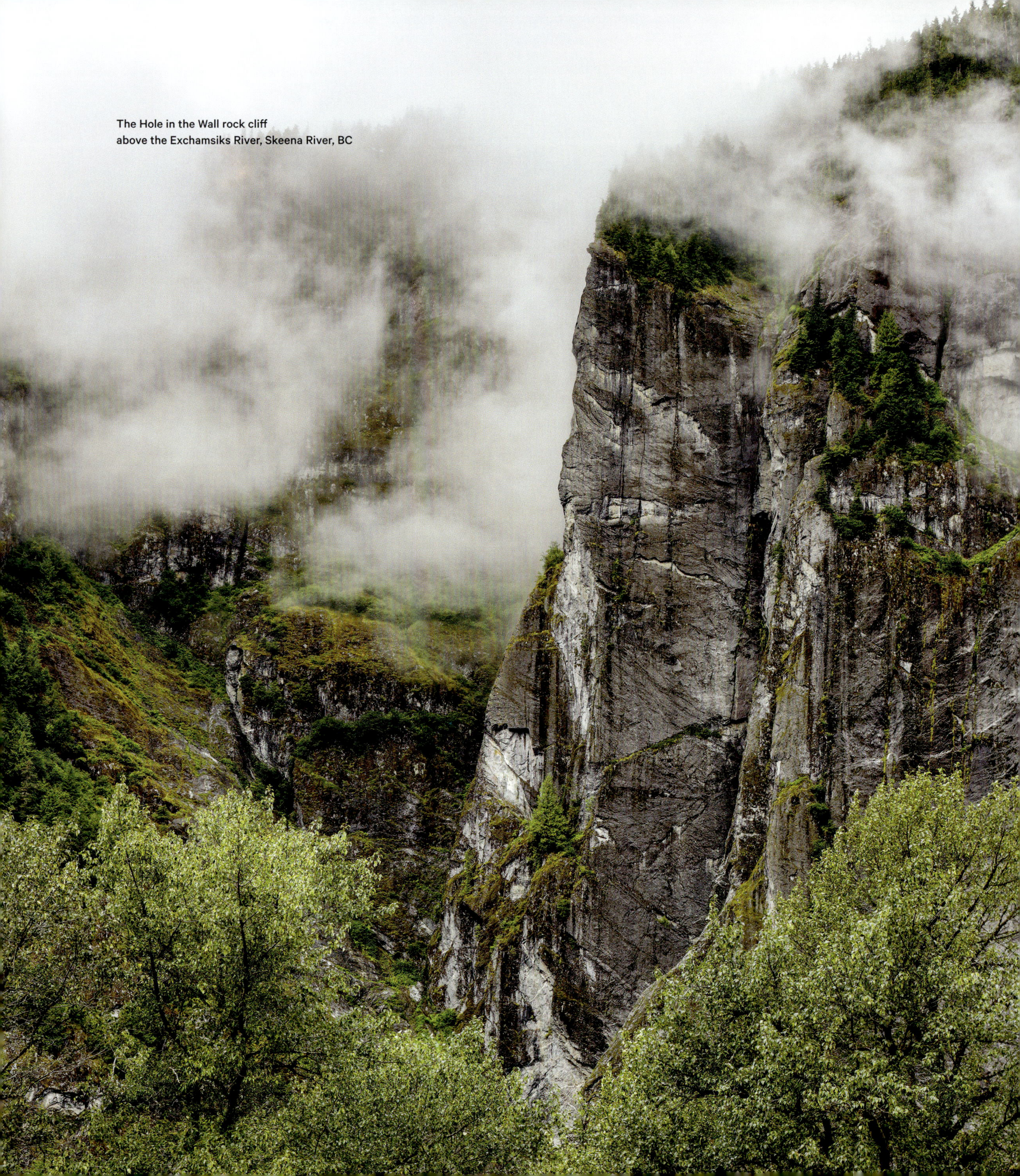

The Hole in the Wall rock cliff
above the Exchamsiks River, Skeena River, BC

This book is dedicated to the memory of my grandparents Julia and Johnny Sinkoots Carlick; my mother and father, Flossie and Johnnie Bob; and my great-aunts Eva Carlick and Helen Carlick. I dedicate this also to my family—Linda, Virginia, Lovetta, Marie, Merle, Charlie Pete, Willie, Tony, and Lorgan—and to my wife, Margaret, my children, David and Tanya, and my grandchildren, Grayson, Roy, Keely, and Nate.

DEMPSEY BOB

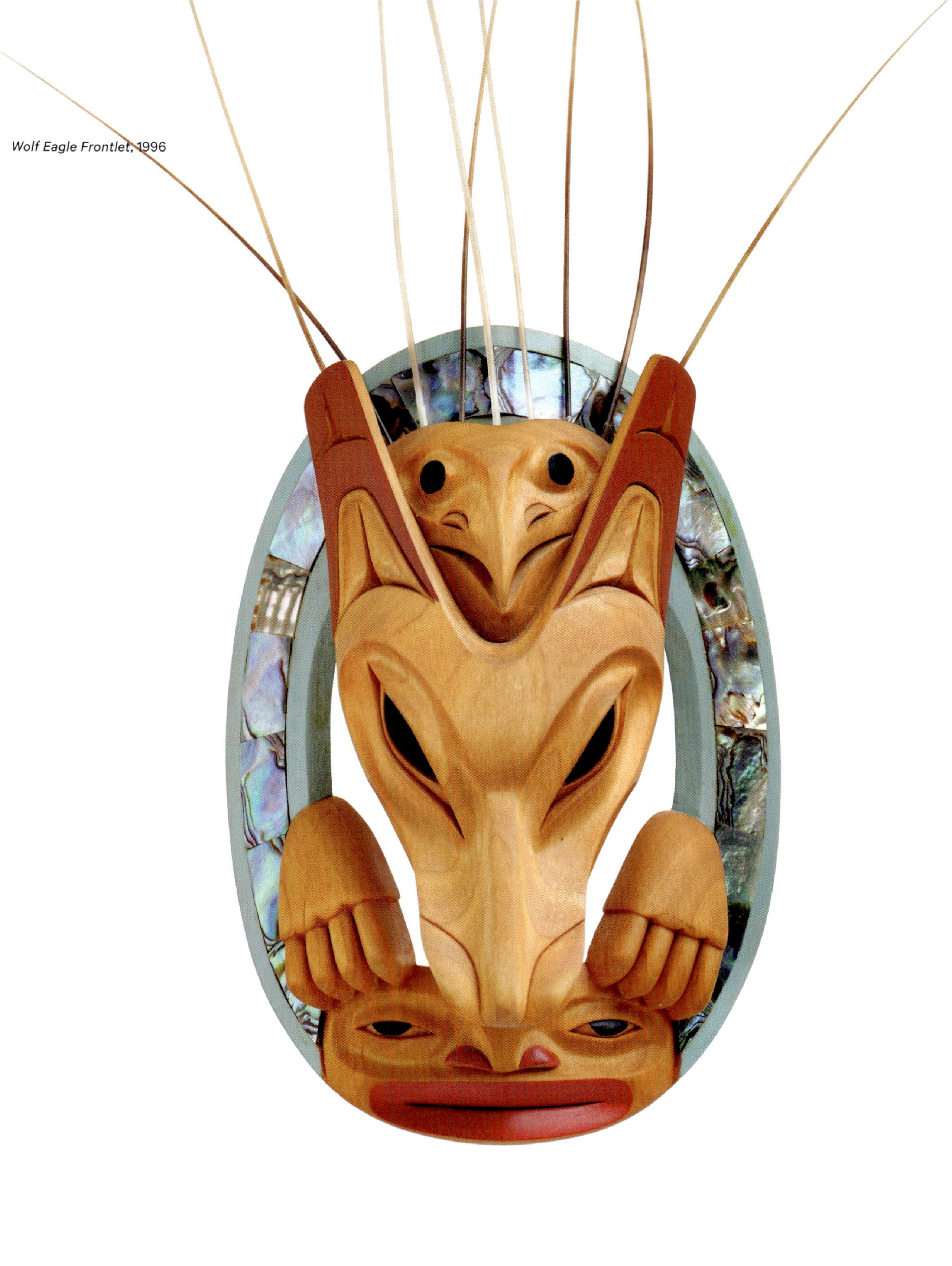

Wolf Eagle Frontlet, 1996

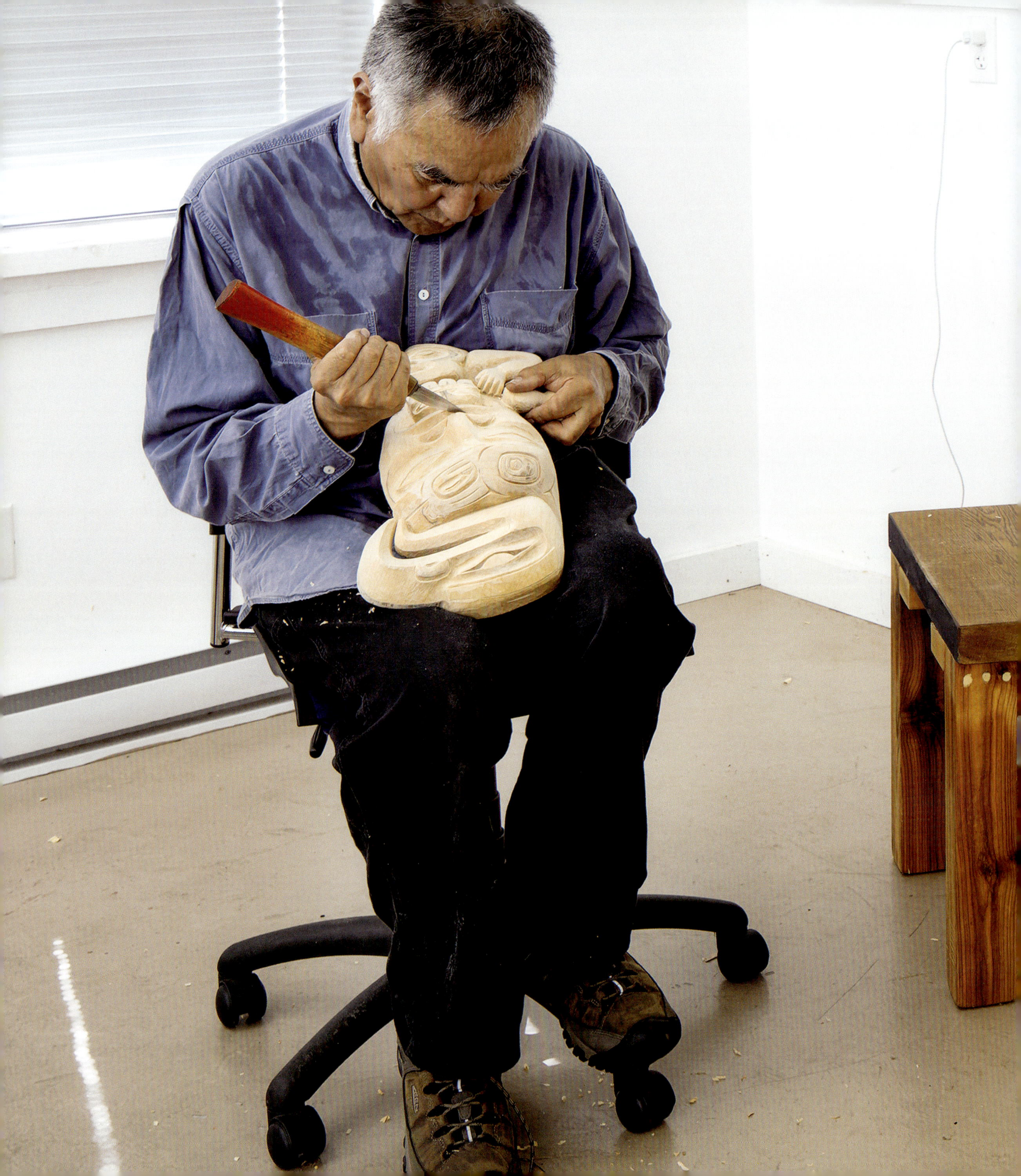

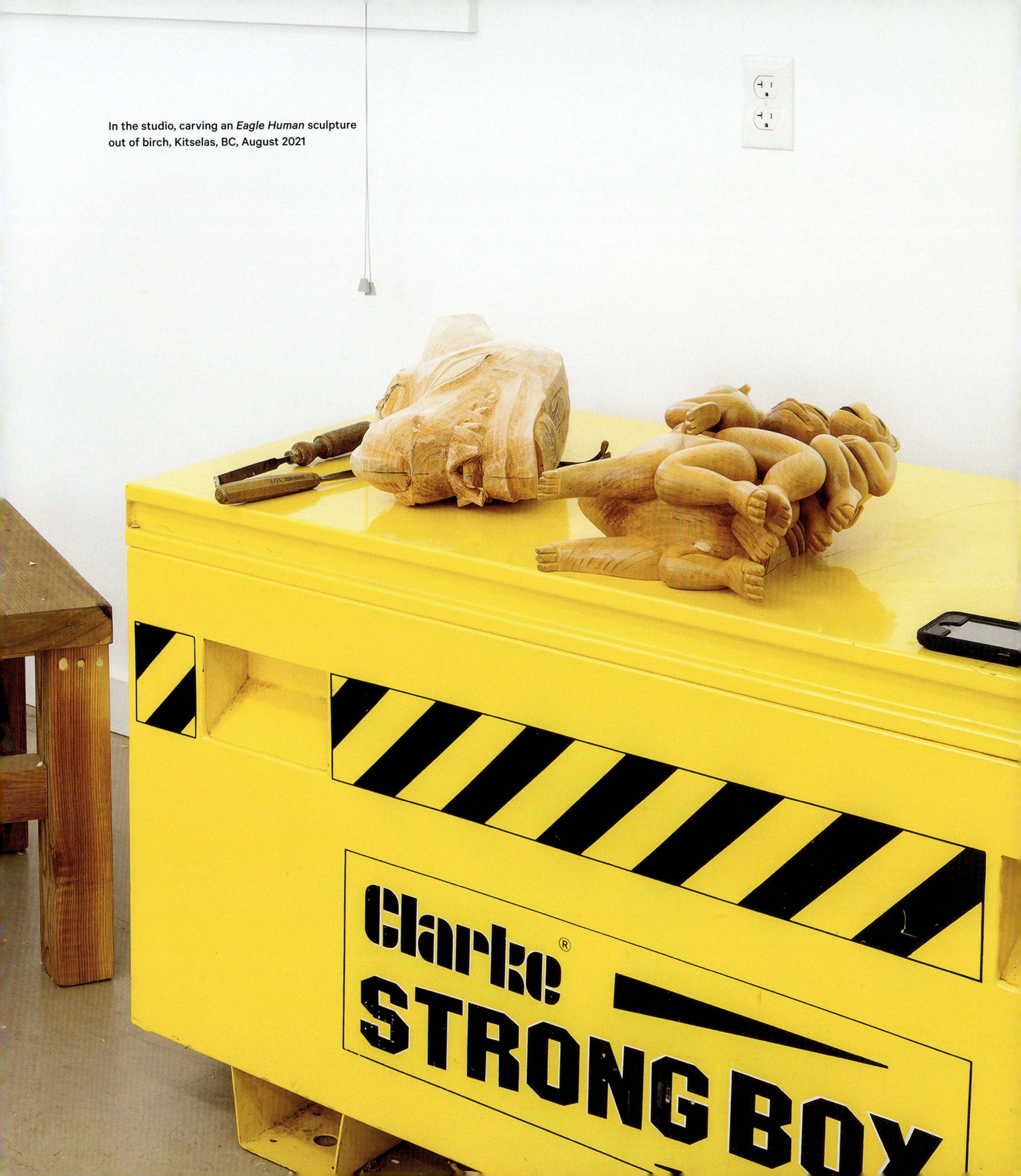

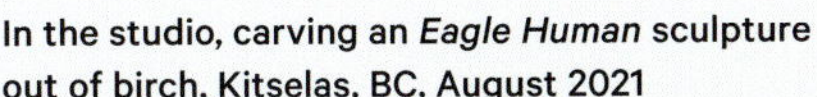
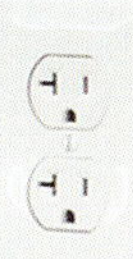

In the studio, carving an *Eagle Human* sculpture out of birch, Kitselas, BC, August 2021

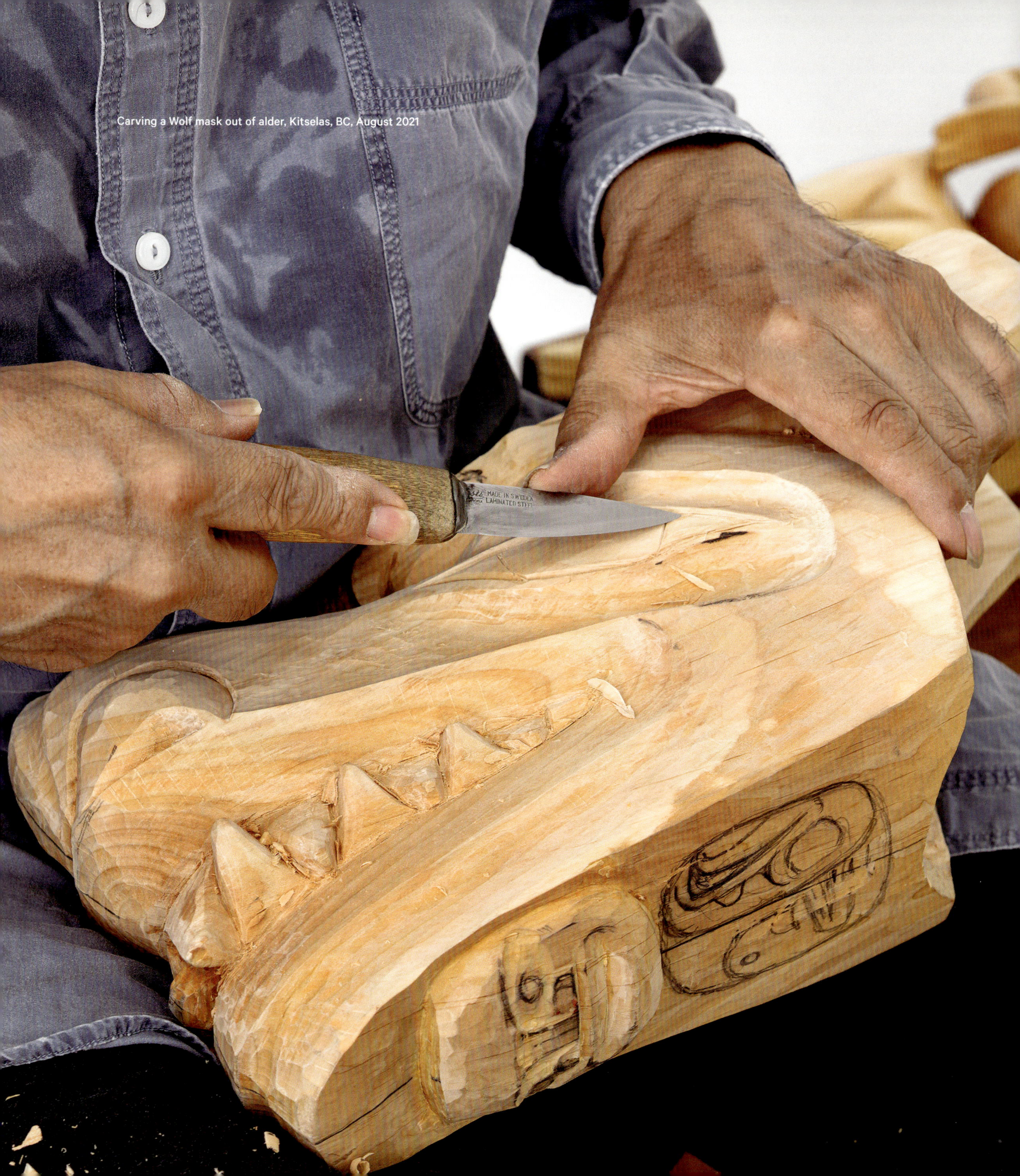
Carving a Wolf mask out of alder, Kitselas, BC, August 2021

CONTENTS

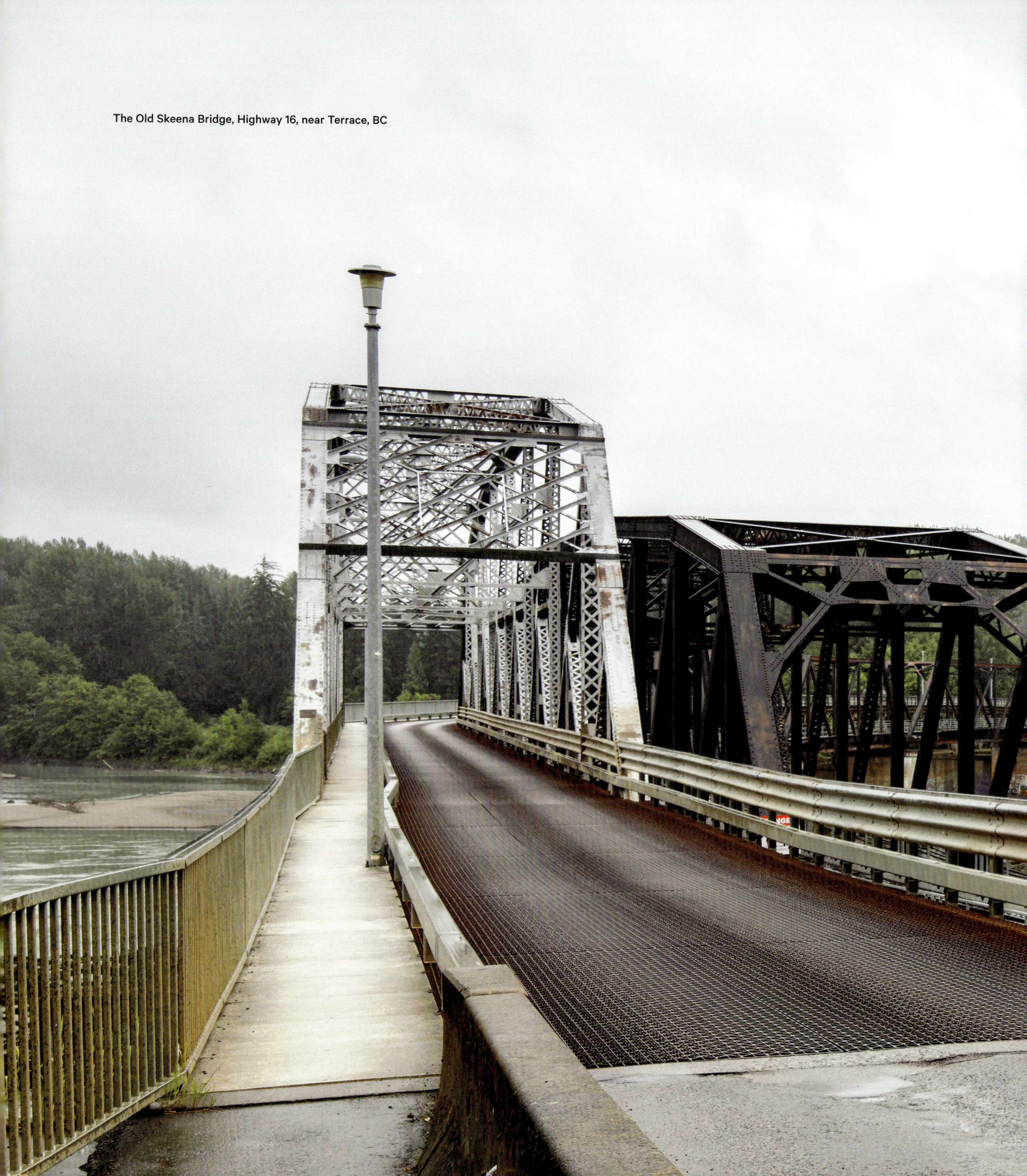
The Old Skeena Bridge, Highway 16, near Terrace, BC

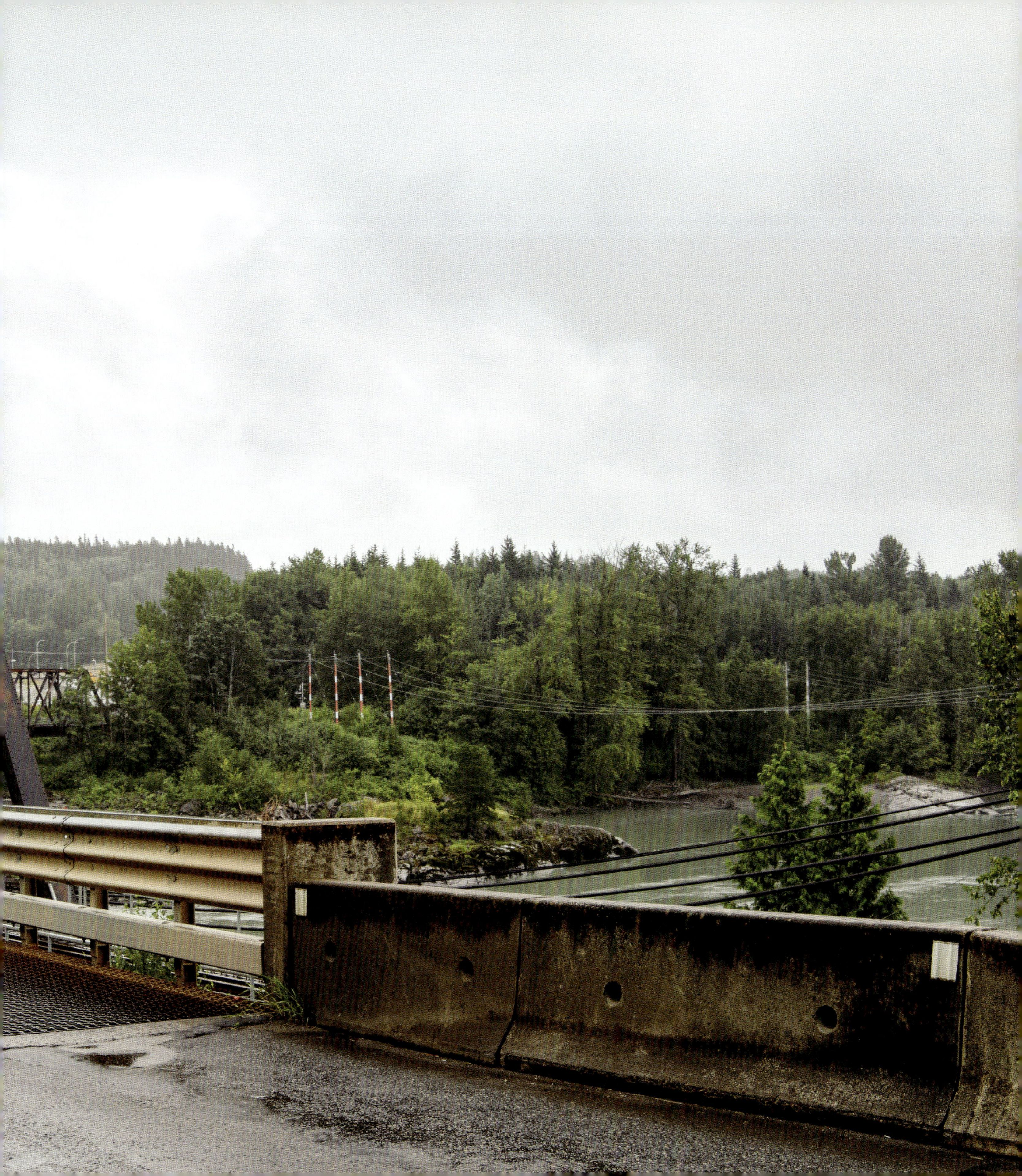

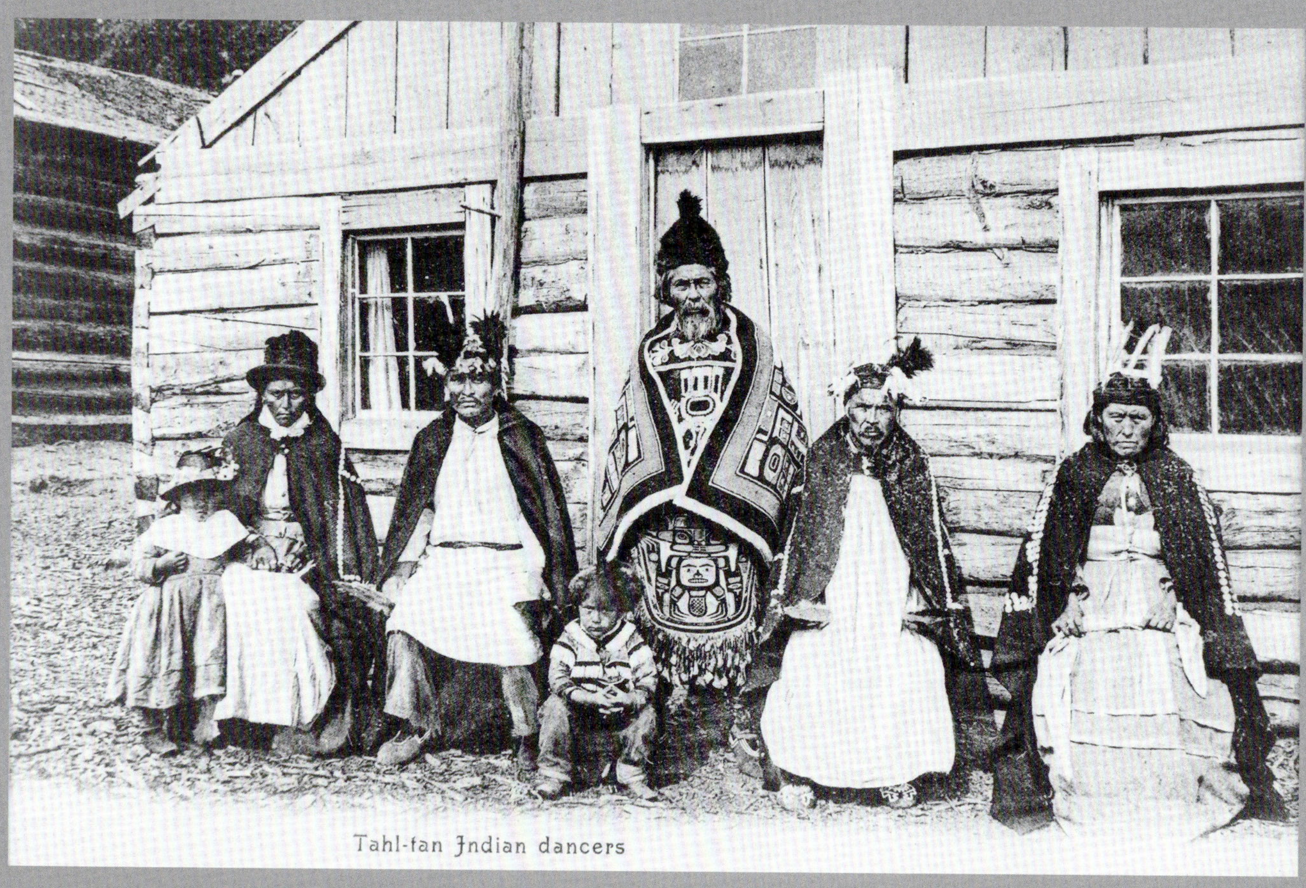

My maternal great-great-grandfather, Étmatá Sinkoots (centre), and my grandfather
Johnny Sinkoots Carlick (the little boy in front), Tahltan village, BC, 1893

16

OUR FAMILY AND CLAN

We get our clans and our traditional names and also our songs from our mother's side of the family. That's how we get our crests.

I am a Wolf, because my mother was a Wolf. Her name was Flossie Carlick, later Flossie Bob. And her mother was a Wolf— Julia Carlick was her name. She was from Atlin, BC.

My father, Johnnie Bob, was a Raven, and my mother's father, Johnny Sinkoots Carlick, was a Raven. He was Tahltan. We don't marry the same crest. That is against our laws. We marry the opposite clan—that's how our system works. I am from the Yin-ya-dee house. We have the Wolf and the Grizzly Bear as our crests and names. I have a traditional name too. It means "watching out for war."

This picture (opposite) was taken in 1893 at Tahltan village. At the centre is my great-great-grandfather Étmatá Sinkoots on my mother's side. The little boy in front is my grandfather Johnny Sinkoots Carlick. His grandfather was a healer. If your leg was broken he could set it, and he could give you medicine.

Some of the meanings of the family names got lost with the sickness. Sometimes now we just have the names. Dr. Sinkoots: Étmatá was his traditional name. In the picture there you can see his chilkat blanket, his ceremonial clothing. He was a Raven.

Dr. Sinkoots had three chilkat blankets—those are chief's robes. He is wearing his apron here too (p. 18); it's now in the Smithsonian, and his blanket may be there too. The apron was collected by George Emmons[1] around the turn of the twentieth century. The shirt he's wearing here is a Raven shirt. It's now in the museum in Victoria, the Royal BC Museum [#14832].

My great-grandfather on my mother's side was named Judson Ward, a Raven, and he was a carver. He came from Hoonah, Alaska, up near Juneau, a Tlingit village. He made sheep-horn spoons, masks, small totem poles. All of it is lost now, like so many things.

My grandmother Julia was originally from Atlin in northwest British Columbia, and my grandfather Johnny Sinkoots Carlick —we called him Johnny Sinkoots—lived in Telegraph Creek, 270 miles away. Before they were married, he used to go over

1. George Thornton Emmons (1852–1945) was an American ethnographic photographer who collected Tlingit and Tahltan cultural materials from the late nineteenth and early twentieth centuries. He sold much of his collection to the American Museum of Natural History in New York City and the Field Museum of Natural History in Chicago. Years after his death, a book of his writings, *The Tlingit Indians*, was published in 1991.

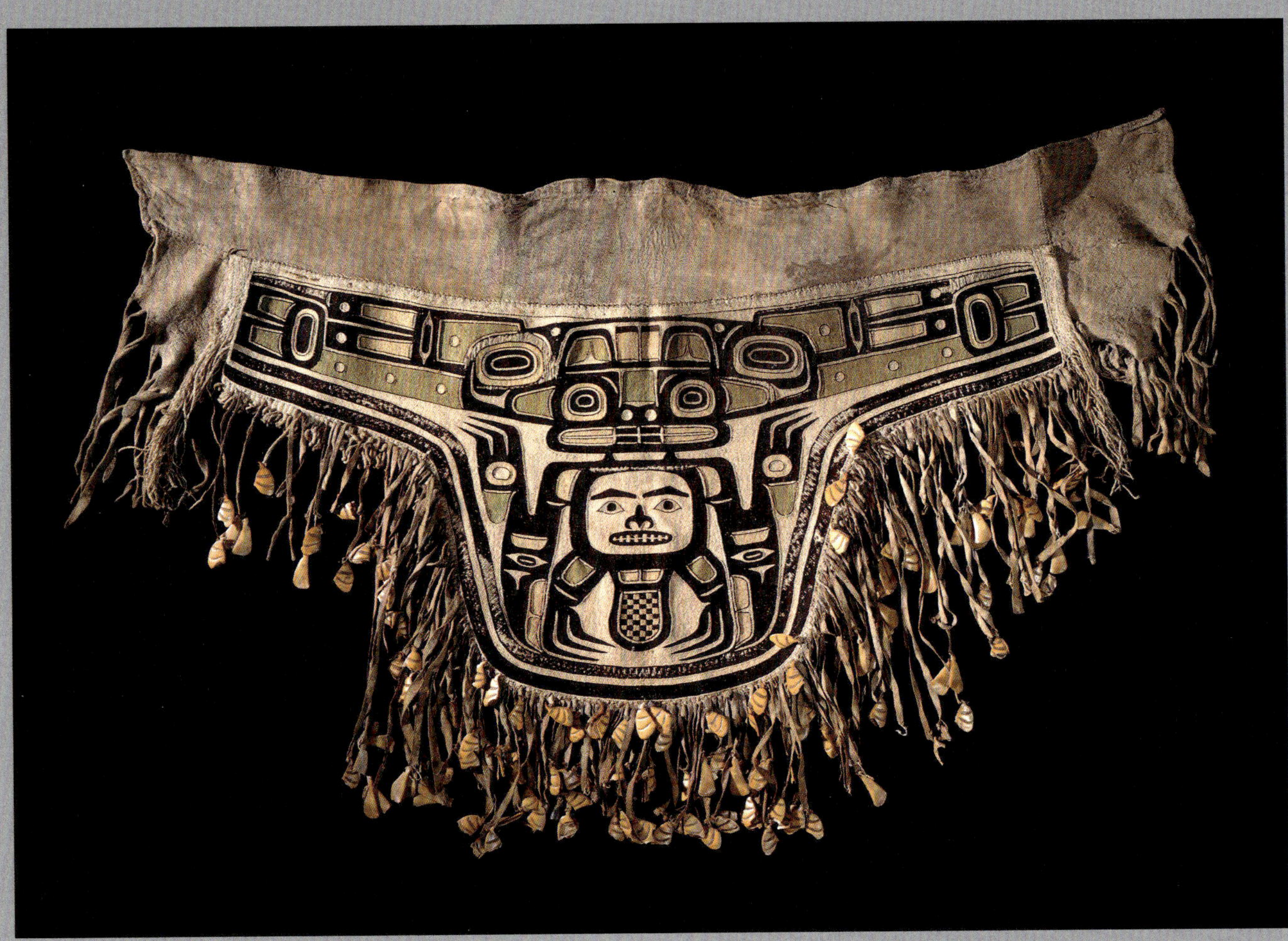

Unidentified Tlingit / Tahltan Maker, *Dance Apron*, late 19th century: cultural belonging of Étmatá Sinkoots; see photograph, p. 16

there to see her by dog team in the wintertime. It was cold—sometimes thirty, forty, fifty degrees below—just to see my grandmother. He used to walk there, too, in the summer. Just him and his dog. He used to say, "Boy, was I in love!" There has always been intermarriage between our communities. There was always trade and travel. Bringing in new blood, you are keeping the bloodlines strong.

My grandfather's village got its English name because they had built that line across to Europe, and it crossed the river there at Telegraph Creek.[2] That was way before we were there, back in his time, but you could still see the wires when we were going to our traplines. They looked like big telephone lines up on poles.

2. In 1866 an American–Russian telegraph line, meant to connect San Francisco to Moscow and then to Europe, was built from California up through the western United States, British Columbia, and Russian America (now Alaska). It was to connect to Russia via the Bering Sea. Part of the line was installed through the BC homeland of the Tahltan people, which led to their community being named Telegraph Creek. That line was abandoned in 1867, after a transatlantic telegraph cable had been successfully completed by American interests in 1866.

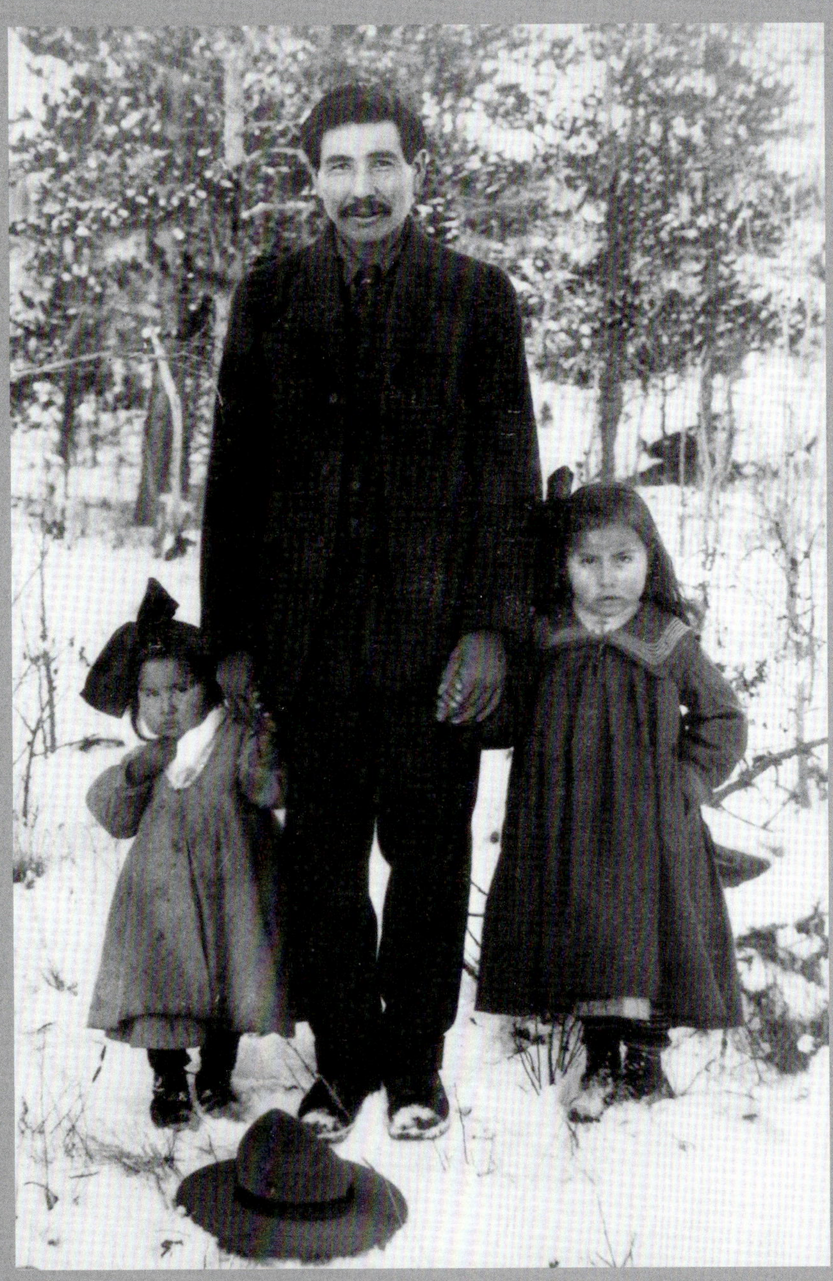

My maternal great-grandfather, Judson Ward, a carver from Hoonah,
Alaska, with his daughters Helen (left) and Julia, who would be the wife
of Johnny Sinkoots Carlick, and my grandmother, undated photo

THE EPIDEMICS

After the First World War, there was that big flu, the Spanish flu,[3] and it was killing a lot of people. Before that there was the smallpox. My great-grandfather Judson Ward, he took my grandmother Julia out on the trapline, with the other children and my great-grandmother, up in the mountains near Atlin.

My grandmother was just a little girl, and he made them all stay in the camp up there, and they kept that camp spotless. They had to wash and bathe all the time, sterilize their pots and pans. He boiled the knives and forks in hot water. He knew about germs; I don't know how he knew.

He kept people away with his gun. If anyone came into the canyon, he would go down there with his gun and he would chase them away. That's how he saved my grandmother from getting sick.

When they went back to Atlin, half our people were gone from the sickness going around. We were related to almost everyone in that village. That's why my grandmother left Atlin. My grandfather was Tahltan, from Telegraph Creek. That's where they started their family.

3. The Spanish influenza pandemic, which began in 1918 and lasted for nearly two years, killed an estimated fifty million people worldwide. Indigenous communities in Alaska were particularly hard hit, representing an estimated 80 percent of those who died from the flu in the state.

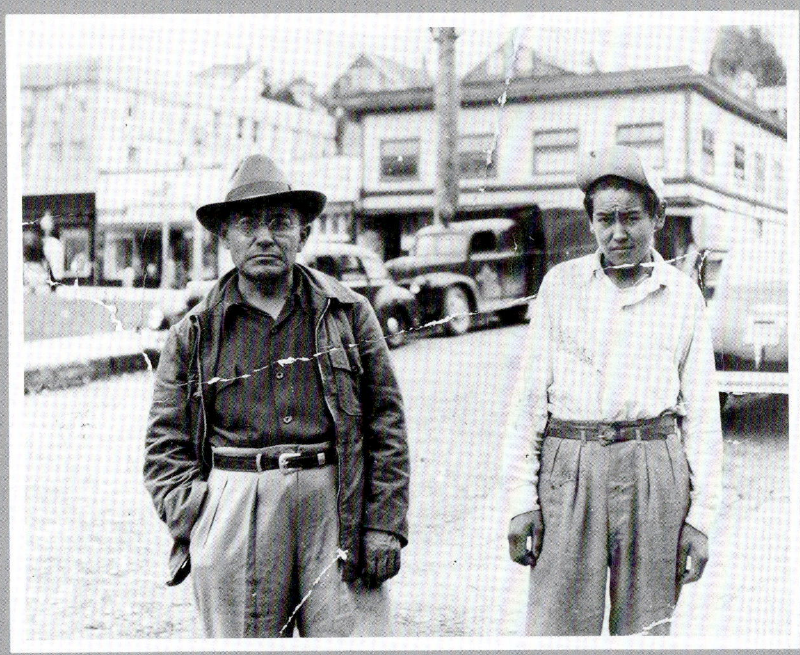

Johnny Sinkoots Carlick, my maternal grandfather, and his son
Herbert Carlick, my uncle, on Fulton Street, Prince Rupert, BC, 1950s

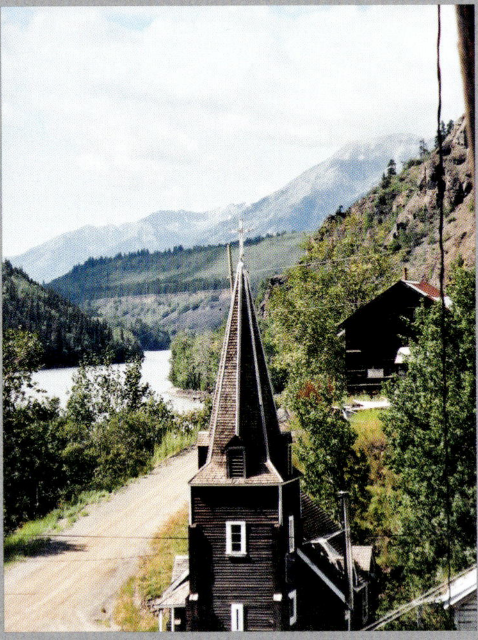

St. Aidan's Anglican Church (still standing) and the
mighty Stikine River, Telegraph Creek, BC, undated

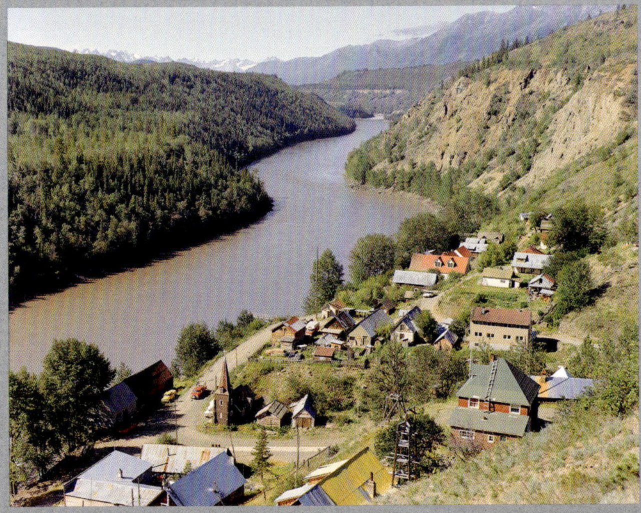

Telegraph Creek and the Stikine River, 1971

WHY WE LEFT TELEGRAPH CREEK

I was born in Telegraph Creek but grew up down in Port Edward. I still have a brother, nieces, and nephews living up there, and a brother in Lower Post. Back then, there were ten of us altogether, and I am nearer in age to the younger ones. I'm the fourth youngest.

Growing up, I got to hear stories from my mother, from the Elders at Port Edward, and after we moved down there, from my grandfather Johnny Sinkoots, and from the Elders in Port Edward too—they all started telling me stories. When we were washing dishes my mother would tell us stories. I was lucky. When the television came in, the stories stopped. But I was living in Prince Rupert by then.

I'll tell you why we left Telegraph Creek. They had taken some of the children to the residential school in Lower Post, near the border of the Yukon. Bad stuff happened there. It still affects us. We weren't allowed to speak our language, sing our songs—all that stuff. So we moved down to Port Edward. I was four or five years old. Otherwise, I would have had to go to residential school. Now they've destroyed that building.[4]

4. The Lower Post Indian Residential School opened in 1951. It was operated by the Catholic Church until 1969, when it was taken over by the federal government, which closed the school in 1975. In 2021 the building was demolished, to be replaced by a community centre.

So we left Telegraph Creek in 1952, on the riverboat down to Wrangell, Alaska. I remember leaving that morning, walking down to the creek, and then to the riverboat. We didn't know we were going for good, and we had never seen anywhere else. When you're a kid you don't realize stuff like that until later. But I knew I didn't want to leave.

There are sandbars outside of Wrangell, and I remember we got stuck there until the tide came in. Then we flew from Wrangell down to Ketchikan, Alaska, and from Ketchikan to Prince Rupert. We had never been on a plane before. People were telling us about the ocean, that it was salty, and we couldn't believe it. We had to taste it.

My dad had been working at the cannery in Port Edward; he had a job there at Nelson Brothers.[5] Before that, my mother's father, Johnny Sinkoots, had worked there too. My great-aunt Eva Carlick—she was married to Tom Carlick, Johnny Sinkoots's twin brother. They worked in Ketchikan, they worked all over in the canneries in the summer, and then went back home to Telegraph Creek to trap and hunt in the winter.

My grandfather Johnny Sinkoots loved travelling, he loved working and doing stuff. That's where I got it from, always working like he did. He would come back to Telegraph and tell everyone there that there was work down in Port Edward.

Johnnie Bob, my father—he left for Port Edward because the fur market was down.[6] They just weren't getting the prices. My dad had been trapping beaver, but he couldn't make a living. My uncle has told me that the last time they went trapping they made $7 and their grocery bill at the Hudson's Bay store was $20 and they couldn't even pay that. So what they did was cut wood, and they made enough money to travel. And that's when my dad left and went down to Port Edward, because of the canneries. They needed a lot of men.

In those days they had to work the fish right away, otherwise it spoiled. You had to work till it was finished, no matter what time of day it was. He had been down there for about a year on his own and had saved enough money to bring us down too.

5. The Port Edward cannery was operated by Nelson Brothers between 1943 and 1981. Nelson Brothers had plants in Masset on Haida Gwaii and Prince Rupert on the British Columbia mainland; these were among the most important fish-packing companies on the West Coast.

6. The fur trade in the Canadian North had been in steady decline from the mid-1950s. The decreased need for furs during the Second World War had caused several larger northern fur companies to stop operating, and the Hudson's Bay Company closed many of their trade businesses in favour of retail outlets.

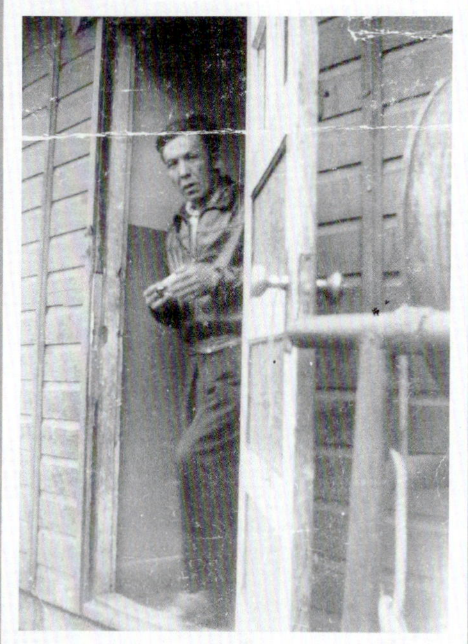

EMPLOYMENT RECORD			FORM 544-A. 2M. 6-51. JACKSON'S.
Last Name	First Name		Middle Name
BOB	Johnnie		

Address		Phone	White	MaleX
Telegraph Creek. B.C.			Native X	Female
			Chinese	Dependents
Date of Birth	Place of Birth		Japanese	XX 8 9
AUG 15, 1907			S. MX D. W.	
Payroll Classification			Rate of Pay	
Labourer			Starting Date	1952

New		In Case of Emergency Notify
Re-Hire	X	
Transfer		
Re-classified		U.I.C. No.
Plant	P.E.	A-847-435

Dad's employment record from the Nelson Brothers Cannery, Port Edward, BC

My father, Johnnie Bob (Raven Clan), at the Nelson Brothers Cannery, Port Edward, BC, early 1950s

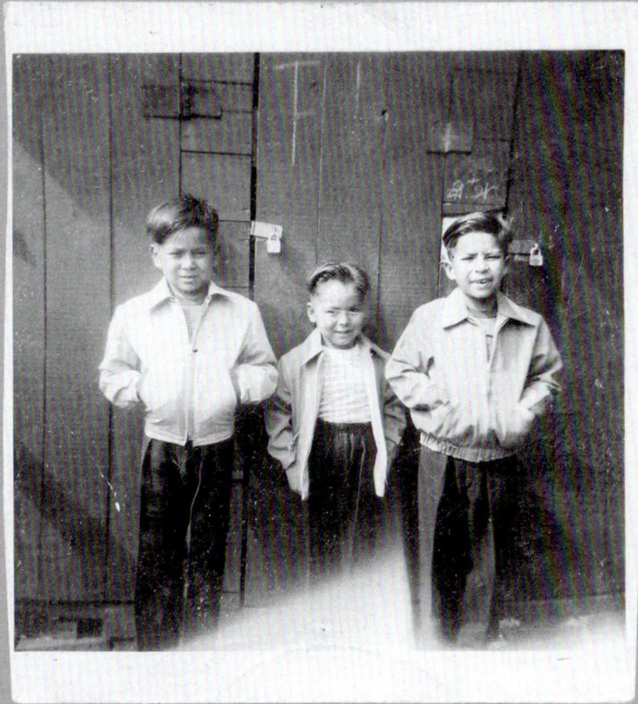

Cannery kids: me, age eight (left), with two of my brothers, Lorgan (centre) and Tony, Nelson Brothers Cannery, Port Edward, BC, about 1956

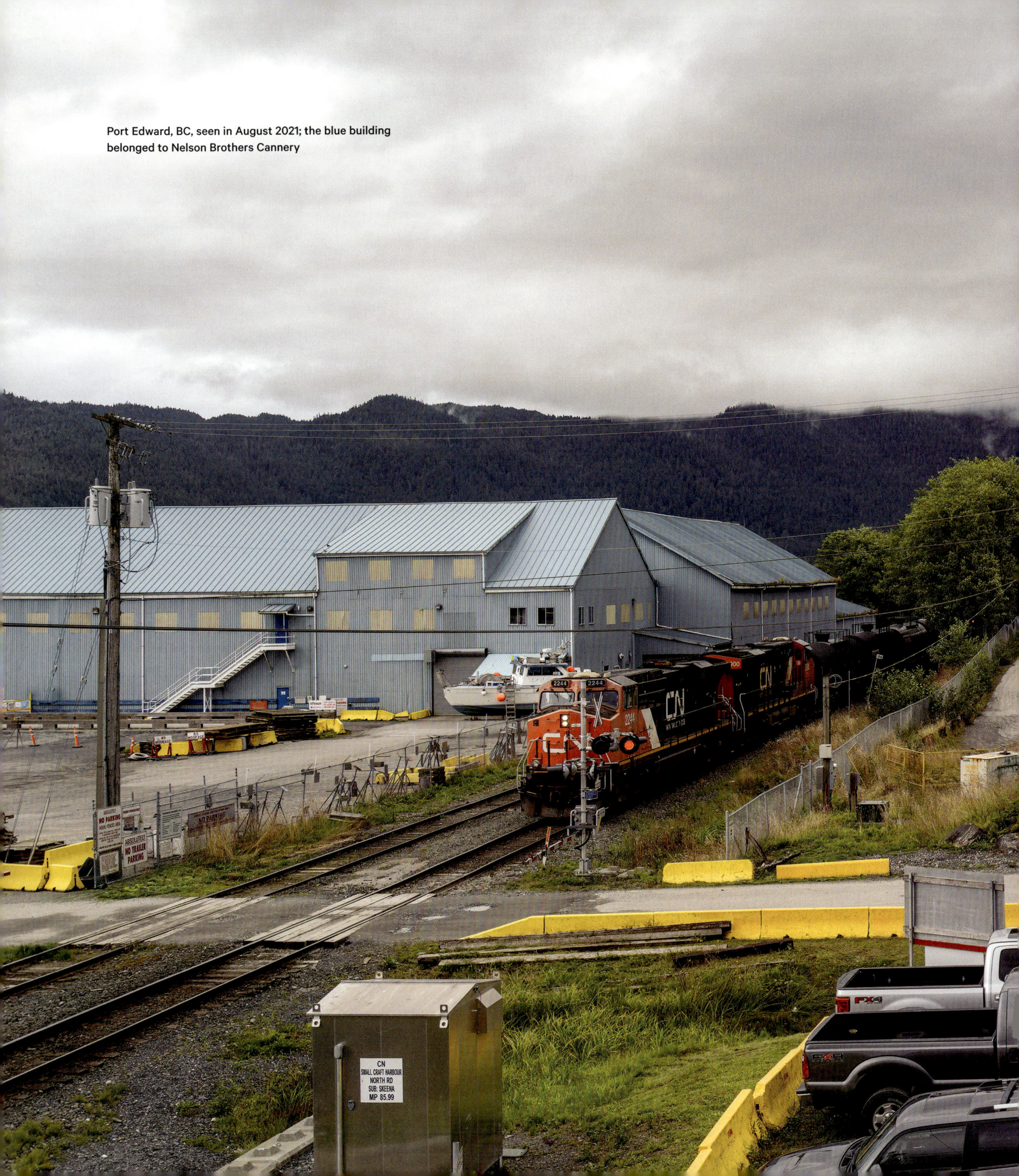
Port Edward, BC, seen in August 2021; the blue building belonged to Nelson Brothers Cannery

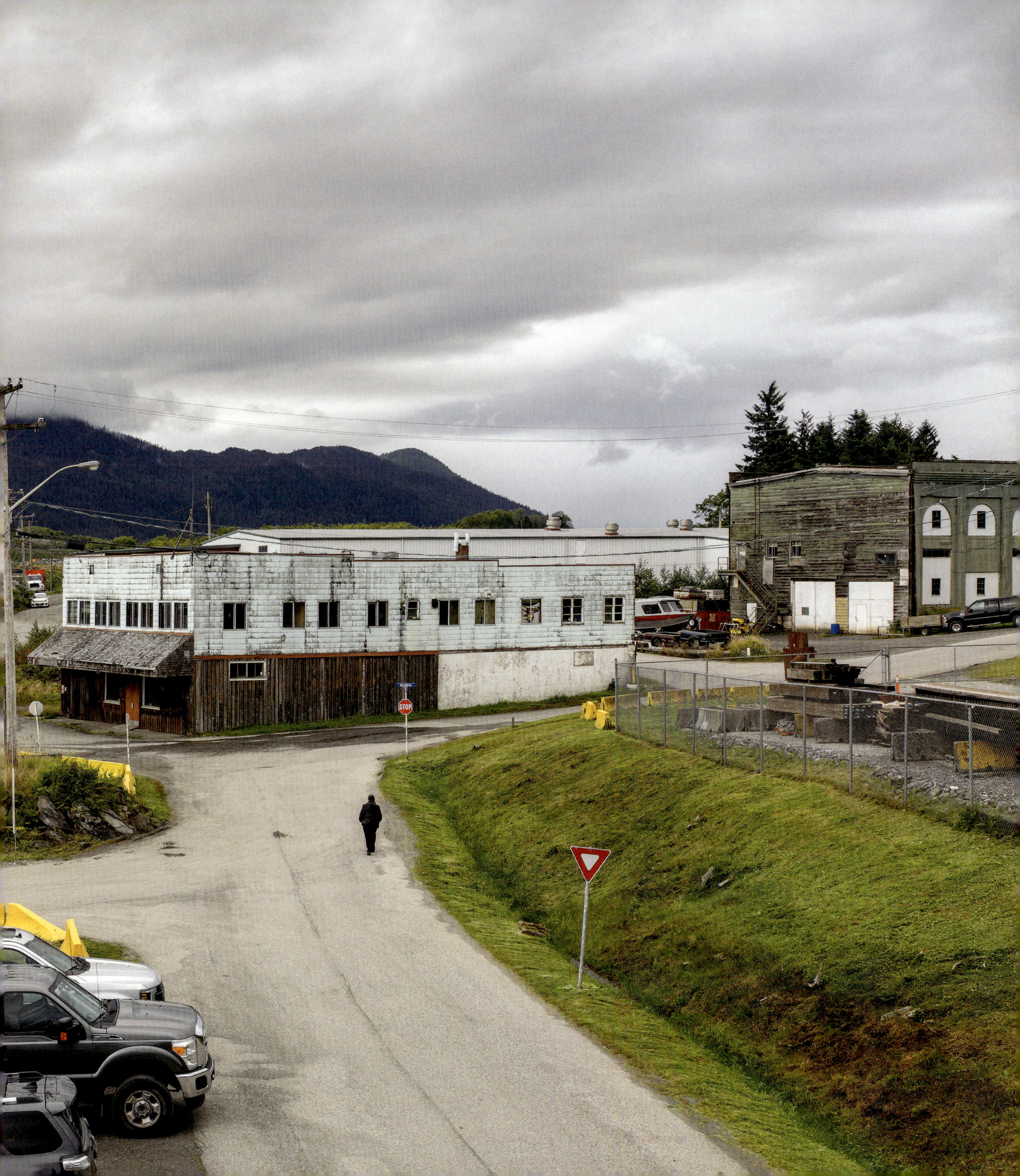

So that's how we got to Port Edward. My mum, Flossie Bob, she worked at the Port Edward Cannery. Everybody worked there—all my relatives, my sisters, my brother, my uncles, my aunties, even my grandpa worked there.

We were only ten kilometres from Prince Rupert. At the cannery at Port Edward we were all segregated. There was a Native village in the cannery, and there was a white village, a Japanese village, a Chinese village.

The women did the cleaning of the fish—that was the more labour-intensive part. They worked fourteen-, sixteen-hour days and then they'd get up in the morning and do it again. The Chinese and the Japanese—you know how many they cleaned in ten hours? Two thousand fish an hour. This was the first time the Japanese were allowed to come back onto the coast after the Second World War, in the early 1950s.[7] All the kids went to school together in the school in Port Edward.

There used to be five canneries in Prince Rupert and another five up along the Skeena River.[8] They had started back in the 1880s and '90s—that's when they came. This was Cannery Row. Different tribes tended to work at different canneries. Some of them were mixed but a lot of them would go to one village to recruit, and they would all come down together. Hazelton would come down here and work in the Cassiar Cannery. The Nisga'a would be at North Pacific. It went like that. That way the communities could stay together. But there was mixing too.

The Inverness Cannery was one of the earliest ones; it opened in 1876.[9] That's where Charles Edenshaw worked,[10] with his wife. There were lots of Haida there. No one has really written the history of it. The Nelson Brothers Cannery in Port Edward was mostly where my family worked. One summer my sisters Linda and Virginia worked at the North Pacific Cannery, hand-canning, because the cannery where they worked in Prince Rupert burned down. They broke a world record hand-canning that summer—the machine-canning operation had shut down at North Pacific in 1971. There was a bunch of them—there was Sunnyside Cannery, Oceanside Cannery, Cassiar Cannery.

When you go visit these old canneries now you can feel how hard these old guys worked, man. Holy shit, they were tough.

7. In 1946, following the dispossession and internment of twelve thousand Japanese Canadians during the Second World War, Prime Minister Mackenzie King announced that Japanese Canadians based in British Columbia had to relocate east of the Rocky Mountains. Although the policy was overturned in 1949, and Japanese Canadians were allowed freedom of movement along the BC coast, the effects of the policy caused lasting damage to the Japanese Canadian community.

8. The fishing industry and canneries employed thousands of people in Prince Rupert beginning in the 1940s. Some of the notable canneries there included the Prince Rupert Fisheries Plant (1940–42, 1950–71), Seal Cove Cannery (1943–53), Babcock Fisheries (1975–93), and Prince Rupert Fishermen's Co-Operative Plant (1961–89). There were several canneries built along the Skeena River in the late nineteenth and early twentieth centuries, which resulted in the area being called Cannery Row.

9. The Inverness Cannery was the first of its kind north of the Fraser River. It employed many people until it closed in 1950.

10. Charles Edenshaw (1839–1920) was a renowned Haida artist and carver born in Skidegate on Haida Gwaii. Edenshaw produced ceremonial items but also made artworks specifically for trade with settlers. His work can be found in museum collections around the world.

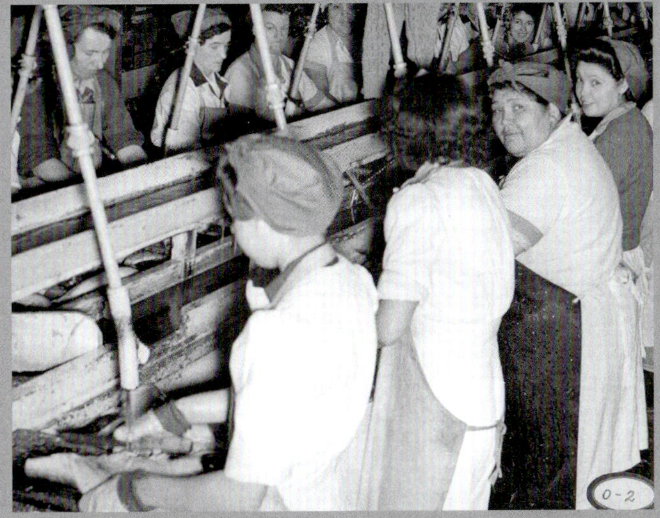

A Northern BC fish-packing operation, 1930s

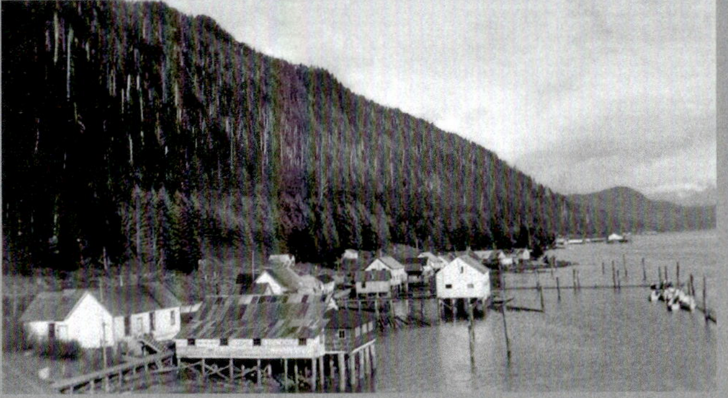

The North Pacific Cannery buildings and docks, 1947

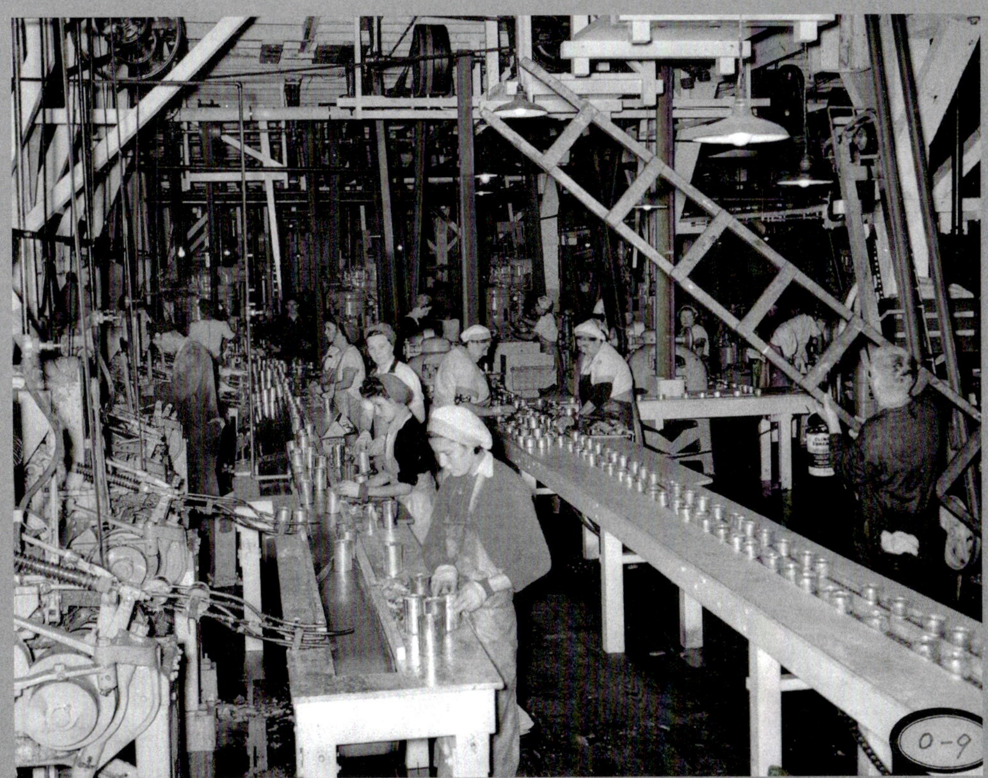

A Northern BC fish-packing operation, 1930s

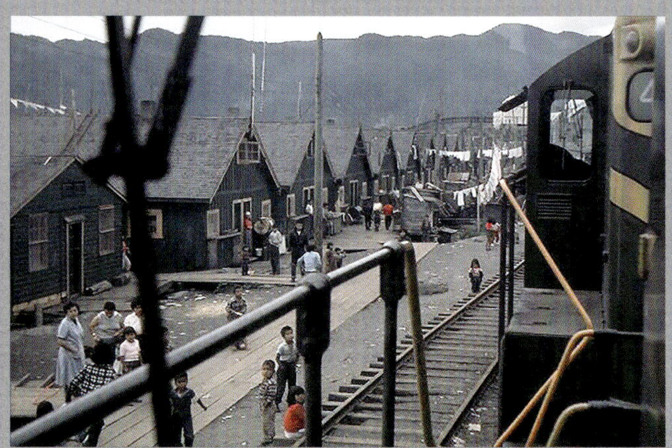
The village, Nelson Brothers Cannery, Port Edward, BC, undated

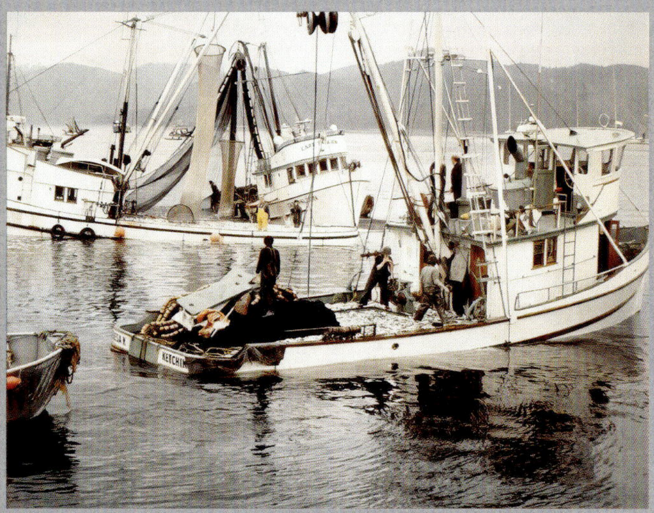
Commercial fishing boats weighed down with deck loads of fish, Skeena River, 1950s

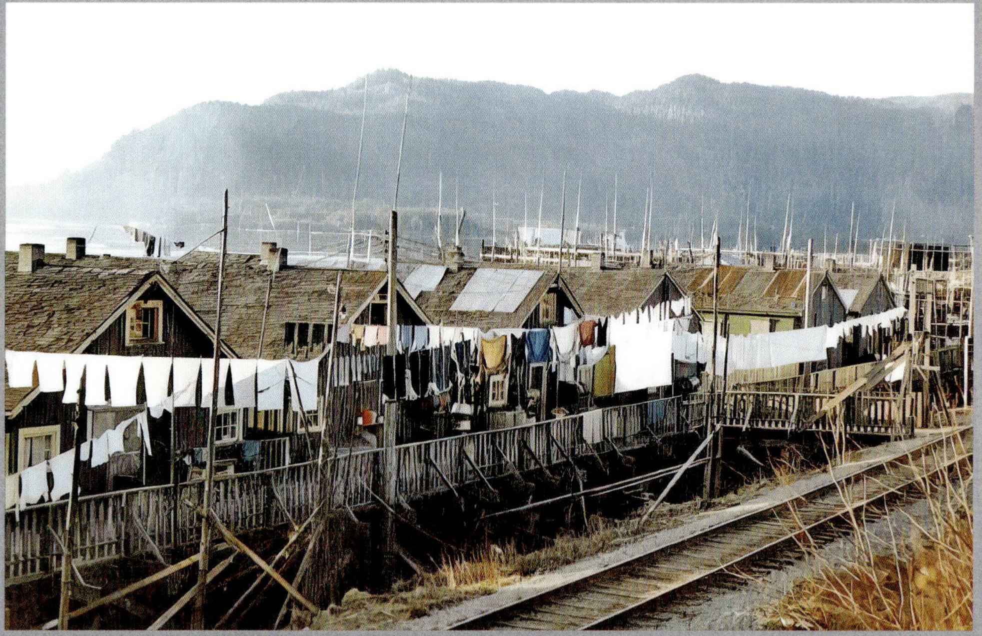
Old Port Edward cannery village, BC, undated

The Japanese workers were good fishermen and boat builders. They did everything too. In those little tiny houses down on the docks, there'd be thirteen, fourteen people in there.

Freda Diesing,[11] the carver who was my teacher later on, had lived in Port Edward before I knew her. Her mother also worked in the cannery there. Don Yeomans,[12] Ken McNeil,[13] James Lewis,[14] Paterson McKay,[15] his son George McKay,[16] Bob Jackson,[17] Alver Tait,[18] Norman Tait,[19] Dale and Terry Campbell,[20] Larry Derrick,[21] to name some of them—there were more than twenty carvers that came out of that village. There were Haisla, Tsimshian, Tahltan, Tlingit, Nisga'a, Haida, Nuxalk, Gitxsan—they were all drawn for work at the canneries. It was a melting pot.

Now all these working canneries are gone. The way they've been doing it with the fish now is just freezing it and shipping it out to China. They don't even process it here anymore. And they're doing that with our logs too—just shipping them out.

This is all part of my heritage now. Someday no one is going to know about the canneries and all the people who came together there. I feel like I was lucky that I was part of it. We lived it. We had lots of fun too. That's how we survived. Our humour.

11. Freda Diesing (1925–2002 Haida)

12. Don Yeomans (b. 1958 Haida)

13. Ken McNeil (b. 1961 Tahltan-Tlingit-Nisga'a)

14. James Lewis (Tsimshian-Tahltan-Tlingit)

15. Paterson McKay (Nisga'a)

16. George McKay (Nisga'a)

17. Bob Jackson (b. 1948 Gitxsan)

18. Alver Tait (Nisga'a)

19. Norman Tait (1941–2016 Nisga'a)

20. Dale Marie Campbell (b. 1954 Tahltan-Tlingit), Terrence Campbell (b. 1956 Tahltan-Tlingit)

21. Larry Derrick (Nisga'a)

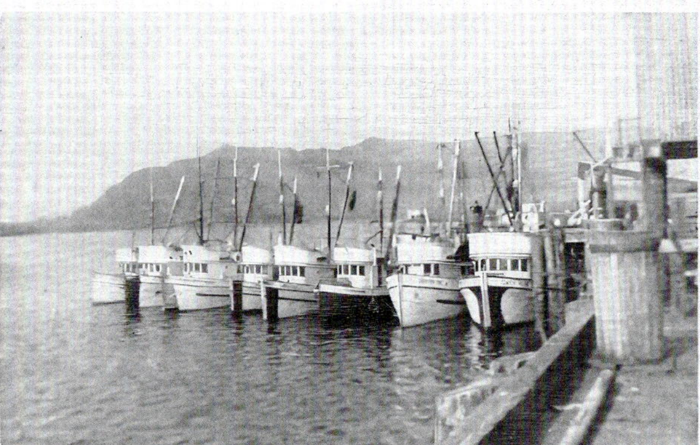

Masset Boats at Port Edwards ——

Massett fleet of seiners call in at the Nelson Bros. Fisheries Ltd. plant at Port Edwards. From the wharf and extending seaward are: "Gwen-Rose", Peter Jones. "Davidson Girl", Robert Davidson. "Western Rover", Wilfred Parnell. "Adelaide J.", George Jones. "Chief Weah", Alec Yeoman. "Masset Maid", Ernie Yeltatzie. "Haida Warrior", Jeff White. On the outside is Jeff Benson's seiner "Finella" who makes his home on the Naas River. Photo taken by Capt. Adolph Price who was skipper this year on Geo. Jones "Adelaide J."

Boats from Masset, Haida Gwaii, at Port Edward, BC, undated

Cleaning the nets on the floats outside the net lofts, Nelson Brothers Cannery, Port Edward, BC, undated

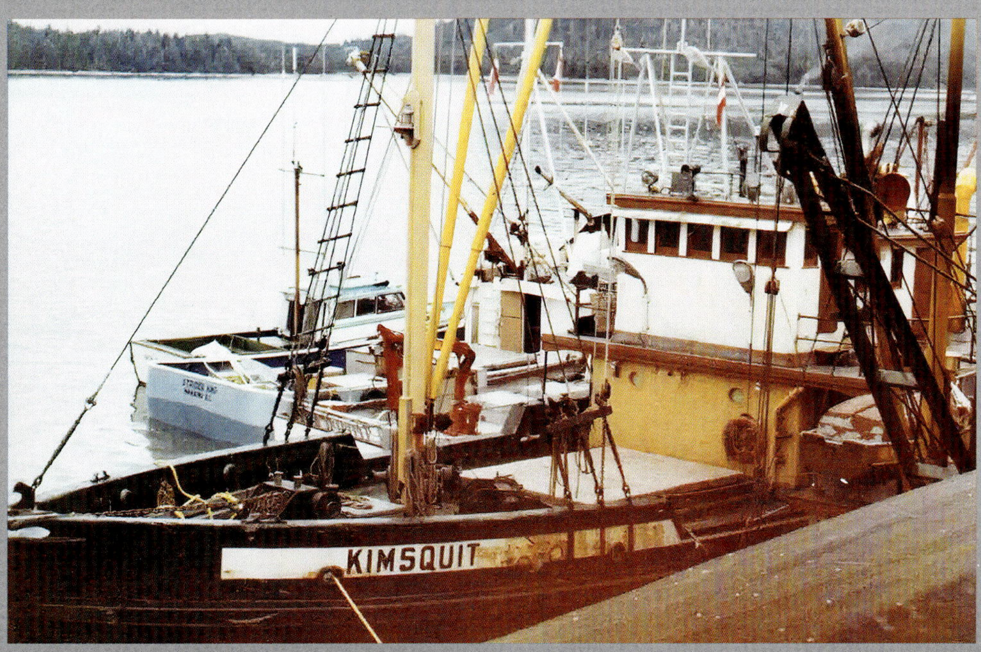

Kimsquit, a fishing boat, Skeena River, BC, undated

32

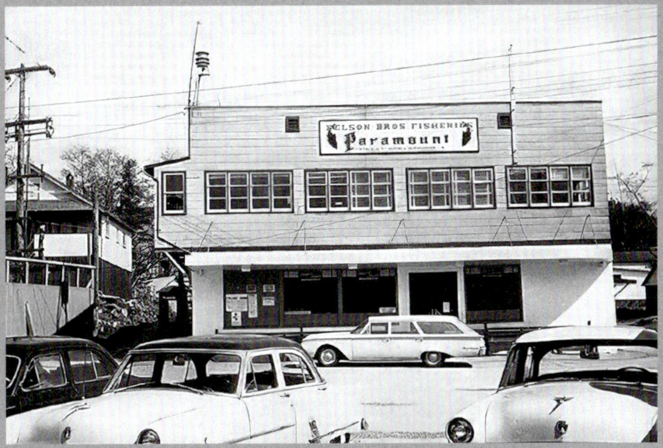

Port Edward general store and post office, with
the Nelson Brothers offices upstairs, 1950s

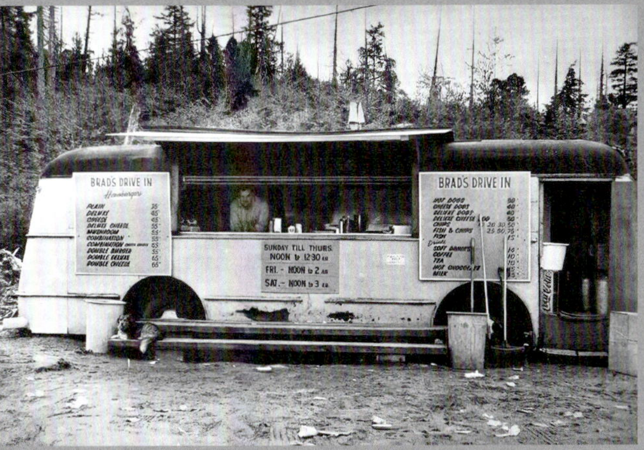

Brad's Drive-In, famous for the best hamburgers,
on Highway 16 near Port Edward, BC, undated

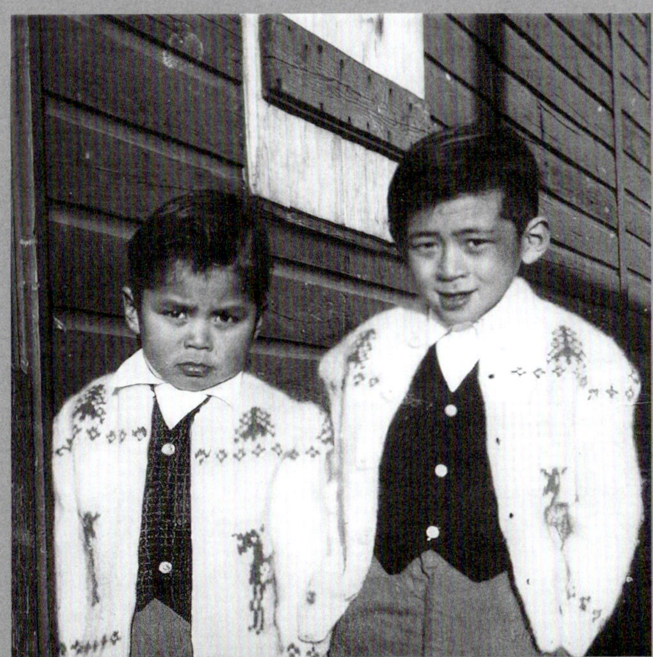

My friends Clarence Martin (left) and his brother
Harry Martin, now a carver, at Nelson Brothers Cannery,
Port Edward, BC, early 1950s

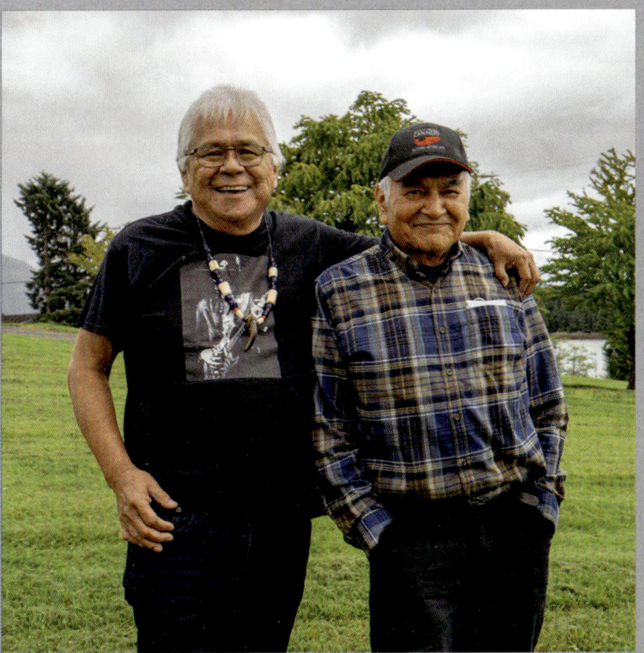

Clarence Martin and me, August 2021

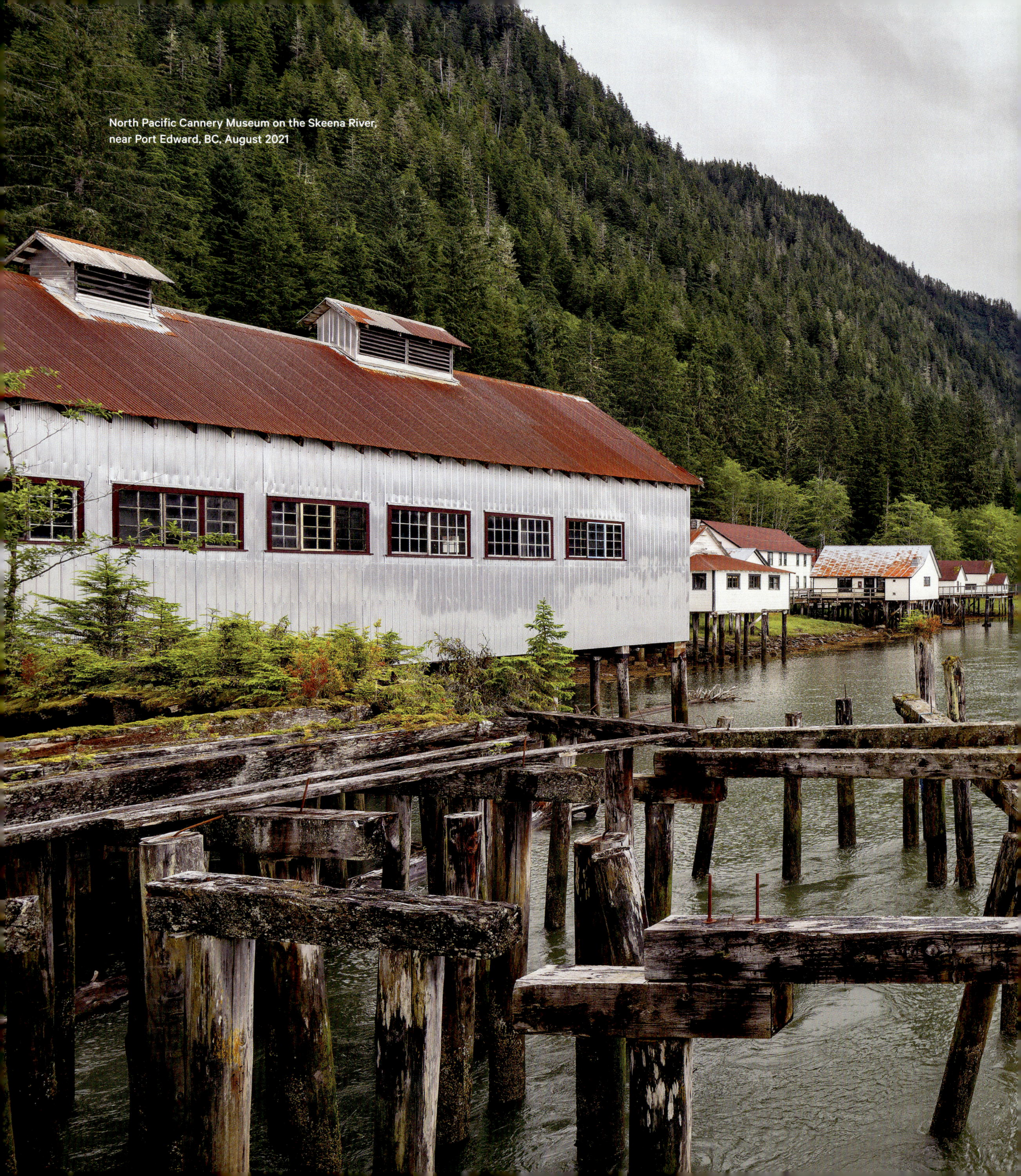
North Pacific Cannery Museum on the Skeena River,
near Port Edward, BC, August 2021

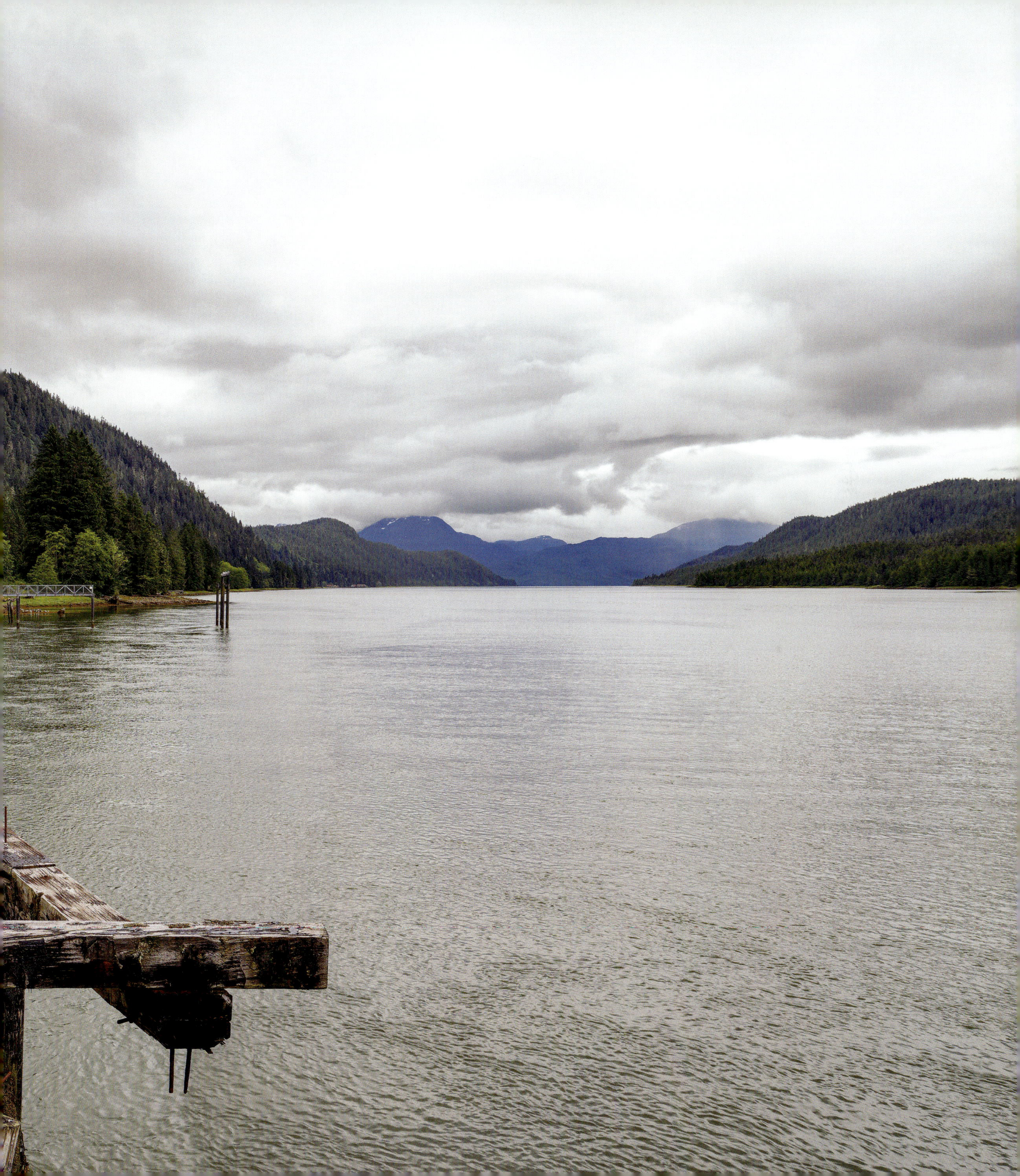

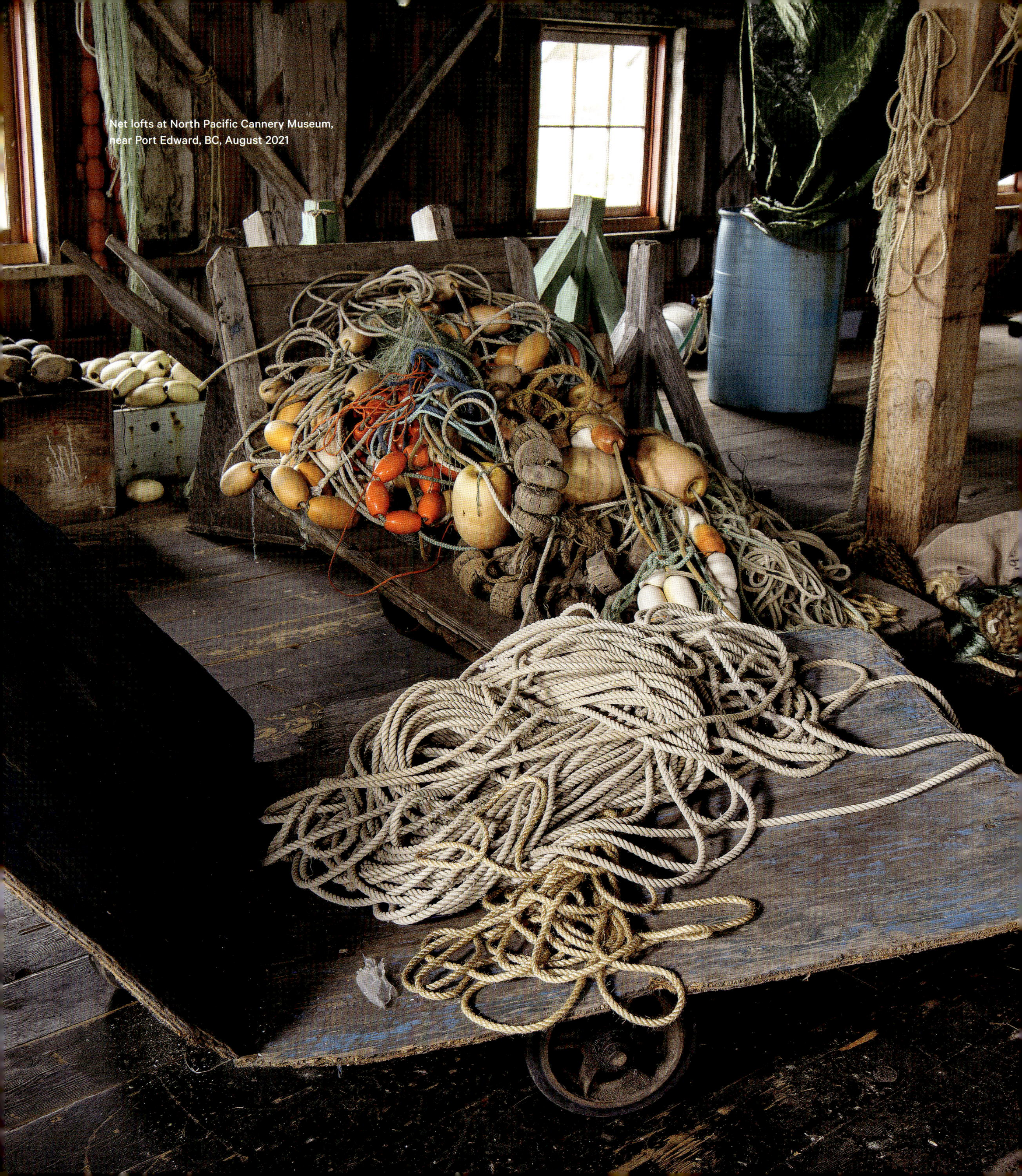
Net lofts at North Pacific Cannery Museum,
near Port Edward, BC, August 2021

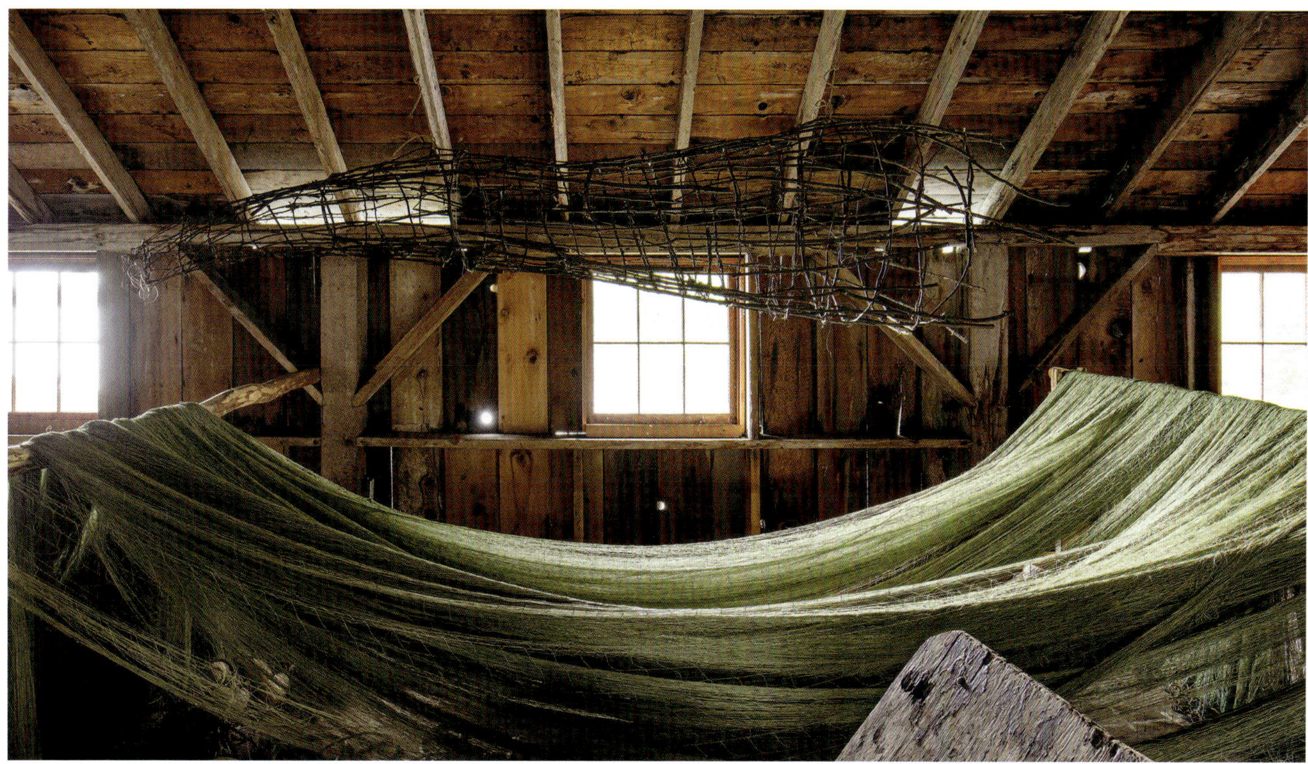

Net lofts at North Pacific Cannery Museum,
near Port Edward, BC, August 2021

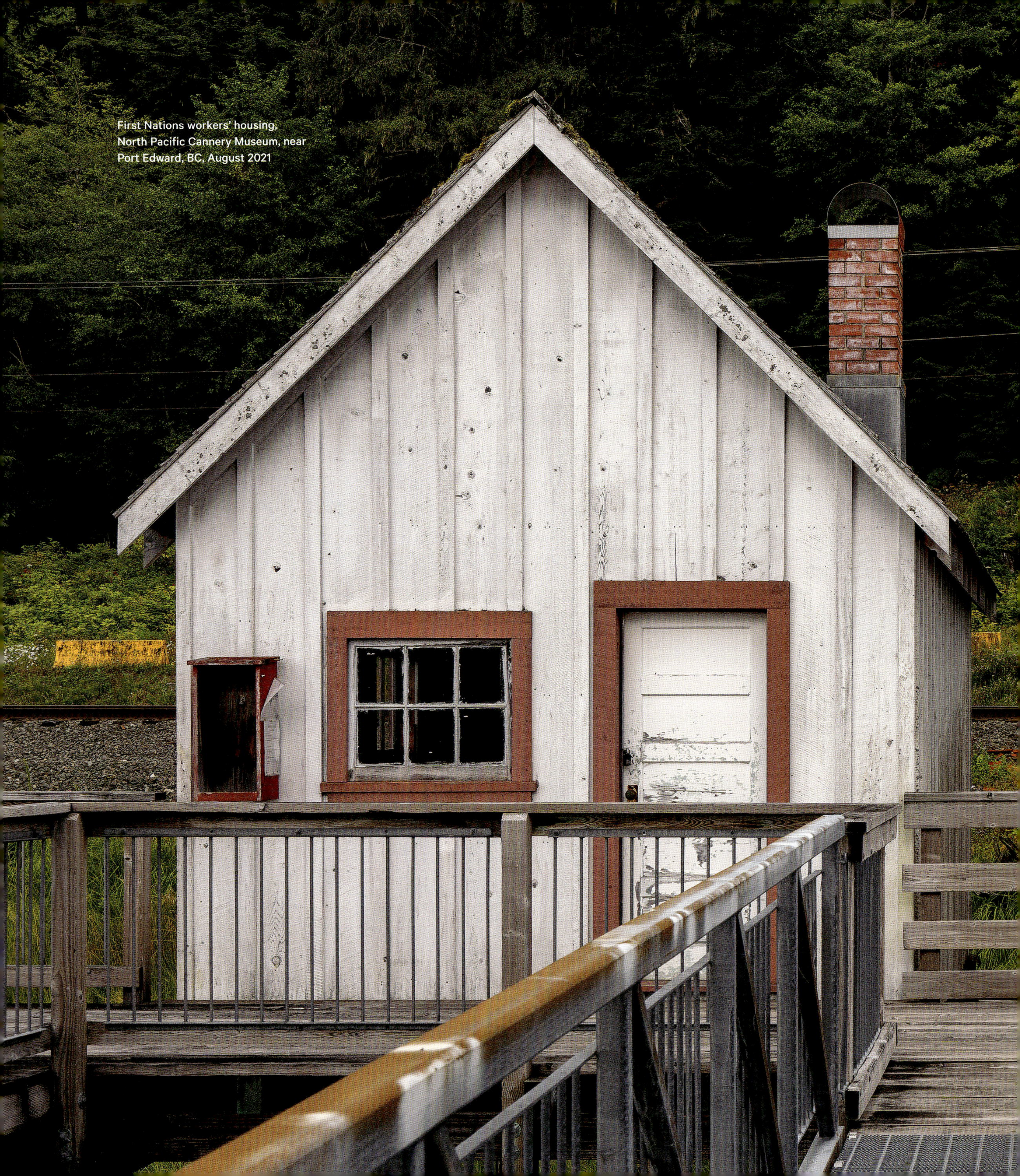

First Nations workers' housing,
North Pacific Cannery Museum, near
Port Edward, BC, August 2021

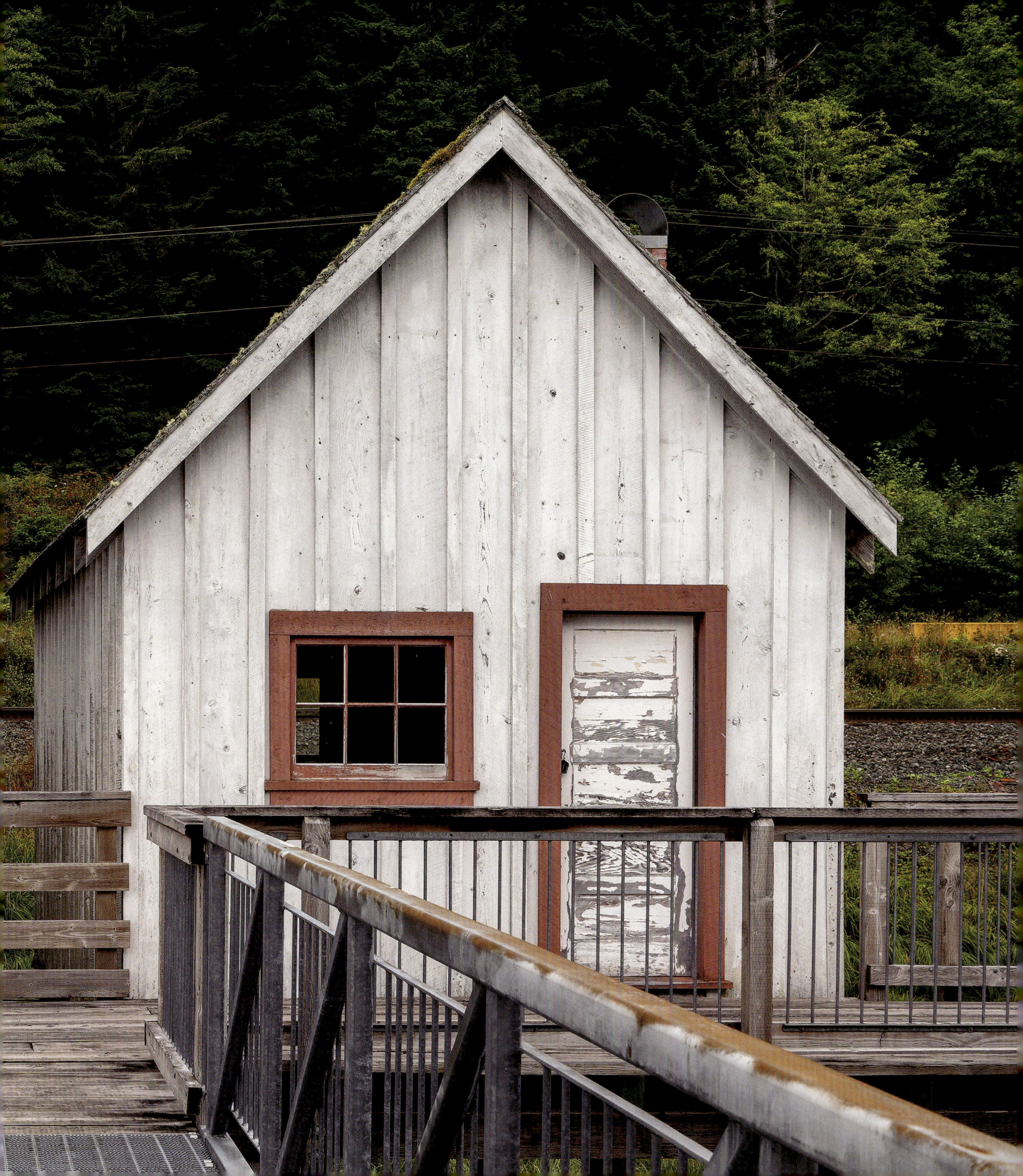

British and Japanese trade goods,
general store, North Pacific Cannery Museum,
near Port Edward, BC, August 2021

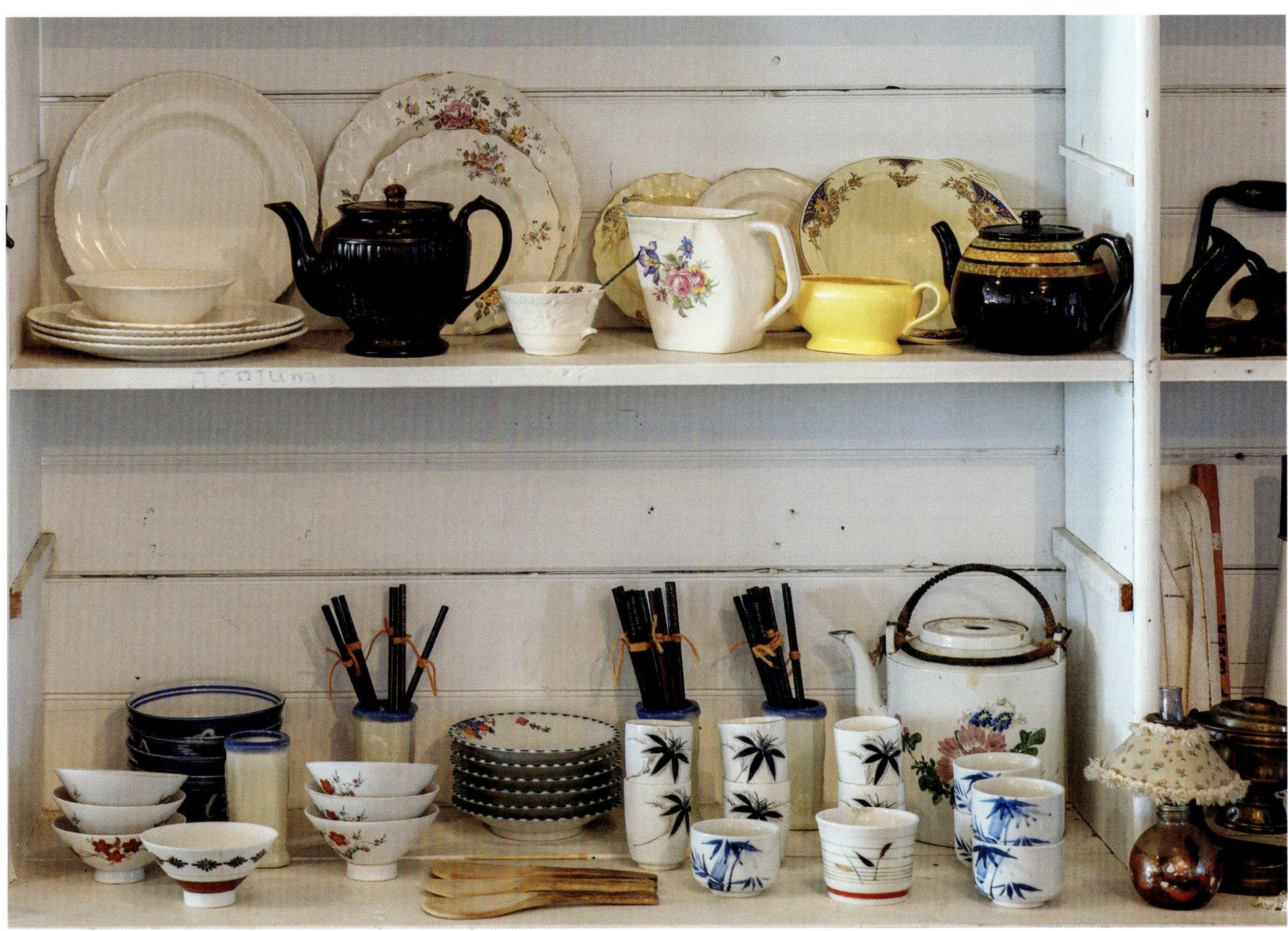

40

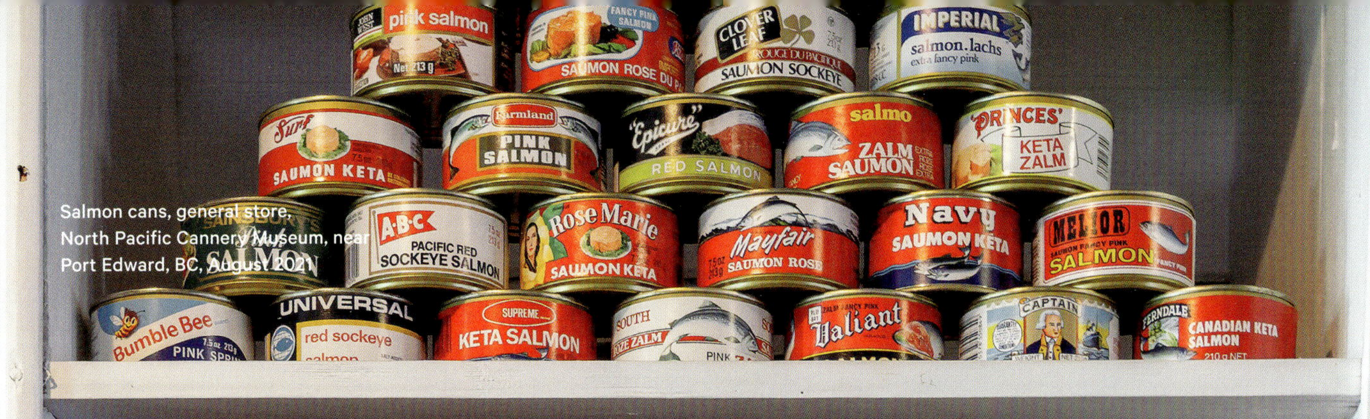
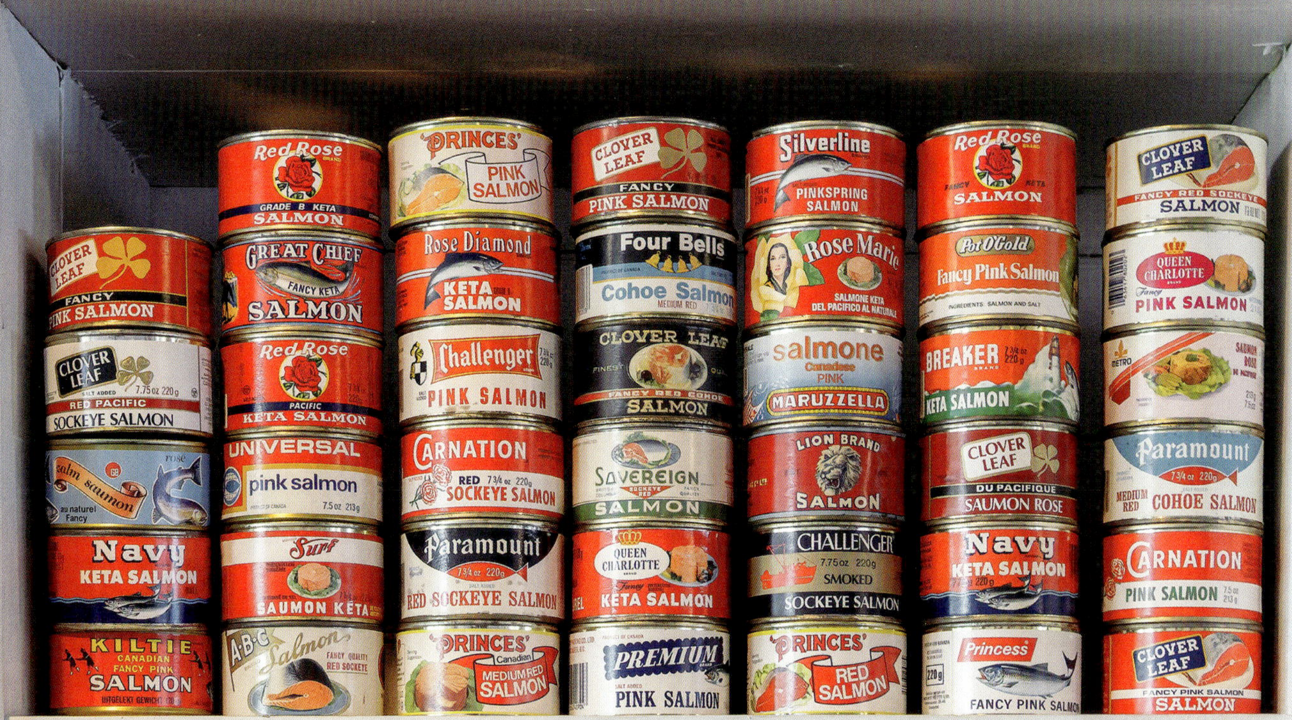
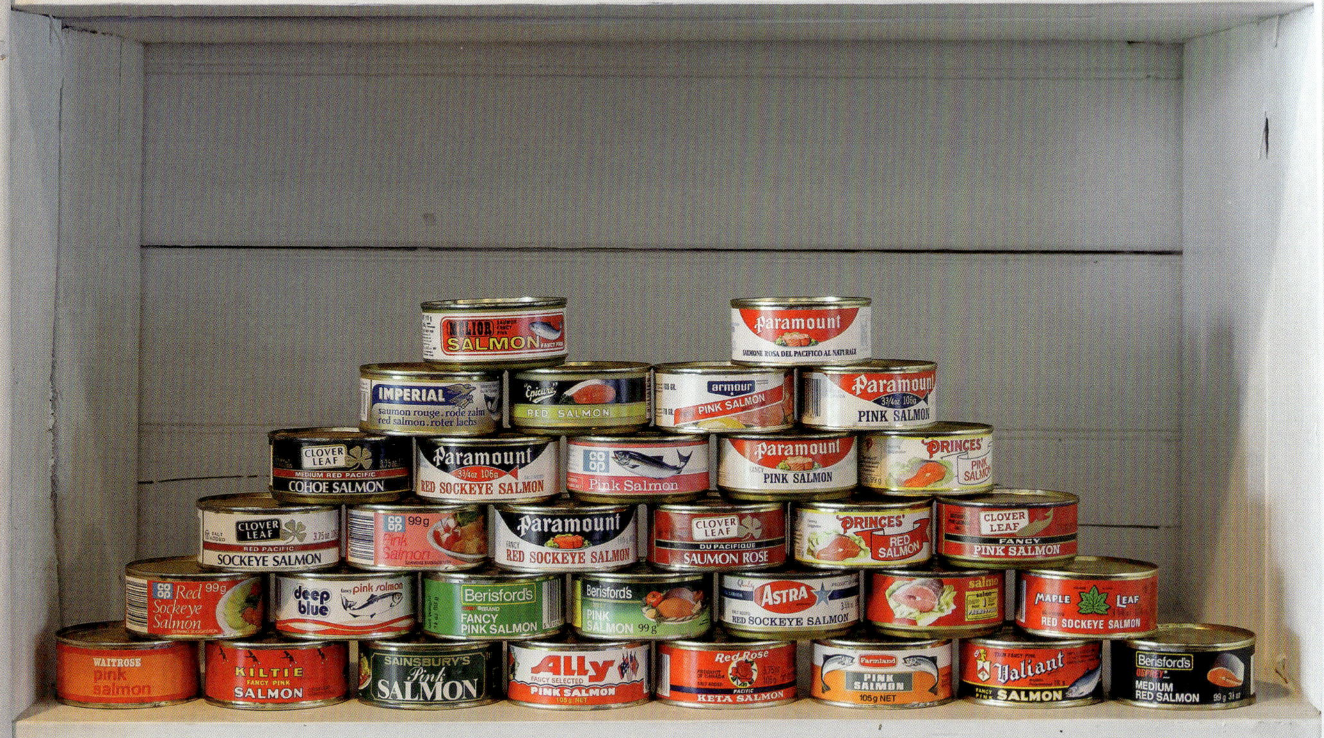
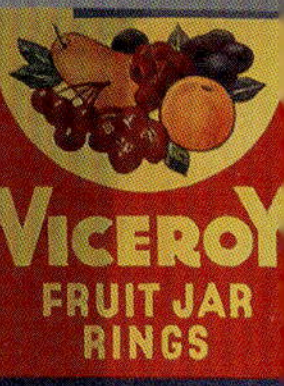

Salmon cans, general store,
North Pacific Cannery Museum, near
Port Edward, BC, August 2021

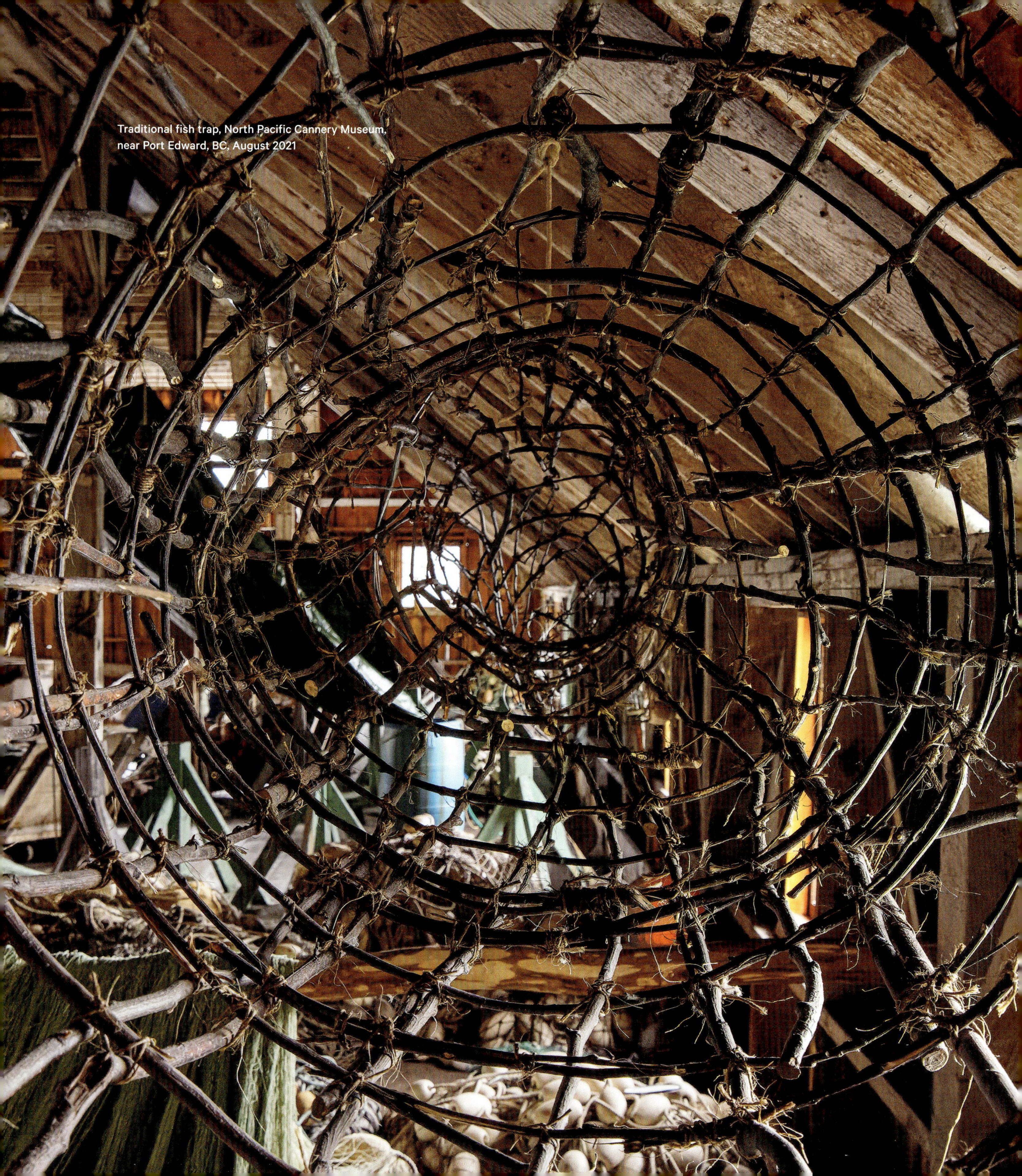

Traditional fish trap, North Pacific Cannery Museum,
near Port Edward, BC, August 2021

Remains of the gas dock, North Pacific Cannery Museum,
near Port Edward, BC, August 2021

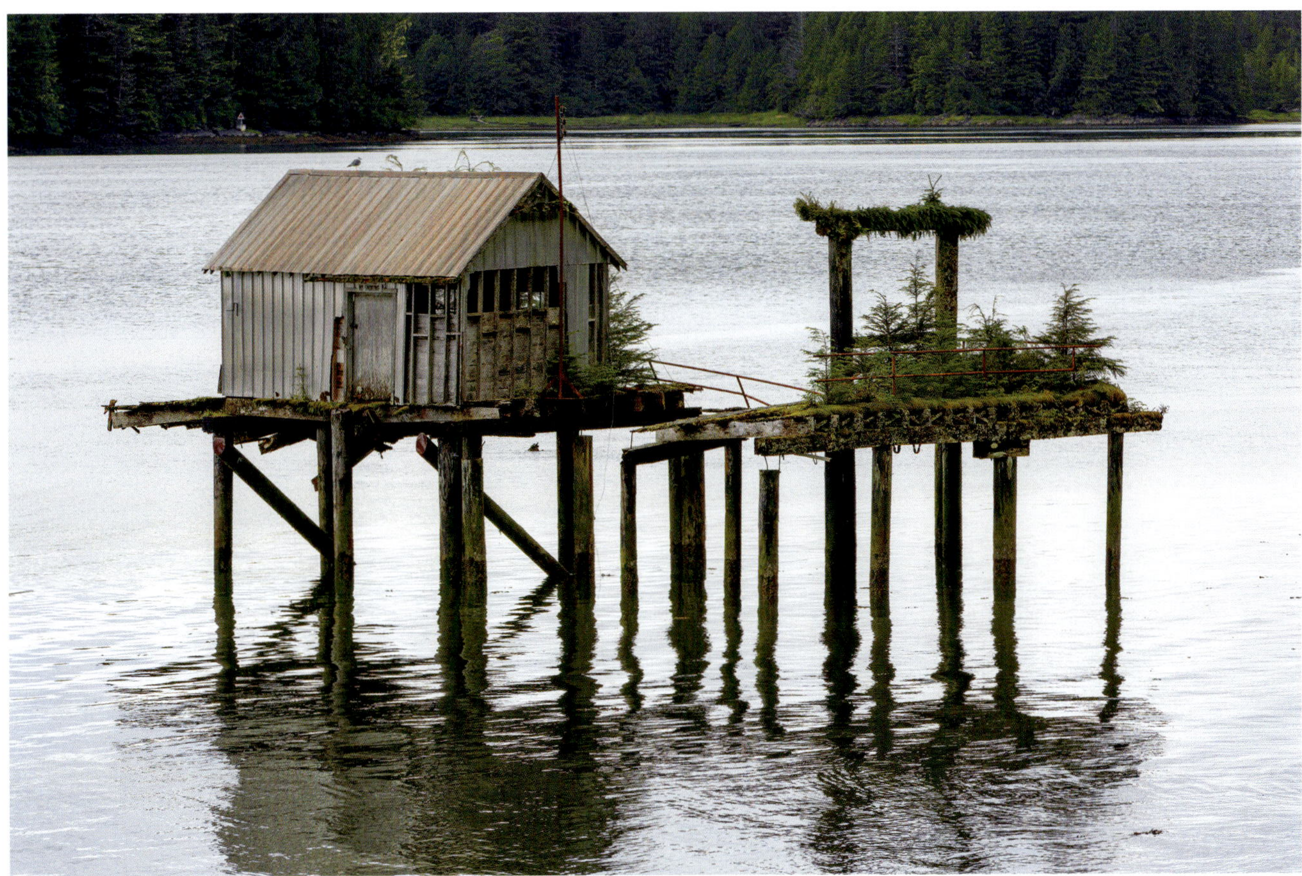

43

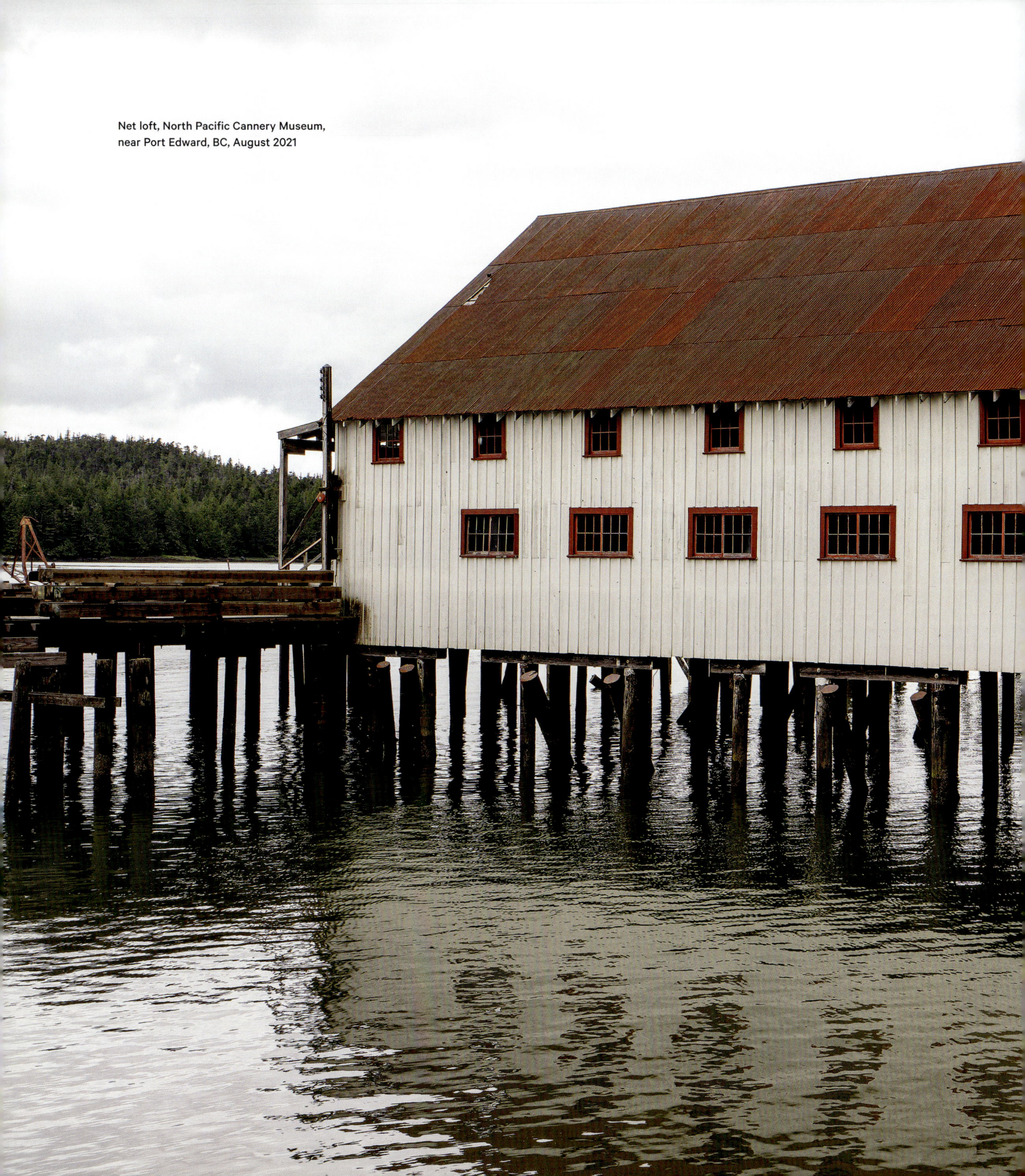

Net loft, North Pacific Cannery Museum,
near Port Edward, BC, August 2021

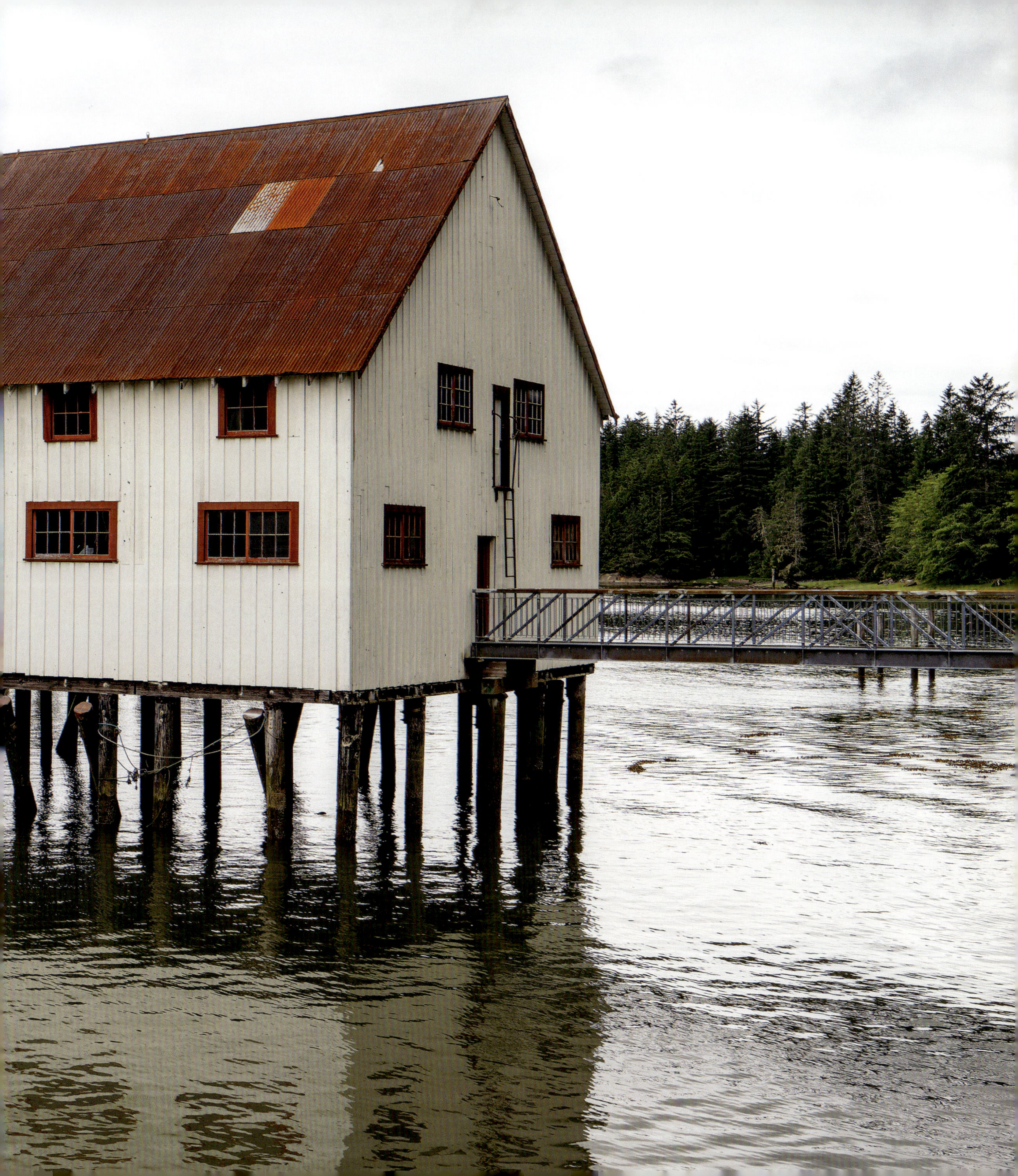

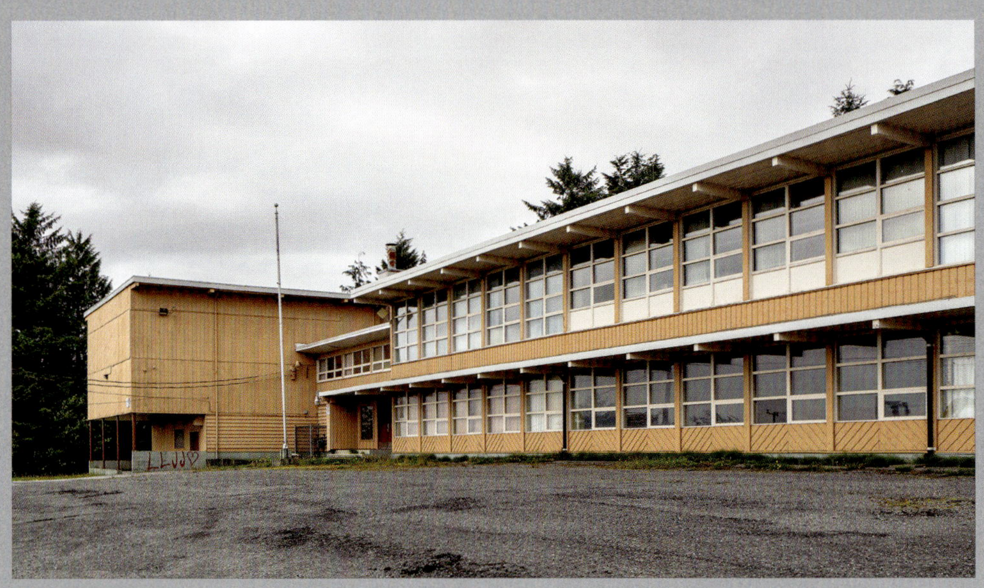

Port Edward Elementary School, where I started Grade 1, seen in August 2021

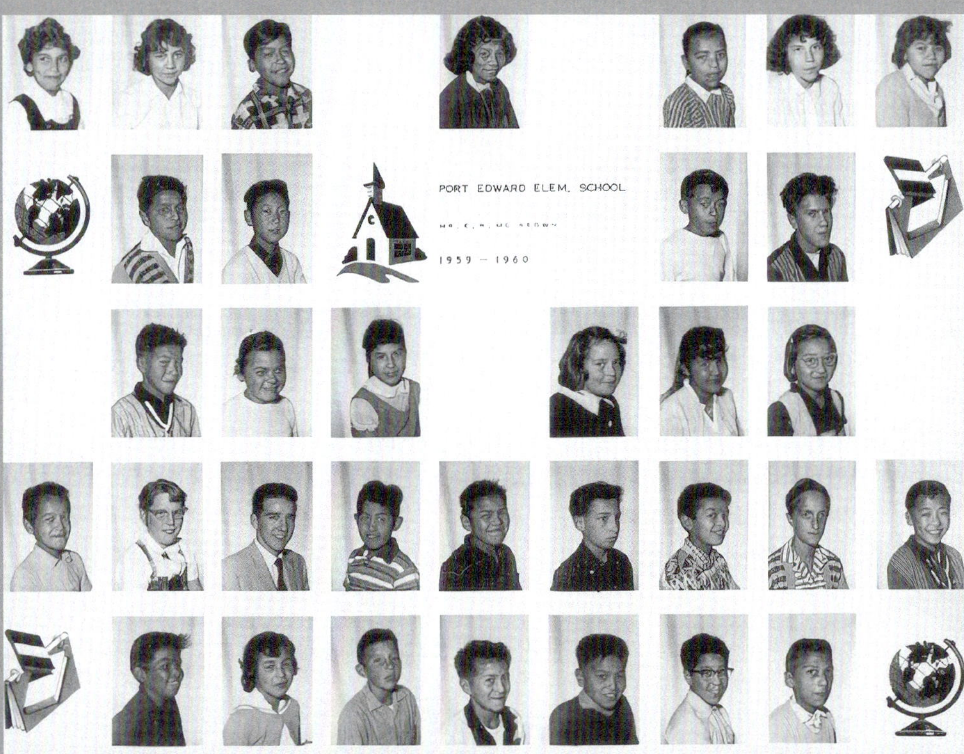

My Port Edward Elementary School class photo (I'm in the bottom row, third from right), 1959–60

46

I started Grade 1 at Port Edward. As a kid I was always curious. I've always liked reading. When my dad was finished with the newspapers I'd read them after him. We had no money. There was no television, there was nothing. The only thing was movies, and we couldn't afford them. We had no money to go but we would sneak in. Then we used to play Tarzan of the Apes—we'd seen it in the movie theatre.

And we drew; we drew and we painted. We drew cars and hot rods and fishing boats and wildlife, and we made our own toys. We just got a little knife and started carving. We would look in a catalogue, like the Simpsons-Sears catalogue—we called it the Wish Book—and then we would see something and draw it, and then we would start carving it out.

When we were working with wood, we got this really good feeling. Me and Bob Jackson—he was a good friend of mine. His grandmother used to tell us good stories, even though we stole her blueberry jam. She told us stuff about our culture, tradition, protocols, and beliefs, how the chiefs were trained.

When Bob and I were about ten, we were playing with boats one day, and he asked me what I was going to be. He said he was going to be an electrician, I think, or a fisherman. I told him, "I think I'm going to be a carpenter like my dad, because I like working with the wood."

That's what my dad did. He taught himself carpentry and mathematics. He only went to Grade 3, but he could build anything. I used to watch him when I was little—he would make shavings to start the fire in the mornings very fast. These were survival skills in those days. You had to know how to do things for yourself. Back in Telegraph we used to pack water up from the creek for cooking on the stove. In winter, we used to wait until the water froze and then transport the ice by dog team back to the village. All that stuff. In my life I've gone from dog teams to cellphones.

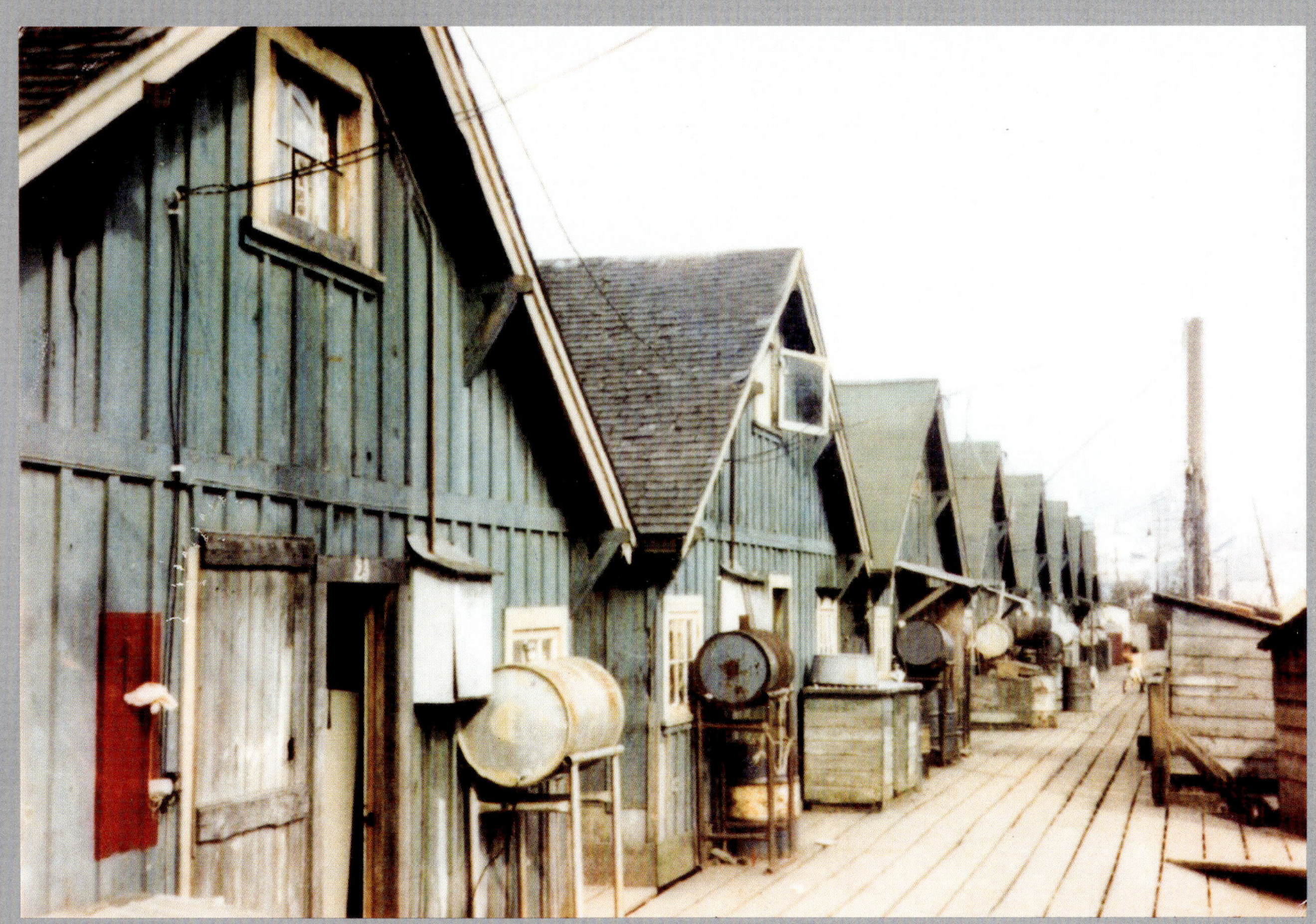

First Nations workers' housing, where I lived, Nelson Brothers Cannery, Port Edward, BC, undated

We were so poor that we didn't even know we were poor!
We were so poor that we weren't allowed to get sick! Everybody
worked. If you didn't work you starved. We'd get one thing for
Christmas—a little toy and that was it. But lots of good food.
Now the kids have everything and they don't even look after it.
And they're bored. We were never bored.

I think we were some of the last children to have a real
childhood, outdoors. We always played Cowboys and Indians,
and no one wanted to be Indian because they always got killed.
And we didn't even realize we were all Indians! Now when I
see those guys I used to play with, I say to them, "Remember
when we were all cowboys?"

A DIFFICULT CHANGE

I lost my dad when I was ten years old, when we were all living
in Port Edward. They say that creative people who lose their
fathers when they're young—it accelerates your creativity. We
had to grow up fast. We couldn't live in the cannery village in
Port Edward anymore, even though my mother was working
there. The head of the family wasn't working there, and that
was the rule. So we had to move out. That's when we moved to
Prince Rupert. In 1960.

I went to the Catholic school there, in Prince Rupert, the
Annunciation School.[22] I was about twelve years old. I used
to draw there too. I liked social studies. I liked history. And I
liked reading.

22. Annunciation Catholic School opened
in Prince Rupert in 1917. It was the first non-
residential Catholic school in the region.

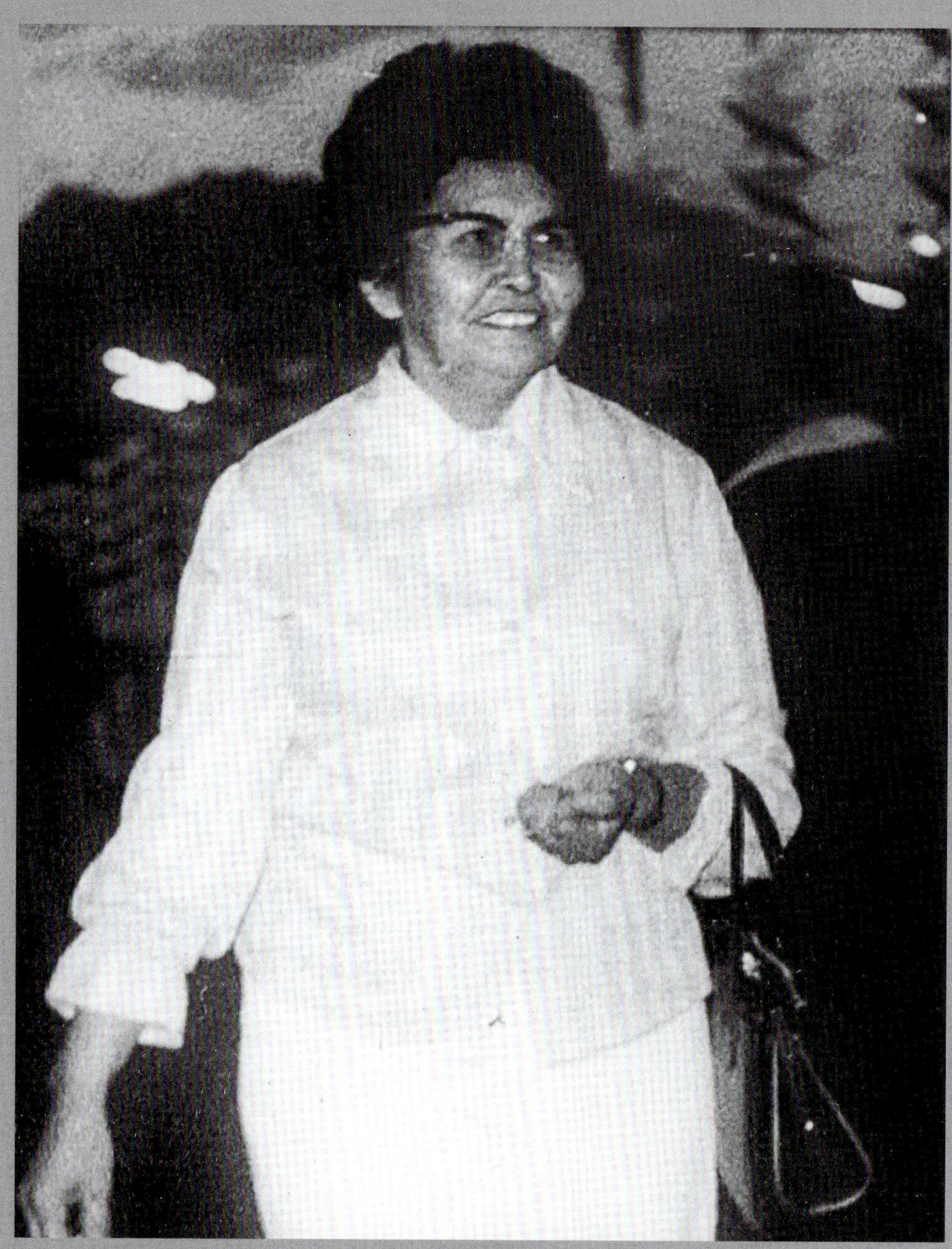

My mother, Flossie Bob (Wolf Clan), about 1965

MY MOTHER

My mother was one of the greatest supporters of my work. She was a real inspiration for me. She taught me how to work and do jobs the right way. She gave me our stories and taught me our culture. I was lucky I listened to her. She gave me good cultural values, and I thank her for that because culture is life and life is culture.

She told me to always wash my face in the morning to be clean, otherwise you won't see anything—you won't be awake. She gave me the hard-work ethic—she had ten kids and she was working all the time—and also the curiosity to learn new things.

When we were young she made our clothing, she made our moccasins for the winter, and she was always doing her beadwork. I remember watching her drawing her designs and cutting them out. She would tell us stories after supper. She knew and understood the spiritual ways and the culture. She lived it. She made really good oatmeal cookies with raisins in them, and she made good Tahltan stew out of moosemeat, and really good bannock. I think she was one of the best bannock makers.

She used to get up at about four in the morning, and she would listen to country music. She also played the guitar. There was this disc jockey down in the Carolinas—his name was Dempsey. He was her favourite disc jockey. That's how I got my name.

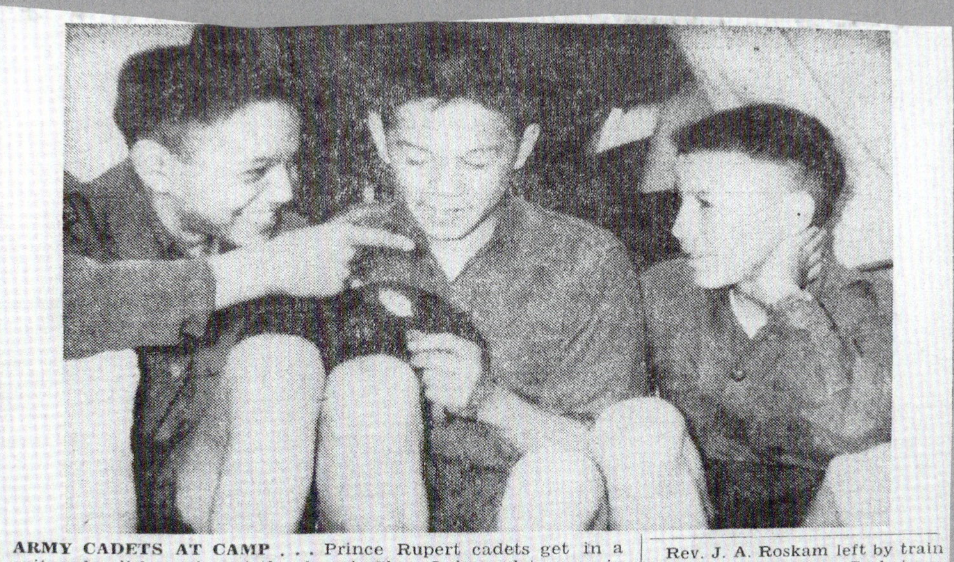

ARMY CADETS AT CAMP . . . Prince Rupert cadets get in a spit and polish session at the Army's Clear Lake cadet camp in Riding Mountain National Park, Man., where they are taking a two-week junior leader course. About 800 western Canadian cadets are attending the campsite this summer. Left and right respectively, are Dempsey Bob and Ellery Day of 855 Second Avenue West, and centre, Dale Chen, of 648 Fulton Street.
—National Defence Photo.

Rev. J. A. Roskam left by train this morning for Saskatoon, Sask., where he will attend a Baptist Union convention August 22 to 26.

Newspaper clipping from the *Prince Rupert Daily News*, 1962—me at fourteen (left), with Dale Brooks (centre) and Ellery Day, the Dundurn Platoon, Clear Lake Cadet Camp, Wasagaming, Manitoba, 1962

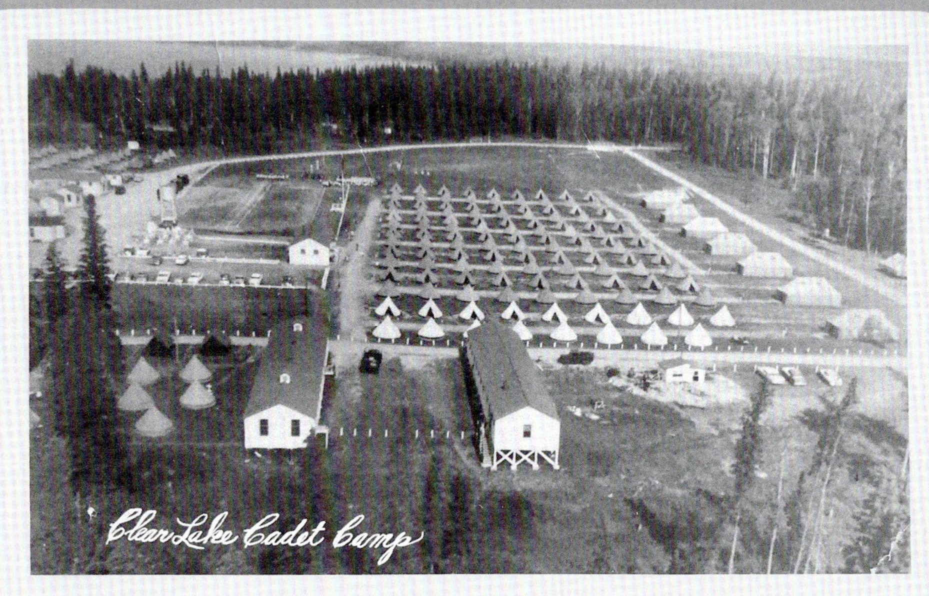

Clear Lake Cadet Camp, Wasagaming, Manitoba, about 1962

In 1962 a lot of my friends joined the army cadets, and I did too. We would meet once at night mid-week at the armoury and then one afternoon on the weekend. If we went to the summer camp in Vernon, BC,[23] they gave us $100. We never had $100. We never had $20! So we thought that was a whole pile of money. And they fed us good.

I was a cadet for two years. In 1962 they took us to Clear Lake Cadet Camp in Manitoba for two weeks.[24] I won the Most Improved Cadet; I got a trophy. We flew from Prince Rupert in a big plane down to Vancouver, and they put us up in East Vancouver. We had our uniforms on, so nobody bothered us. I went to visit the relatives of my buddy Dale Brooks, and we saw a television there. It was the first time we saw TV.

We stayed at the Jericho Beach army barracks in Vancouver for one night. I remember we met some cadets from Jamaica that were on their way to the cadet camp in Vernon. That's where the older boys went, and I did, too, the following year, for six weeks.

After Vancouver, we went on the train all the way to Clear Lake Cadet Camp, near Brandon, Manitoba. This was in 1962. Going through the Rockies—well, we'd never been anywhere. What was really strange was waking up in Regina and there were no mountains. We'd never been in a place with no mountains. We had no money but they fed us good. Some of the other kids were complaining about the food, but we thought we were in heaven. We could eat all we wanted.

That's where I got my discipline: cadets. But I got it from my family too. From my dad. He used to make us sweep the floor properly, and if you didn't do it right you'd have to do it again—mop the floor and keep it clean. He always expected us to do something with our lives. He wanted us to be educated, not just sit around.

My great-aunts Eva and Helen Carlick, my grandpa Johnny Sinkoots, and my mum told me all these stories, all these things over the years. I used to stay with family in Terrace and Prince Rupert. My grandpa knew so much. He told me about the Flood

23. The Vernon Cadet Camp opened in Vernon, BC, in 1949. Every summer more than a thousand cadets from across British Columbia and Alberta travelled there to learn infantry basic training, driver mechanics, and signalling. From 1962 to 1996 it was known as the Vernon Army Cadet Camp.

24. Clear Lake Cadet Camp opened in 1945 in Riding Mountain National Park, north of Brandon, Manitoba. Cadets travelled from across Canada to attend summer courses and training workshops there until its closure in 1968.

—he told me all kinds of stuff. I remember one Sunday morning
we heard the church bells ringing and he said to me, "I don't
have to go to church because wherever you pray, that's your
church. If you pray by the mountain, that's your church. If you
pray by the river, that's your church. God knows Tahltan." He
used to say, "I pray in Tahltan as soon as the sun comes up, as
soon as the sun goes down. I don't have to dress up and show
off and go to church." He used to say, "Anyways, they just stole
our stories and put them in the Bible to make them their own!"
We knew about the Flood, we knew about migration, we knew
it through the animals, we knew it through nature. My mum
went to church but the rest of us not really, because of the
church taking our people. We couldn't understand how they
could say *this* and then do *that*.

GROWING UP AND STARTING OUT

As I got older I worked at the canneries and at the fish plant.
I did all kinds of stuff in the summers. I unloaded the boats,
worked with the women, worked on the line making the cans,
putting the cans in the machine. In 1973 I worked at the pulp
mill, Canadian Cellulose,[25] near Port Edward: I worked in
the wood department there, where the chips are. We cleaned
up. Earlier, I'd worked at the sawmill here in Terrace, Skeena
Sawmills,[26] when I was seventeen. That was my first job. My
sister's husband was working in the sawmill and he got me a
summer job, so I stayed with them, piling lumber. By that time
I was going to school in Prince George, at the Catholic school,
Prince George College.

I went there when I was fifteen, in 1963. It was Grade 9. My
older brother Tony and my sister Linda were there, too, and my
younger brother Lorgan went there later on. A lot of the kids
that came to that school came from residential schools all over
the North, but it was also not just for First Nations kids. I liked
the history classes and the woodworking there. I had always
liked reading, since I was young.

25. Canadian Cellulose operated a sawmill and pulp mill in Port Edward, BC, from 1946 to 1973, when it was taken over by the government of British Columbia.

26. Skeena Sawmills was founded in Terrace, BC, in 1960. After being sold and temporarily shuttered several times, it is still operational.

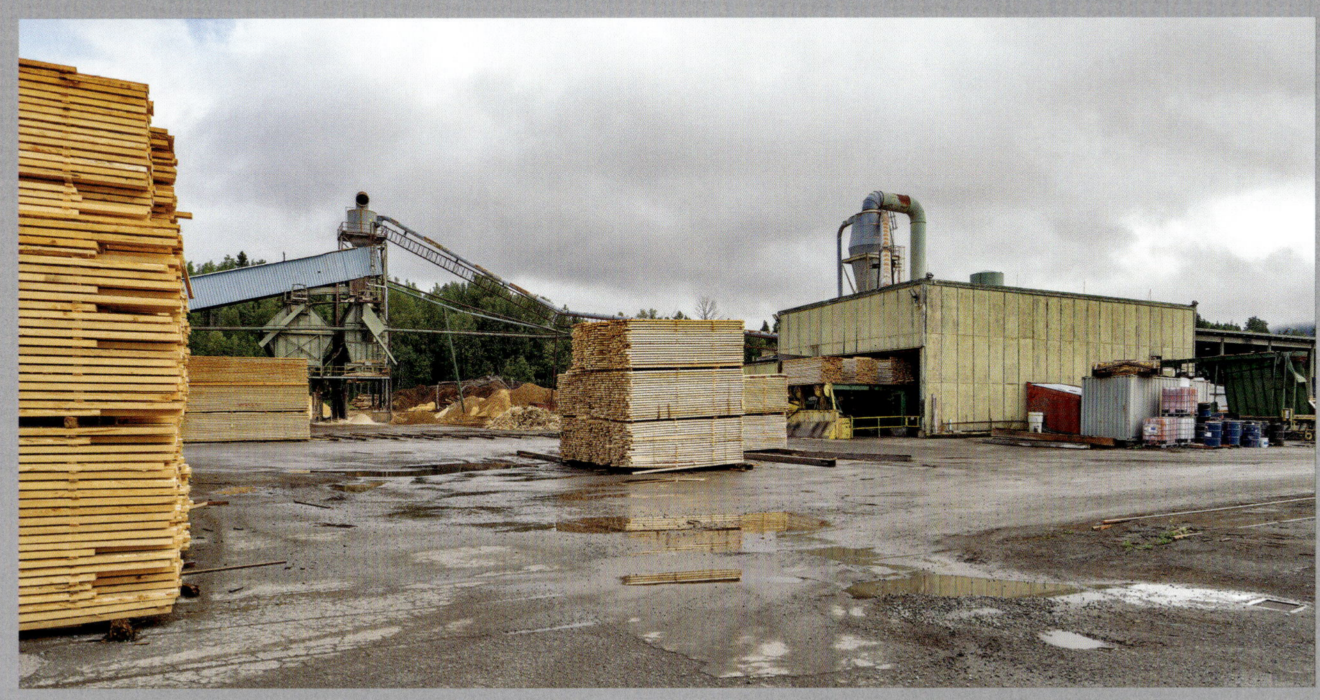

Skeena Sawmills, where I had my first job, at seventeen, Terrace, BC, August 2021

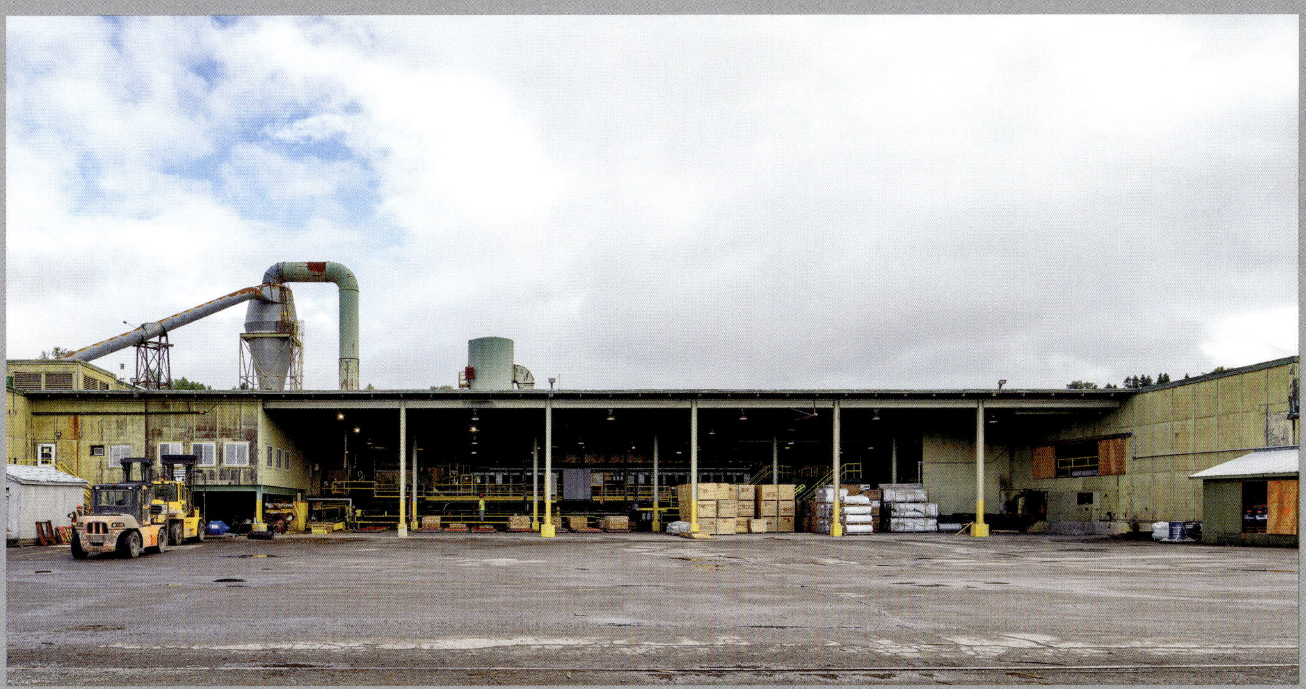

The green chain, which moves lumber to be graded and sorted, at Skeena Sawmills, Terrace, BC, August 2021

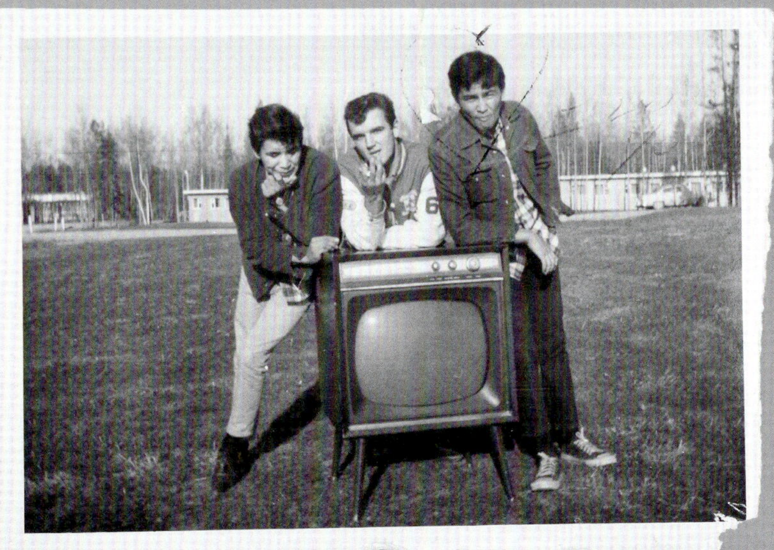

Thomas Pierre, a.k.a. Smiley (left), Mike Shephard (middle), and me
in front of the student residence buildings, Prince George College, 1967

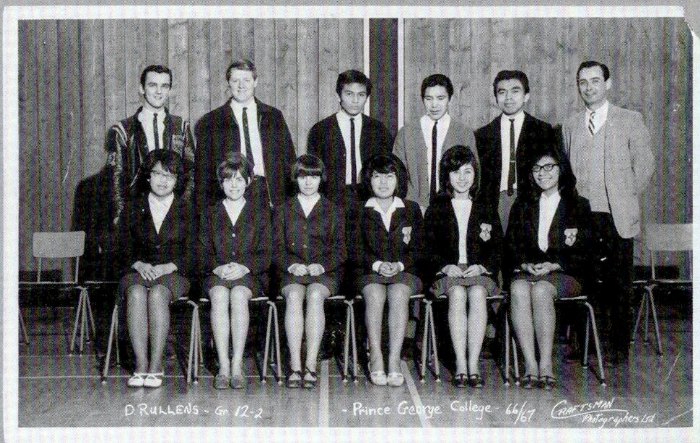

Prince George College class of 1966–67; Mike Shephard (top row, far left),
me (top row, third from left), Thomas Pierre (third from right)

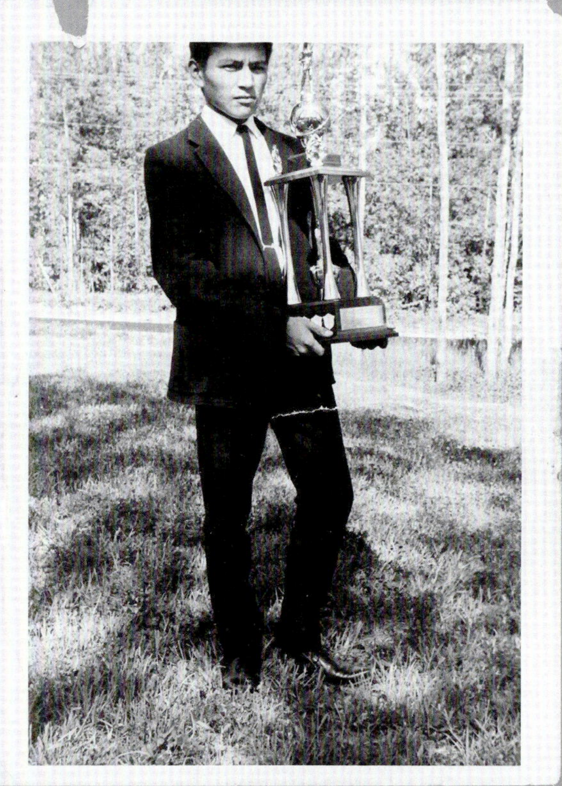

Me with my basketball championship trophy,
Prince George College, about 1966

I remember the day that John Kennedy died. I was in social studies class, and Mr. Shields—he was our teacher, an American from New York—he came in that day and he was crying. It was just before lunch. He told us that Kennedy had been shot and killed. I had seen Kennedy on TV; I knew who he was. Mr. Shields also talked to us about segregation. And he knew the music of that time; we knew about it too. He was a very good teacher; he had a very positive effect on my life.

We had a band and one day we went to visit one of the residential schools, to perform for them—Lejac Residential School, near Prince George.[27] I played the drums. While we were playing, a kid in the audience started making sign language with his hands. He was telling us they were hungry. They were asking for help.

We were hungry too. Just eating sandwiches, baloney, pancakes with white flour. No fruit and vegetables. The school was given money by the government to take care of us, but they barely fed us. But they always had lots to eat. Bacon and eggs in the morning. We could smell it. We used to walk down behind the school and go hunting for grouse. We would hunt them with a sling shot and roast them to eat.

Once my art teacher called me in and said she had to give me a C-minus because I didn't draw the way she wanted me to draw. I told her I'm Tahltan and I'm Tlingit, and I can't deny who my grandmothers are. I just stuck to my guns. It made me determined to get better. Later on I went back to my school reunion but she wasn't there. When I got that Order of Canada I thought, That's pretty good for a C-minus in art.

We had an incredible coach for basketball, Mr. Bewen—he was from the States too. He was pretty strict—he taught us how to work together, how to be team players, how to help each other to improve. The things he taught us—no smoking, no drinking, no staying out late—he was teaching us how to be good people. He was teaching us about life through basketball. When we went down the court, he used to say, "You have to make it count. Two points can win you the game."

27. Lejac Residential School was open between 1922 and 1976 in Fraser Lake, BC, west of Prince George. The children were taken to the school from local Dakelh, Sekani, and Gitxsan communities.

We played hockey in our outdoor rink too. Most of the athletes there were hockey players, because they had grown up in the Interior. I had a friend called Thomas Pierre—he was a really good hockey player from Fort St. James. He was a big reader too; he got me back into reading again. All kinds of books.

I did my first totem pole there. Mr. Shields wanted a totem pole for a friend of his. He thought every Native person from the coast could carve totem poles. I made him one maybe ten inches tall. I just looked at a picture in a magazine to figure out how to do it. Someone had carved something on the sign for the school as well, so I looked at that too. Fifty years later he gave me back this pole, and we had a big unveiling in front of the grandchildren. They thought it was pretty funny.

I graduated from Prince George College in 1967. Many years later I met one of my classmates, Shirley Joseph, from Hazelton. We had graduated together. She said, "I remember you started up slow, but I remember seeing you drawing all the time at school. It seemed like it started slow and then, boom. You just blossomed."

When I graduated I was eighteen. I went back up to Telegraph Creek. I didn't know what to do, so I went to see my family there. I worked for a while at Cassiar, up near the Yukon border. I worked building houses, doing roofing. I did all kinds of jobs. And then I went back down to Prince Rupert.

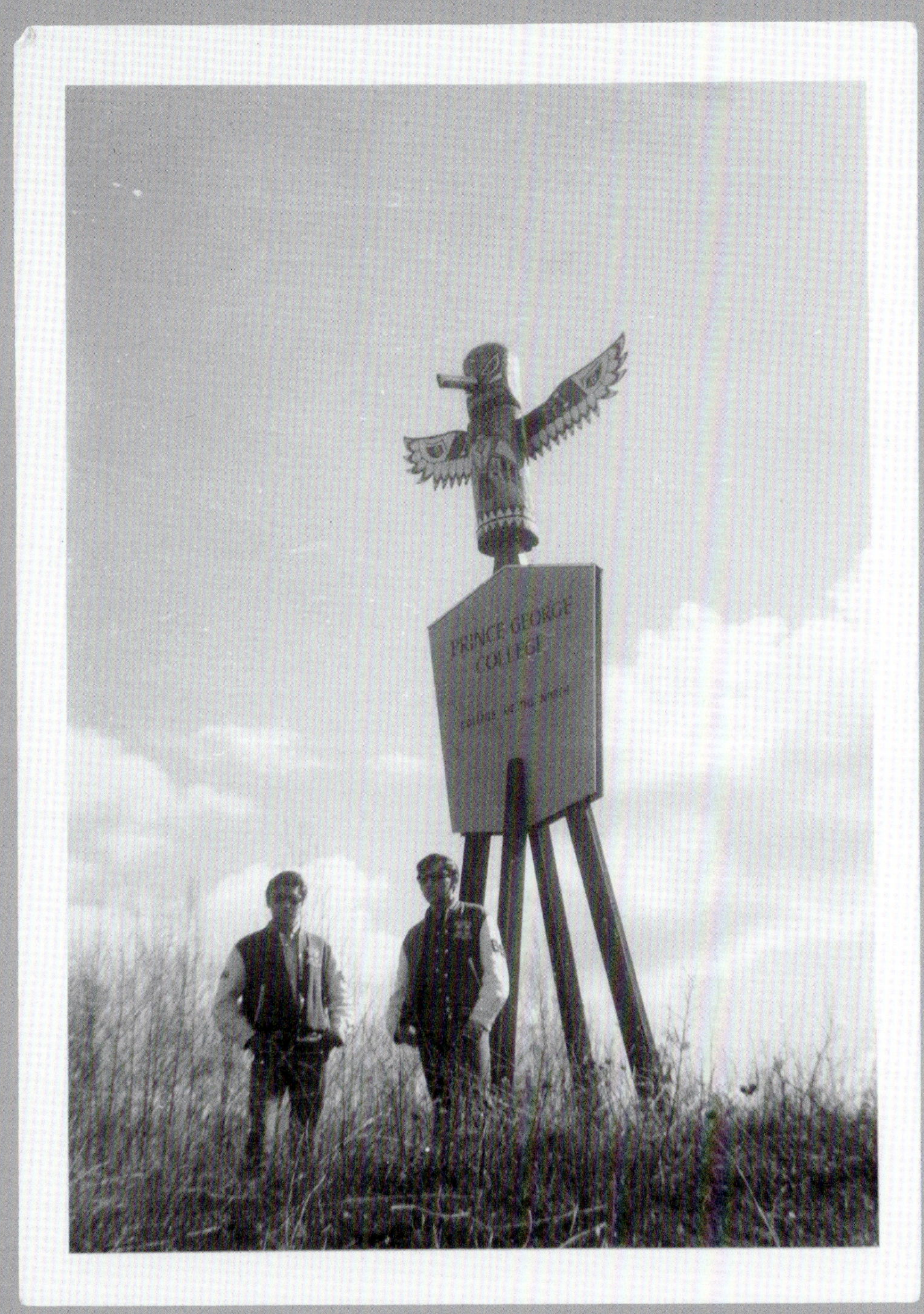

My friend Antoine and me (right), Prince George College, about 1967

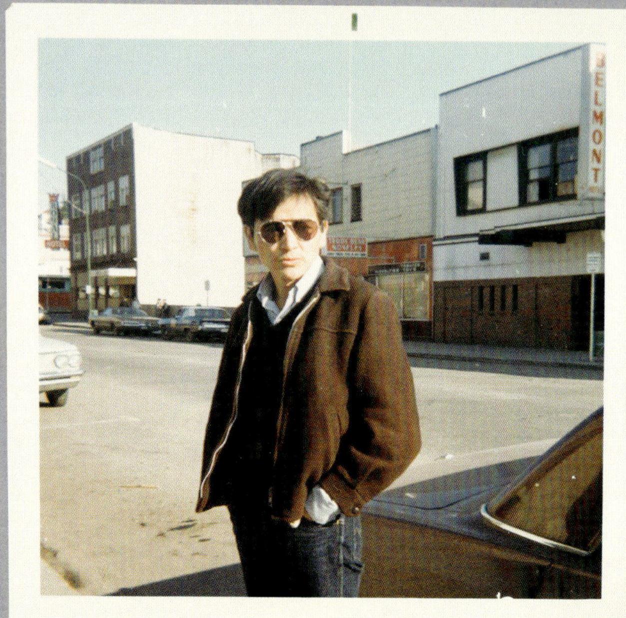

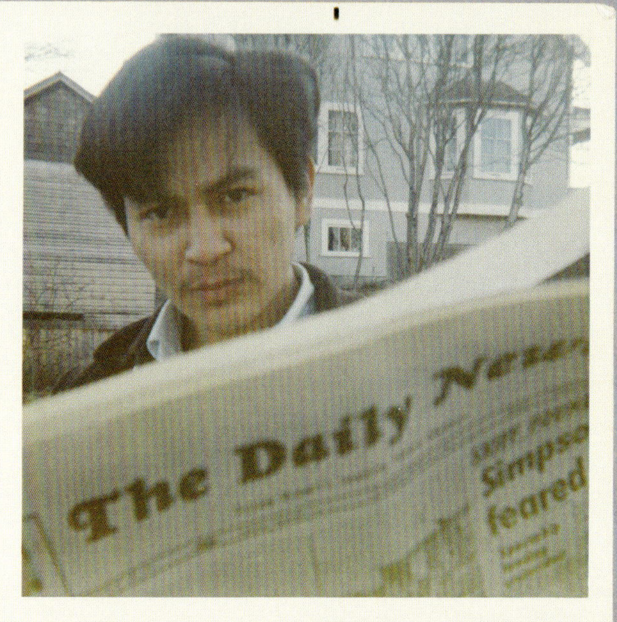

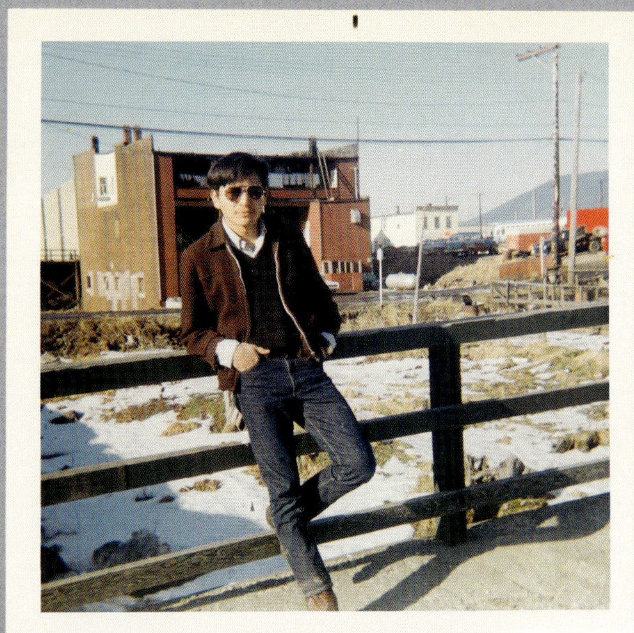

Three photos of me in downtown Prince Rupert, BC, about 1969

Everything from that time—there was just a feeling like you were part of something, part of history. It was a creative time. There was a feeling that if you believed in yourself, and you did the work, you could do anything. Music was changing. Rock 'n' roll was the thing. We had these big dances. Some of the guys had sideburns like Elvis and dyed their hair. When they started sweating, the black stuff would run down their faces.

I liked the blues then and I still do. Everything came out of the blues. I like the old guys like Howlin' Wolf and B.B. King. Also Sonny Terry and Brownie McGhee, and Tina Turner. The old guys have got soul. To make really true, great art—you couldn't create the blues if you didn't live it. It isn't real. In the '80s, years later, I remember I was in Copenhagen and I was taken to this club called the Mojo Blues Bar. And there were all these blond-haired guys playing the blues. Everything was technically perfect, but there was no feeling, there was no energy. It has to come from truth, otherwise it has no power. You can't play the blues if you didn't live it. You have to earn it with struggle and hard work.

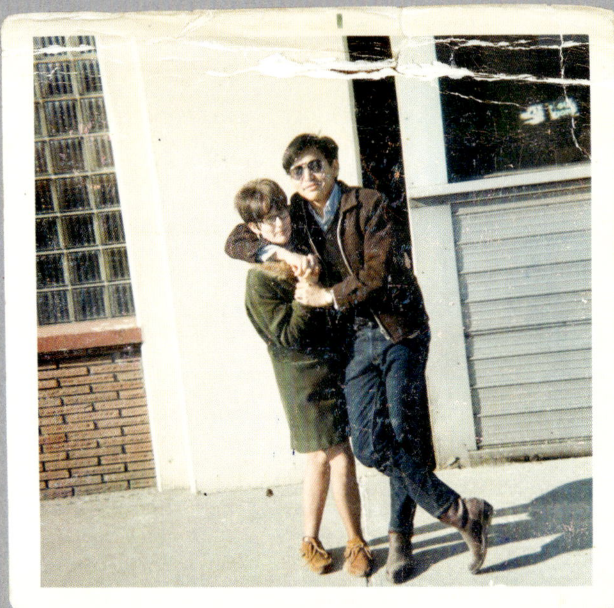

Margaret (Pie) and me, about 1969

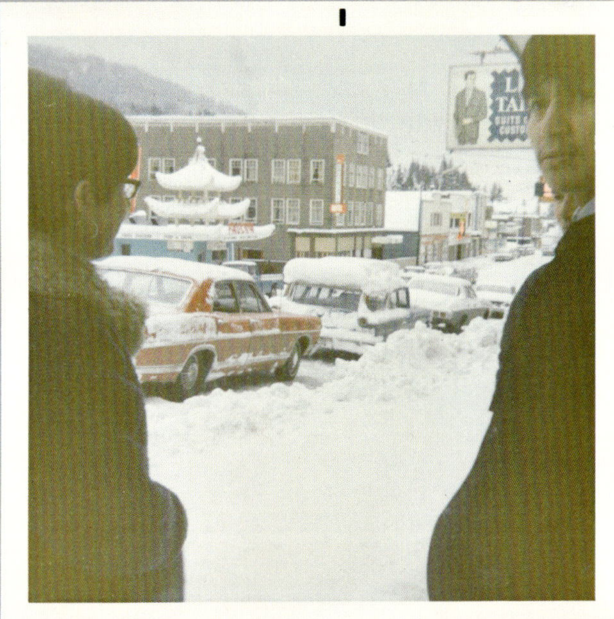

Pie and me in front of the Pagoda restaurant and the Royal Hotel
after a snowstorm, Prince Rupert, BC, about 1969

Pie and me after a snowstorm, Prince Rupert, BC, about 1969

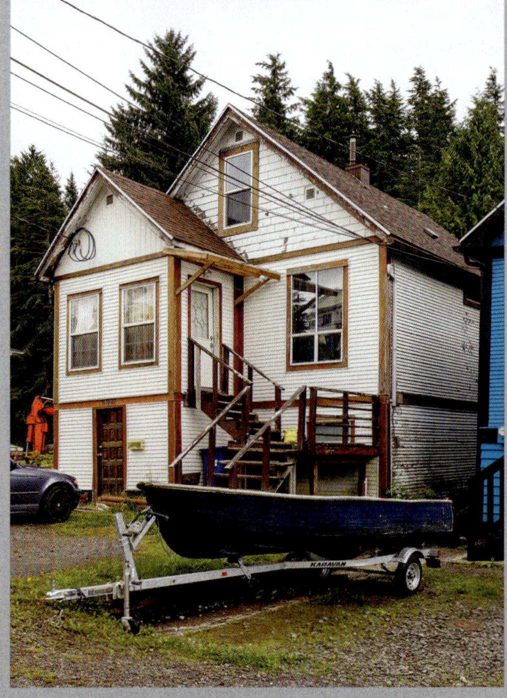

My and Pie's house on Ninth Avenue East,
Prince Rupert, BC, undated

I didn't meet Margaret until '68. She's a real Rupertite—born and raised in Prince Rupert. When I met her she was still going to high school. There were lots of rock 'n' roll dances, there were battles of the bands, and they would play all night. So I think that's where we met. One night we were listening to the song with the line "Bye bye, Miss American Pie," and I said, "I should call you Pie," and I've called her that ever since. A lot of other people call her that too.

There was also an All Native Basketball Tournament there every year, in Rupert—a big feast—and tribes came from all over. After the games they had dances. They still do it—2021 was the first year since 1960 that they haven't done the all-Native tournament, because of COVID. There was a team that came from Metlakatla, Alaska. We used to sneak in there and watch the games.

We've been together since then, since 1968. Our son, David, was born at the end of 1968, and our daughter, Tanya, at the end of '74. Now we have four grandchildren: Grayson, Roy, Keely, and Nate.

Me and Pie got our first little place together in 1973. I used to carve in that basement apartment, on a little table. Then we moved upstairs, and I had a better place to carve. I used to carve up in the attic. The rent was $75 a month, and then it went up to $85 and we protested. But in the end, we stayed there anyway.

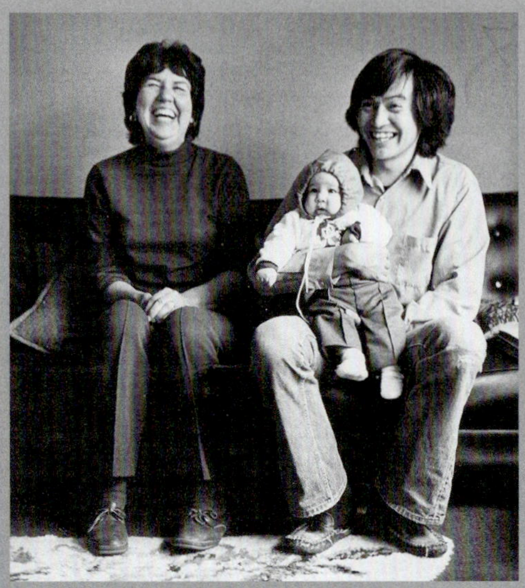

Freda Diesing with me and my daughter, Tanya, Prince Rupert, 1975 (Photo: Ulli Steltzer)

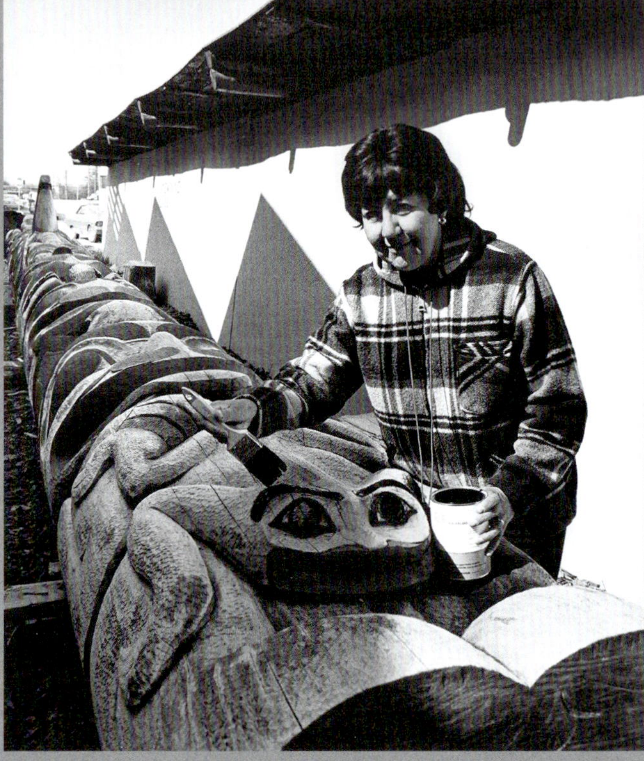

Freda Diesing with the totem pole she and Josiah Tait carved for the city of Prince Rupert, 1975, still standing in Moose Tot Park, Prince Rupert. Freda was the first woman to carve large totem poles on the Northwest Coast. (Photo: Ulli Steltzer)

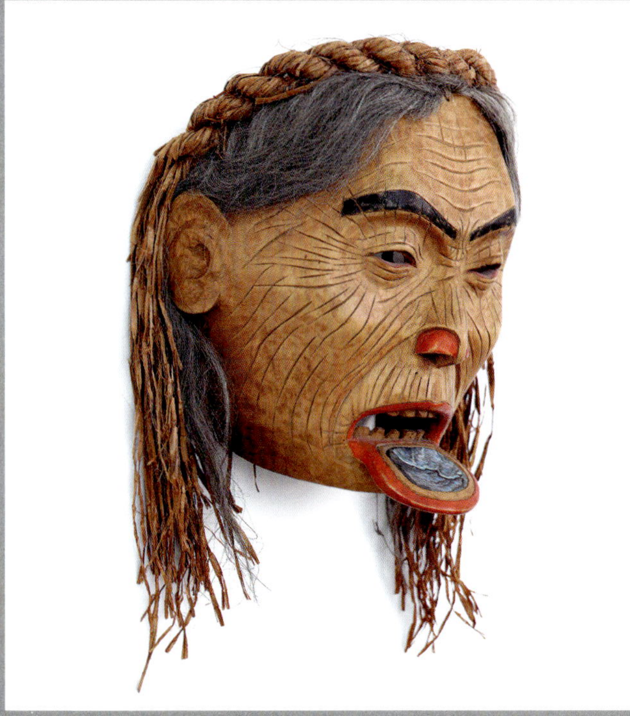

Freda Diesing, *Old Woman with Labret*, 1973

When I started making art, it sort of happened by accident. Freda Diesing was teaching in Prince Rupert but I didn't know her. My friend Tommy Reece was going to her carving class. He's Tsimshian from Hartley Bay, and his brother Danny was going there too. Freda was teaching then at the Friendship House in Prince Rupert. Tommy bugged me for months to go with him, and I said, "I've got no tools! How can I carve when I have no tools?" My brother Tony used to carve a bit. He had some gouges and chisels. So I went there and I borrowed his tools, and I finally learned carving with Tommy and Freda.

She must have been around forty-three years old when I met her. I started talking with her and I liked her. She was a good person, a good human being. And she was very smart and she knew exactly what was happening. Freda Diesing has never gotten the recognition she deserved, but she was a key person in the revival of mainland carving. She taught so many artists: Don Yeomans, her nephew, and Norman Tait, me, Alvin Adkins,[28] his brother Richard Adkins,[29] Norman Jackson,[30] and Gerry Marks.[31] She did both teaching and carving. Her students were like her children.

All her students were part of that generation born just after the Second World War: Norman Tait, Robert Jackson, me, Gerry Marks—a lot of us were born in the late '40s. Robert Davidson,[32] the Haida carver, was part of that generation too. We were the second wave, after Freda and Walter Harris,[33] Earl Muldon,[34] and Bill Reid.[35] I was lucky that I met her and we became friends. Freda wasn't pushy about recognition but she was a truly great teacher. She taught us how to make tools too. Because we had no money, we had to make our own. She taught us how to really see the art, and how to find the information and to learn from good books.

In Port Edward, we used to get leftover cedar from the Japanese boat builders. I got that really good feeling of working with my hands. I knew this was what I wanted to do. With Freda I started drawing again, too, and she liked what I was doing. She pushed me until I hit my own wall. I had to go back and learn to

28. Alvin Adkins (b. 1959 Haida)

29. Richard Adkins (b. 1955 Haida)

30. Norman Jackson (b. 1957 Tlingit)

31. Gerry Marks (1949–2020 Haida)

32. Robert Davidson (b. 1946 Haida-Tlingit)

33. Walter Harris (1931–2009 Gitxsan)

34. Earl Muldon (1936–2022 Gitxsan)

35. Bill Reid (1920–1998 Haida)

draw properly to get anywhere, because sculpture is all about the lines. As artists, we look for the magic line. That's what gives it life. You've got to live the line—that's what Rembrandt said. I think that's what Picasso meant when he said that you have to draw like a child, with that wonder and innocence and that total freedom.

Freda really knew her stuff. She knew the history, but also she could relate to people. To be a good teacher, you have to be able to think on different levels. Also, you've got to be able to share. She was generous. And she was strong in a gentle way. We loved her. We'd do anything for her. The best thing I did was to stay up north and work with her. Other carvers were moving down to Vancouver then, but I think I went further working with our people here than if I had left to go to the city. But I didn't do it for money. I did it for my people and for our culture.

Freda was always interested in what we were doing. We would visit her in her house—we wanted to see all her carvings, and all her old books. We had no way to see our own art. Our art is all over the world now, but not here. We learned it from books—that's all we had. We would sit there and drink tea and wait for her to show us all of her stuff, and then we'd tell her, "We're going to do one like that, only better!"

She knew how to make a helmet, a hat, to make the proper shape of a bowl. You have to know form. You might think it's easy but it's hard! Her carving was the best stuff that we could see at that time, and she gave us the tools to look at the best pieces. She gave us that good eye. And she believed in us. And if we carved something wrong we'd say, "Come and save us!" And she would fix it all up.

While I was studying with Freda I also worked in the fish plant and I worked in the pulp mill, Skeena Cellulose,[36] just to survive. My brother was really mad at me for deciding to go to art school. He would say, "You think that's going to do you any good? You could have a steady job, and get a pension." But I realized that if I stayed at the pulp mill I would just be doing the same thing over and over, repetitive and empty. I didn't want to be given a gold watch for my life.

36. Skeena Cellulose was a forest products company that operated on Watson Island at Prince Rupert. The mill was the largest employer in Prince Rupert until its closure in 2001.

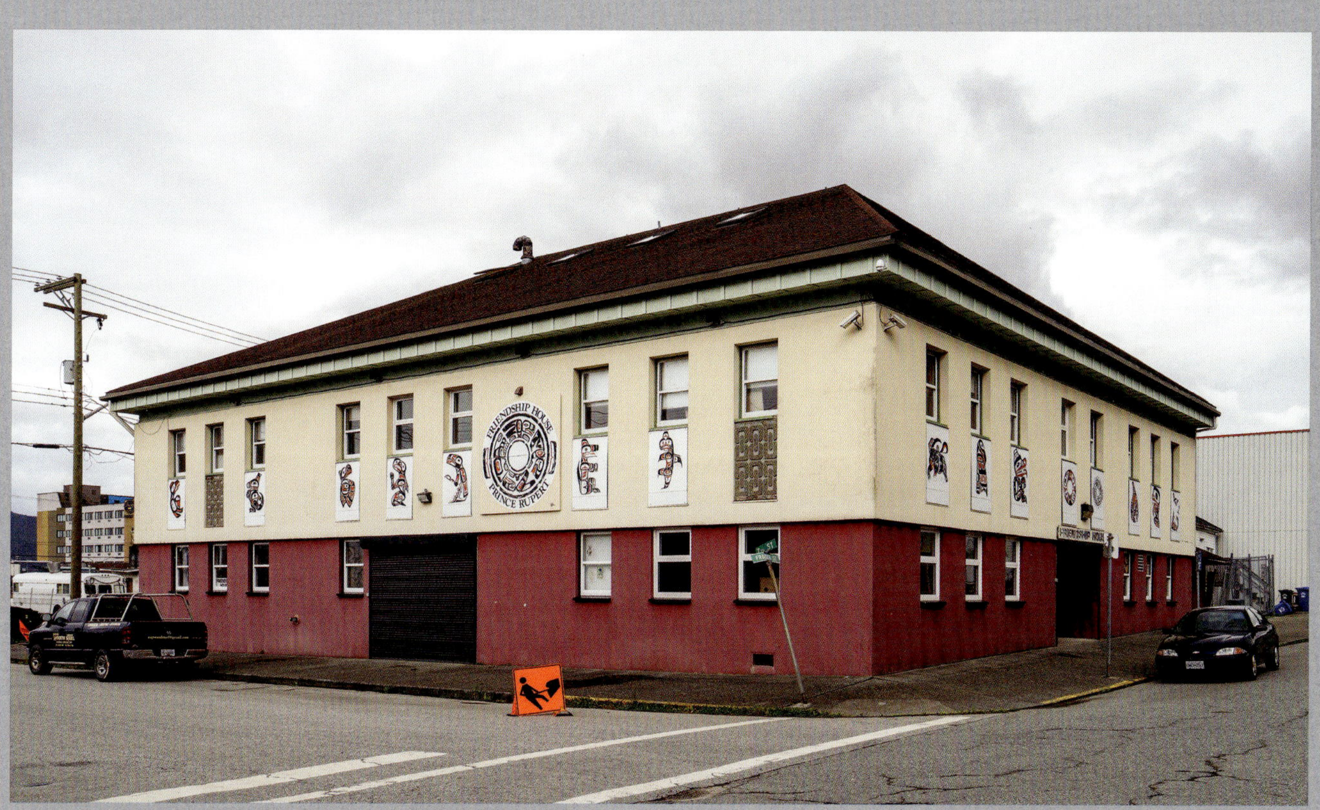

Friendship House, where I first started teaching, Prince Rupert, BC, seen in August 2021

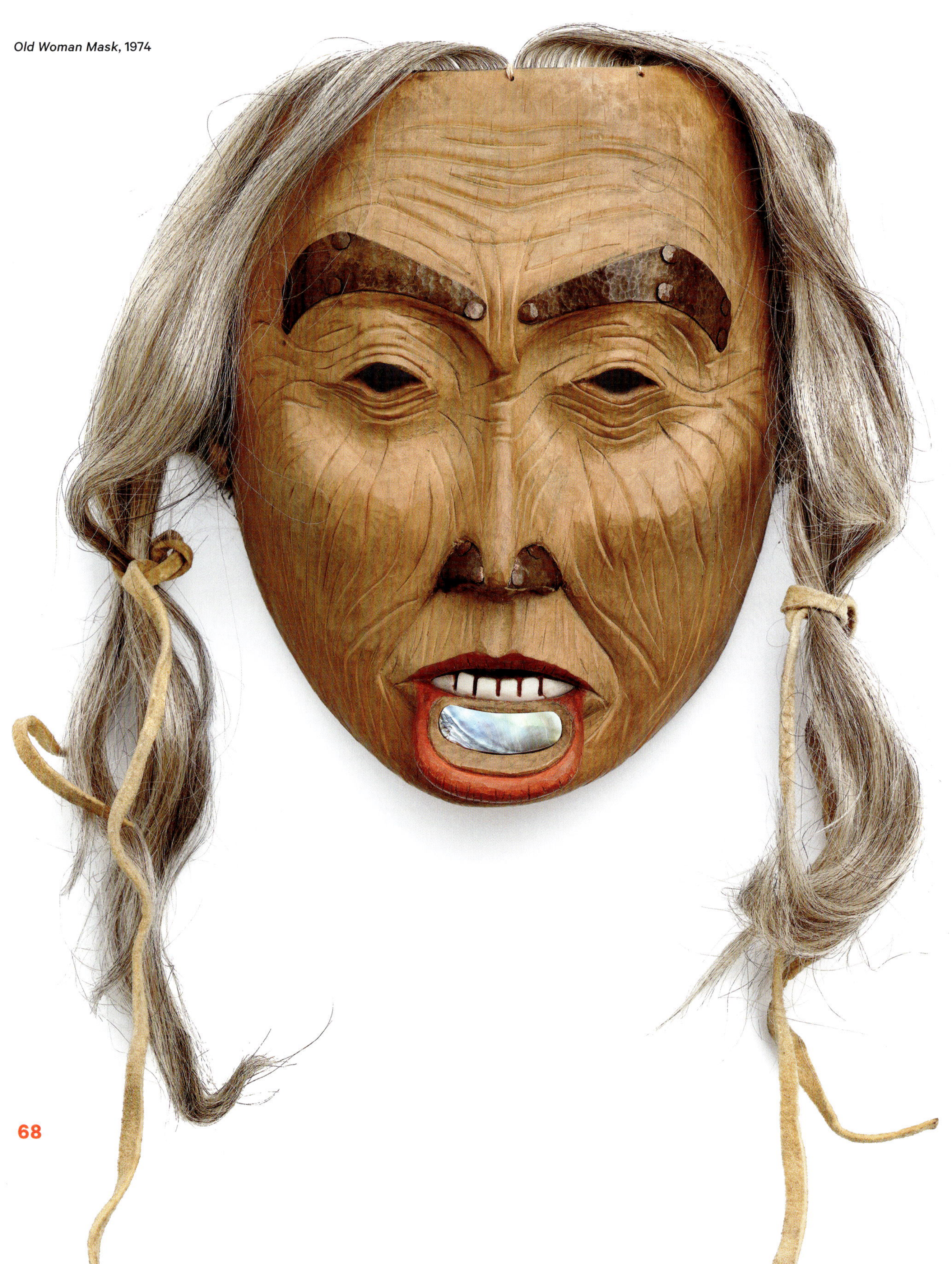

Old Woman Mask, 1974

This is a very early mask of mine. Freda Diesing at that time was making old woman masks.[37] Our people made them; there's images of them in books. What happened was that Freda told me about the Gitanmaax School in Hazelton.[38] I went there in '72, and again in '74. In between I worked with Freda in Prince Rupert. But I made this mask at Hazelton.

They were teaching us portrait masks—we had two weeks to make one. If you finished one, you could make another. I finished mine, so I made the old woman mask next. I thought of my ancestors and my great-aunt Eva and my grandmother.

I'd seen some of Freda's old woman masks—she would always tell us, try this, make that. You have to make a spoon, make a plaque, make a moon mask, make a small totem pole. That's how we learned. I wanted to learn and I wanted to make something different. My teacher wanted to buy it, but I thought, No, I'm going to keep it.

Eventually I gave it to my daughter, Tanya. People asked me to make another old woman mask and I said, "I can't. That's done, in that time and that place. I can't make another one."

37. Beginning in the early 1970s Freda Diesing made several masks that depict matriarchs. Diesing adorned her masks of elderly women with abalone labret piercings, hair, and cedar bark.

38. The Gitanmaax School of Northwest Coast Indian Art in 'Ksan, Hazelton, which opened in 1970, was the first school to offer formal instruction in Northwest Coast art.

People's Moon Mask, 1980

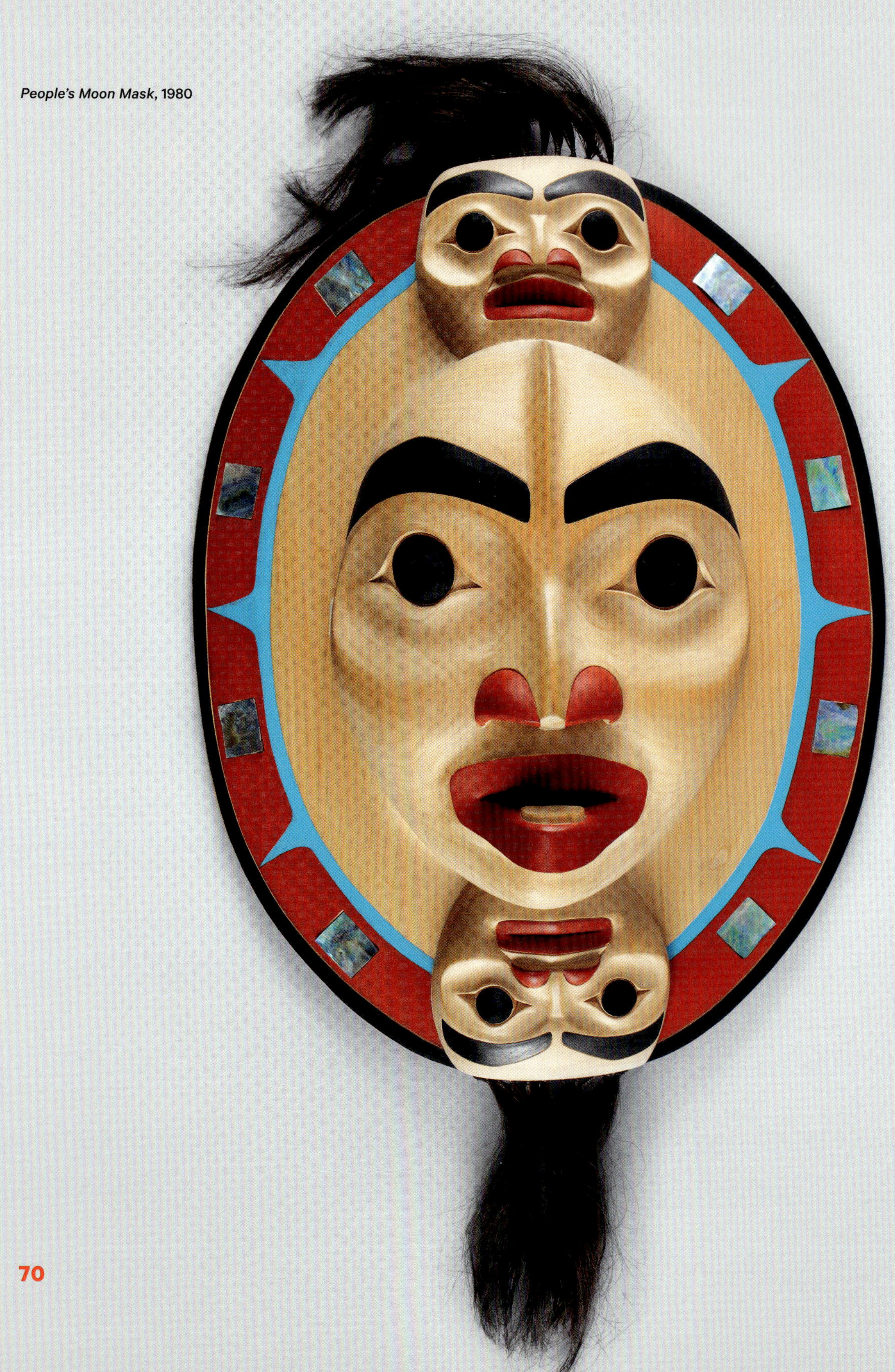

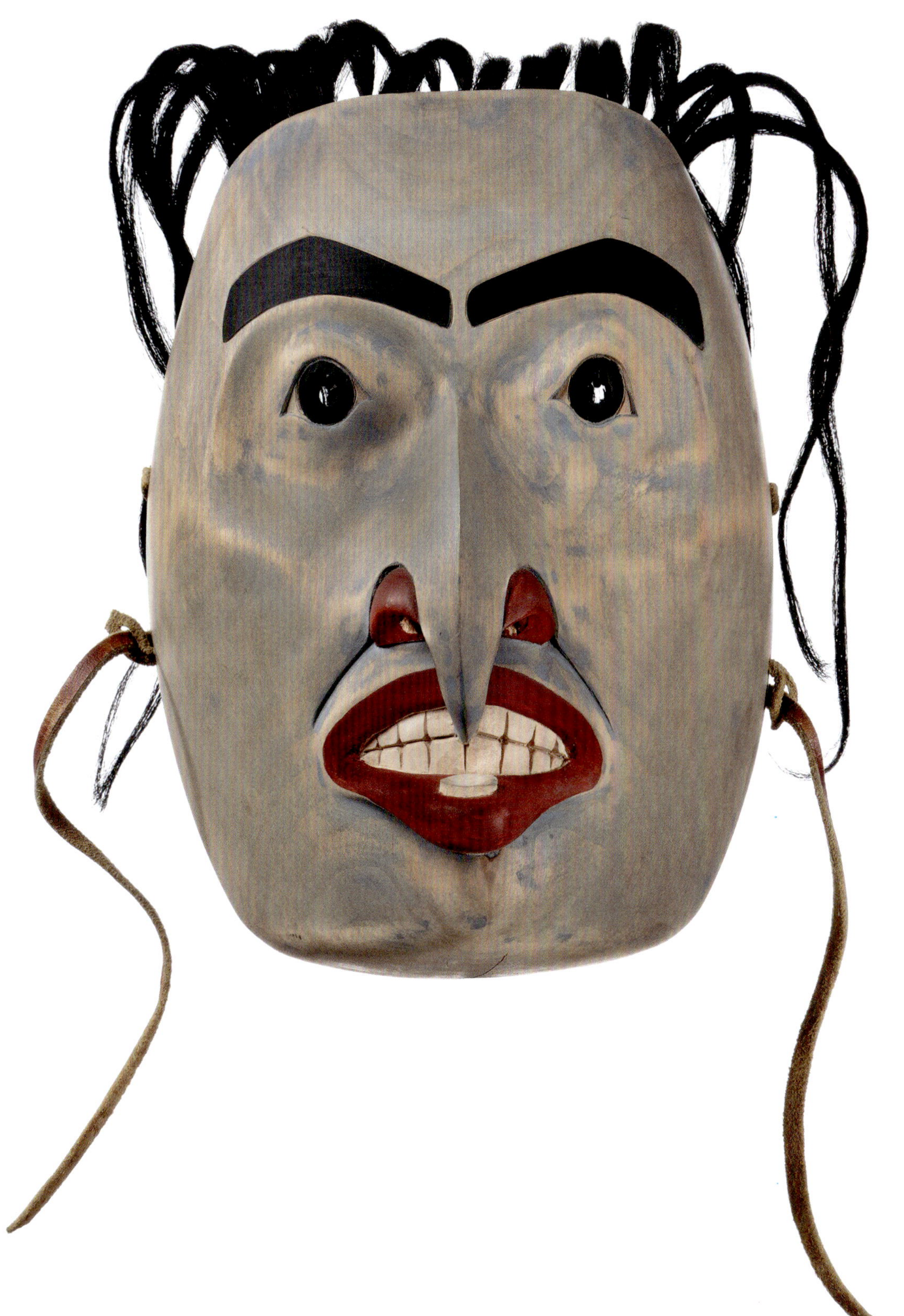

Hawk Portrait Mask, 1974 or earlier

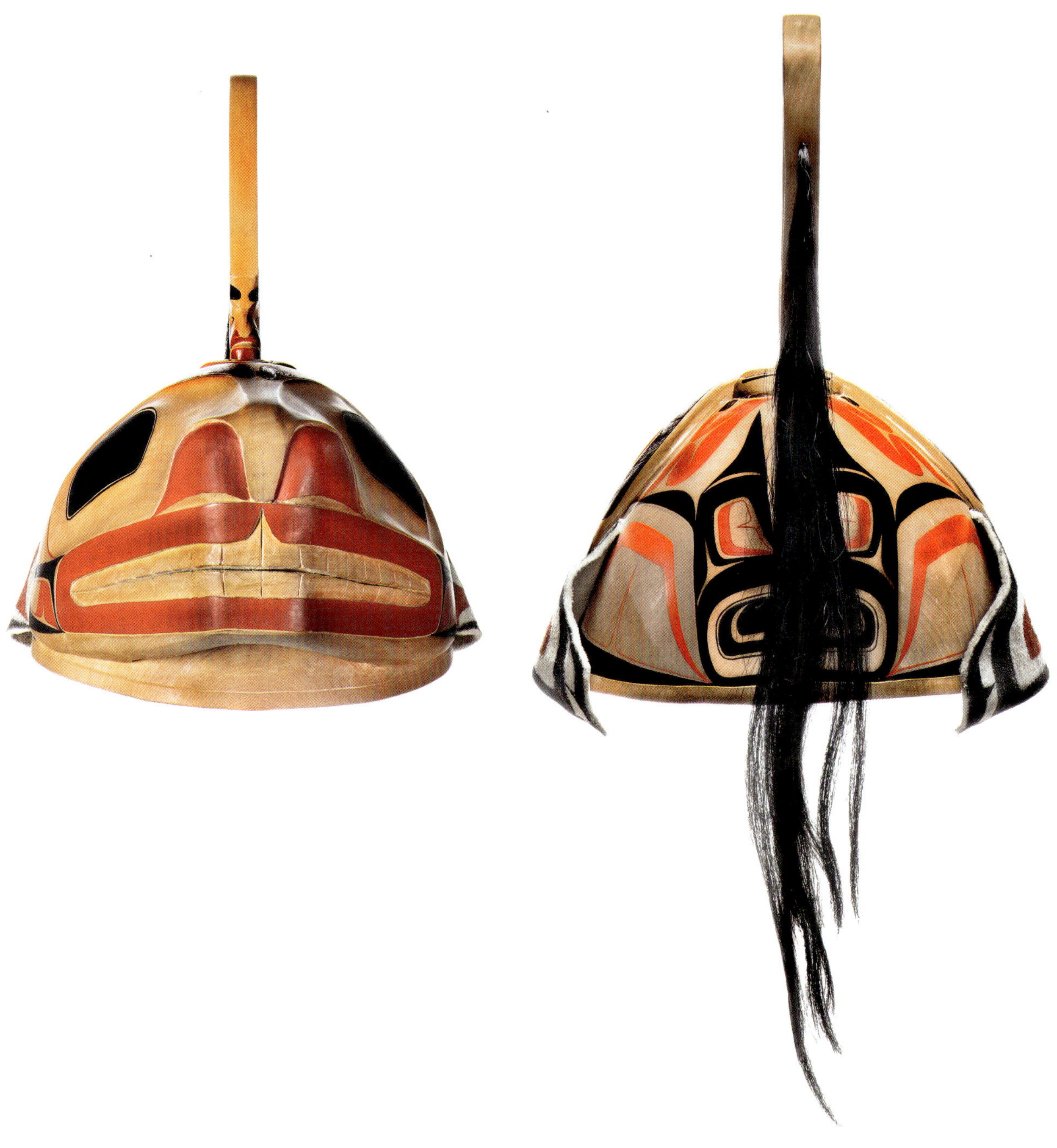

Killer Whale Helmet, 1977 or earlier

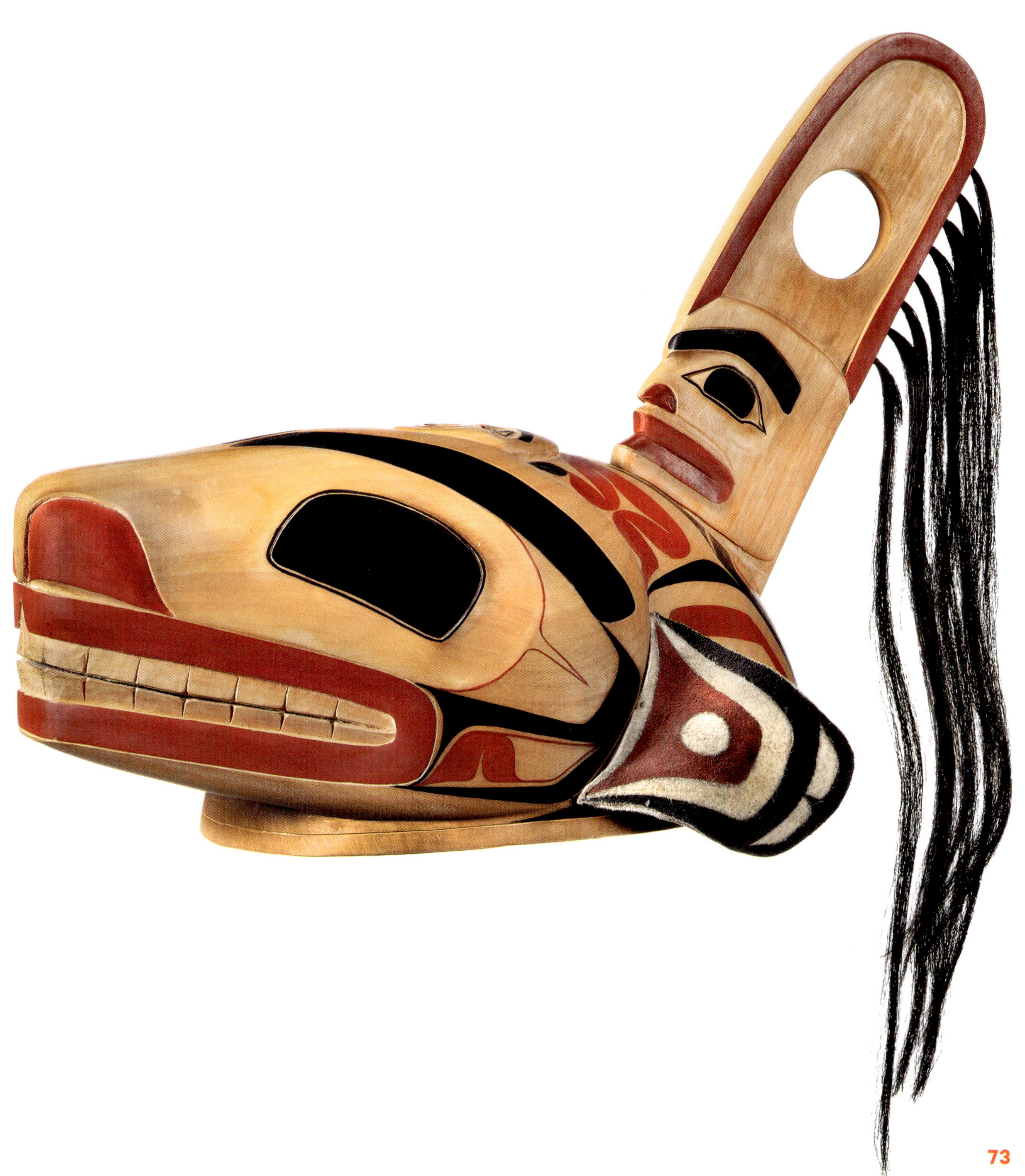

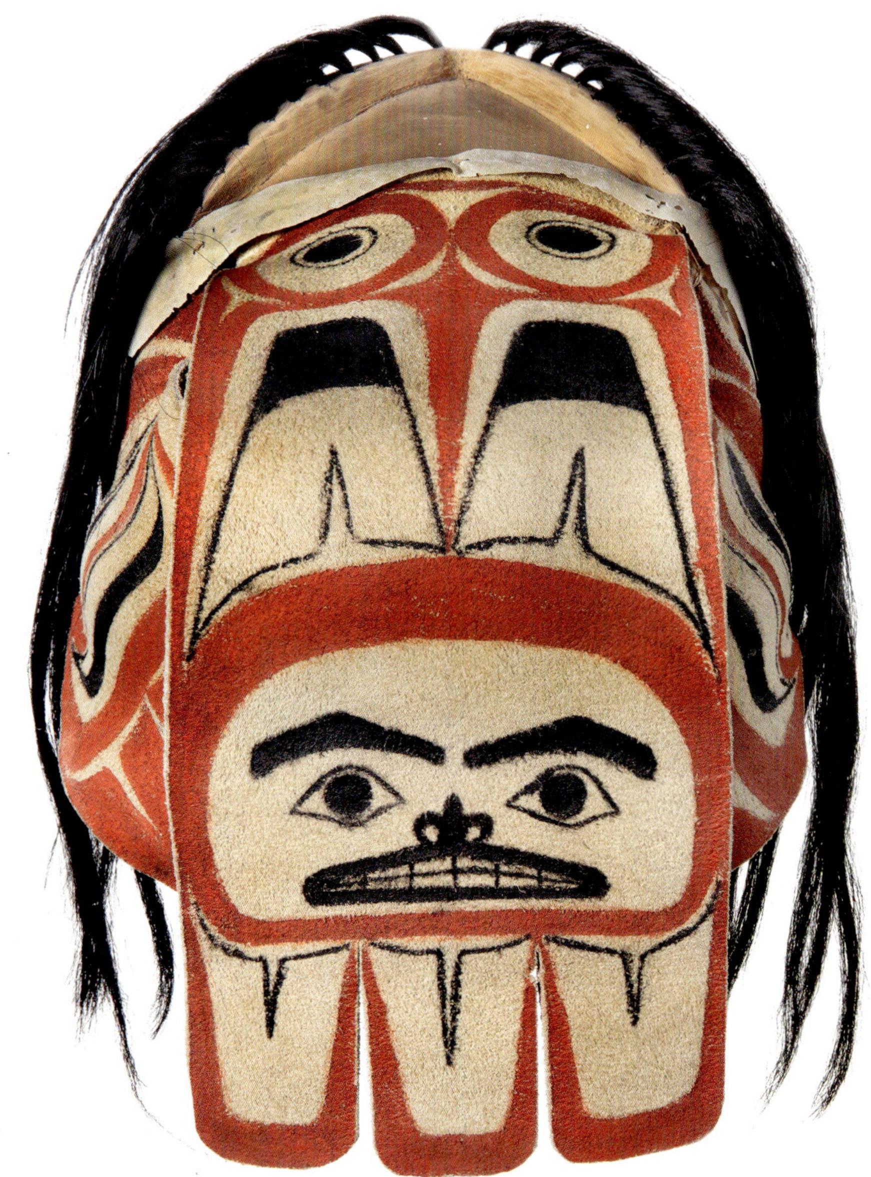

Raven Forehead Mask (back view), 1982 or earlier

74

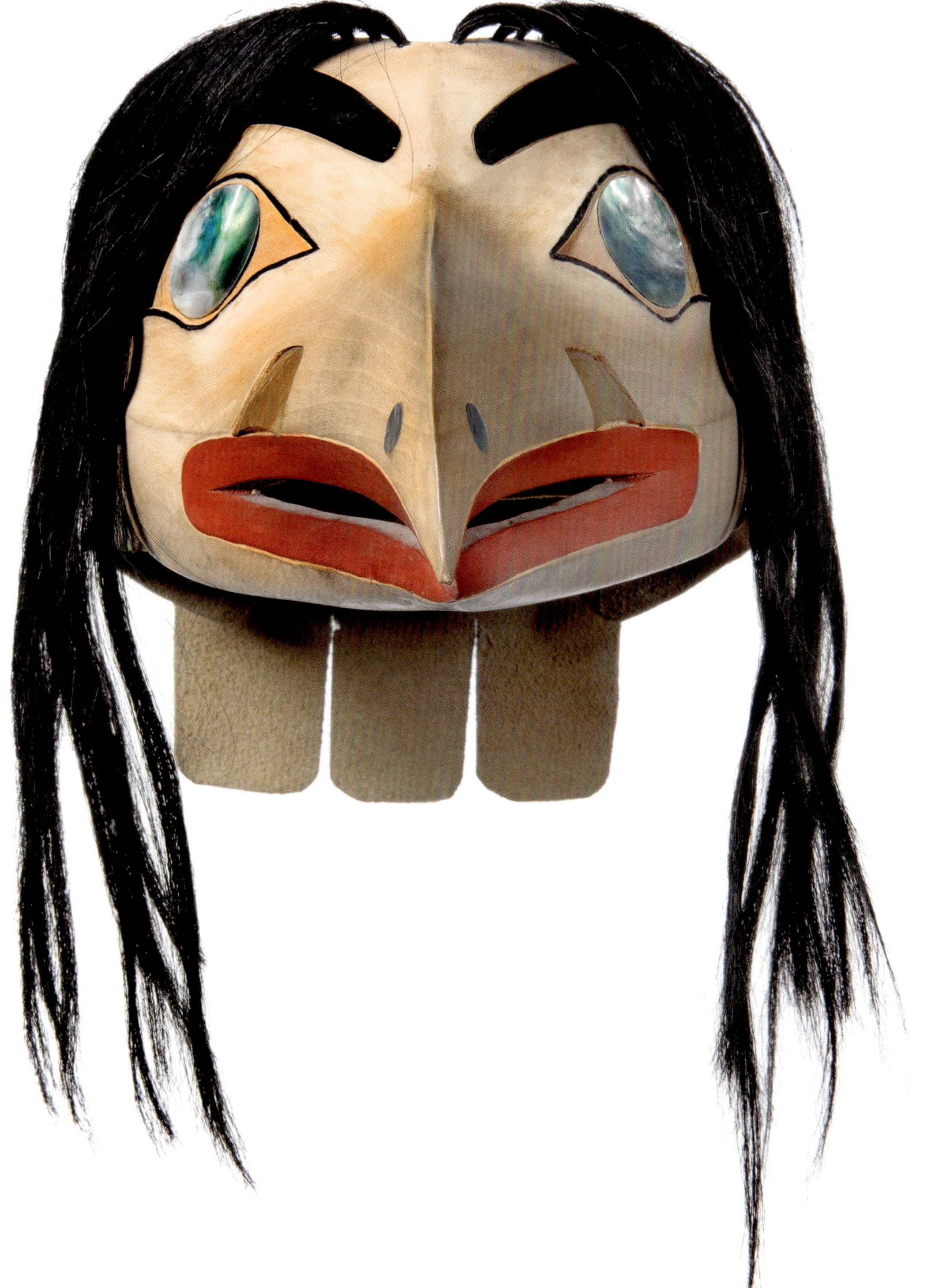

Raven Forehead Mask (front view), 1982 or earlier

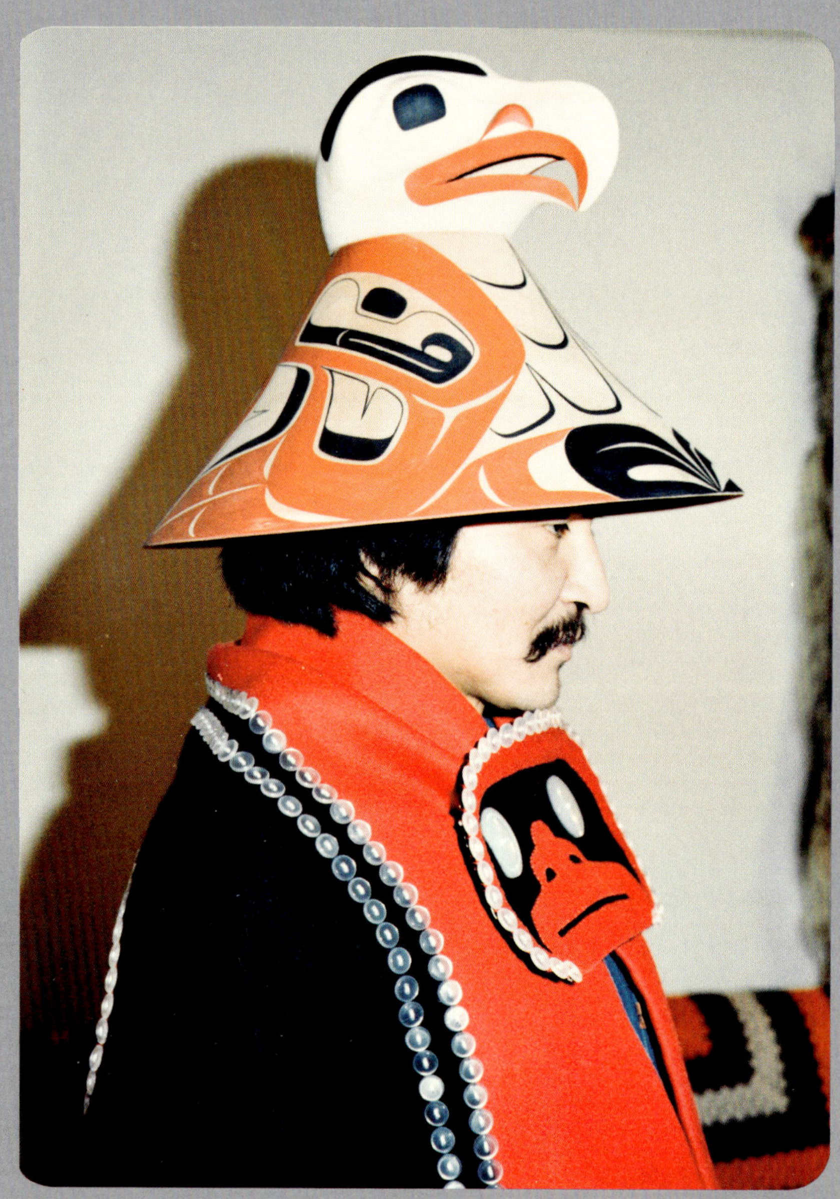

Wearing my *Eagle Chief's Hat*, now in the collection of the
University of British Columbia, Museum of Anthropology, Vancouver

Eagle Chief's Hat, 1982

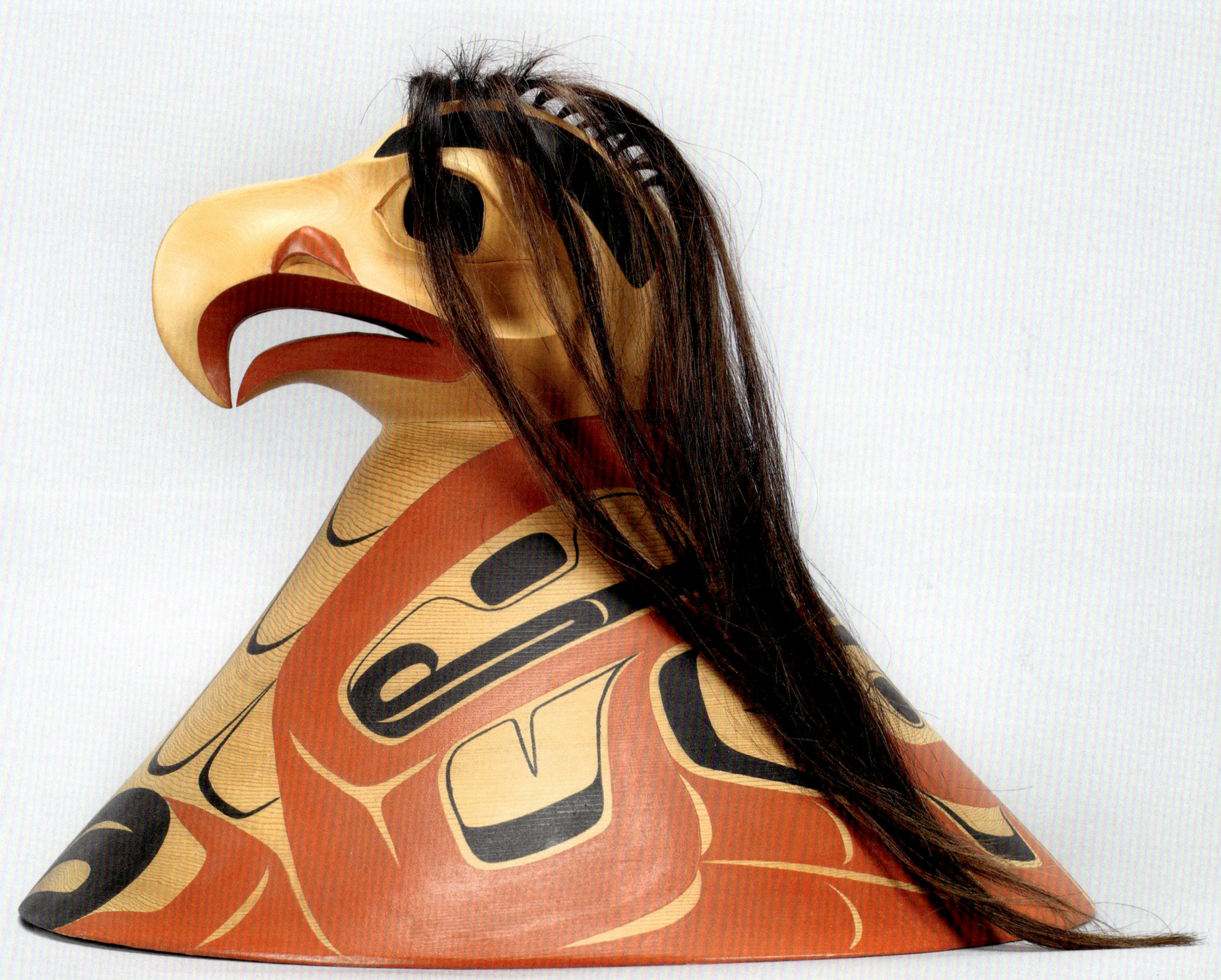

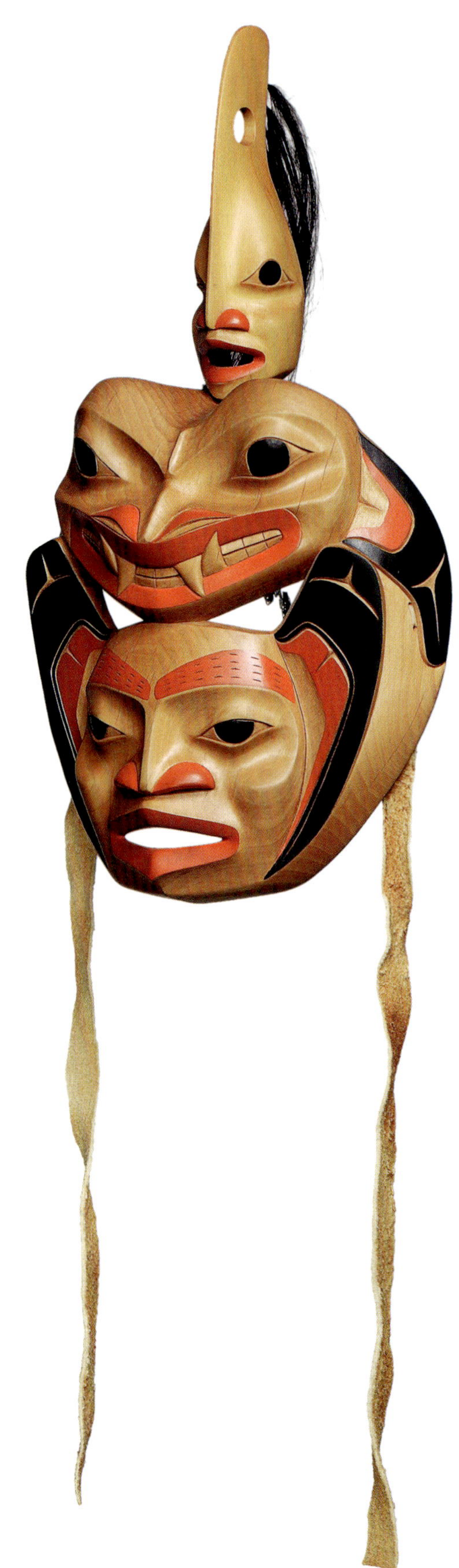

Young Killer Whale Mask, 1986

Eagle Human Mask, 1987

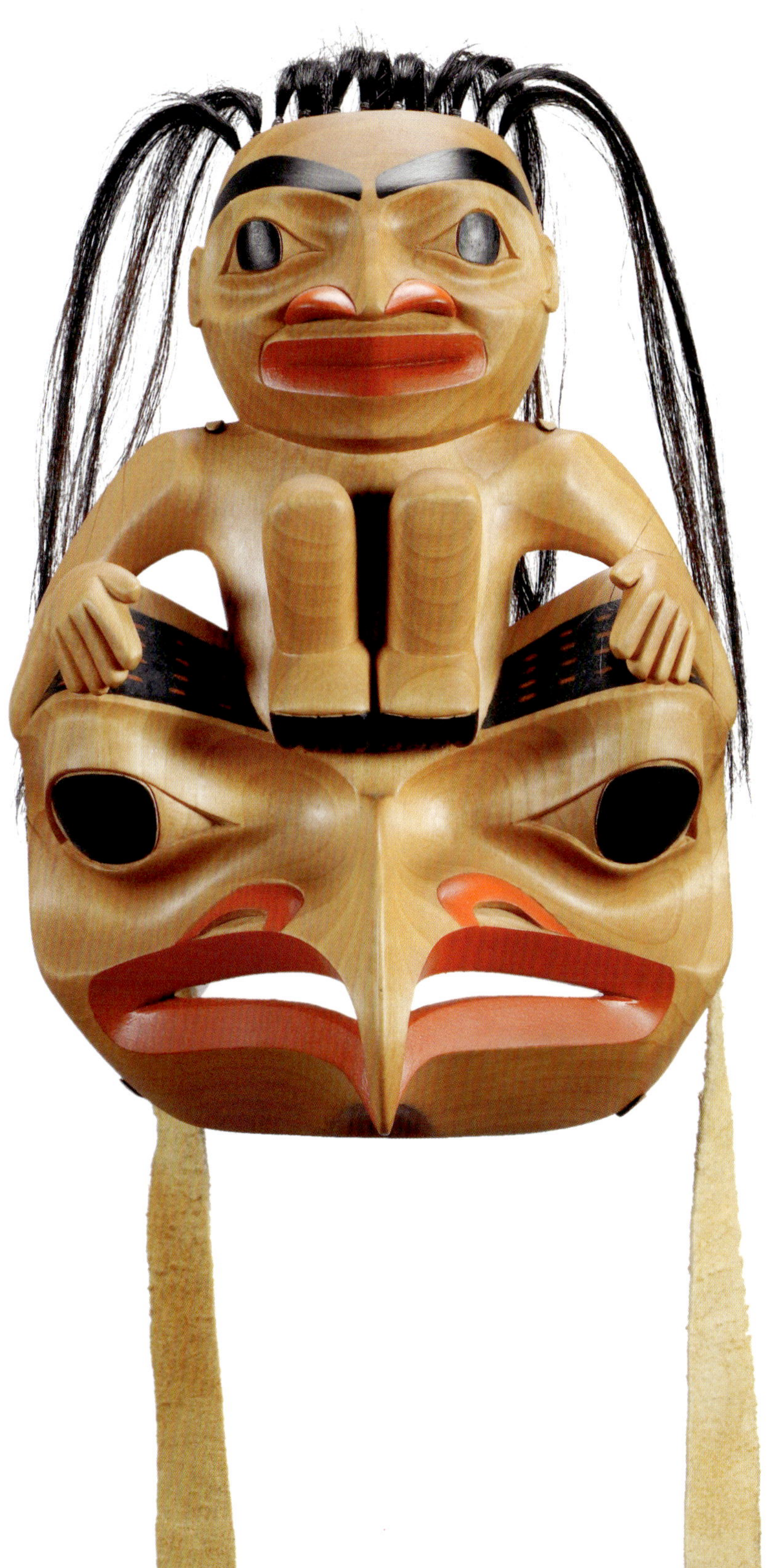

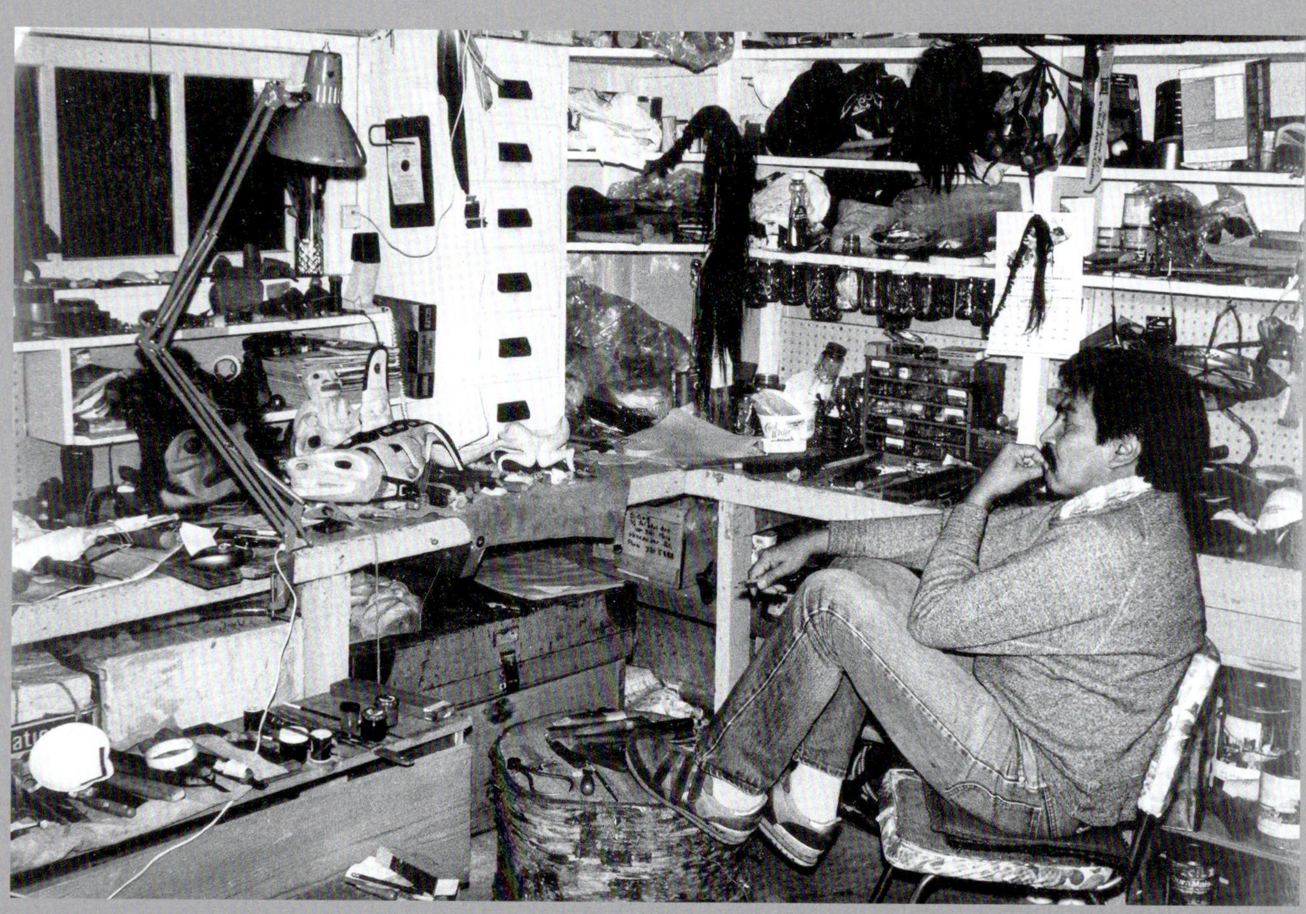

The carving studio in the basement of my and Pie's house on Ninth Avenue East, Prince Rupert, BC, with *Eagle Bear Mask, Eagle Human Mask,* and *Killer Whale Headdress,* about 1986

Killer Whale Headdress, 1987

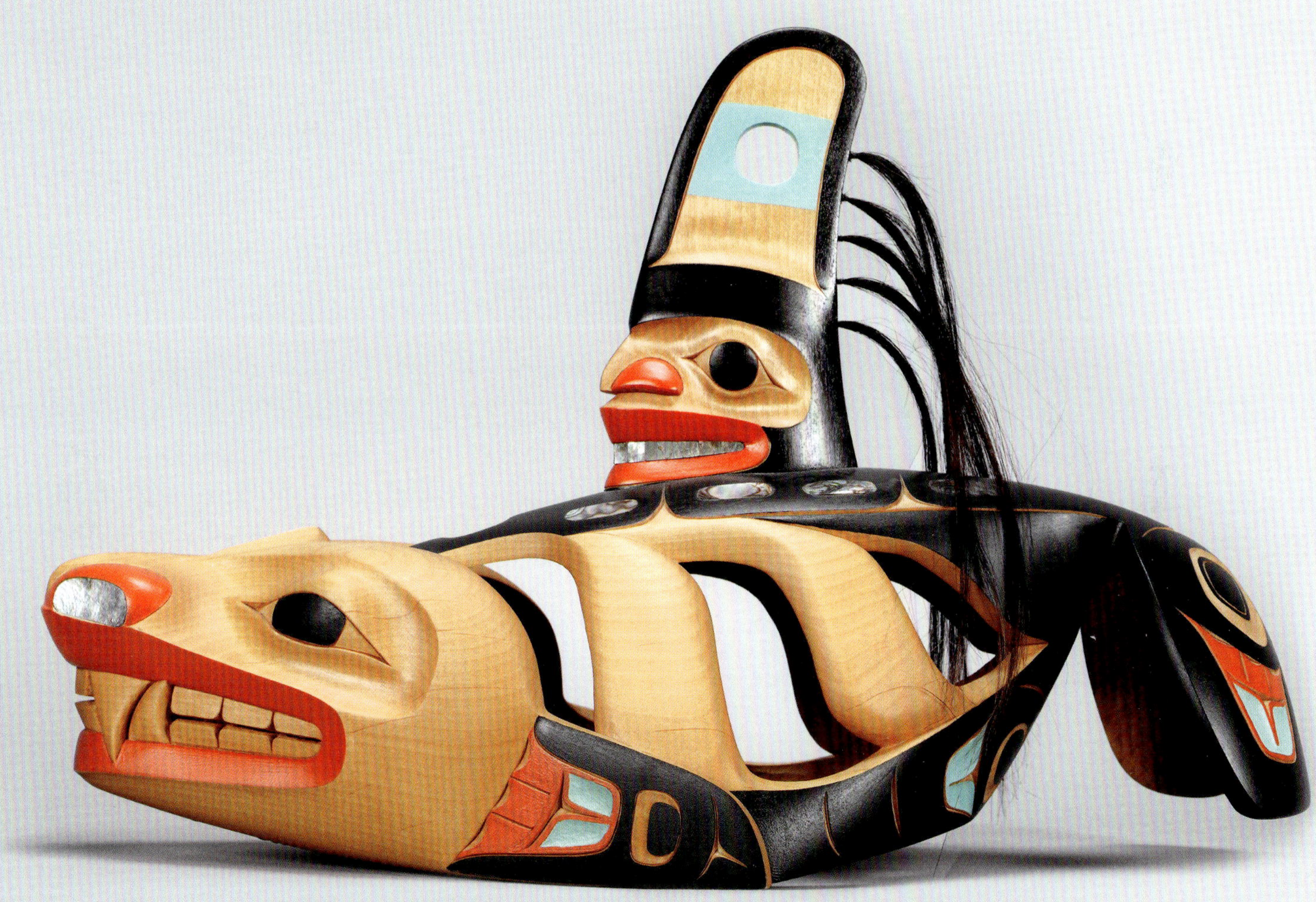

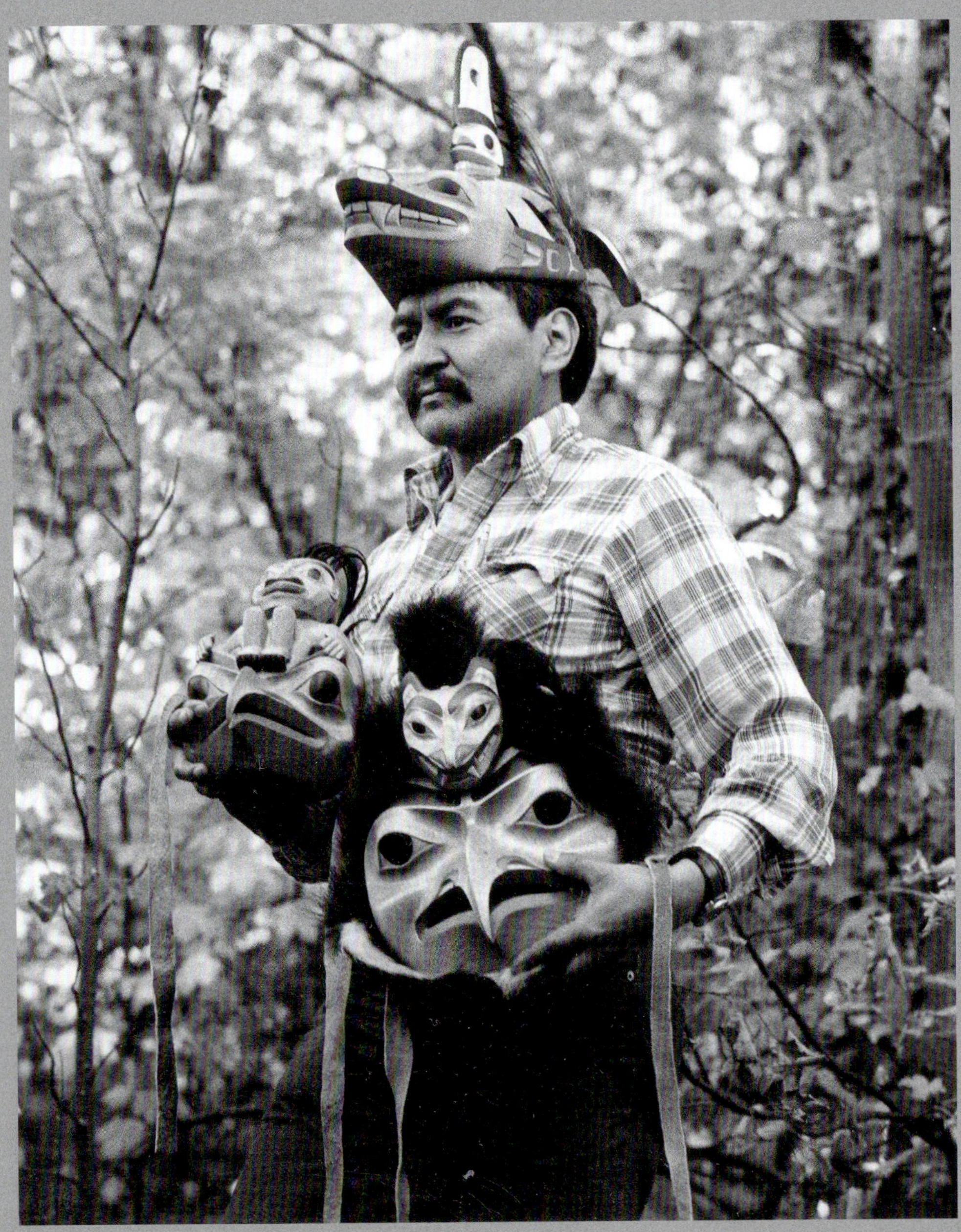

Wearing my *Killer Whale Headdress* and holding my *Eagle Human Mask* (left) and *Eagle Bear Mask*, all from 1987, and all now in the collection of the University of British Columbia, Museum of Anthropology, Vancouver

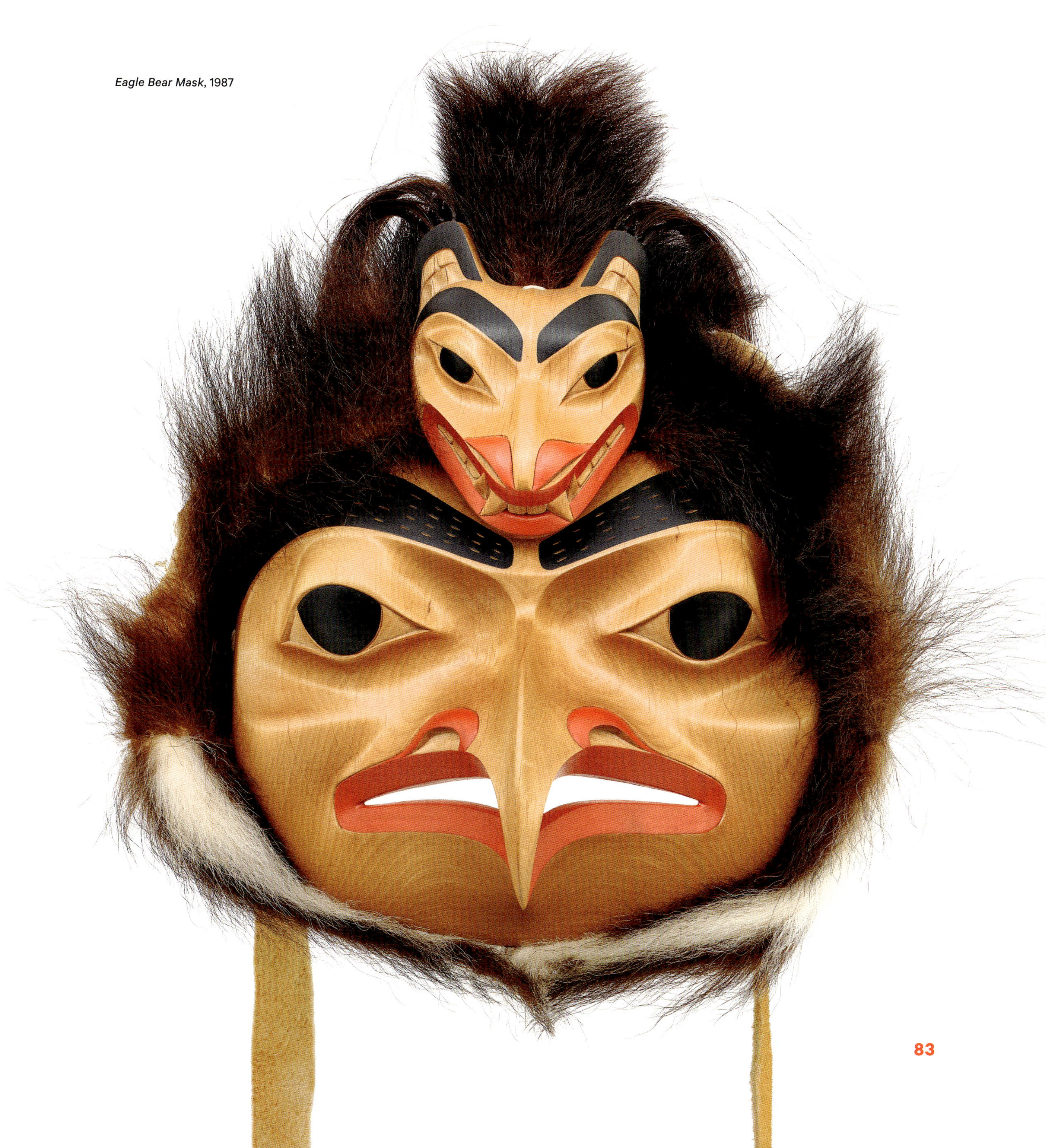

Eagle Bear Mask, 1987

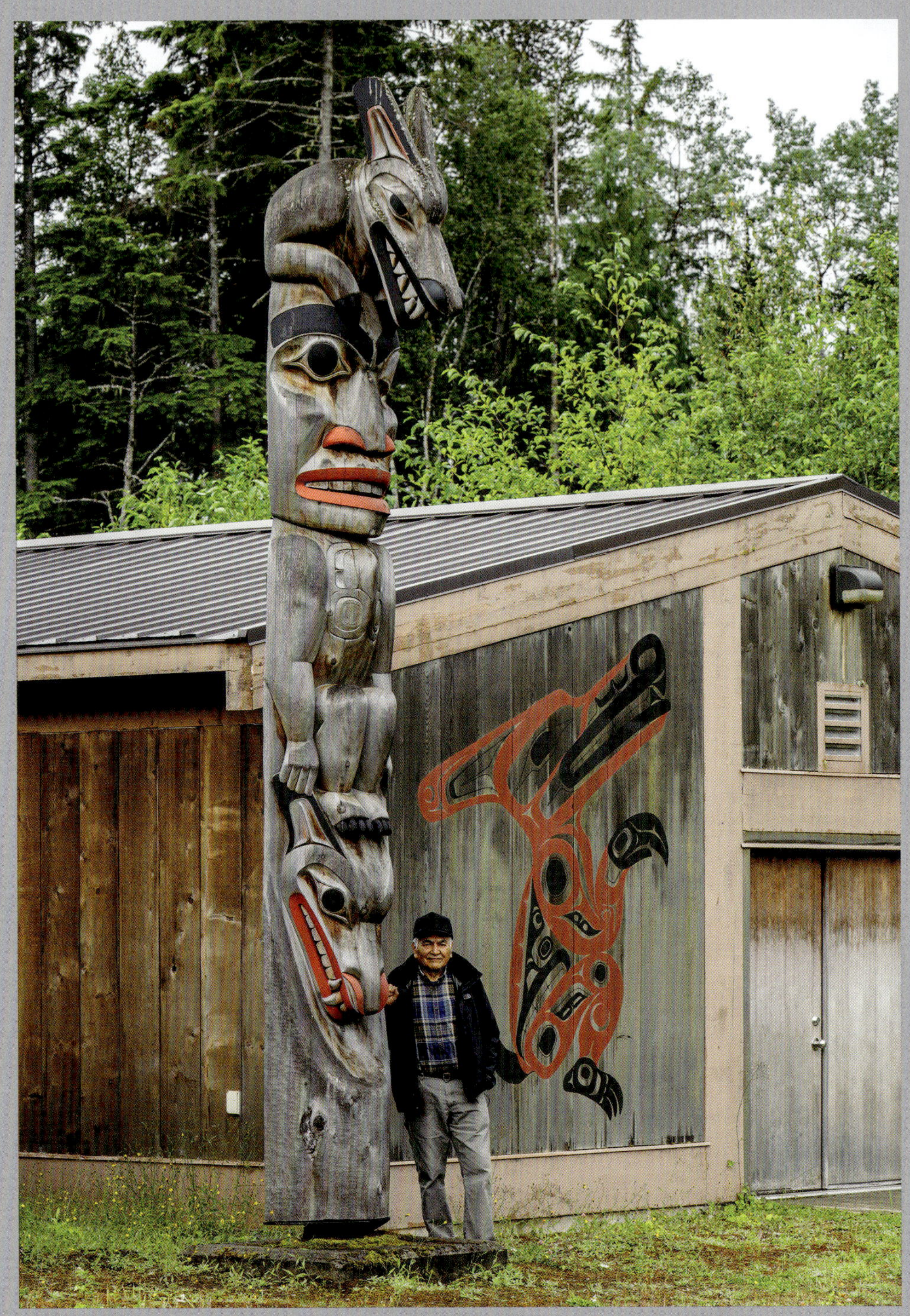

My Wolf pole and Wolf design on a longhouse, Kitselas Canyon, BC, August 2021

In 1976 I made a big pole in Prince Rupert. It was a copy of an old pole that fell down and broke. The city of Prince Rupert commissioned it. It was an eagle pole, and its historic name was *Eagle on the Decayed Pole*. It was large, fifty-two feet high, and it had a lot of figures on it. I carved half of the pole and Glen Wood carved the other half. It's in the Prince Rupert Museum now.

Up in Telegraph we didn't have poles but more sculptures, like the big raven. Down by the Taku River, near Atlin, my grandmother's people, they had the big cedars, so they had poles. Most of those old poles were taken, and some of them were destroyed. My grandfather told me about things being taken—he remembers Emmons, when he came up there. That's how our apron ended up at the Smithsonian. He didn't say too much about it. I don't know how he got it—the pieces are supposed to go to the next generation in the clan. But when so many people died, those lines were broken. And the church people didn't want us to have those things. Some people let their poles go because the church was going to burn them.

There were a couple of big fires up in Telegraph in the 1940s and another in the '50s, and a lot of our old regalia was destroyed —the blankets the drums, the masks. That's how we lost a lot of stuff. And people just sold these things for money. The Totem Pole Gift Shop in Prince Rupert was able to buy a lot of stuff for nothing because people here were having a hard time.

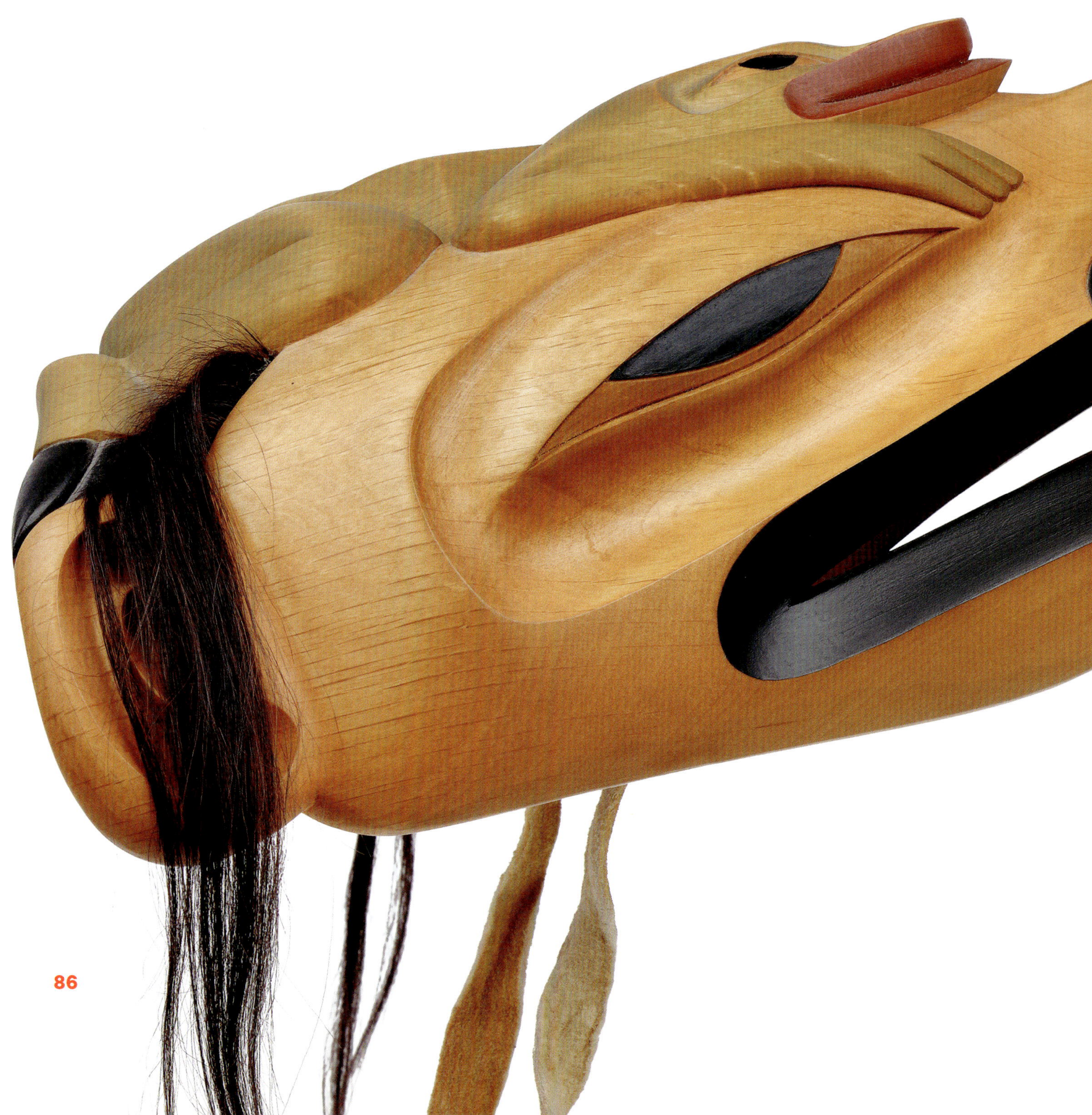

86

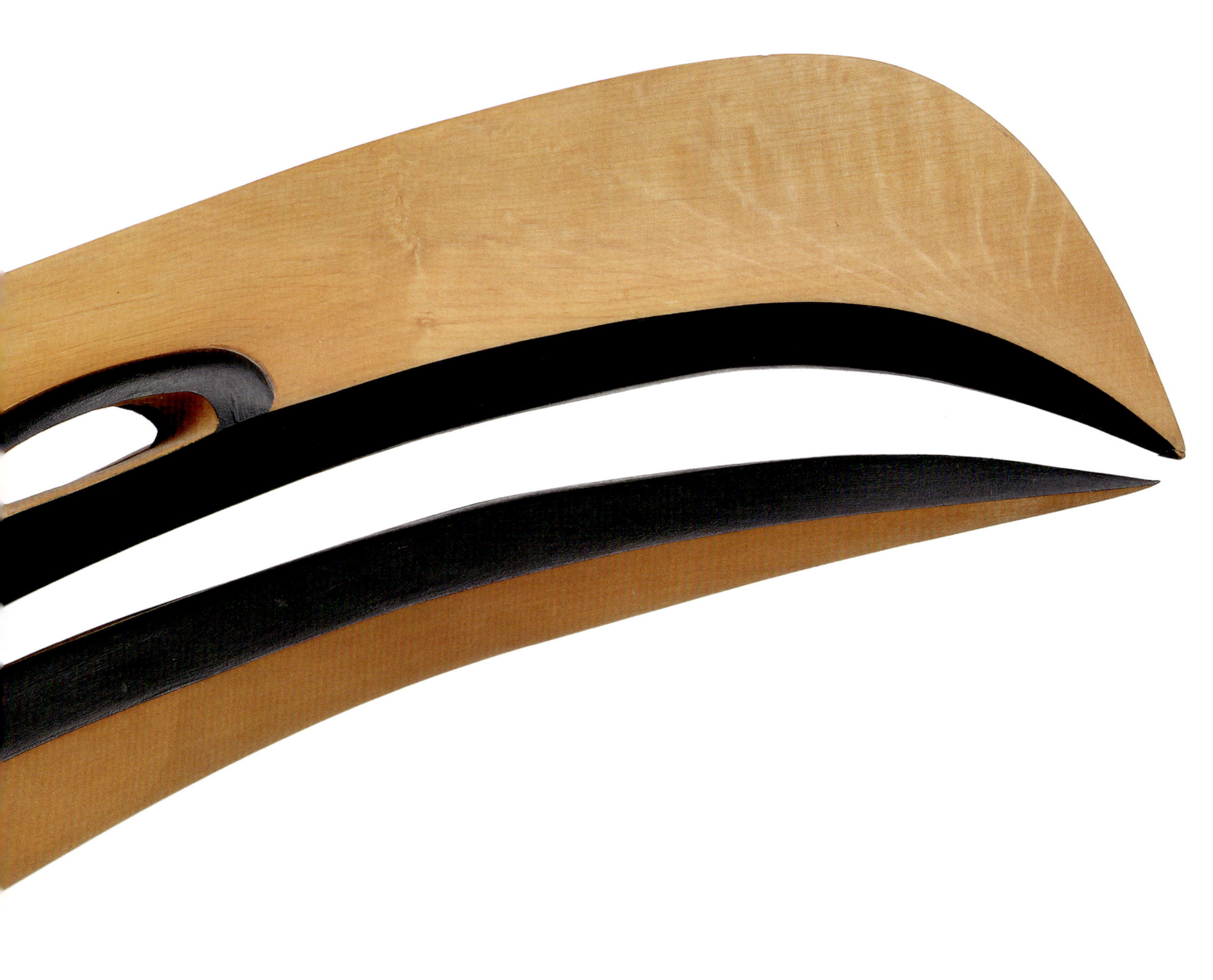

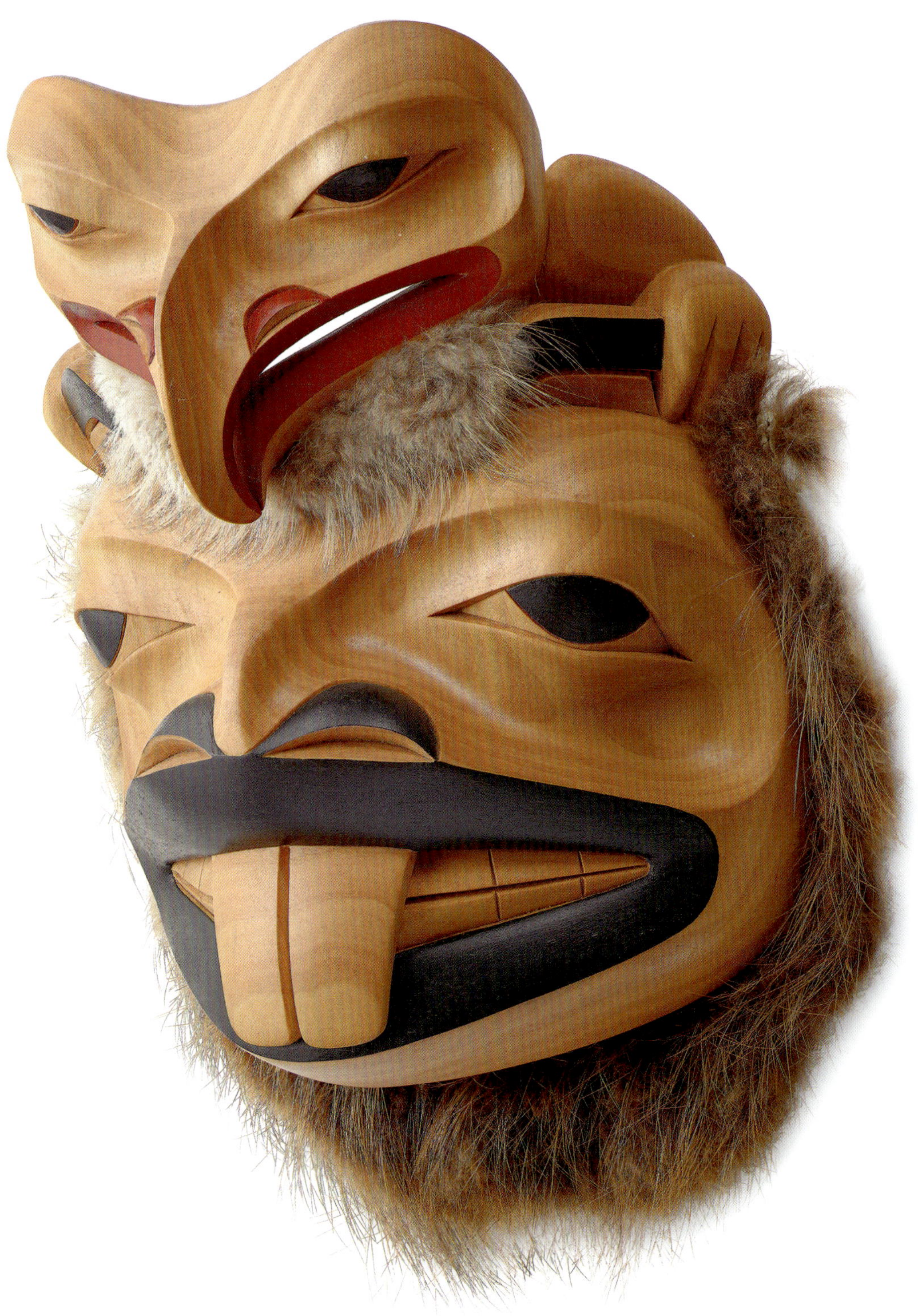

Beaver Eagle Mask, 1989

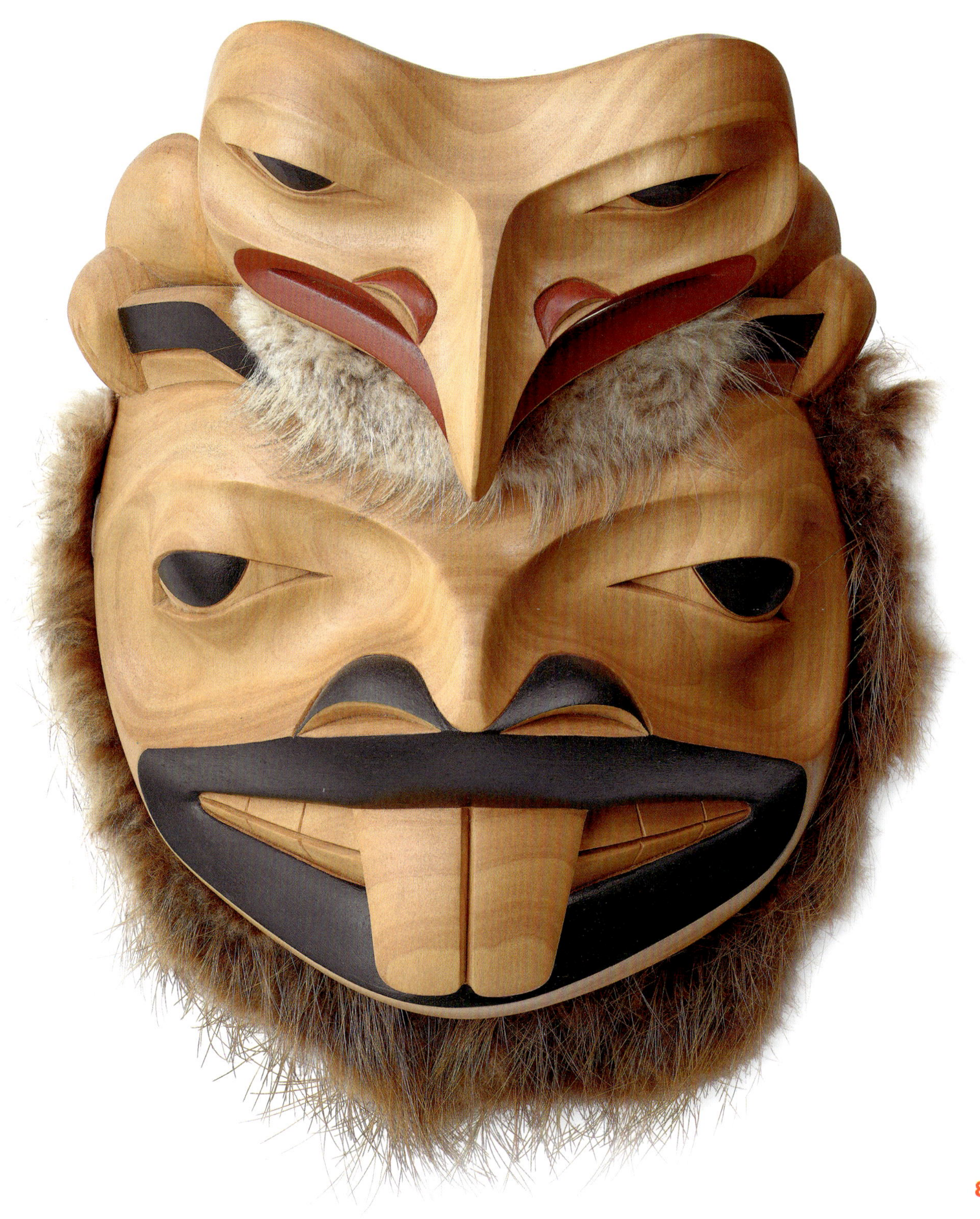

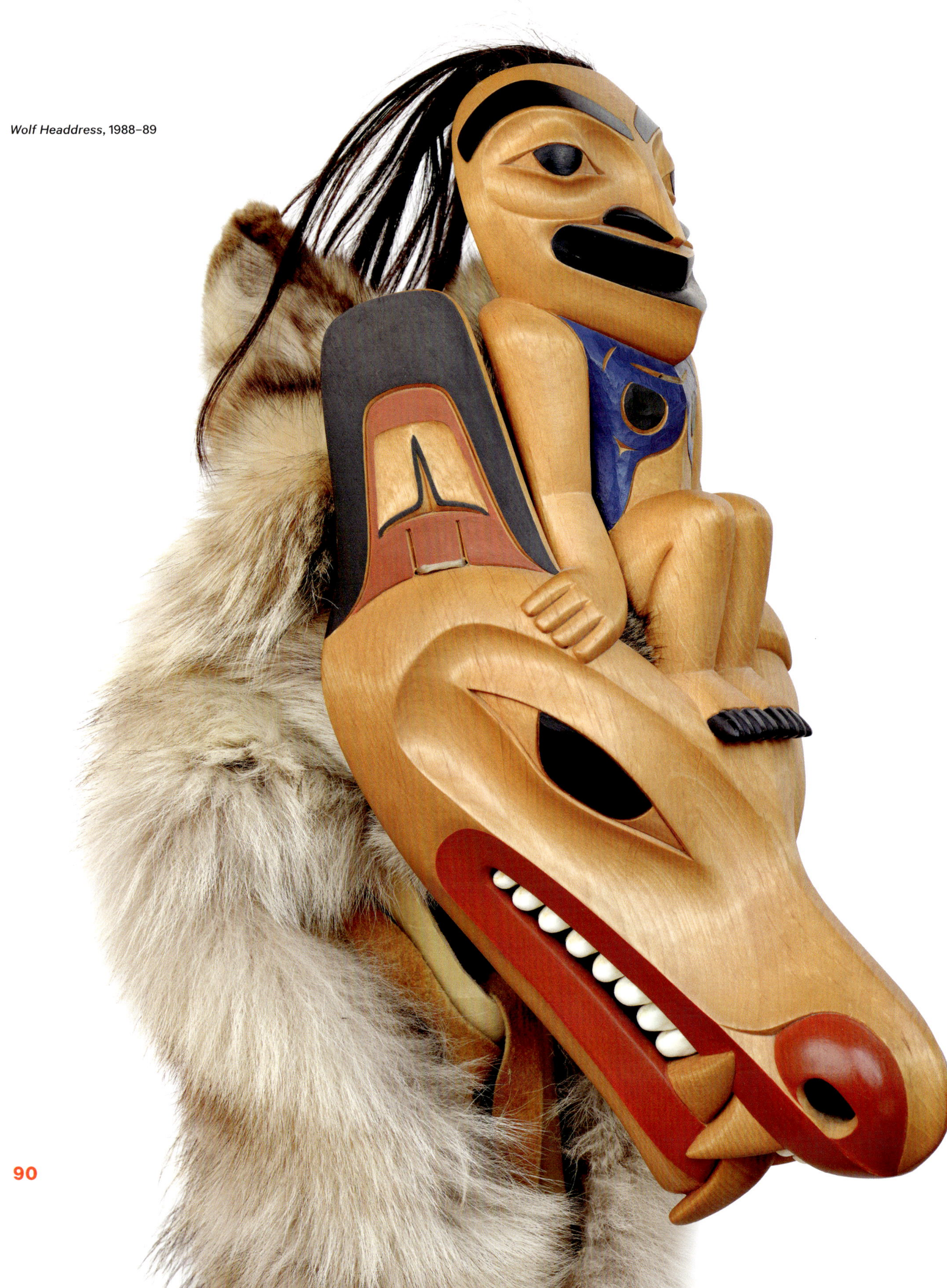

Wolf Headdress, 1988–89

They know stuff. They'll come. I've seen some packs running on the ice on the lake, coming down from Telegraph Creek—it gives you a different feeling. It's not very often that you see it. It feels like a special thing when you do. I realize how strong they are and how smart they are too. They are looking for moose. They will work a whole area that is wide and they will funnel the moose down and chase him right out onto the ice. Moose can't stand on the ice, and when they fall down, that's when the wolves attack. Usually it's about ten or twelve wolves—something around that. They work in families.

I like the beautiful lines when they're moving, and the lines of their faces. When I carve I try to stylize it—what I see and also what I think of them, to bring that together. I try to get those beautiful lines that are flowing, that are moving. In the eyes I see the intelligence, the strength too. They are each different characters. The eyes are very important. I've dreamed them. I've seen them looking at me.

They each have their own traits, their own ways of doing things. And I think about the true freedom they have still, living in the wild and by themselves. The wolves are bound by love, too, for their pups, for the pack.

I have seen how they work their country; they know how to scare the game out. One would scare the game, the other would chase it, one would be waiting up ahead and would take over, and then another would be ahead of that. They would run a moose or a deer like this until it was tired out and then they would get it. They know all kinds of tricks like that. They used to chase the deer into deep snow, too, and then get them.

Their family unit is very, very close, and they can work together. There's a leader of the family—they work like we do. But you hardly ever see them, unless they want to be seen.

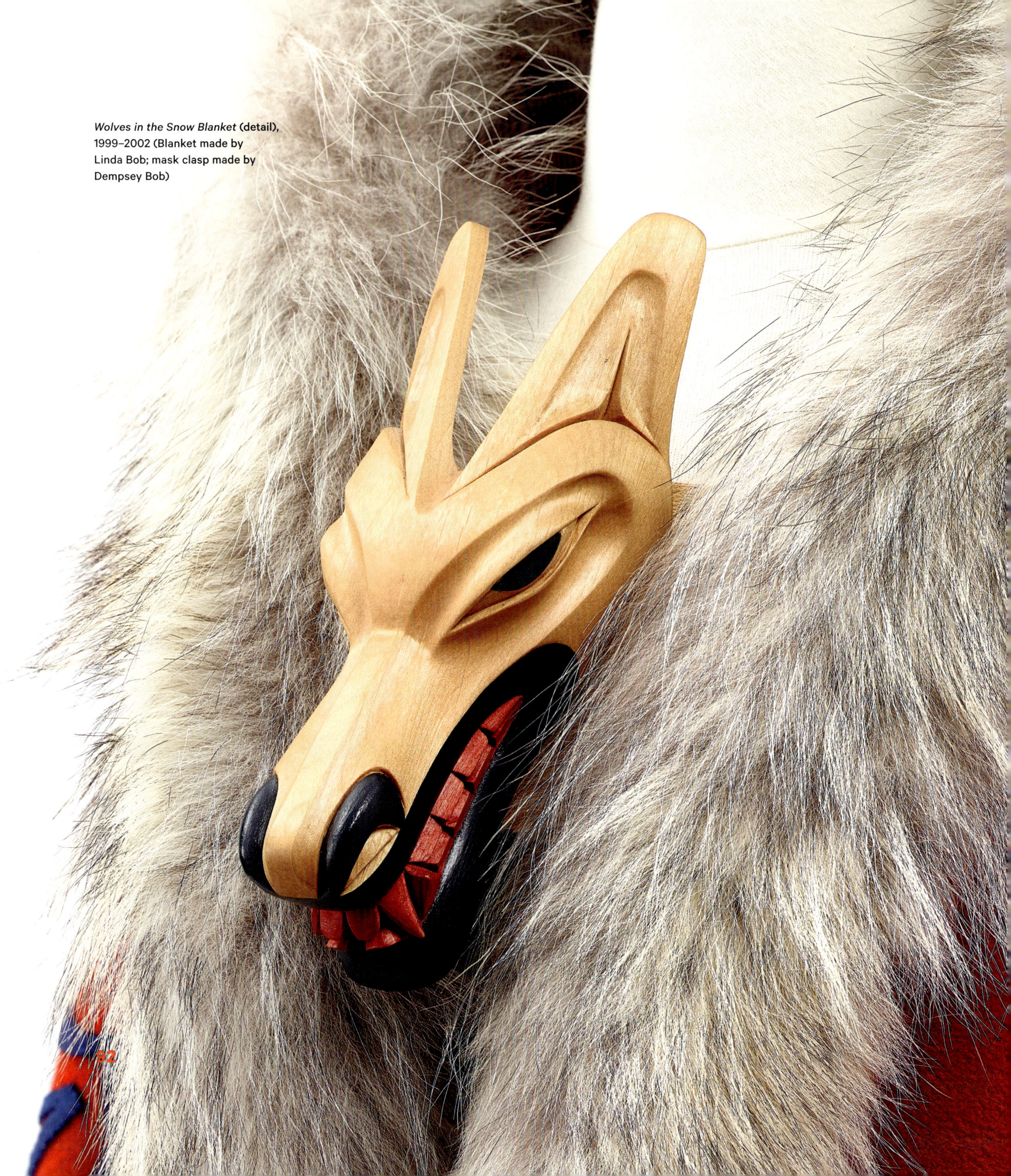

Wolves in the Snow Blanket (detail),
1999–2002 (Blanket made by
Linda Bob; mask clasp made by
Dempsey Bob)

A WOLF STORY

We were out driving to Ridley Island once, near Prince Rupert, and we were going along, and right beside the road—just up on the bank above the road—we saw a wolf. So we stopped the car and went back and he didn't run away. Usually they will run away. He just stood there and looked at us.

We thought about it—what does that mean? Animals will come to you sometimes. So we left and came back and he was still there; we had been gone about an hour. The traffic was going by.

I'm a Wolf, that's my crest. The next day we heard about my first cousin, my mother's sister's son. He had died. That's why the wolf was there. That son was a Wolf.

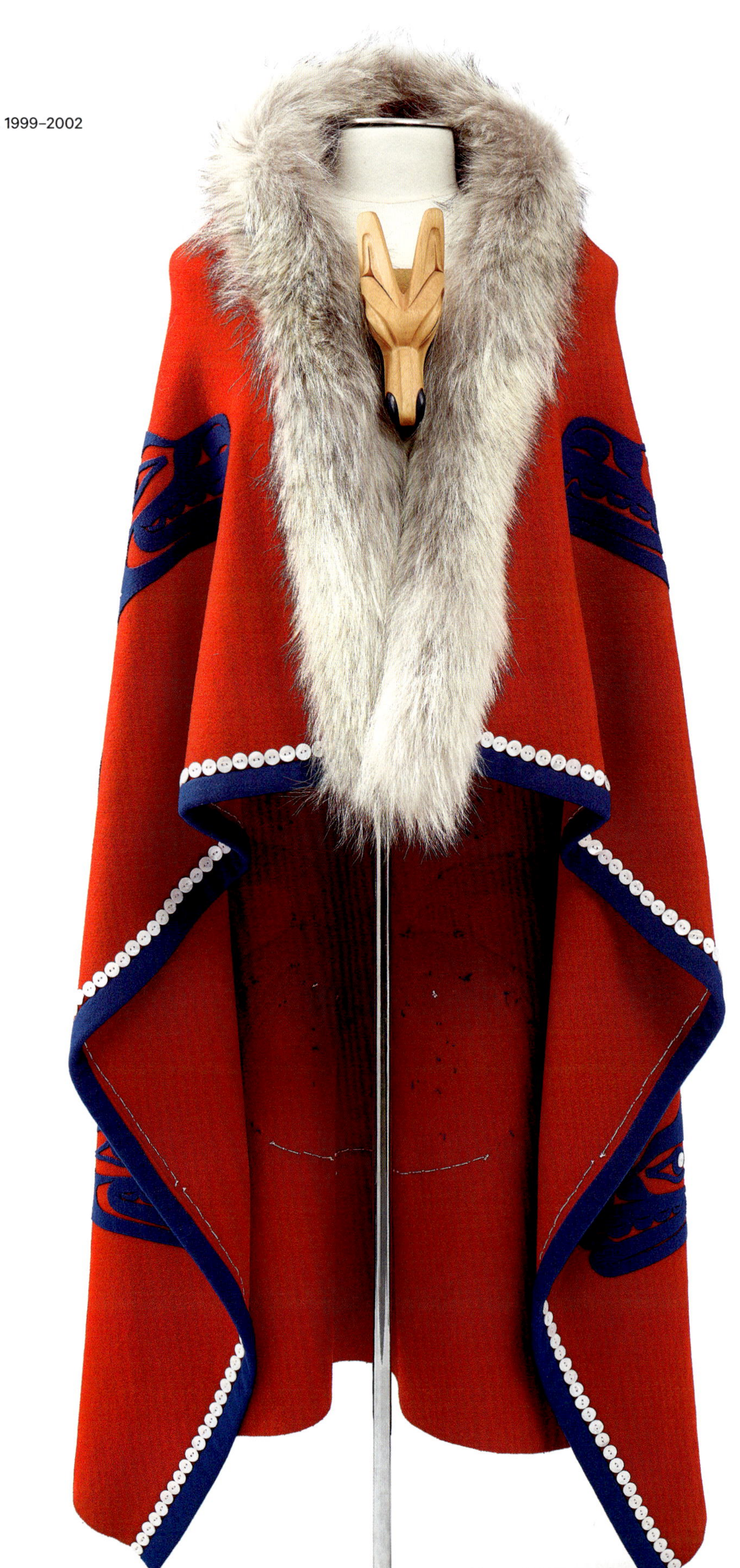

Wolves in the Snow Blanket, 1999–2002

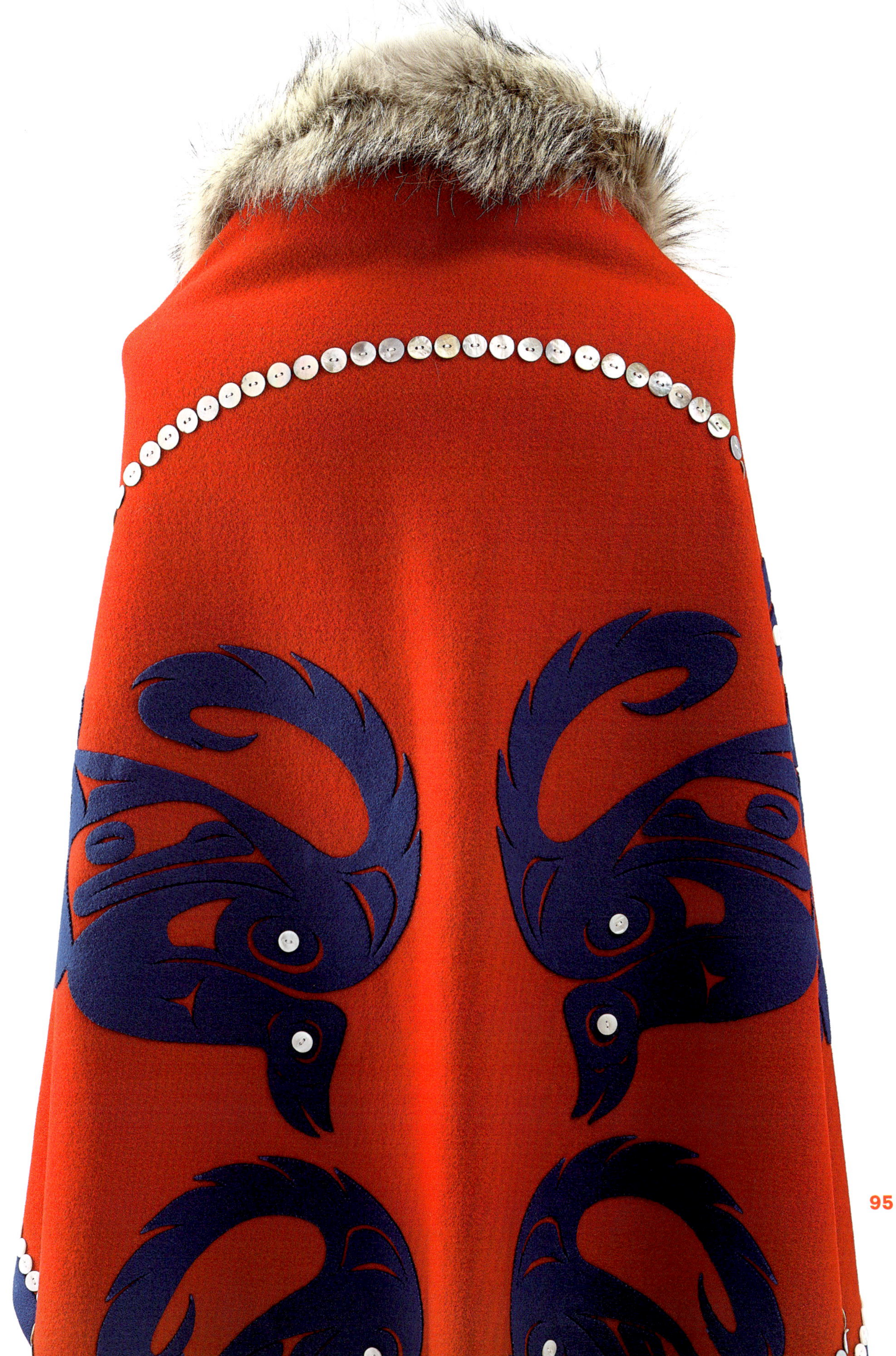

In 1972 I realized I needed to take the next step. I thought, If I don't go now, I'll never go, and Freda encouraged me. So I enrolled in the Gitanmaax School of Art in Hazelton—that's farther inland from Terrace. I only took the traditional beginner's design course there. But then after about ten weeks, Pie said I had to come home. She said, "We're starving—you've got to come home and get to work!"

I didn't want to quit, but I went back home for a while, two and a half years, and just worked like hell, and then I went back to Hazelton in '74 for five more months. That's when I finished the advanced carving course.

I did a pole up in Hazelton, my first big work. It was our last project before graduation. I did it with my teachers: Earl Muldon, Walter Harris, and Victor Mowatt.[39] These guys were all Gitxsan. Vernon Stephens[40] was teaching there too—he was a bit younger than us. We got unemployment insurance so we could go to school instead of looking for a job, so that's what we did. Vernon Stephens would dock us pay if we were late and missed school.

None of us were really known, so people shared and we helped each other. Today some artists are better known and people are jealous. They are teaching competition—it's so different now. After that money gets in there, it changes everything. There's rivalry, and the BS starts.

Earl and Walter were both important teachers to me. Walter would teach us how to make a bowl; Vernon Stephens would teach us to design and draw and paint. Victor Mowatt taught us big totem pole carving, Kenny Mowatt[41] some design plus panel carving, Phil Janze[42] taught me jewellery techniques, and Earl did too. You learned not just from one teacher. You learned in depth from each teacher. They taught us well, in the very traditional way of using bent knives and gouges. We worked nine to five and then again after dinner, every day for five months.

39. Victor Mowatt (Gitxsan)

40. Vernon Stephens (1949–? Gitxsan)

41. Ken Mowatt (b. 1944 Gitxsan)

42. Phil Janze (1950–2016 Gitxsan)

I think that school was the only Native-run art school in Canada. They started it. It's closed now. Freda taught there, too, sometimes; she did workshops. Walter, Earl, and all these guys—they were all part of that revival. When I finished, they wanted me to stay and carve. I worked hard, but I soon realized that since I'm not Gitxsan I had to learn my own style.

Freda told me that among all the people she taught I had gone the furthest in my own style. That's why she supported me. But eventually Freda said, "I took you as far as I can. If you want to go the rest of the way, you have to go by yourself." She kicked me out of the nest! It was the best thing she did for me.

She sent me up to Alaska, because that's where my people were from, my mother's people. She sent me to teach at Totem Heritage Center in Ketchikan[43] and at the University of Alaska. I was learning my culture, my mother's culture. They had all the Tlingit totem poles under the building there at the Totem Heritage Center, in storage—the old traditional ones. That was in 1976.

I studied those old Tlingit poles. I studied the masks, everything I could see up there, and I found some of my relatives. Teaching also really made me do my homework and work hard and learn my drawing. That's what had been holding me back. I also taught at Hoonah, Alaska, and at Whitehorse, at Skookum Jim Friendship Centre there,[44] and at a middle school at Ross River. And I taught at Metlakatla, Alaska, at Sitka, Alaska. I taught in the jails up there in Alaska, too, and also up in Whitehorse.

That was a challenge, because those guys in the prisons, they know if you're bullshitting. You've got to know your stuff, or they'll be right on you. There were some really good artists there too. They drew all the time, because they had the time. I learned a lot from them about drawing and how important practice is.

I can remember seeing those guys standing in line, waiting for their food. It reminded me of the residential schools. People's thinking became institutionalized in those places. I was grateful I had grown up with my family. At Prince George

43. The Totem Heritage Center is a museum in Ketchikan, Alaska, that opened in 1976 to preserve totem poles relocated from uninhabited Tlingit and Haida settlements.

44. The Skookum Jim Friendship Centre in Whitehorse is the oldest Indigenous organization in Yukon. It provides services for Indigenous community members.

College, I had a friend who had been taken to residential school when he was five years old. When we graduated, I said, "Aren't you going home?" He said, "No." I said, "What about your parents?" He said, "I don't know them."

After 1974 I only had one or two more little paying jobs, but I never really worked again after that. I just made my art and taught. We had little shows. There was a salmon festival in the summertime, and we sold our work at the museum in Prince Rupert too. Sometimes they would accept our stuff for sale. After that, there was just the Totem Pole Gift Shop in Prince Rupert, and they ripped us off. We had shows up in Terrace too. We had shows wherever we could. Then we started meeting people. Buyers would come up from Vancouver and buy stuff. And the people on their way to Alaska on the cruise ships—they would buy stuff too.

FINDING AN AUDIENCE

It was in 1980, when I was thirty-two, that I got my carvings into *The Legacy* exhibition at the Royal BC Museum in Victoria.[45] Bud Mintz[46] was the one who got my pieces into that show. He was the first one in Vancouver to put on a Northwest Coast commercial gallery show. He just piled everything in there—we called it the art warehouse, at Main and Southeast Marine Drive.

I had a show there in the early '80s, me and Reggie Davidson. He called it *Northern Comfort*. "Southern Comfort is a whisky," he said, "so we'll call it *Northern Comfort*."[47] Until then, our people weren't even really allowed into art galleries. They wouldn't accept our work. Bud Mintz—he taught at Langara College as well. He's the one that got us into the Inuit Gallery in Vancouver too.[48] He introduced us to Joe Murphy; it was his place. The Americans were buying our work there, but the Canadians weren't. We had to get recognition outside of the country first to get attention here. Vancouver was close to the American border, so they came up and bought our pieces. If they liked your work they would pay and they would not complain.

45. *The Legacy: Tradition and Innovation in Northwest Coast Indian Art*—curated by Peter L. Macnair, Alan L. Hoover, and Kevin Neary in 2007—was a major exhibition organized by the Royal BC Museum, Victoria. It toured internationally and was accompanied by an illustrated catalogue.

46. George Austin (Bud) Mintz was the founder of the Potlatch Arts gallery. He was a supporter of and advocate for Northwest Coast artists and was responsible for printing many silkscreen works for First Nations artists in the 1980s and 1990s.

47. The exhibition *Northern Comfort* opened in March 1982 at Potlatch Arts in Vancouver.

48. The Inuit Gallery opened in Vancouver's Gastown district in 1979. It specialized in works made by Inuit and Northwest Coast artists.

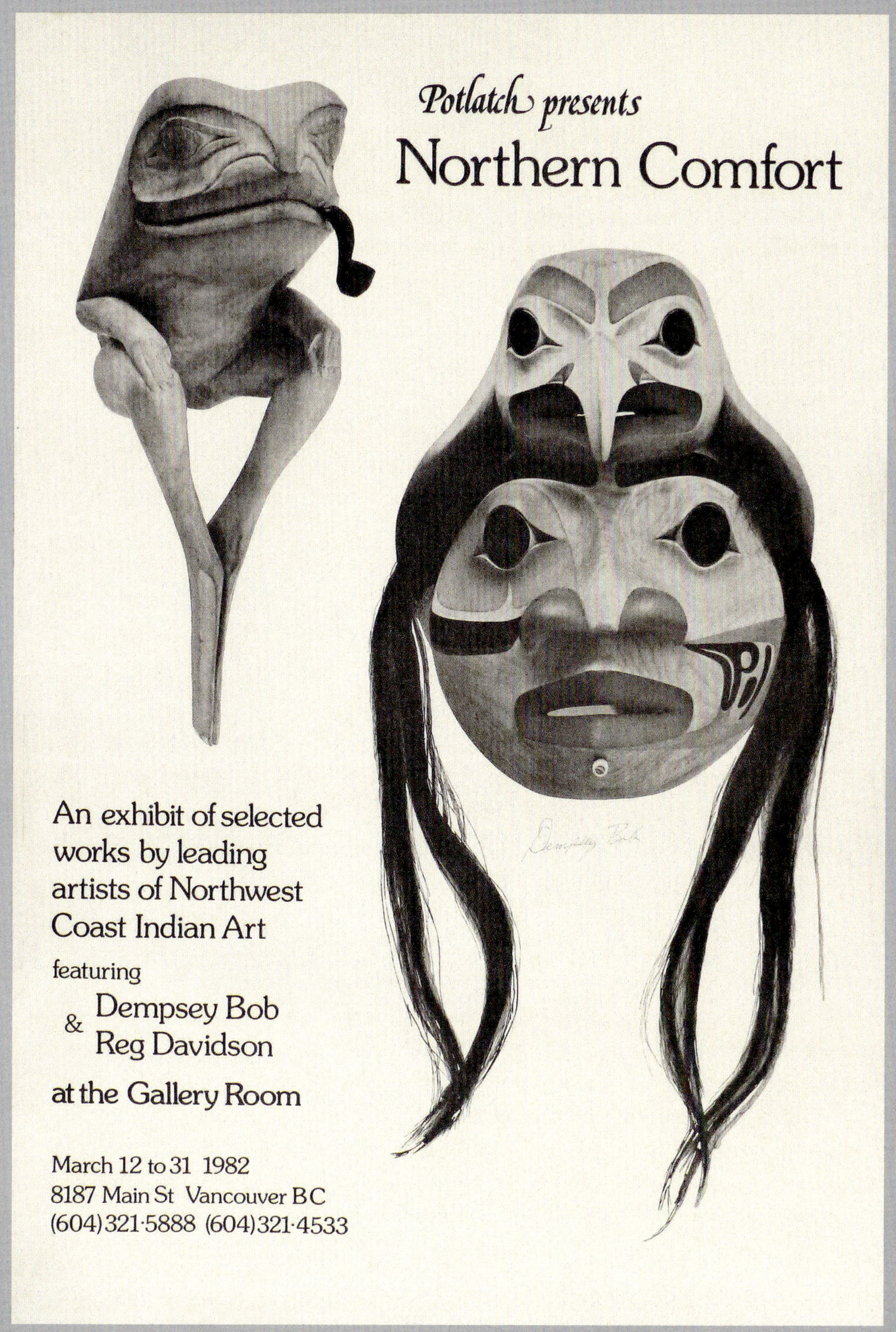

Northern Comfort exhibition poster from my first art gallery show, with Reg Davidson,
at the Potlatch Arts gallery, owned by Bud Mintz, Vancouver, 1982 (Courtesy of Harold Demetzer)

The Legacy was a really important show. Those of us who got into that show are the best-known artists today. Some guys didn't want to be in the book because they were worrying about copyright and so on, and they missed the boat. Freda also got us information on opportunities like that; she encouraged us. Bud was kind of like those old guys that sold modern artists in Paris. He knew the art, and he could promote it. He was the pioneer, he helped us all—Don Yeomans, Robert Davidson, Reggie Davidson. Ulli Steltzer's photography book *Indian Artists at Work*[49] was another critical project, because the artists that got into that book also got a big push.

A little later in life, in the '80s, I met the American collector George Gund.[50] He was my first big collector. At my first solo commercial show in 1989, he bought the whole show. The exhibition was at Grace Gallery; there were thirty-two pieces.[51] The dealer's name was Grace Mooney. That's where I first showed *The Smart One*—I knew it was one of my great ones. That, and the wolf forehead mask. I had offered them both to George MacDonald in Ottawa.[52] I took them down south; he was supposed to come look at them in Vancouver but I never heard from him. So I took the pieces back and I put them all together at Grace Gallery.

The day of the show a guy phones up from San Francisco and says, "I want to look at the show." "Well," we said, "you have to be here by seven o'clock tonight." It was George Gund's representative. He flew up that morning, and he got to the gallery at around 4:00 p.m. Twenty minutes before opening we had sold the whole show for more than $300,000. That was the turning point for me. It established me, and it set the values of my pieces.

George used to come to town from time to time. He owned the San Jose Sharks, so he came up to Vancouver when they were playing. He was on the board of the MoMA in New York, and I think his sister was too.[53] I think she was the chair of their board. George knew art and he just loved my work. He owned the Cleveland Cavaliers basketball team too. I got to know him a bit. I wish I had spent more time but I was too busy working. He'd phone Inuit Art Gallery, and Gary Wyatt[54] would open

49. Ulli Steltzer began photographing Indigenous artists after she moved to Vancouver from Germany in 1972. Her book *Indian Artists at Work* was published in 1977.

50. George Gund III was an American businessman, sports entrepreneur, philanthropist, and art collector.

51. *Dempsey Bob: Tahltan-Tlingit—Master Carver of the Wolf Clan* opened in November 1989 at the Grace Gallery in Vancouver. It featured masks, bowls, panels, blankets, and small works in gold.

52. George MacDonald was President and CEO of the Canadian Museum of Civilization (now the Canadian Museum of History) in Gatineau, Quebec, from 1983 to 1998. He was a trained anthropologist who specialized in the First Peoples of the Pacific Northwest.

53. Agnes Gund, sister of George Gund, is President Emerita and Life Trustee of the Museum of Modern Art in New York City.

54. Gary Wyatt was co-owner of Spirit Wrestler Gallery in Vancouver and worked with many Northwest Coast artists to promote and sell their work.

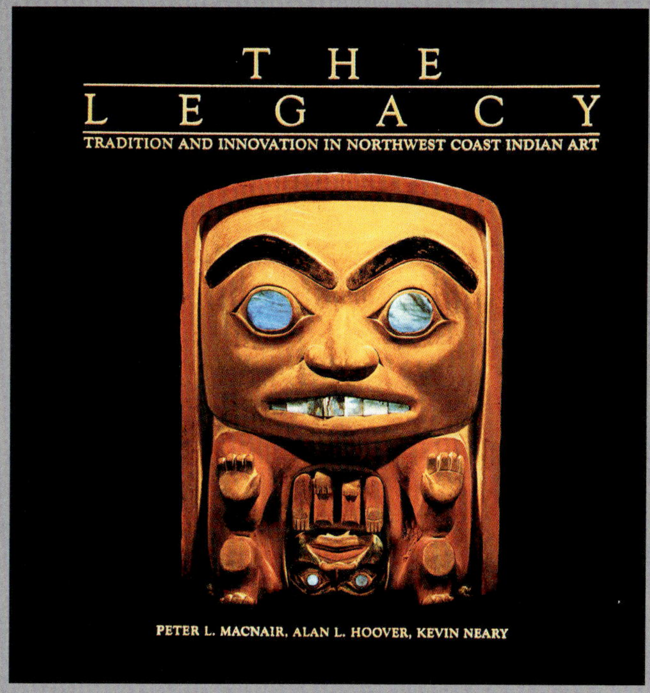

Book cover of *The Legacy: Tradition and Innovation in Northwest Coast Indian Art,* by Peter L. MacNair, Alan L. Hoover, and Kevin Neary (1984)

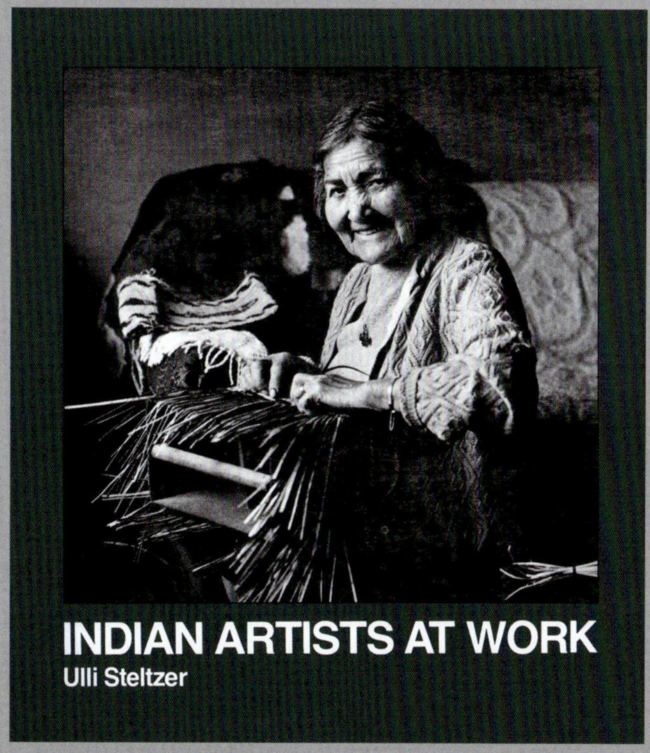

Book cover of *Indian Artists at Work,* by Ulli Steltzer (1977), which features some of my work

Wolf Chief's Hat, c. 1993

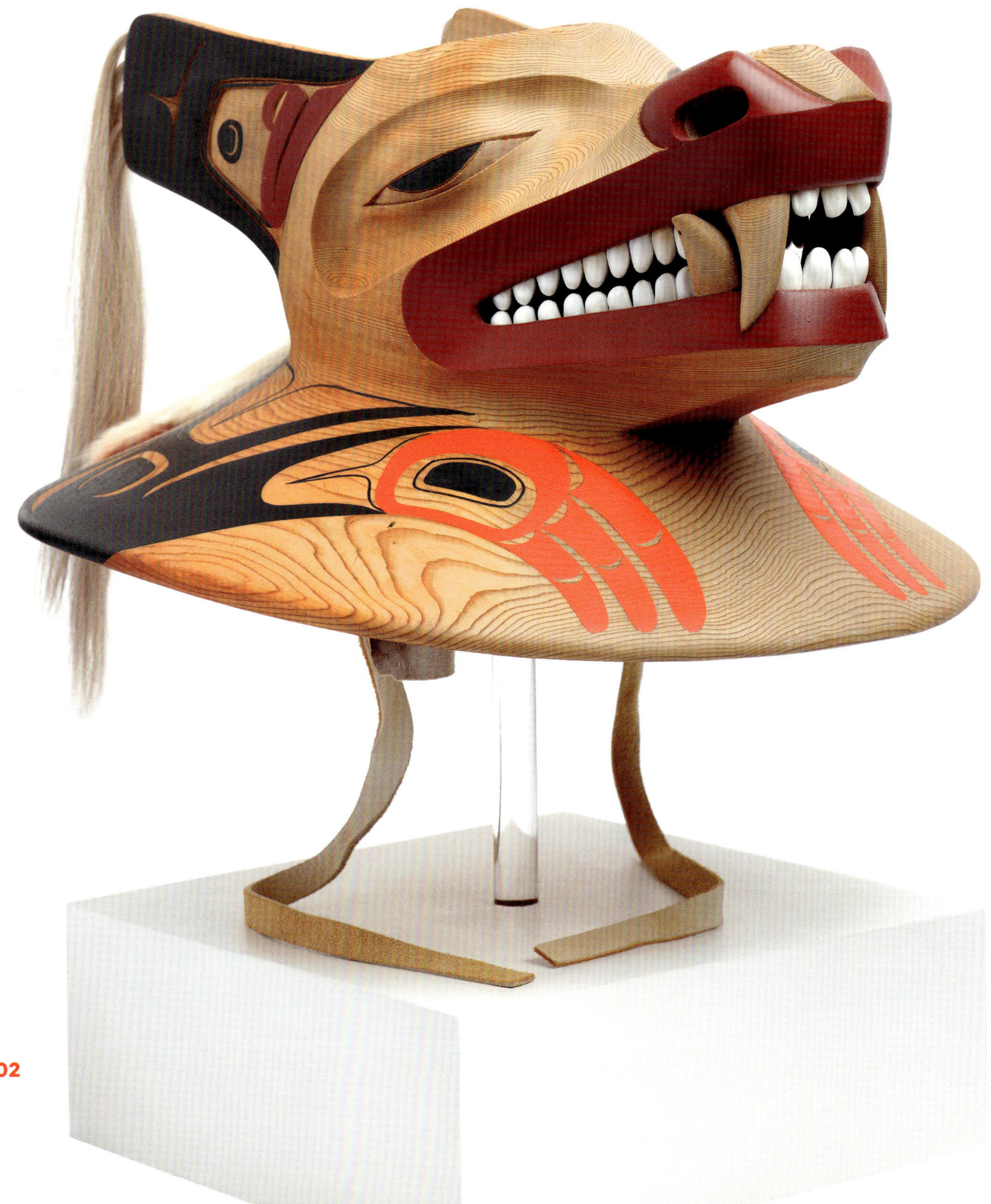

the gallery up in the middle of the night and sell him tens of thousands of dollars' worth of art at a time. He didn't just buy my stuff—whatever he liked, he bought it. He took my pieces with him wherever he lived.

Eric Savics[55] was the other big buyer of my work. He was on the board of the Vancouver Art Gallery when I met him. I had done some pieces for some lawyers—a big panel and some other pieces—and they were disbanding their company, so they were selling their art collection and Eric bought them. When I had a show in Vancouver in 1993,[56] Eric bought the whole show, including my *Wolf Chief's Hat* (opposite), and he has continued to buy work from me over the years.

55. Eric Savics is Vice-President and Director of Haywood Securities in Vancouver and the owner of Tantalus Vineyards in the Okanagan Valley, one of the oldest continuously producing vineyards in the province. For many years, images of Dempsey Bob's carvings have adorned the labels of Tantalus wines.

56. In 1993 *Dempsey Bob: Myth Maker and Transformer* opened at the Vancouver Centennial Museum, now the Museum of Vancouver.

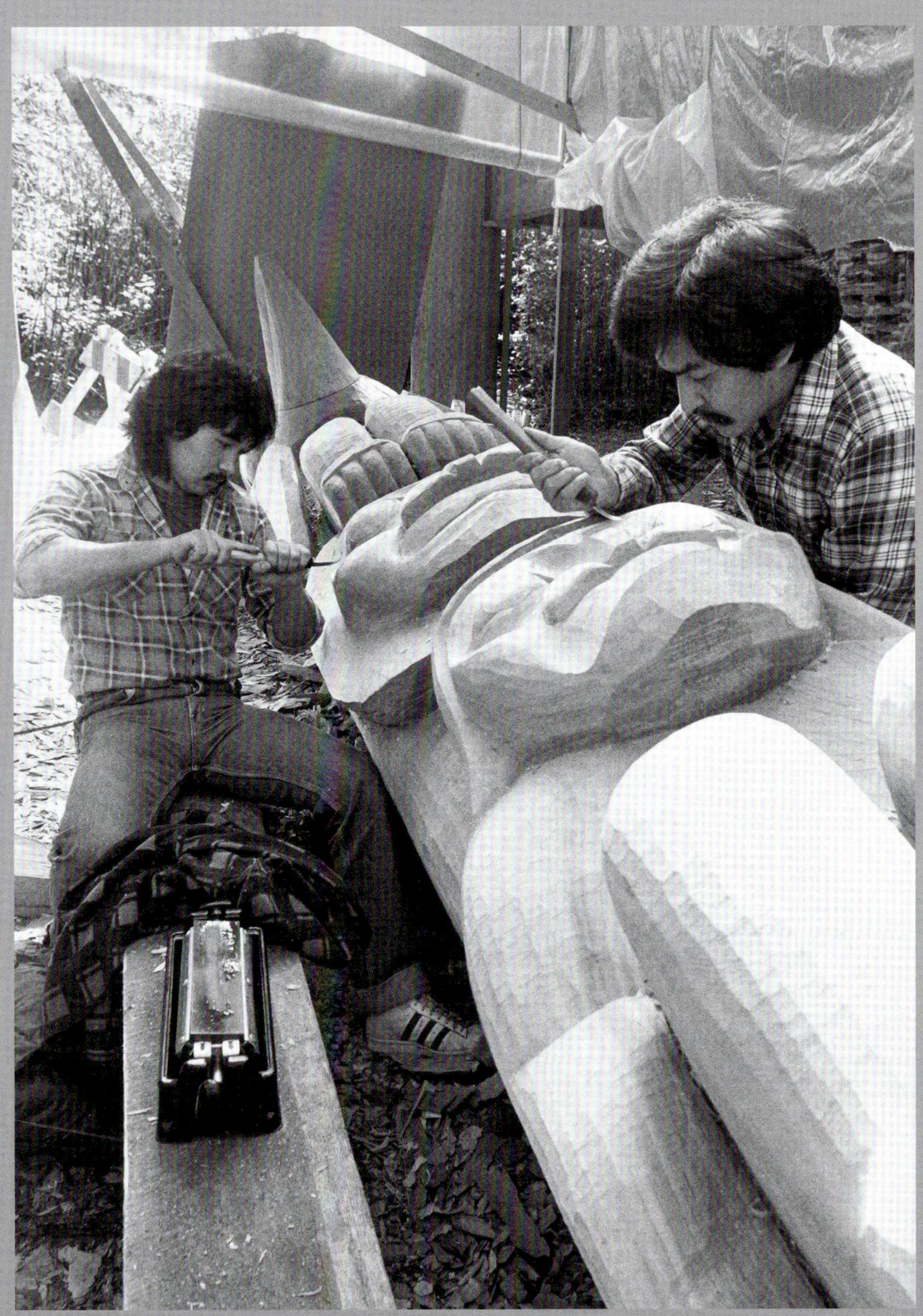

My nephew Stan Bevan and me carving the *Raven Stealing the Sun Pole* in 1982
to honour the Tongass tribe in Ketchikan, Alaska. The pole was raised in May 1983.

WIDENING CIRCLES

In the 1980s I started travelling outside of BC and going back East—to the Native Business Summit in Toronto.[57] I gave workshops at the Saskatchewan Indian Federated College in Regina;[58] I was invited by Bob Boyer[59] there, in the mid-'80s. I went to a big workshop in Yellowknife. I travelled to teach at Fort McMurray, at the community college.[60]

They used to have these SCANA conferences, starting in 1985, the Society of Canadian Artists of Native Ancestry.[61] There was an early one held up in Hazelton. SCANA lobbied for funding from the Canada Council and for attention from museums. I remember they had a feast and a show, and there were a lot of good talks about the art and what we were trying to do. Up until then, we had all been working individually. That's when we really got started in organizing to get our work recognized. I would go to the Native Business Summit, and I would show some of my work and meet all these guys, and then I'd be invited to a conference in Ottawa or in Toronto. That's how I met the other artists in different parts of the country, like Bob Boyer and Robert Houle,[62] David General,[63] Gerald McMaster,[64] Alex Janvier,[65] Daphne Odjig,[66] Norval Morrisseau,[67] Allen Sapp[68]—I met all those guys.

In around 1999 they finally opened some galleries of our Native art at the British Museum in London—it was not just our art from the Northwest Coast but from cultures all over North America. They have so much there that nobody sees. When they opened the new galleries, we all ended up there, beside our traditional art forms. What was really sad was that we *felt* those pieces. They hadn't been on our land sometimes for centuries.

Today I like to look at the old pieces. I don't look at the contemporary pieces much. Some people think that Northwest Coast carving is too traditional, but if you understand art you know that everything that was ever done was contemporary to that time. What I'm doing now is contemporary to our time. I was giving a talk in Toronto and someone asked me, "Do you still use stone tools?" I said, "I didn't come here in a canoe. I came here in a jet, and that changes everything about who I am."

57. The Native Business Summit is an annual conference and trade show held in Toronto from 1986.

58. The Saskatchewan Indian Federated College opened in 1976 in Regina. It was designed to serve First Nations students. In 2003 the school was renamed First Nations University of Canada.

59. Bob Boyer (1948–2004 Métis)

60. Keyano College in Fort McMurray

61. SCANA was founded in 1985 as a national artist lobby group.

62. Robert Houle (b. 1947 Saulteaux)

63. David General (b. 1950 Haudenosaunee, Kanien'kehá:ka-Onayotekaono)

64. Gerald McMaster (b. 1953 Plains Cree-Siksika)

65. Alex Janvier (b. 1935 Denesuline)

66. Daphne Odjig (1916–2016 Odawa-Potawatomi)

67. Norval Morrisseau (1931–2007 Anishinaabe)

68. Allen Sapp (1928–2015 Cree)

In the '80s, the singer Buffy Sainte-Marie came up to Telegraph. She came to support our people. I met her up there, and she knew about me because she had seen my art. BC Hydro wanted to dam our river, the Stikine, which would have killed all our salmon, and we stopped them.

The river is under threat again, now from mining. There are so many mines up there—gold, everything. We've got lots of coal up there too—the good coal that they use for making steel. The Stikine, the Nass, and the Skeena—we call it the Sacred Headwaters. It's the place where the Raven came from, when he brought the light. Those whole mountains are all full of coal. They want that coal.

We have fought for a long time to protect the Stikine. They wanted to flood the canyon—the Grand Canyon of the Stikine. It's almost fifty miles long. When the volcano erupted a long time ago, when the lava came down, it went up both sides about two hundred feet high. The lava rock is porous, so there are caves underneath; we don't know where they go. The mining company had said it was safe to dam the river there, but the consultants will write anything you want for money. So we hired our own consultants. We found out that the weight of the water would have collapsed the land.

There are goats that live in that canyon. They live on the rock walls, the cliffs. Most live way up in the mountains; they eat the lichen. It's amazing where they can go.

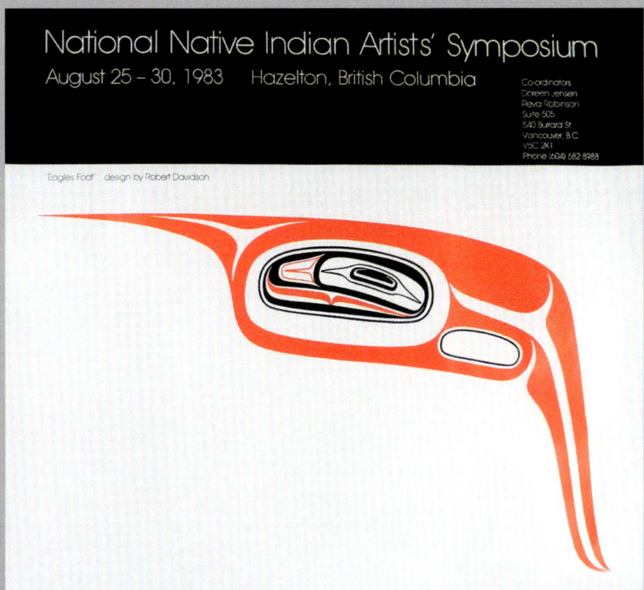

National Native Indian Artists' Symposium brochure, Hazelton, BC, 1983
(Courtesy of Harold Demetzer)

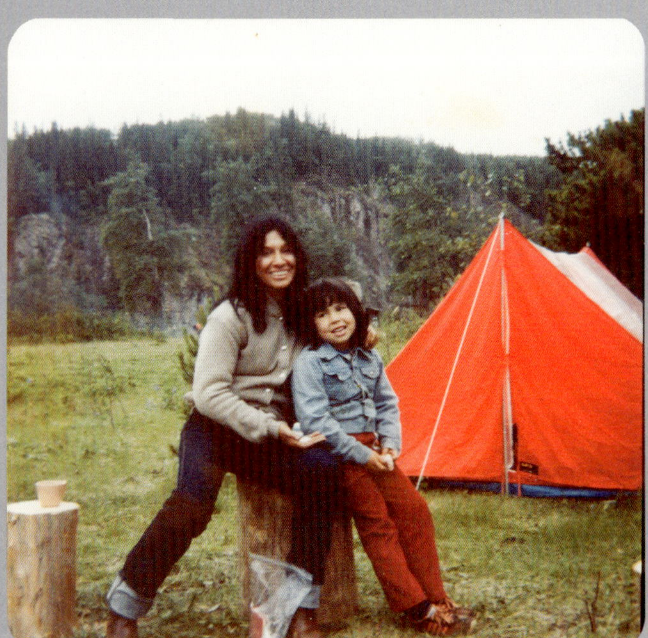

Buffy Sainte-Marie and my daughter, Tanya, Telegraph Creek, BC, 1980s

Daily Activities
(except arrival and departure days)

- 6:00 a.m.-6:30 a.m.   Meditation and spiritual preparation for the day
- 6:30 a.m.-7:15 a.m.   Fun Run
- 7:30 a.m.-8:30 a.m.   Group breakfast at campsite
- 10:30 a.m.-11:00 a.m.   Coffee at Hazelton High School
- 12:00 noon-1:30 p.m.   Lunch at Hazelton High School

Note: All sessions take place at Hazelton High School.

Thursday, August 25, 1983 — Arrival Day

- 9:00 a.m.-7:00 p.m.   Registration and settle into camp
- 7:45 p.m.   Gather in Ksan Village
- 8:00 p.m.-11:00 p.m.   **Traditional Welcome Feast** — Hosted by the people of Ksan

Friday, August 26, 1983 — Day One

- 9:00 a.m.-12:00 noon   Morning Session
  "Not Dead — Only Sleeping" Albert Douse - Ksan
  Facilitator: Neil Sterritt
  "Who Started It?"
  Discussants: Tony Hunt:
    - Continuity in personal life history
    - Pride of family
    - Responsibility
    - Connection of art to ceremony
  Robert Davidson:
    - Bringing it back
    - Recreating
  Walter Harris: Connection of art to ceremony
  Tom Hill: "Old Culture - New Images"
  Dr. George MacDonald & Alan Hoover: "Responses & Reflections"
- 1:30 p.m.-3:30 p.m.   Afternoon Session
  The Spiritual Heritage: A Dialogue with Tradition
  Facilitator: Robert Davidson, "Personal Inspiration"
  Participating artists share their inspiration.

  This is a very special session. All are welcome to attend, to listen, and to feel. We ask that you respect the intent of the session by refraining from interruptions and distractions such as recording, photographing or questioning.
- 4:00 p.m.-4:30 p.m.   "Reflections" Dr. Carole Farber
- 5:30 p.m.   Dinner / Group Barbeque at campsite
- 7:00 p.m.-9:00 p.m.   Evening Session
  Exhibit Opening — Northwestern National Exhibition Centre, Hazelton

Saturday, August 27, 1983 — Day Two

- 9:00 a.m.-12:00 noon   Morning Session
  Visions
  Dialogue: Gloria Cranmer Webster & Dr. Marjorie Halpin
    - Getting in touch with your vision
    - "The How of Tradition" How is it happening now?
    - Expressing your vision.
  Discussion: Innovative responses and experiences of participants. Artists are visionaries; they formulate visions for all of us. What is your dream and how do you make it happen?

  Whatever you can do or dream you can do, begin it. Boldness has genius, power and magic in it. Begin it now.   Goethe
- 1:30 p.m.-3:30 p.m.   Afternoon Session
  Visions in Action
  Sharing individual portfolios, ideas and visions.
- 5:00 p.m.   **Traditional Feast**
  Hosted by the people of Kitwancool. Buses leave the campsite at 5:00 p.m. for Kitseguecla, Kitwanga, Battle Hill and Kitwancool.

Sunday, August 28, 1983 — Day Three

- 9:00 a.m.-12:00 noon   Morning Session
  Quality, Authenticity and Commitment
  Facilitator: Carl Beam
  1. "Quality: The Vision of Personal Excellence"
  Discussants: Artists who have earned the right to speak
  2. "Authenticity: Who decides?"
  Discussants: Artists, museum representatives, gallery representatives, government agencies, private collectors
  3. "Commitment: The Double Edge"
  Discussants: Artists
- 1:30 p.m.-4:00 p.m.   Afternoon Session
  Meeting the Challenge
  Facilitator: Alfred Young Man
  Marketing Discussant: Lia Grundle
  Workshops
  1. Training/Apprenticeship
     Resource persons: Robert Davidson, Norman Tait
  2. Professionalism
     Resource person: Maxine Noel
  3. Copyrights, contracts, tariff restrictions, legalities
     Resource person: Legal Advisor
  4. Cottage Industries
     Resource person: Dora Kenni
  5. Co-operative Marketing
     Resource person: Bill Williams, Native Brotherhood of B.C.
- 4:00 p.m.-5:00 p.m.   "Reflections", Dr. Carole Farber
- 6:00 p.m.:   **Banquet at Hagwilget Village**
  hosted by the people of Hagwilget followed by performing artists
    Margo Kane and "Spirit Song"
    Morley Loon - singer, entertainer
    Winston Wuttunee - singer, entertainer
    Sharon Watson - singer, entertainer
  Buses leave campsite at 6:00 p.m. for Hagwilget.

Monday, August 29, 1983 — Day Four

- 9:00 a.m.-11:30 a.m.   Morning Session
  Challenges
  Facilitator: David General
    "Policies for Collections"
  Participants: Art Gallery Representative
    Museums, Gerald McMaster
    DIAND, Jackson Beardy
    Foundation for the Development of Native Art, Allison Bastien
    "A Look at the Applebaum - Hébert Commission Report", Cheryl Brooks
- 11:30 a.m.-12:00 noon   "Reflections", Dr. Carole Farber
- 1:30 p.m.-3:30 p.m.   Afternoon Session
  Visions and Challenges Confronted
  Workshops for drafting resolutions
  Choose the workshop or workshops you wish to attend (others may be added)
  1. Quality and Authenticity - Juried shows
  2. National/Regional Policies for Collections
  3. Marketing Directions
  4. Policies and Grants to Artisans
  5. Forming Regional Groups
  6. Tariffs
- 4:00 p.m.-5:00 p.m.   Closing Session
  Facilitator: Dr. Carole Farber
  Discussion/adoption of resolutions. Conference evaluation by participants. Where to now: Future conferences. Visions.
- 7:00 p.m.   Evening Session
  Banquet and Dance
  "In Celebration of Expanding our Boundaries"
  Hosted by the people of Kispiox Village
  Buses leave campsite at 7:00 p.m. Return during evening.

Tuesday, August 30, 1983 — Departure Day

- 10:00 a.m.   Brunch at campsite
- 1:00 p.m.   Buses leave for airport

National Native Indian Artists' Symposium

Name ______________________________
Address ____________________________ City __________
Prov. _________ Postal Code __________ Telephone __________

Please make cheque or money order payable to The Gitksan-Carrier Tribal Council and mail with this form to
Co-ordinators, National Native Indian Artists' Symposium
Suite 505 - 540 Burrard Street
Vancouver, B.C. V6C 2K1
We would very much appreciate your registration and payment immediately.

Family members and friends accompanying me:
____
____

Please indicate if you wish daycare ☐

Please list your childrens' ages ______________________________

The main form of accommodation will be 2-person tents and billeting.
Please indicate your preference:
Tent ☐ How many ____
Billeting ☐ No. of persons ____

There are limited spaces available for campers. Do you require a camper space? ____

A few hotel rooms are available.
Do you require a hotel room? ____

Arrival date ____
Do you require transportation from the Smithers Airport to Hazelton (50 miles)? ____

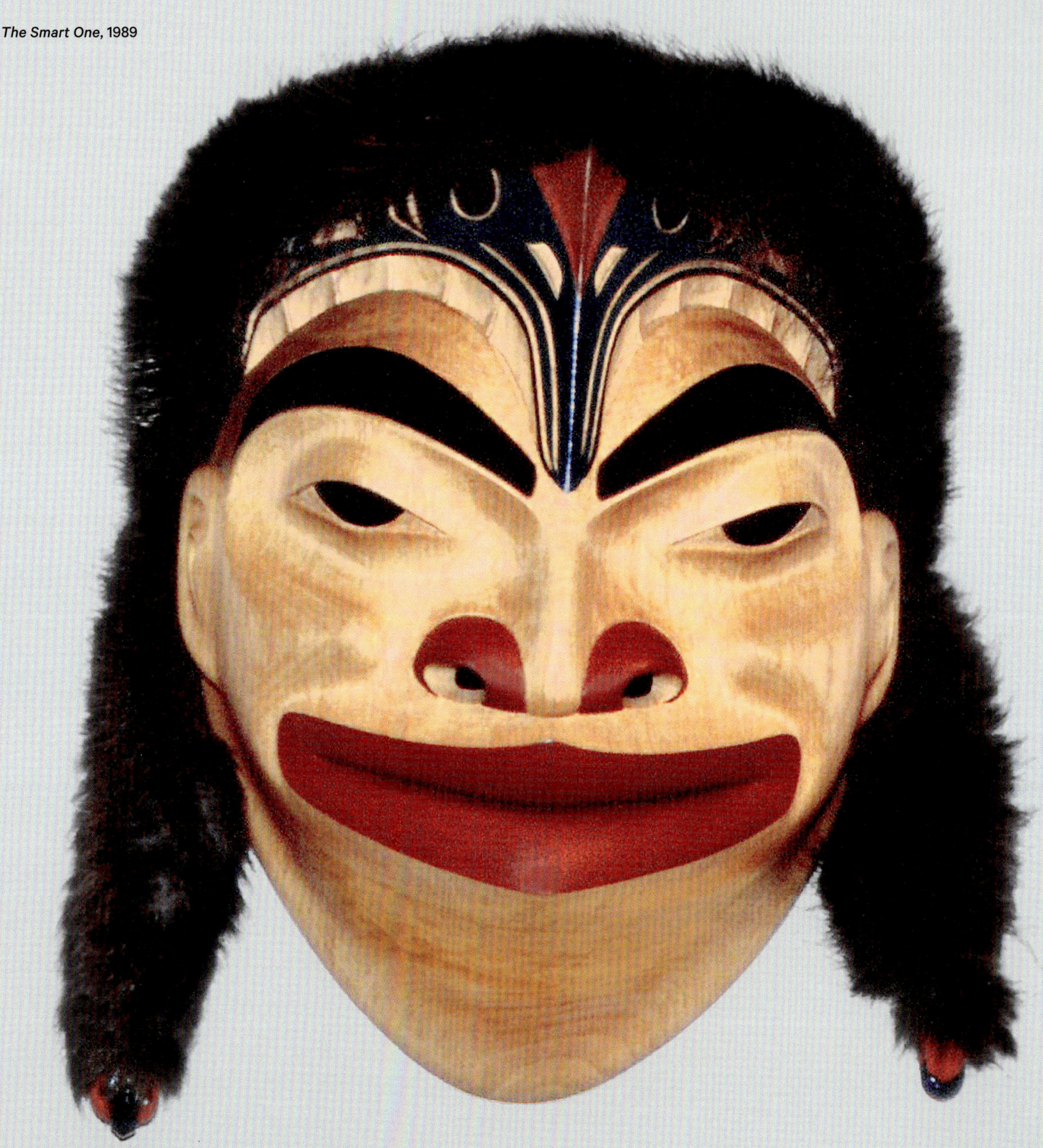

The Smart One, 1989

One Sunday morning I was just sitting, having coffee, and he just came to me. I thought, Who's going to know in the future there was this guy called "the smart one"? I thought I better carve him.

The smart one was the keeper of the stories. He was trained and taught and lived with the Elders, and they related all the stories to him, and he had to learn them word for word or he couldn't be the smart one. If there was a dispute between the clans of the people, once the smart one spoke, that was it and things were settled, and it was done. That's how disputes were settled. If someone was offended there could be a feast to settle differences. There would be a payment at the feast with gifts and food.

The smart one was chosen for his memory and his interest in learning the stories. The Elders would know. What I think about now is that back when I started, it was my great-aunt Eva Carlick, and my grandmother's sister Helen Carlick, and my grandfather Johnny Sinkoots, and my mum, Flossie Bob—these were the people who supported me at the beginning. They told me stories and they helped me. I realize now that in a way I was chosen by them. They knew I was going to do something, but they didn't know what. They kept telling me the stories over and over and over. I see now that those stories all fit together. I was lucky, and I was ready.

I started carving *The Smart One*. I was working on about ten pieces at the same time, but I knew this was his time. When you're hot, you're hot—when you're not, you're not! You have to do it fast; ideas and feelings don't wait for you.

One morning I stopped carving. I had a workbench with a little window above it. I put *The Smart One* there and went upstairs for a coffee. I turned off the lights. When I went back down, I walked in the door and the light from outside was hitting him perfectly from the top—and he was looking right back at me. And I said, "Holy shit, he's there!" I just left him for a while. I let him tell me how to finish him.

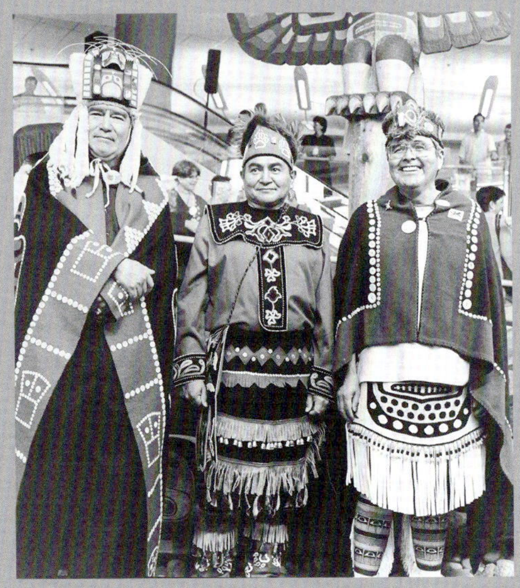

Richard Hunt, me, and Robert Davidson at the unveiling of the YVR commissions, Vancouver International Airport, 1999

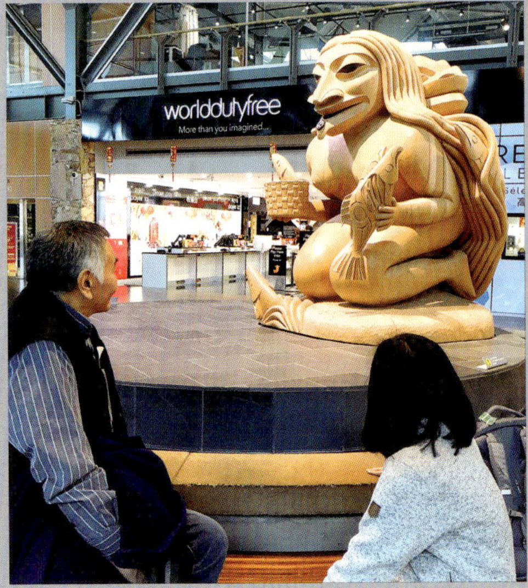

With my granddaughter, Keely, looking at *Story of Fog Woman and Raven*, Vancouver International Airport, 2007

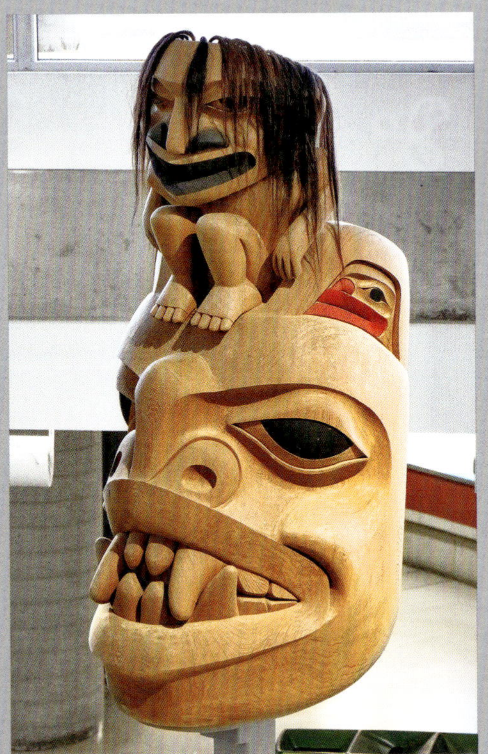

Bear Human Mask,
Vancouver International Airport, 1999

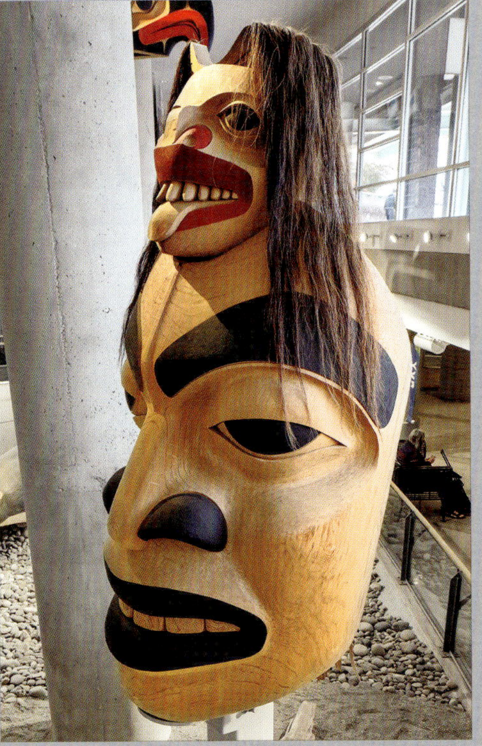

Human Bear Mask,
Vancouver International Airport, 1999

I studied him every morning, in the morning light. The way I did his neck and his head too—the beaver fur. What people said about him was that he *knows*. In his eyes he knows, but he's not going to tell. Some people said it was me in there, because of my knowledge about art, and about the history too. He's a part of me.

I looked at him and what I saw was that he was smarter than me. He ended up exactly the way he wanted to be, not the way I thought of him. I was just the carpenter. It was an honour to be a part of him for a while.

I left him and I didn't see him for a long time. They start out a block of wood and they end up like your children. You have to let them go into the world by themselves.

When I did the fog woman for the Vancouver airport (opposite), it was the same thing.[69] People asked, "How long did it take to make this?" I would say she was my girlfriend for one year. But when I look at her now, she's her own self. She turned out better than I ever thought.

69. Dempsey Bob has made three large commissioned works for YVR Vancouver International Airport: two large mask sculptures for the domestic terminal—*Human Bear Mask* and *Bear Human Mask*, both completed in 1999—and the monumental *Story of Fog Woman and Raven*, 2007, for the international terminal, a work that embodies traditional values of environmental stewardship.

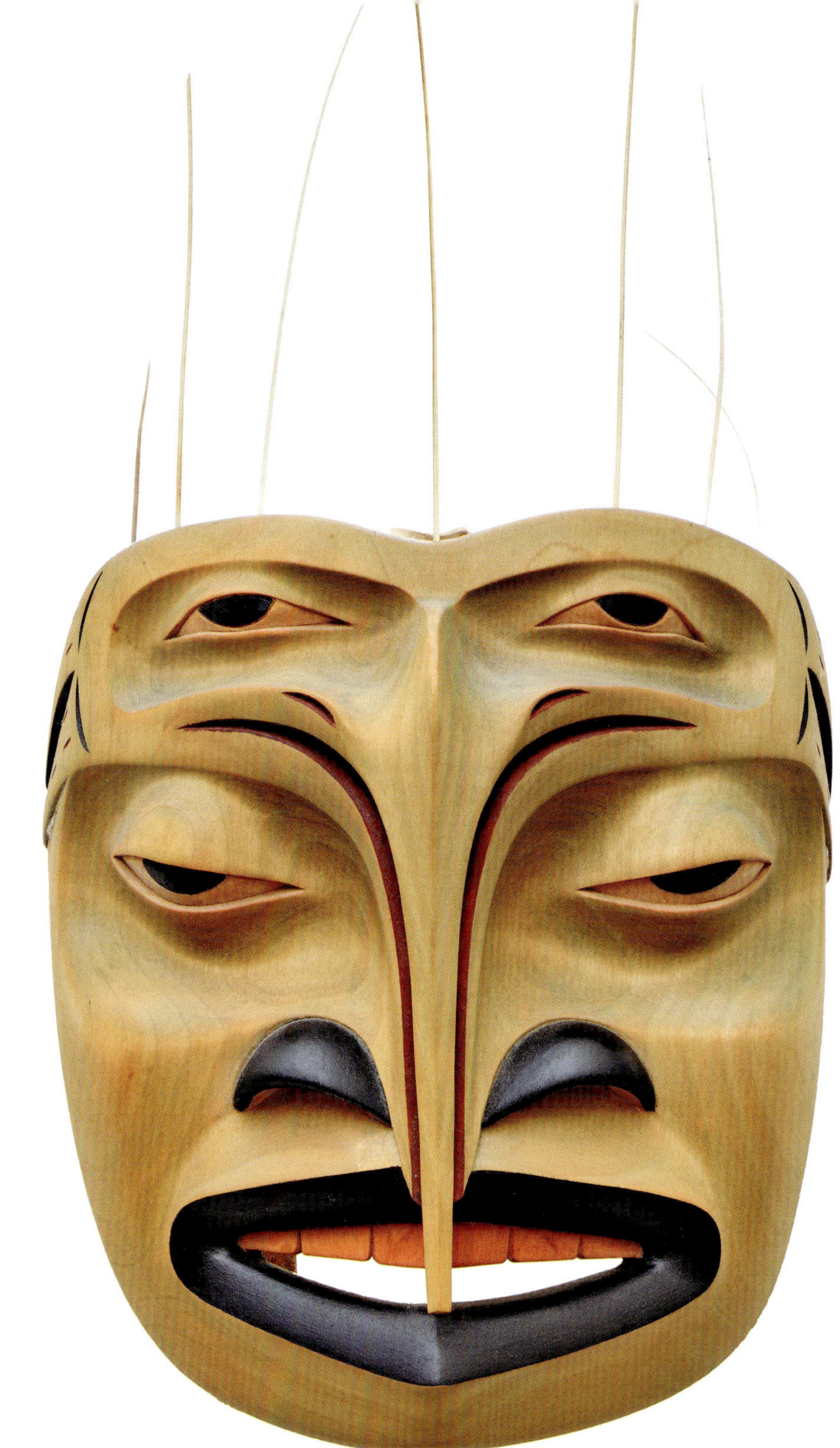

Mosquito Mask, 1989

MOSQUITO MASK

I thought about how to make this mask—that mosquito beak coming right down his nose. It is really strong.

There's a story about a monster that was killing the people and eating them, and all the toughest warriors couldn't kill him. This one guy trained and trained, and he killed him. He cut the monster all up in pieces and burned him on the fire. The ashes that came off the fire turned into mosquitoes. That's where they come from. That's why they sting when they bite.

ALDER WOOD

Alder wood is a very hard wood, and that's the wood I usually use. It's one of our traditional carving woods. It's really beautiful. It's strong and it's crisp—you can make very clean cuts with it—and we used it for our spoons and our masks and our bowls because it has no taste. Each wood has its own purpose.

Cedar, it has oil. Cedar is better for lasting outside, so that's why we use it for our poles, because it has the resin. Some people also preserved the poles with oil.

You see the beauty of the tree? We borrow the beauty of the tree from Mother Nature. We carve our history on our poles. Then we raise them to stand again. When we pull up the pole we pull up the pride of our people. The pole raising is a special day because it's the first time people are going to see it standing like a tree in nature. When it falls down, we give it back to Mother Nature.

Raven Frog Chief's Hat, 1989

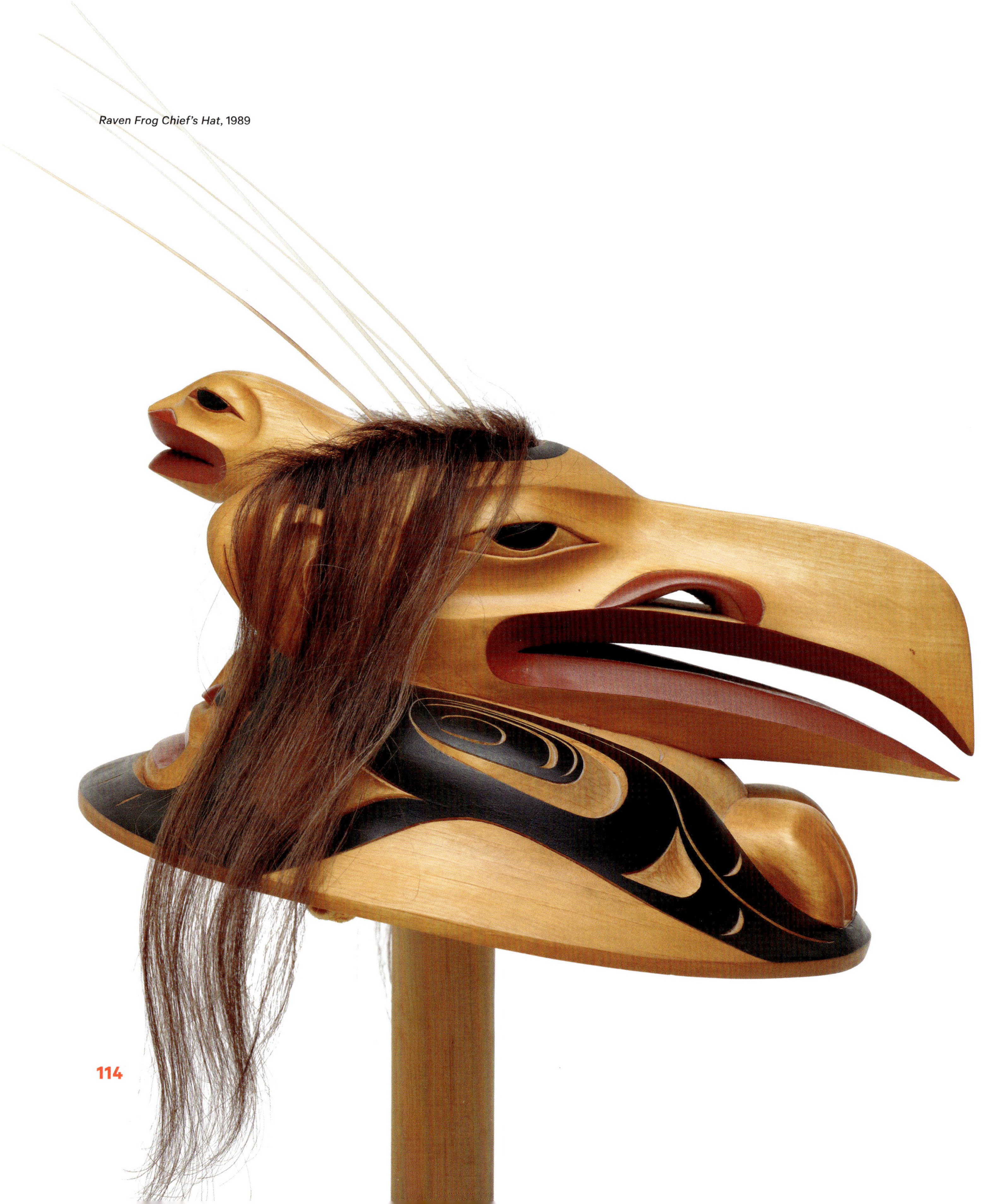

When I decided to make those helmets, I looked at some of the old Tlingit helmets to see how they did it. I knew it was like a mask on a helmet, but your proportions are different. Every time I would figure out how to do something new, I would then do it five or six times in a series. If you just do one, then you have to reinvent every time. If you do enough in a row, you can really draw on the knowledge from one piece to another. It stays with you.

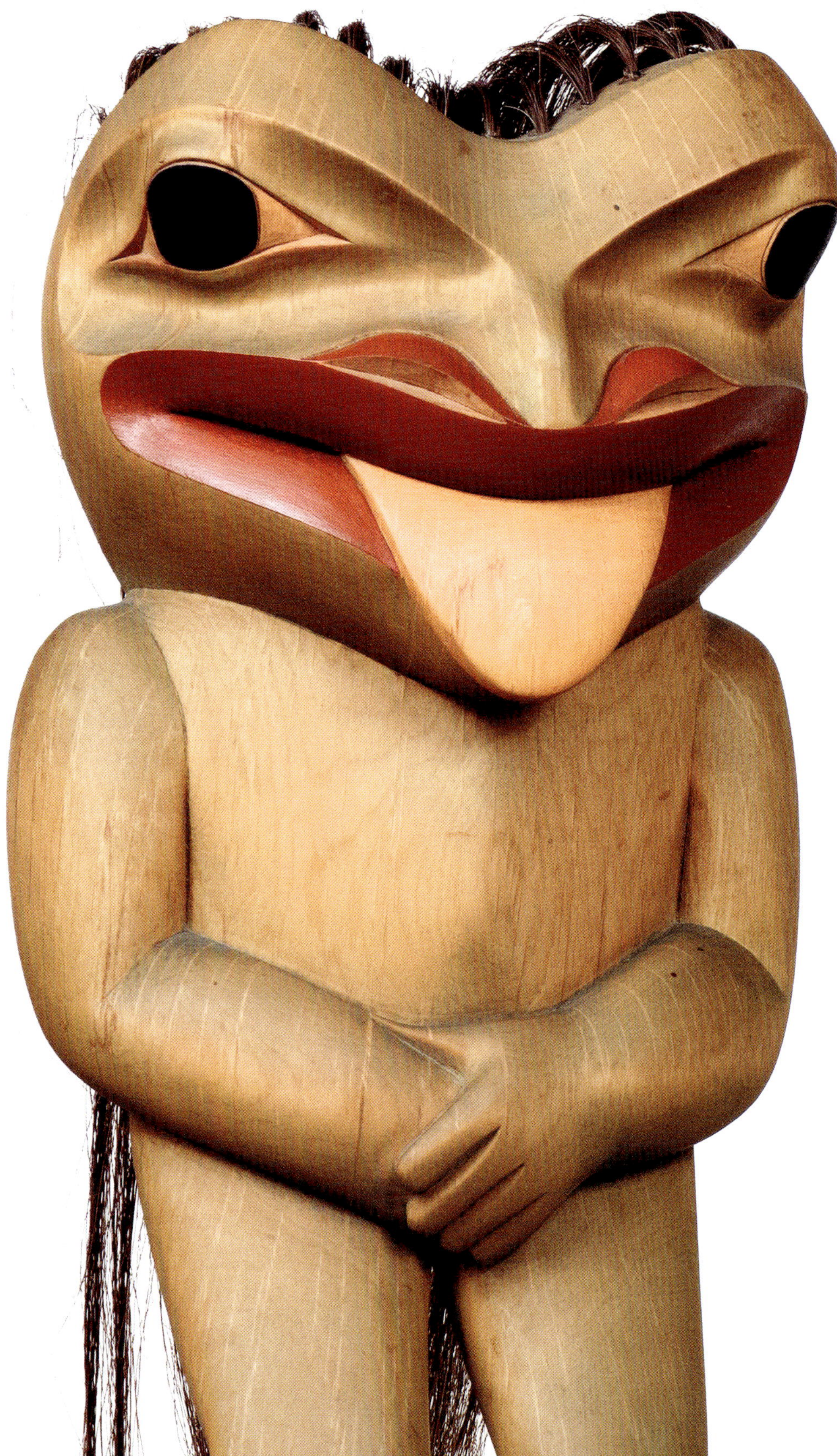

Little Frog Sculpture, 1989

LITTLE FROG SCULPTURE

I made him in my basement—he was so alive—and I used to pack him around like he was a little kid when I was making him. I finished him and I put him in a show at Vancouver. The lady there said, "That's not Northwest Coast art!" She said, "It's not a totem pole." I said, "It's not supposed to be a totem pole. It's a sculpture." I knew he was going to make it on his own. And he got into that show at the National Gallery of Canada, *Land, Spirit, Power*, in 1992.[70] He became famous!

That little frog sculpture is now owned by my friend Harold Demetzer. I first met him back at the *Northern Comfort* exhibition at Potlatch Arts. He has been collecting Northwest Coast art for a long time.

70. *Land, Spirit, Power: First Nations at the National Gallery of Canada* was curated by Diana Nemiroff, Charlotte Townsend-Gault, and Robert Houle for the NGC in 1992. It was the first major exhibition of contemporary Indigenous art at the gallery.

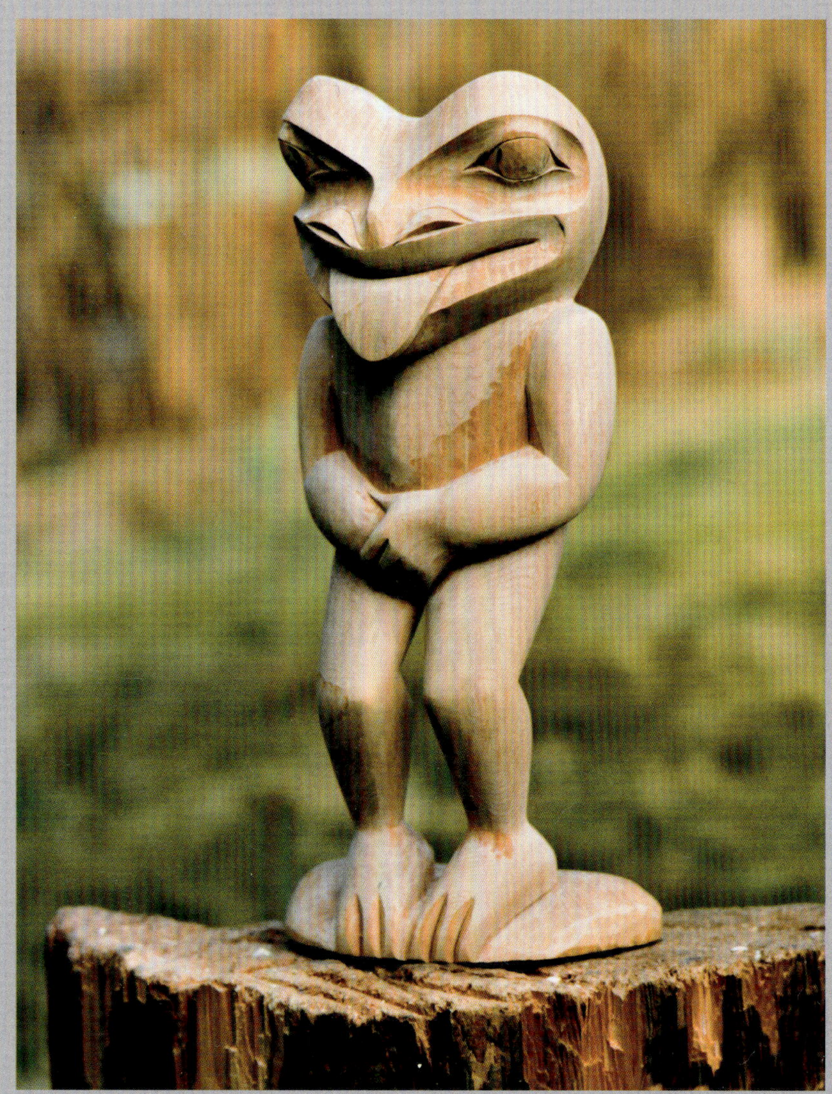

Little Frog Sculpture in progress, Prince Rupert, late 1980s

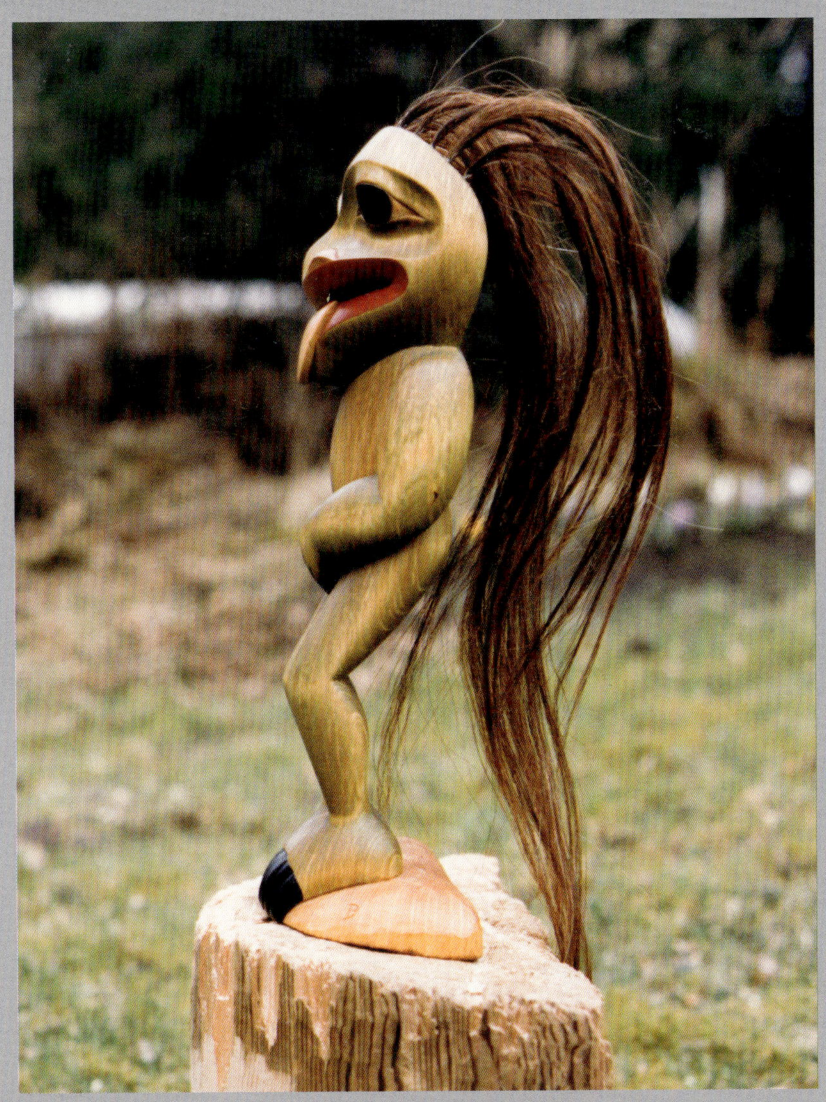

Little Frog Sculpture in progress, Prince Rupert, late 1980s

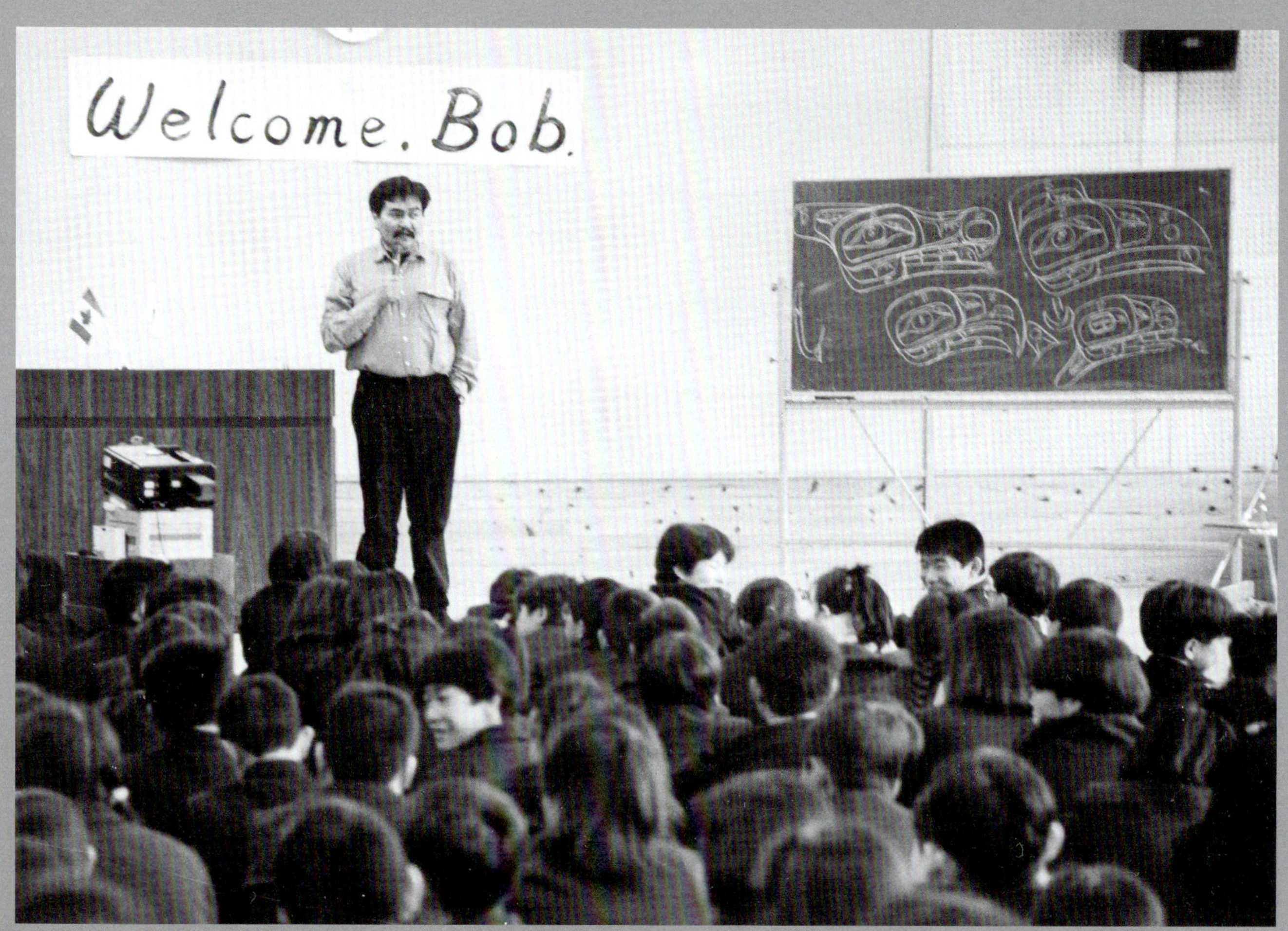

Speaking at Owase High School, Owase, Japan, 1993

TRAVELLING TO JAPAN

In 1993 I carved a pole for the city of Owase, Japan.[71]

We carved it in Prince Rupert and then we took it on a ship that April. We went over there, and we danced.

Our daughter, Tanya, had gone there on a school trip in Grade 12; Owase and Prince Rupert are sister cities. The mayor, Haruo Sugita, asked the teacher if they could get a totem pole for the new cultural centre in Owase, and so the group was asked if they knew anyone that could carve a pole, and Tanya's teacher, Larry Hope, said yes!

We carved the pole in Prince Rupert, and then they flew us all over there and we had a pole raising. The pole has the eagle on the top, and then a man with salmon, and then a bear and a little human on the bear, and then a salmon below the bear. It's one of our stories of a man who was helped by the bear and the eagle, giving him salmon.

There was this Japanese Elder from Owase—she looked at us and she could dance with us. She could feel it. My nephews were dancing too. There were about ten of us altogether, and the mayor of Prince Rupert, Pete Lester, came, too, and my friend Norman Jackson from Ketchikan, Alaska.

The Japanese come from a really old culture and ours is strong too. They have their culture still, and there are a lot of similarities. They still have their language and their old songs. They sound similar—the really old ones. When we are dancing the ancestors are with us.

71. Owase is located on Japan's southestern Kii peninsula on the Pacific Ocean.

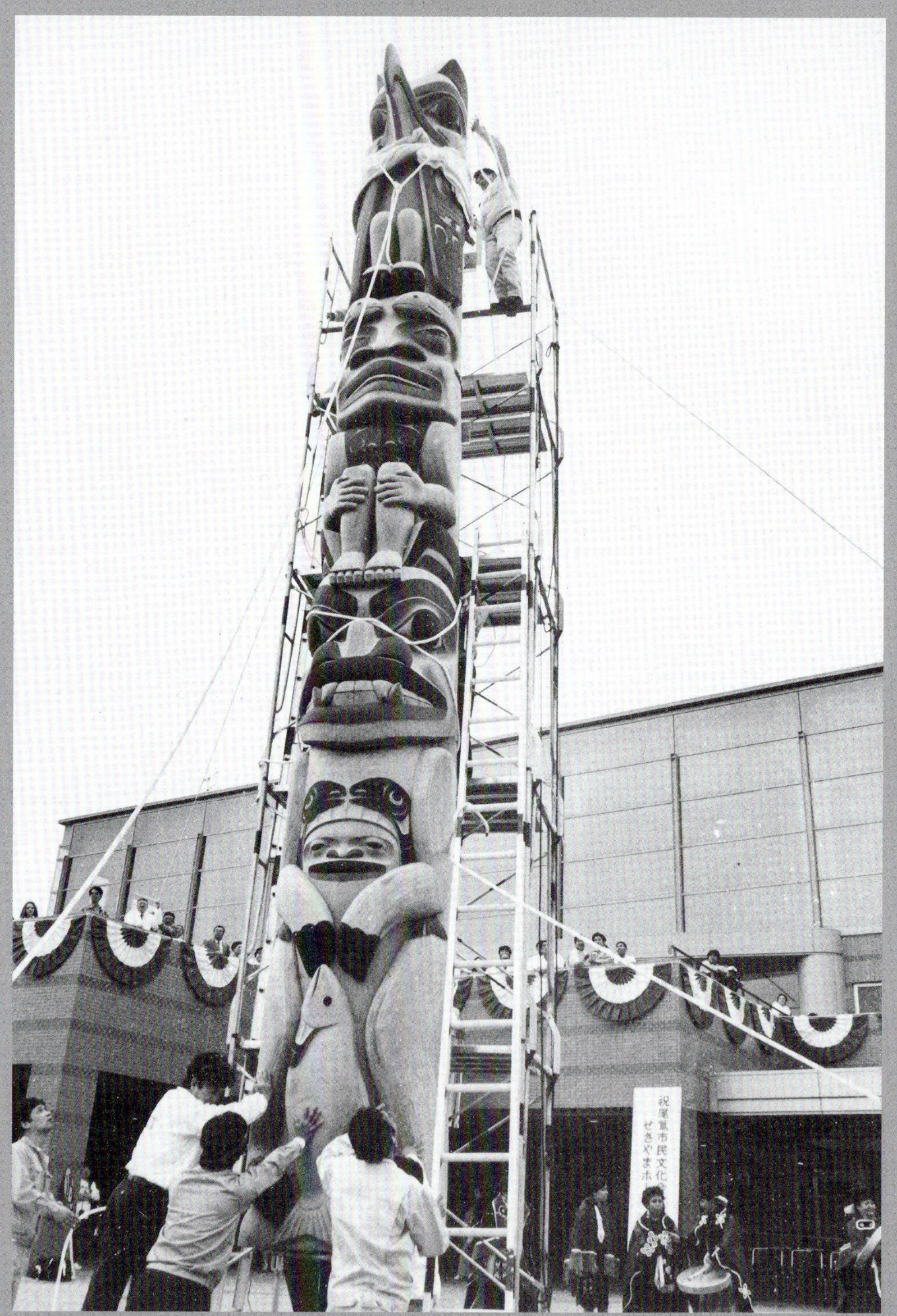

Raising the *Good Luck Pole*, Owase, Japan, 1993

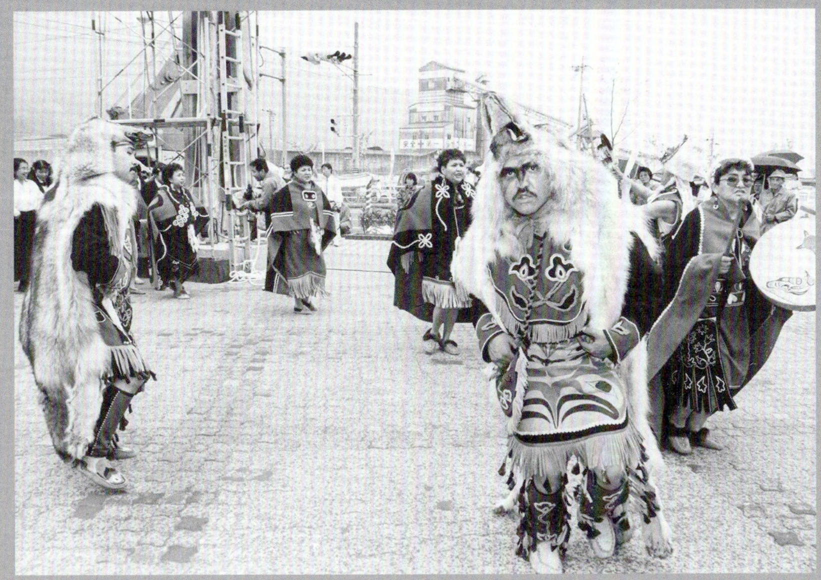

The Salmon Creek Dancers doing traditional dances at the totem
pole raising, Owase, Japan, 1993; (from left) Stan Bevan, Lovetta McNeil,
Merle Bevan, Linda Bob, Ken McNeil, Sheila Frank

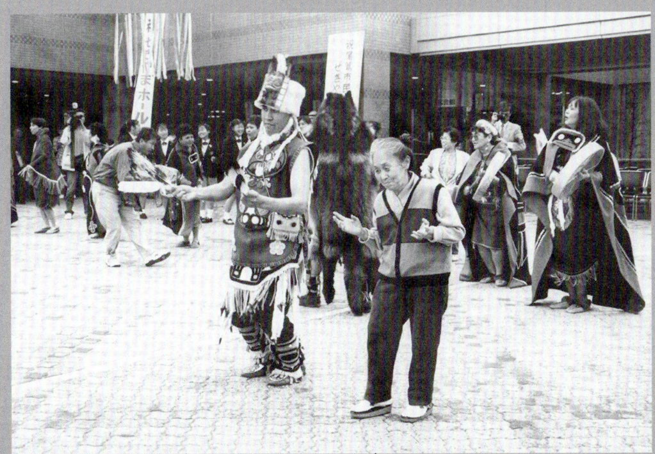

Norman Jackson, of the Tongass Bear Tribe, Ketchikan, Alaska, with a
Japanese Elder dancing at the totem pole raising, Owase, Japan, 1993

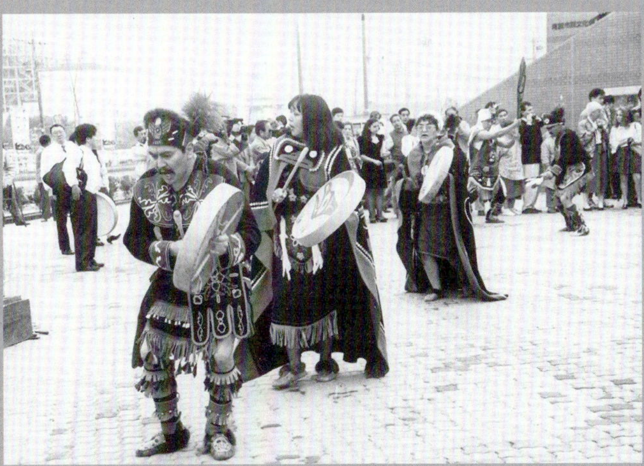

The Salmon Creek Dancers doing traditional dances at the totem
pole raising, Owase, Japan, 1993; (from left) me, my sister Virginia Bob,
Sheila Frank, Ken McNeil (back)

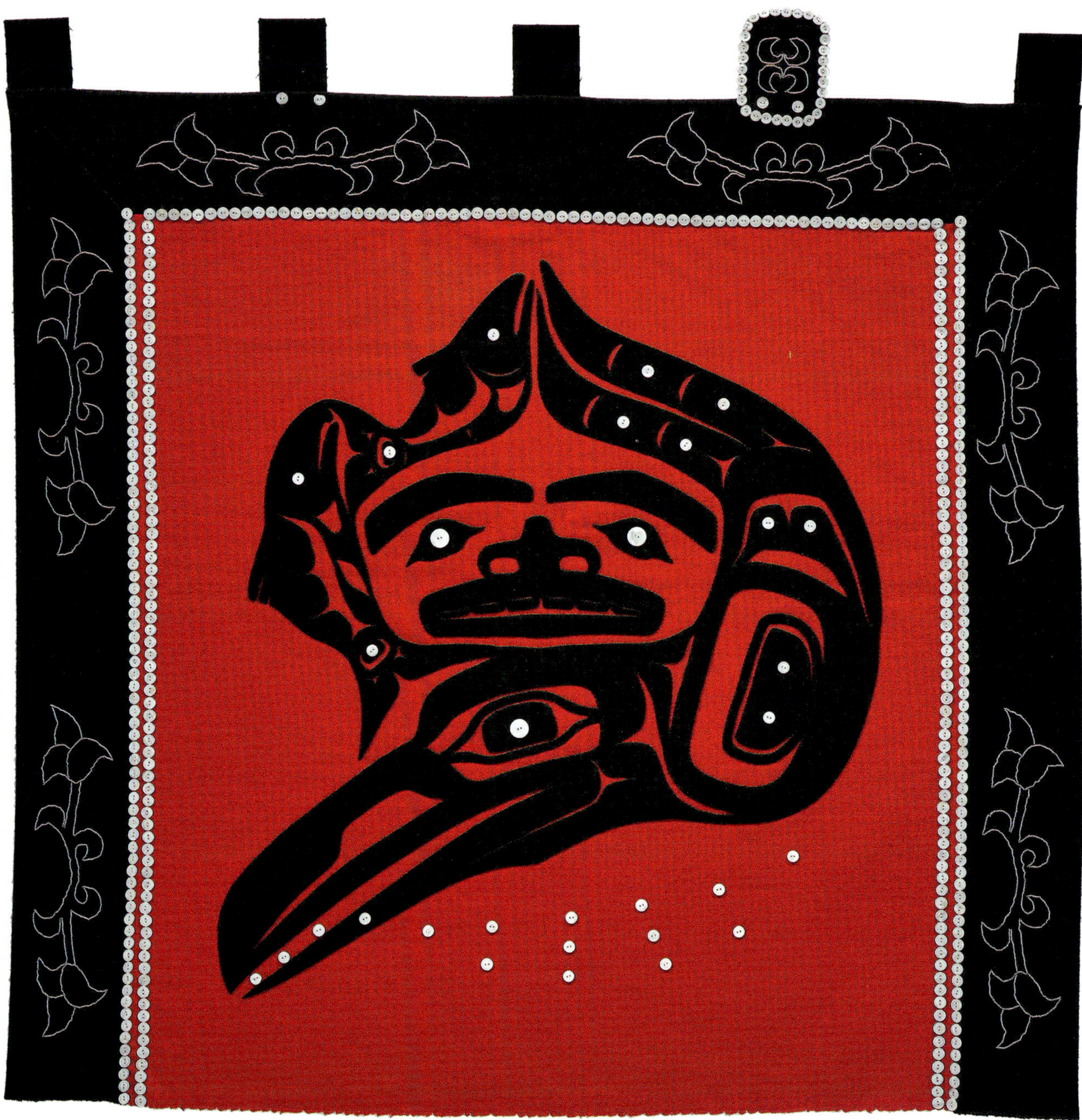

Raven and Salmon Blanket, 1985
(Designed by Dempsey Bob; made by Linda Bob)

Bill Reid said my *Raven and Salmon Blanket* from 1985 at the
Royal Ontario Museum was the best design he had seen in
Northwest Coast art. I've been doing salmon designs a lot lately
because we're losing the salmon and the frogs. We've lost 70
percent of the sharks, the rays too. We've got stories about the
raven bringing the salmon.

The deer is the peace animal. The noise of those hooves
is the sound of peace—that's why we use them in our aprons,
because they come in peace.

Some of the young people are coming in and they want to
do these war dances and songs in the feast, but that's not right.
Feasts were our way of sharing, making peace. The feast was
for healing. The old people measured their wealth by what they
gave away, not by what they had. This one lady, she was poor,
she had nothing. She wanted to go to this feast, so she took wild
rhubarb and gave it away at the feast.

Chief's Headdress—Human, 1993

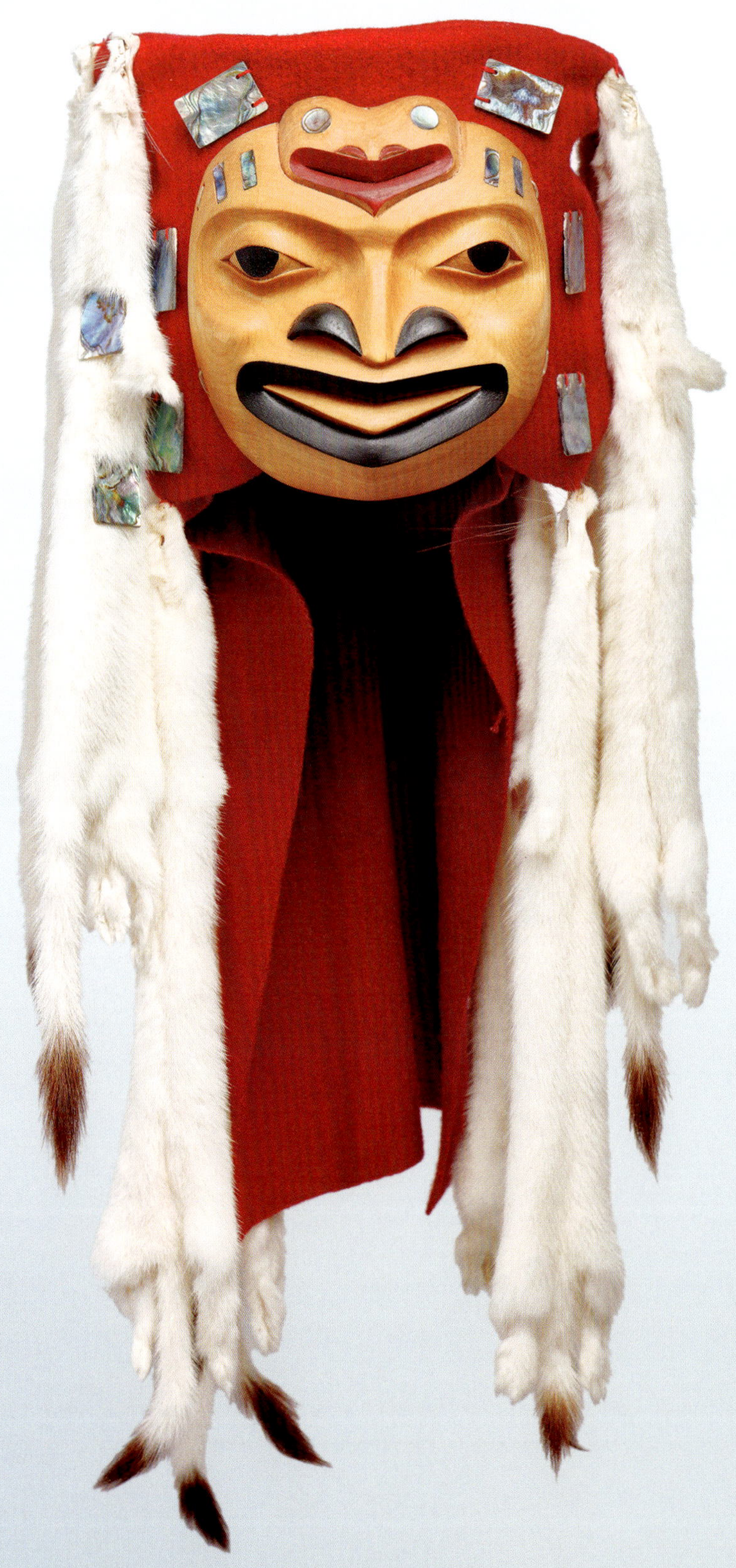

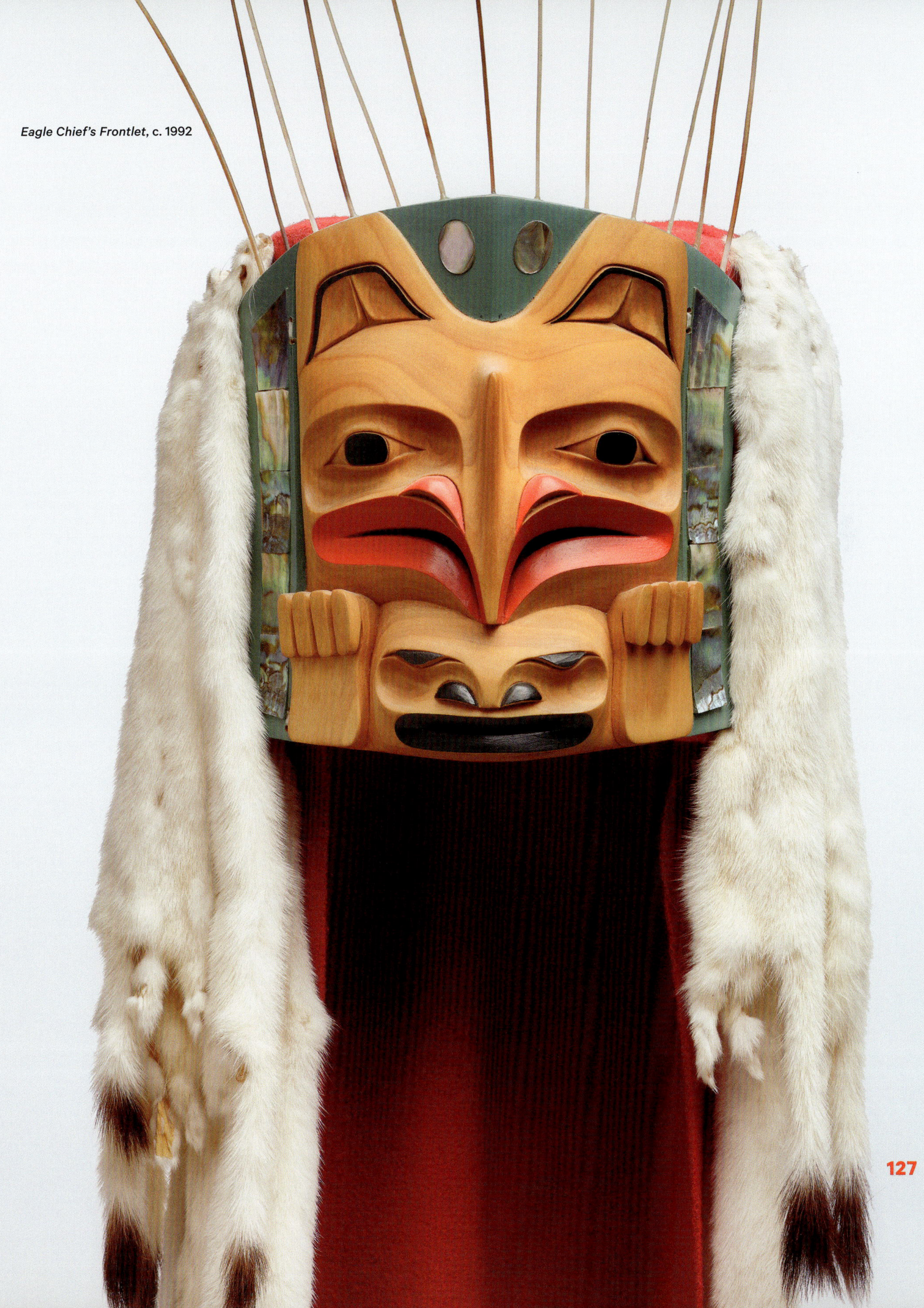

Eagle Chief's Frontlet, c. 1992

127

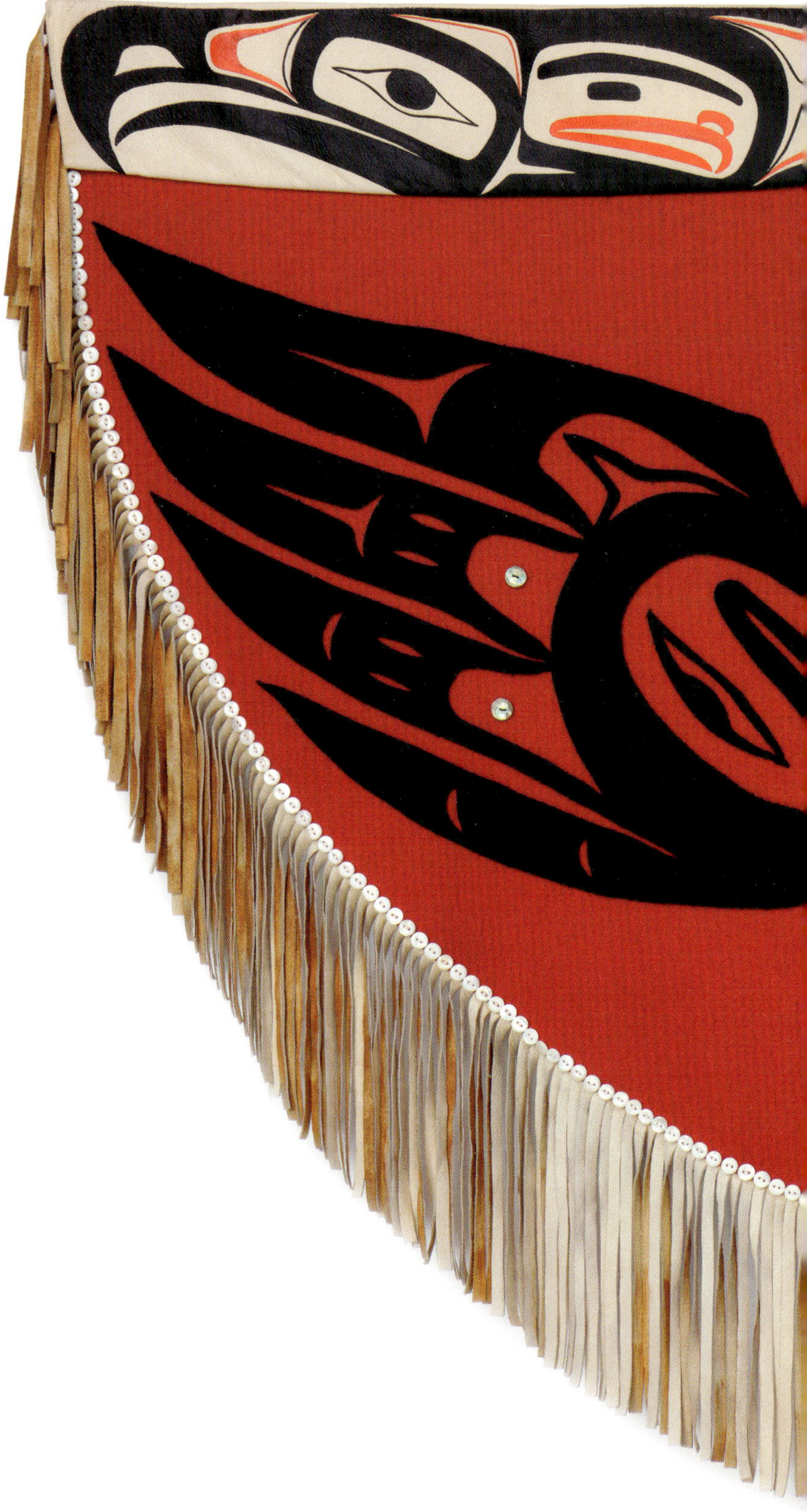

Eagle Chief's Robe, c. 1992
(Designed by Dempsey Bob; made by Linda Bob)

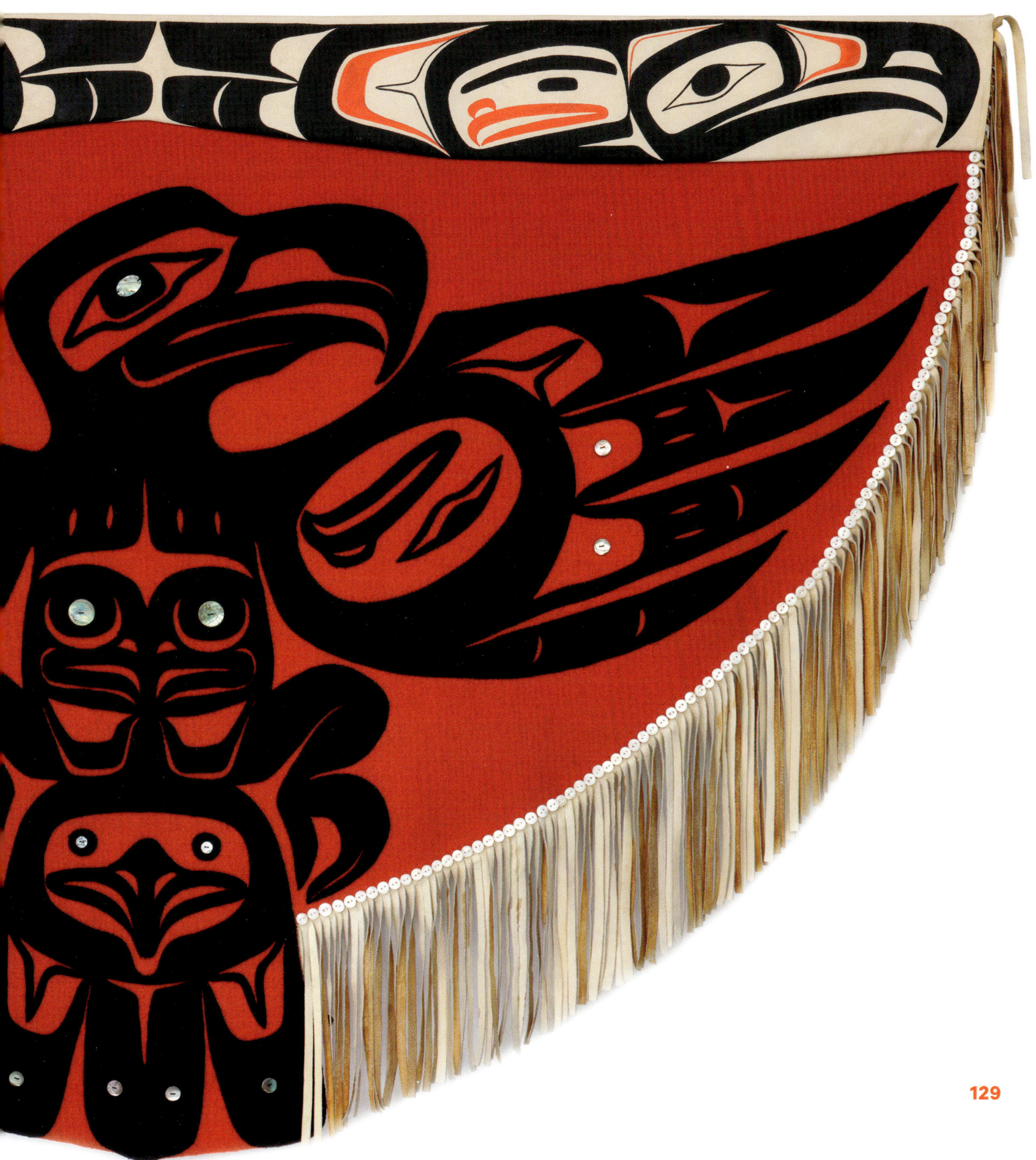

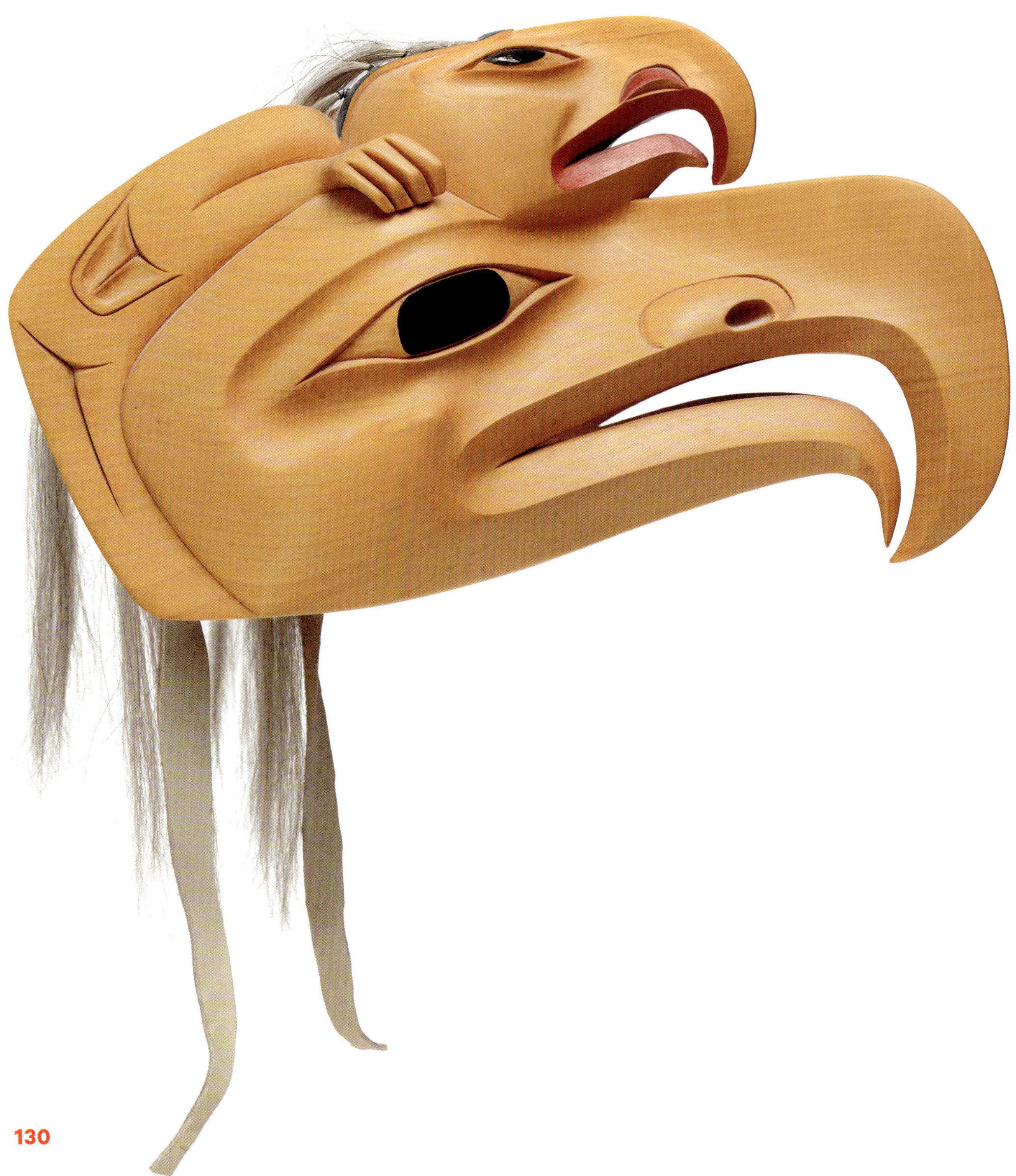

The Eagles Forehead Mask, 1996

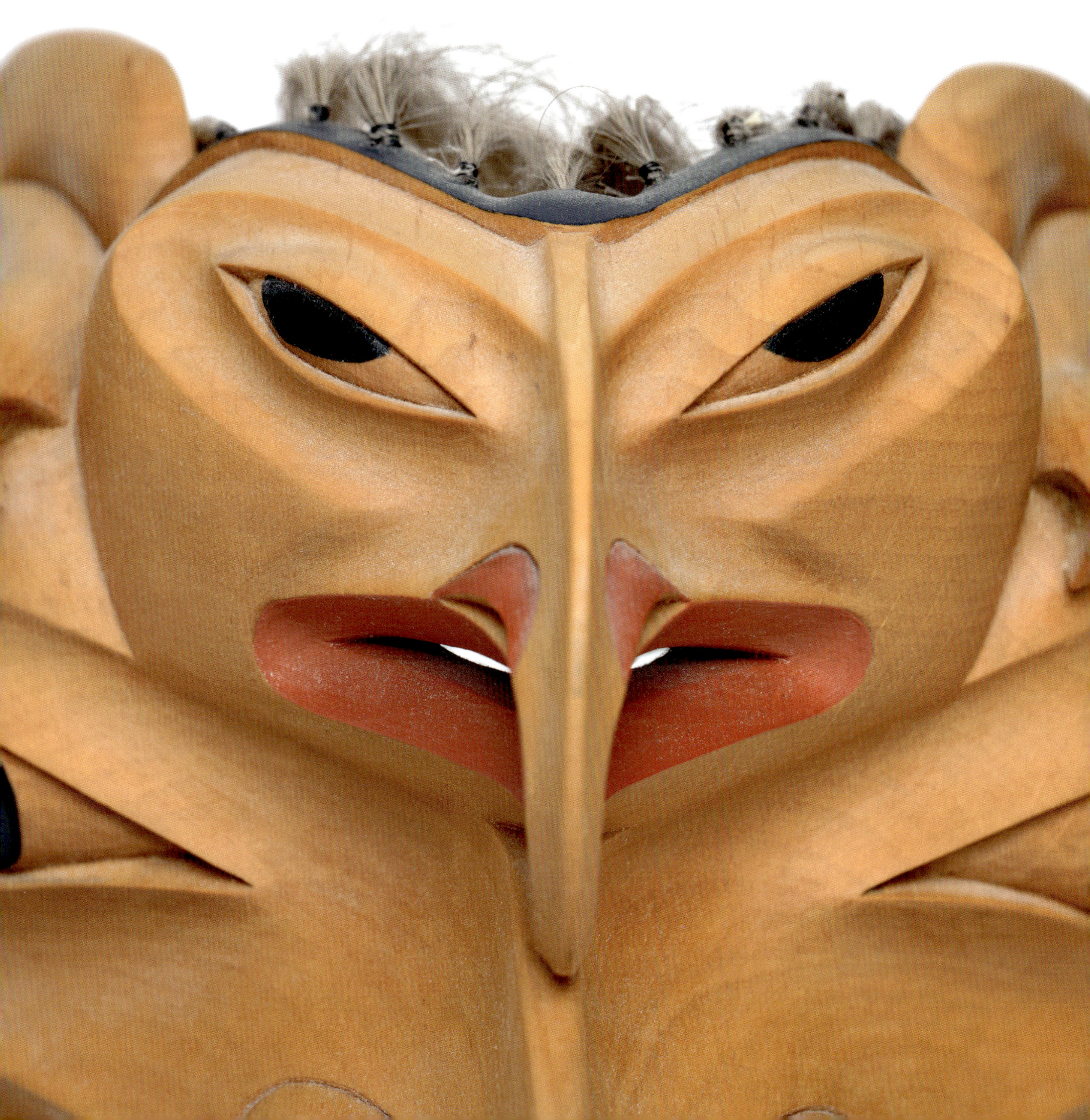

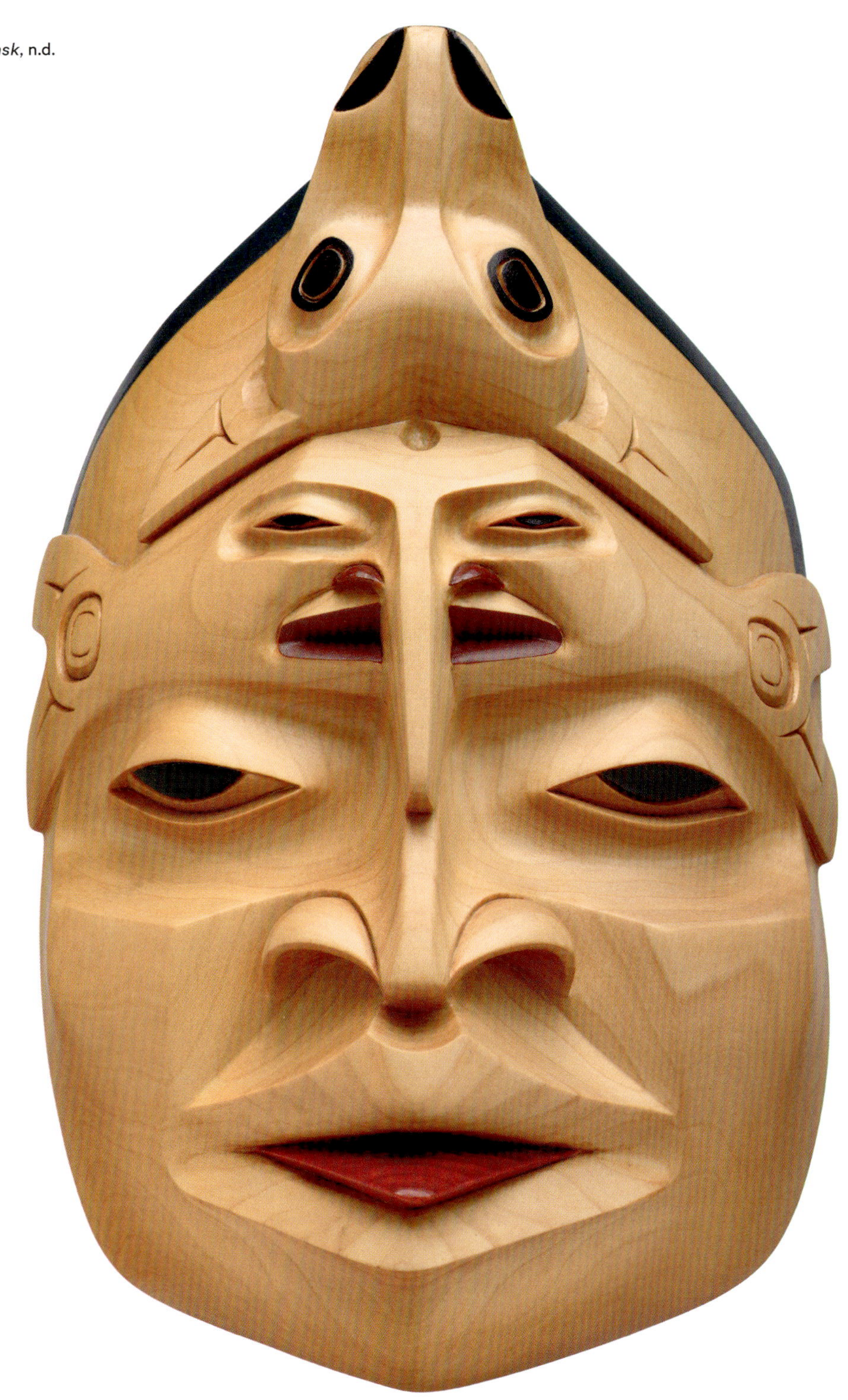

Killer Whale Portrait Mask, n.d.

Wolf, Eagle, and Human Mask, 1997

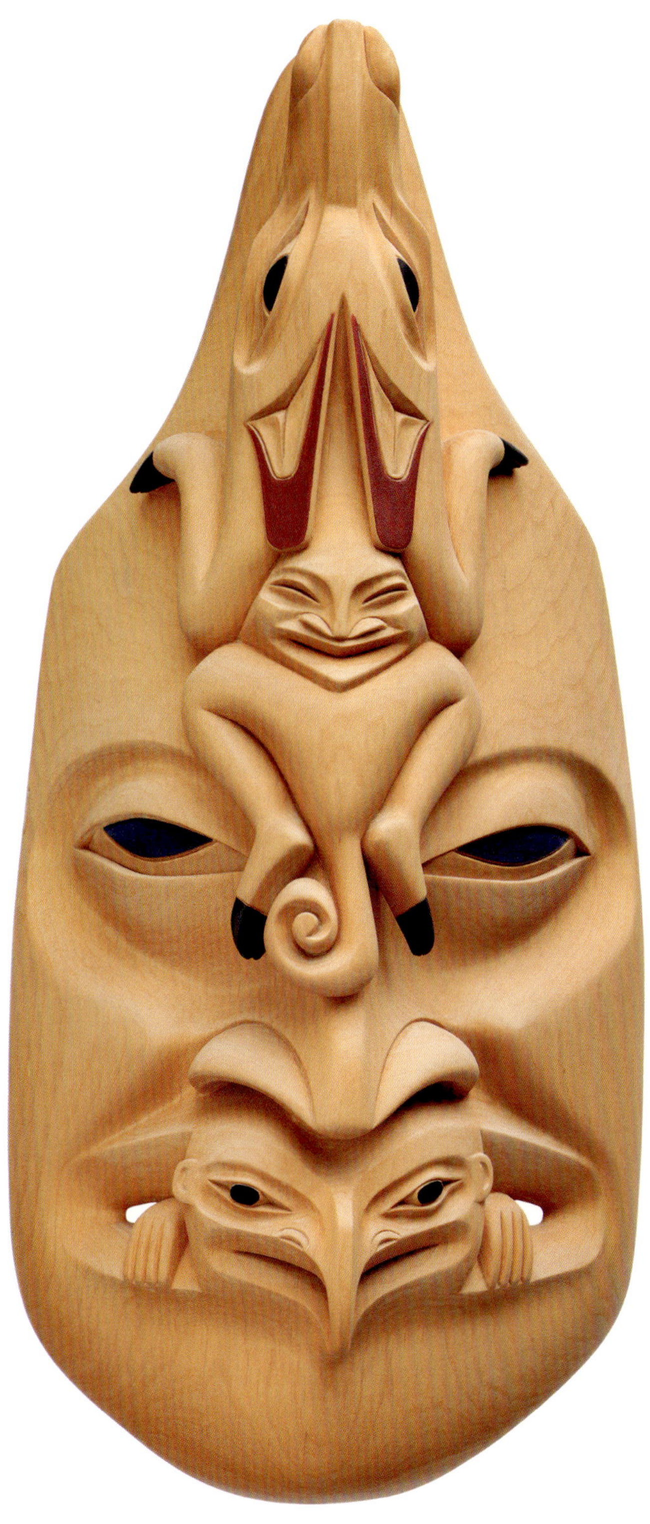

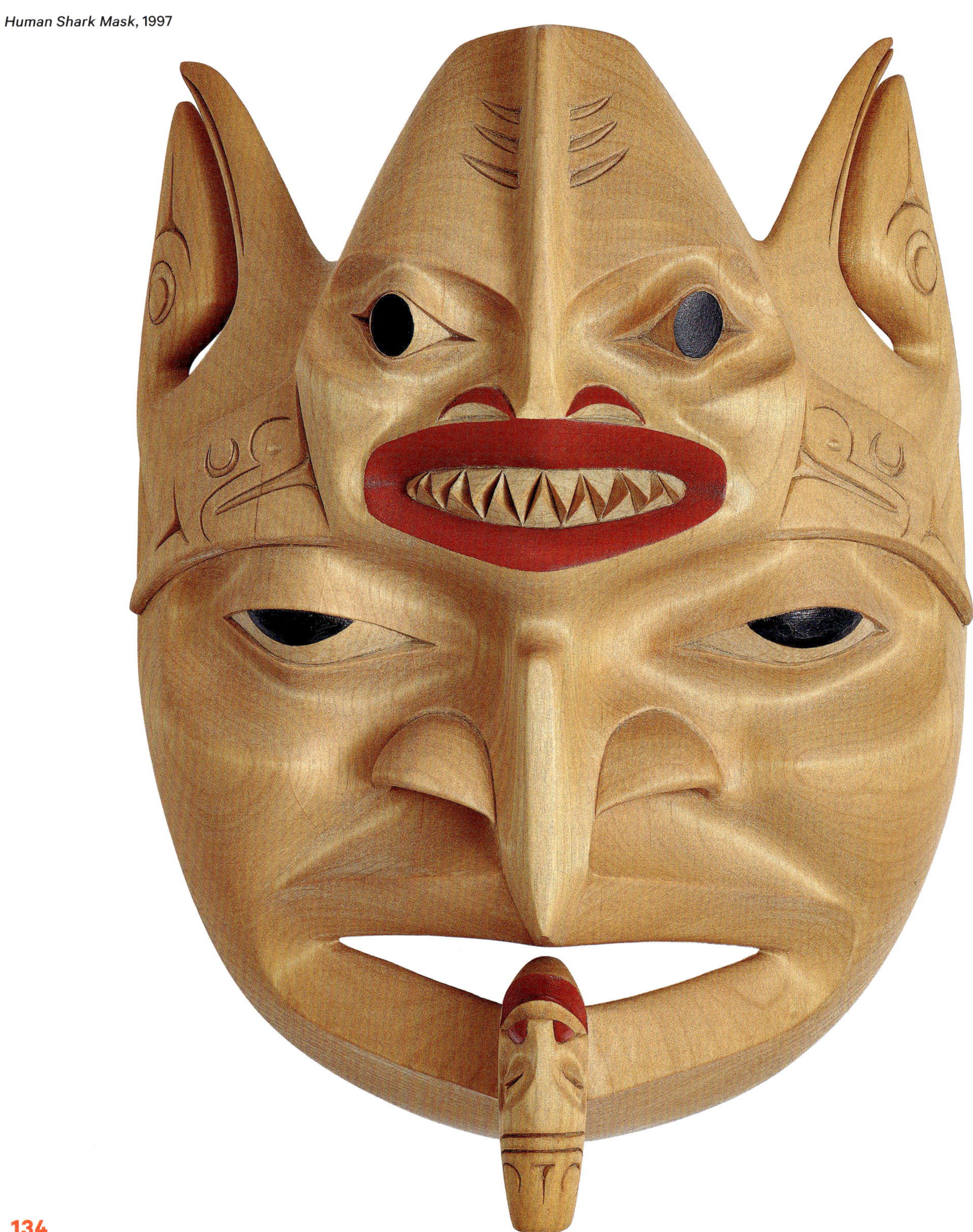

Human Shark Mask, 1997

134

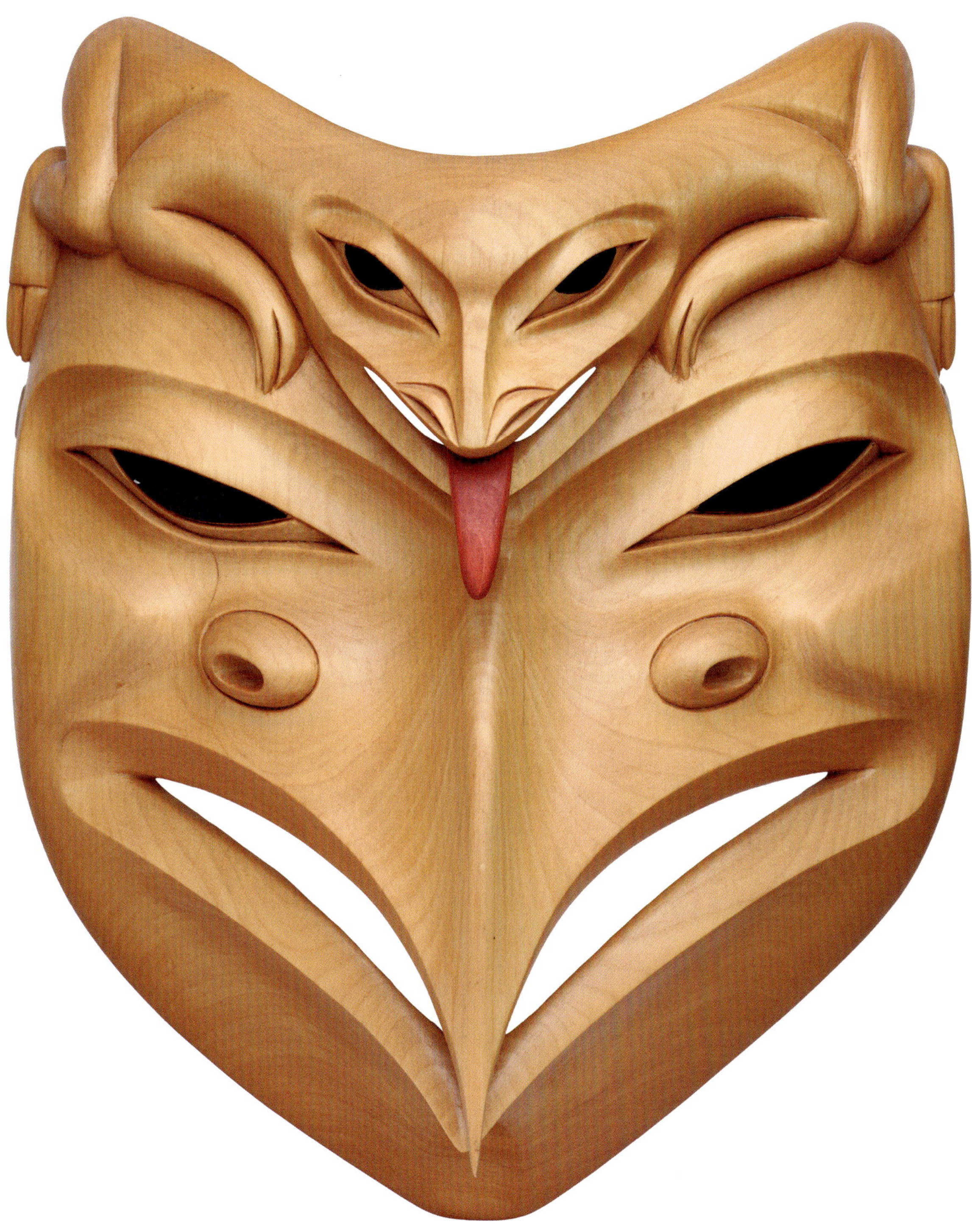

Raven and Frog Mask, 1997

A STORY ABOUT WHALES

One time that I saw whales I was a lecturer on Northwest Coast art on the *Yorktown Clipper,* working up and down the coast.[72] I would demonstrate carving once in a while, talking to the people and basically just hanging around with them. We went down to Seattle, up to Juneau—I went maybe three or four times in the '80s. I met some really interesting people from all over the world.

Once when we were up by Icy Bay, in Alaska, we saw six killer whales coming toward us, and all of a sudden they all dove down together and then came up in a straight line on the other side of the ship and just kept going. There was a little baby killer whale too. You don't usually see them in a row like that, in formation. That's how they hunt. People call them the wolves of the sea. And the eagle is the wolf of the sky. That refers to their way of hunting—they work together in groups.

I was just trying to make different creatures and objects, and I had never done a helmet before—I think the killer whale helmet (pp. 72, 73) I made was one of the first. In the old days, they used to make them out of burls. When you hit a burl, it doesn't split. The wood is very hard. But my ones are made out of alder because they are art pieces. I don't even know how they carved them back then, because the grain is so curled and twisted. It's amazing what they did.

72. The *Yorktown Clipper* was a cruise ship that took passengers along the coast of Alaska and Northern British Columbia.

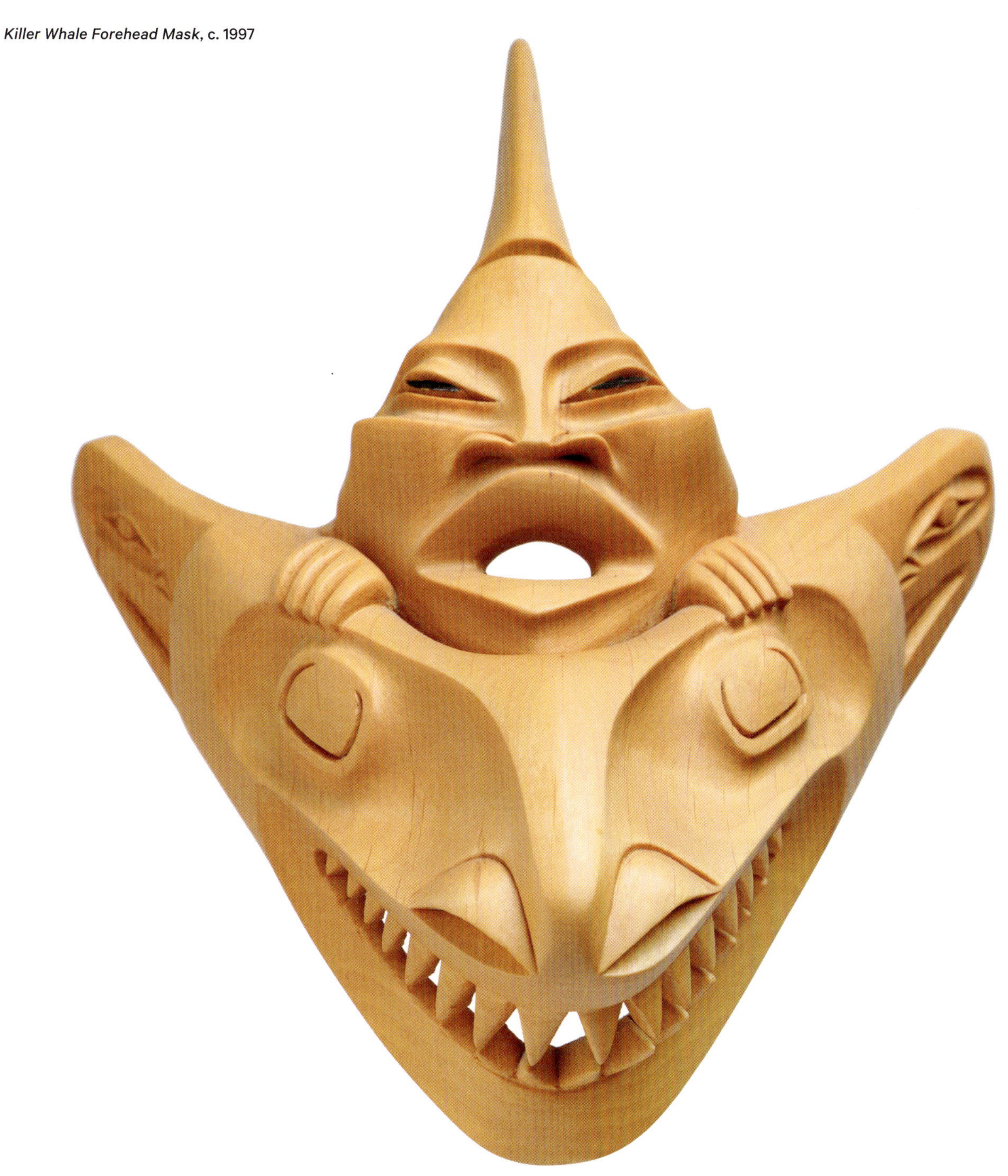

Killer Whale Forehead Mask, c. 1997

Hawk Human Portrait Mask, 2003

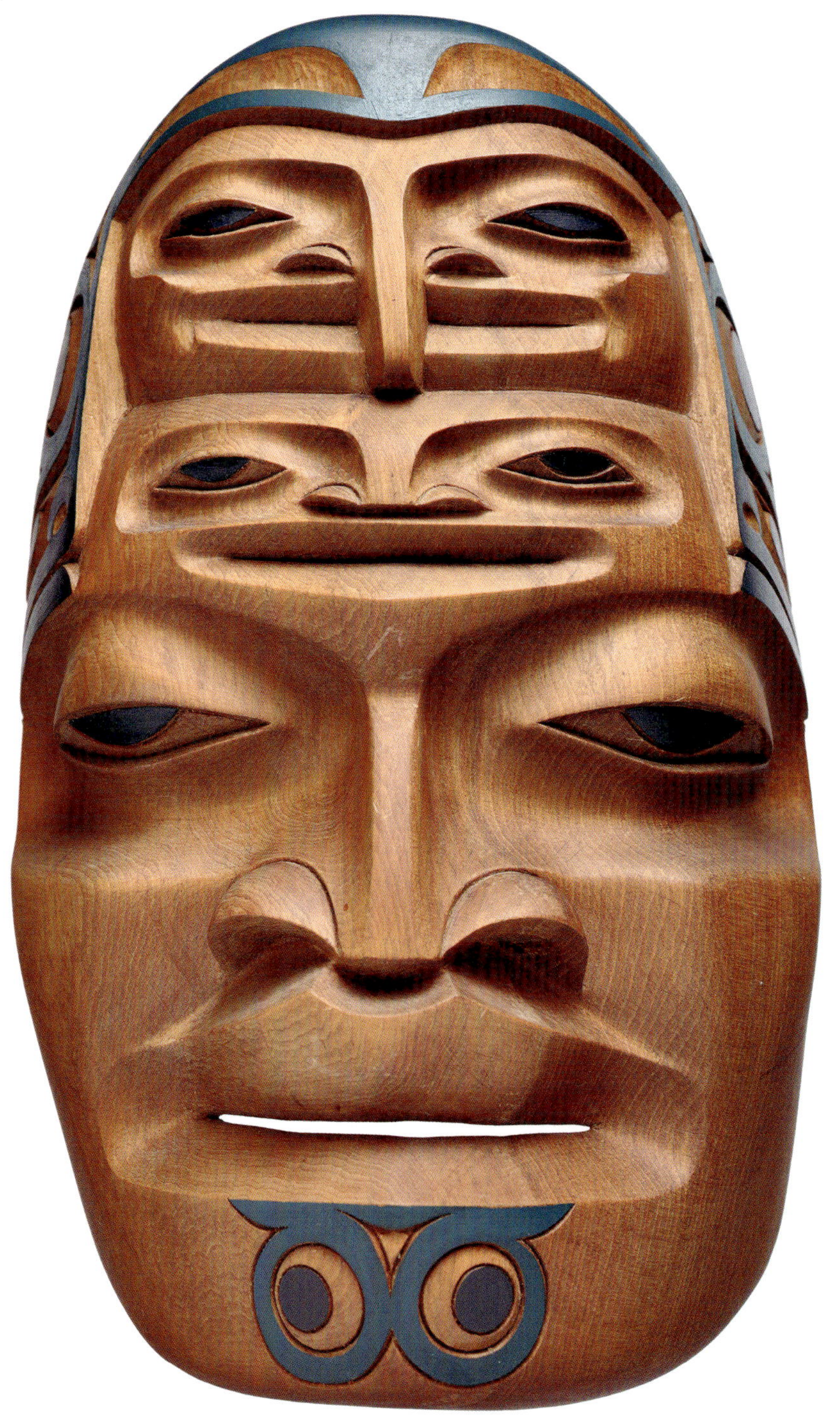

In the early 2000s I had the chance to work in New Zealand. I went to Napier and attended a workshop with Sandy Adsett.[73] He's a Māori artist and a teacher there.

It happened because in 1999 my nephew Stan Bevan[74] and I were at a conference in Ottawa and the Māoris were there too. They wanted to meet us. When we started talking they knew all about us, Freda and me and Bill Reid, and invited us to New Zealand for the 2000 millennium daybreak ceremony.

But they didn't phone; we never heard from them. By chance, I saw Gary Nichols[75] the next year at a workshop at Evergreen State College in Olympia, Washington.[76] We had held a workshop there, about eight days long, really good artists. It was just a magical time and very creative. When Gary saw me, he said, "Weren't you supposed to come to New Zealand?" And I said, "Weren't you supposed to call me?"

So then the next year, 2001, they found the funds to pay for the trip—they have an international art festival there.[77] So we went. Now I have been there twelve times. My friend up in Alaska, Betsy Jackson—she had also been to New Zealand. She had told me about the Māoris, and said they are just like our people. She said, "You have to go there." When I went, I saw that. They were so close to us.

Our culture is a canoe culture, we are a sea culture, longhouse people, we're artists, wood carvers, we are weavers. I checked out their old carving tools, jade tools—they are the same shape as ours. The weaving is the same technique as our Raven's tail. Same weaving patterns in their baskets: they start them a special way in Prince Rupert and in New Zealand and nowhere else in the world. They told us about how they navigate with the stars, and we do that too. And the whale rider story—we have a whale rider story too. The way they conduct their feasts. How they give out the food. I looked at their canoe bailers—so many little things like that. All around the Pacific Rim the Indigenous people have been very artistic. They had to know how to work with trees. When you touch an old tree, for us it's like going to church.

73. Sandy Adsett (b. 1939 Māori)

74. Stan Bevan (b. 1961 Tahltan-Tlingit-Tsimshian)

75. Gary Nichols (b. 1950 Tasmanian)

76. A gathering of Indigenous Visual Artists of the Pacific Rim, 2001

77. The New Zealand Festival of the Arts is a biennial that was started in 2000.

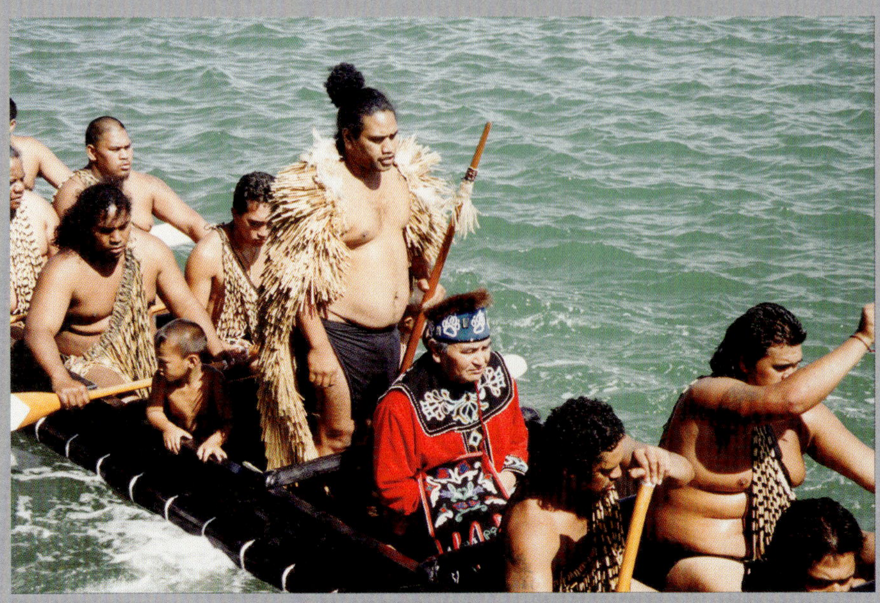

Tai Mamaku (standing) and me in *Mātaatua* (one of the large voyaging canoes in which Polynesians migrated to New Zealand seven hundred years ago, according to Māori tradition), on the day Stan Bevan and I were adopted into the Te Teko Māori community, Whakatane, New Zealand, 2001

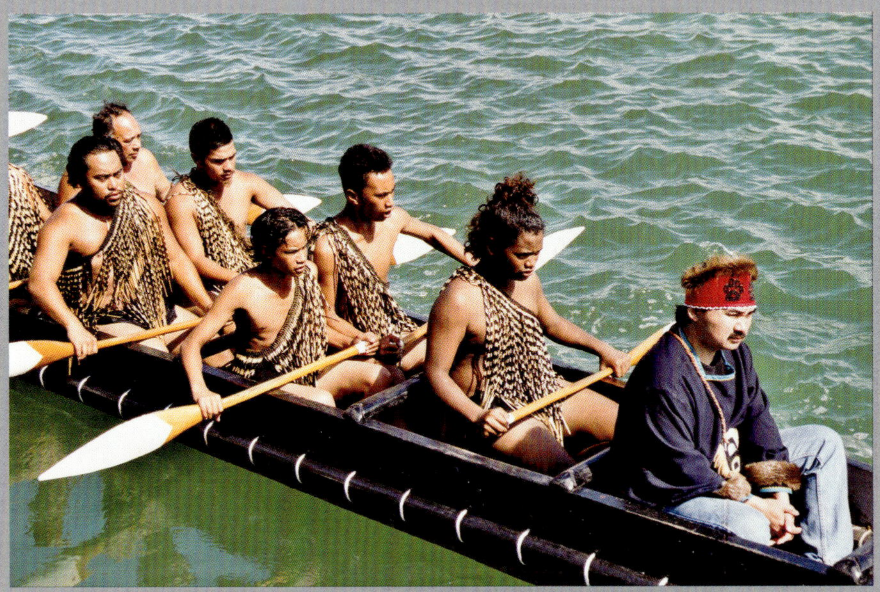

Stan Bevan (front) in *Mātaatua*, Whakatane, New Zealand, 2001

When you have to explain your culture you come to understand it better. They challenged us and helped us to understand them, and ourselves better too. When you share, it makes you stronger. And we have such a similar history, with the English coming to our land. That's why we're so close to the Māoris. They're our brothers and sisters. Their art was outlawed too. Darcy Nicholas[78] and Lyonel Grant,[79] Rangi Kipa,[80] Steve Gibbs,[81] Manos Nathan,[82] Alex Nathan,[83] Sandy Adsett, Derek Lardelli,[84] Joe Harawira,[85] and Ben Mamaku[86]—I liked their paintings and the beauty of their art forms. I studied their old sculptures in the War Memorial Museum in Auckland, too,[87] and at the Te Papa Museum in Wellington.[88] Both of us use two-dimensional design in our sculpture.

When I was at a gathering at Napier in 2008, they gave us a project. I had to carve a three-foot section of a sculpture. It was a three-foot cube in totara wood. I thought, How am I going to get this done?

People talk about the "low man on the totem pole," but to us the bottom figure is the most important. It's the closest to Mother Earth. I was assigned to do the next piece up—the idea was to do a warrior because they come from a warrior society too.

I had a dream and then I knew what to do. I had this idea of a Tlingit warrior with a visor and a helmet on. But how to fit that into that three-foot cube? So I flipped the centre of the design onto the corner of the cube and I added a little eagle on the helmet. That carving is in Napier now. This was the first time that I made a carving that was not symmetrical. It was not a mask in the conventional way—it was a wall sculpture, like *Northern Eagles Transformation Mask* (p. 154). Most pieces until then had always been the same on both sides, symmetrical, but that's when I broke away from that.

Christian White did a three-foot piece, too, and there was a Pacific Islander carver there as well—he was carving flowers. When the Pacific Islanders saw us and what we were doing they

78. Darcy Nicholas (b. 1945 Māori)

79. Lyonel Grant (b. 1957 Māori)

80. Rangi Kipa (b. 1966 Māori)

81. Steve Gibbs (b. 1955 Māori)

82. Manos Nathan (1948–2015 Māori)

83. Alex Nathan (b. 1940s Māori)

84. Derek Lardelli (b. 1961 Māori)

85. Joe Harawira (b. 1956 Māori)

86. Ben Mamaku (d. 2011 Māori)

87. The War Memorial Museum in Auckland, New Zealand, displays more than a thousand Māori taonga (treasured possessions).

88. The Museum of New Zealand Te Papa Tongarewa in Wellington is the country's national museum. It has a significant collection of Māori taonga.

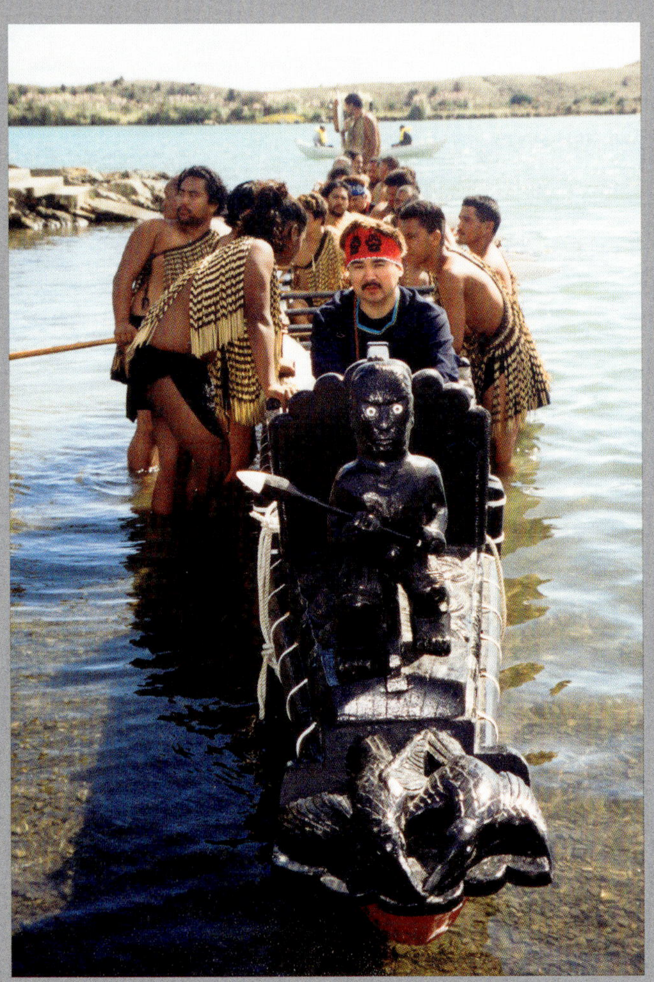

Stan Bevan in the bow of *Mātaatua*, 2001

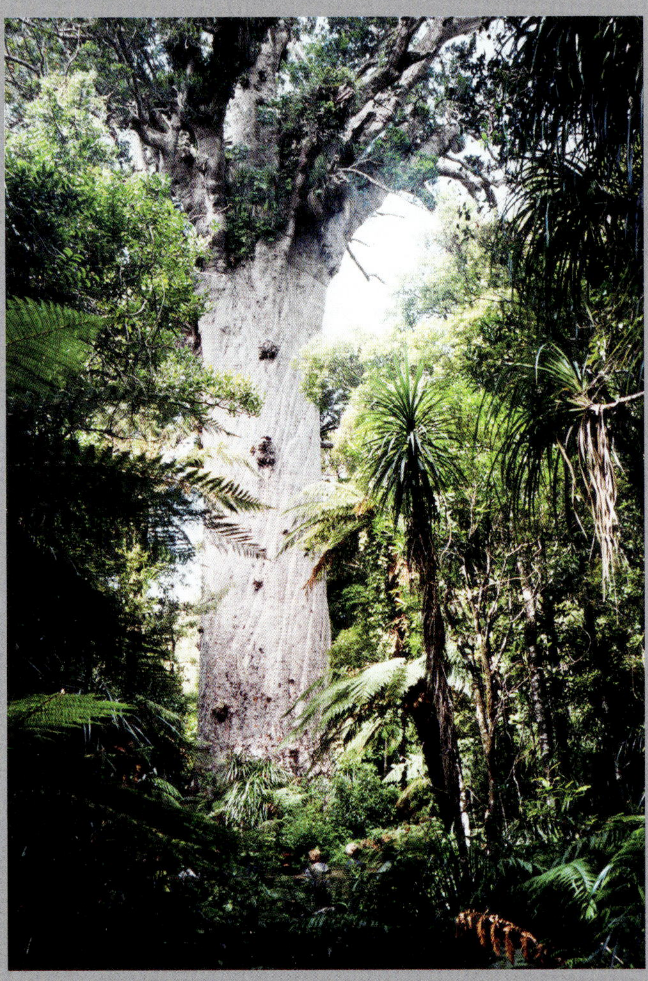

Tāne Mahuta (Grandfather of the Forest), a kauri tree reputed to be more than two thousand years old and the world's largest rainforest tree, Waipoua Forest, North Auckland Peninsula, New Zealand

didn't come the next day. Then they flew in their best carver, after they'd seen us working!

I have been to Hawaii three times also, to lead workshops, invited by the Indigenous Visual Artists of the Pacific Rim group—I met them through the Māoris. Around the Pacific there are a lot of artists, on all the islands.

It wasn't until later in my life that I had this chance to travel, because before that I didn't have much money. When I got older, and people learned more about what I was doing, I was invited places: New Zealand, Italy (to do bronze casting), Denmark, Scotland. Usually when I'm travelling I'm working. In 1992–93 I got into making bronzes and wanted to learn, so I went to Italy. I also took a bronze-casting course in Boise, Idaho.

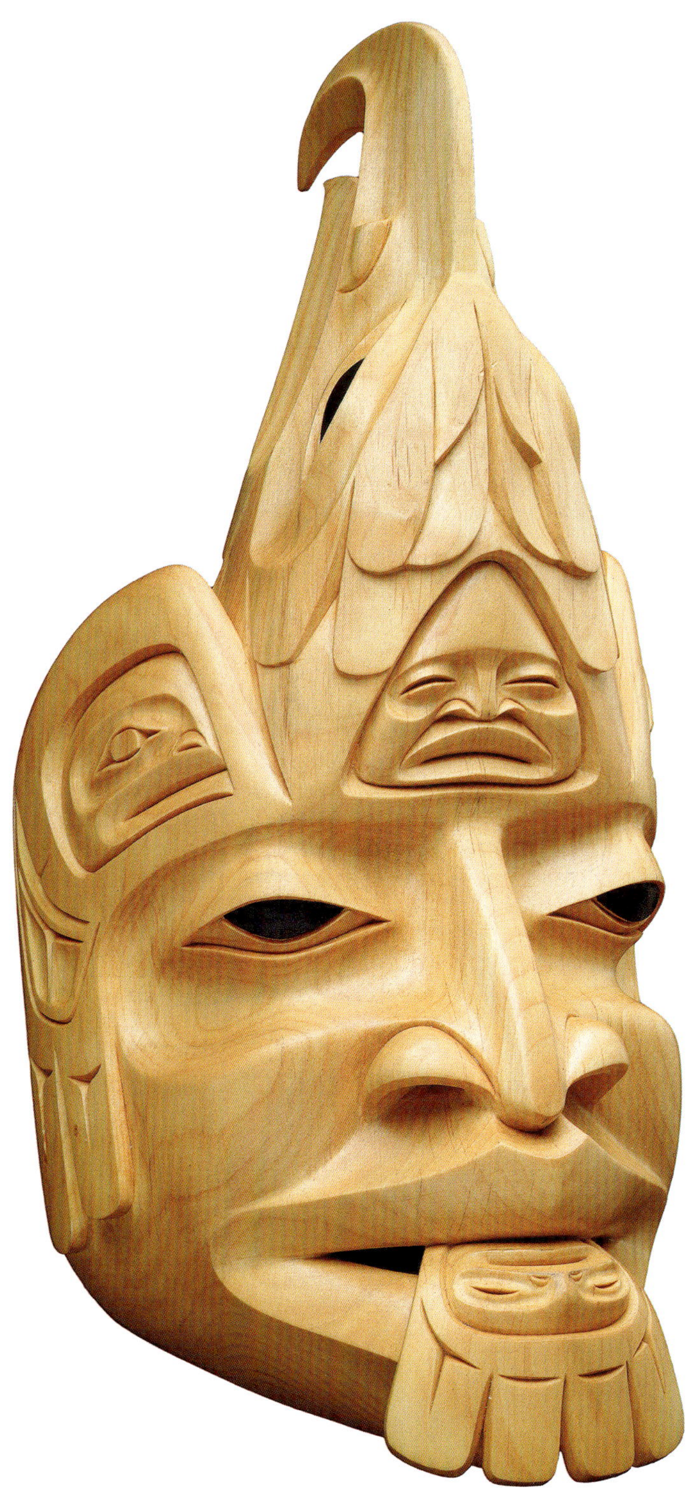

Eagle Mask, 2000

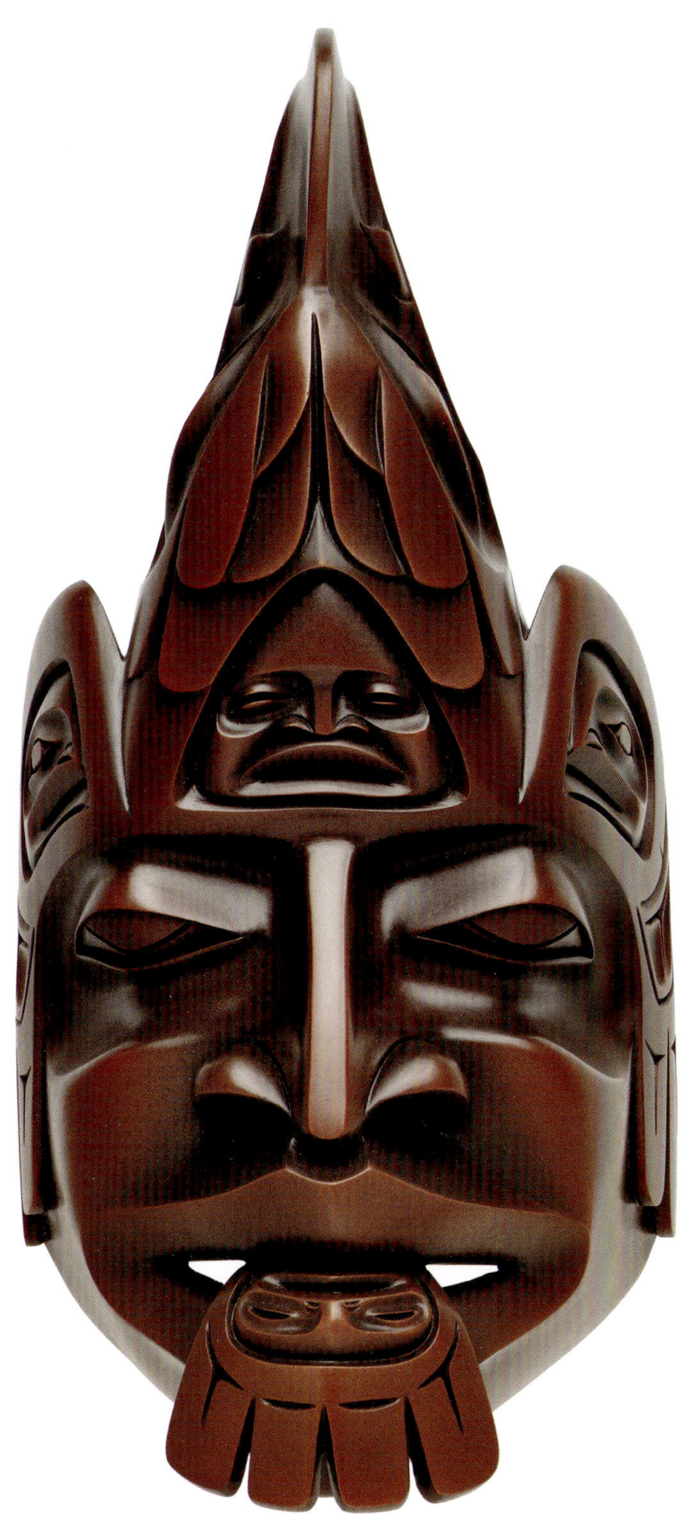

Eagle Mask, 2001

When I was in Italy in 1992, I saw them casting a big bronze of Michelangelo's *David*. I studied it—it was amazing. I put my hand in *David*'s ear and it went up to my elbow—that's how deep it was. It was in a foundry in Pietrasanta, in Tuscany— that's where Michelangelo worked. From the town you can see the mountains where marble is quarried. There are about thirty-three foundries in Pietrasanta, and more than sixty marble workshops and sculpture studios. There are schools there too. It's the mecca for sculptors. That's where Botero worked. He stayed at the same hotel where I stayed, and I ate at the same restaurant. I thought that was pretty neat.

In London, I would visit the British Museum. It's like going to university. We used to go into the storage vaults there with Jonathan King. We could look at whatever we wanted. I saw the depth, the design, and the movement in those great old pieces— the drawing, the lines. When I look at something, I can look at it for hours. I was trying to figure out how the guy did it, or how I would do it. It sparked me to keep learning.

You can really feel the power in those old pieces. It comes from all the ceremonies that they went through—all the songs, all the feasts, all the people. That's what makes them what they are.

Some of my people up in Alaska use my things in ceremony. If a chief or clan leader wants something, they would approach us, and they would ask us, and they would relate their story, and we would come up with a design, and they would approve it, and we would carve it, and the piece would belong to them. We would not copy that piece—the story belongs to them. It's part of their clan history. We would be paid when they had the feast. I made a pole for the Tongass people. You have to know their history and their rituals, and you have to know what is appropriate.

When we raised the pole, our song leader for the dance group was Esther Shea, from the Tongass tribe. She was one of my most important teachers too—we learned not just dancing; we learned our culture there too. She was a regalia maker and she taught Tlingit in the school. Her son Norman Jackson was one of the students at the Totem Heritage Center in Ketchikan; he was a student there with Freda and me. He's like family to us. He's one of the top Tlingit artists in Alaska and a very good dancer, jeweller, and carver too.

At Oxford, I went to the museum there, too, the Pitt Rivers Museum. I went by myself. Then my daughter took some students there and I came too—and the curator there, she said she never comes in this museum at night. You can hear banging and singing and you can see the old people in there. The energy in those pieces is fighting all night. You've got to separate that stuff out. Most of that stuff shouldn't even be shown. These are shaman pieces from all over the world.

Our art was changing already when contact happened. I wonder where they would have gotten to if they hadn't been interrupted. My grandpa Johnny Sinkoots said, "Look at all your fancy tools. The old ancestors, they had nothing—one, two, three tools, and they could still make everything." He used to watch them when they were drilling those old stone pipes. If you go too fast it shatters. He would say, "I bet you can't do that with all your modern tools." He was challenging me.

We have all the tools now but we are losing the culture and the knowledge and the experience. When I think now about the Northwest Coast, I think our people have done some of the greatest sculptures of any time or any place in the world.

What I realized, too, was what modern art stole from us, modern European art—the freedom of forms and ideas, the abstraction. In Australia, we had a show of our pieces along with the Max Ernst collection there. His collection ended up at the National Gallery of Australia in Canberra.[89] He had Tlingit frontlets and spoons, all kinds of stuff. They decided to have a show with these pieces, and the curator said, "I need a few contemporary pieces too." She didn't know if we were even still alive. So they put some of our new work in there, along with the Max Ernst collection.

When I saw his collection with our pieces, I saw what the Europeans had taken from us. They were trying to go into abstraction, but we were already there. We have to take it back

89. In 2006 work by Dempsey Bob was included in the exhibition *People of the Cedar: First Nations Art from the Northwest Coast of Canada* at the National Gallery of Australia. Works were drawn from several collections across Australia, including a collection assembled by the German Surrealist Max Ernst that was acquired by the National Gallery of Australia.

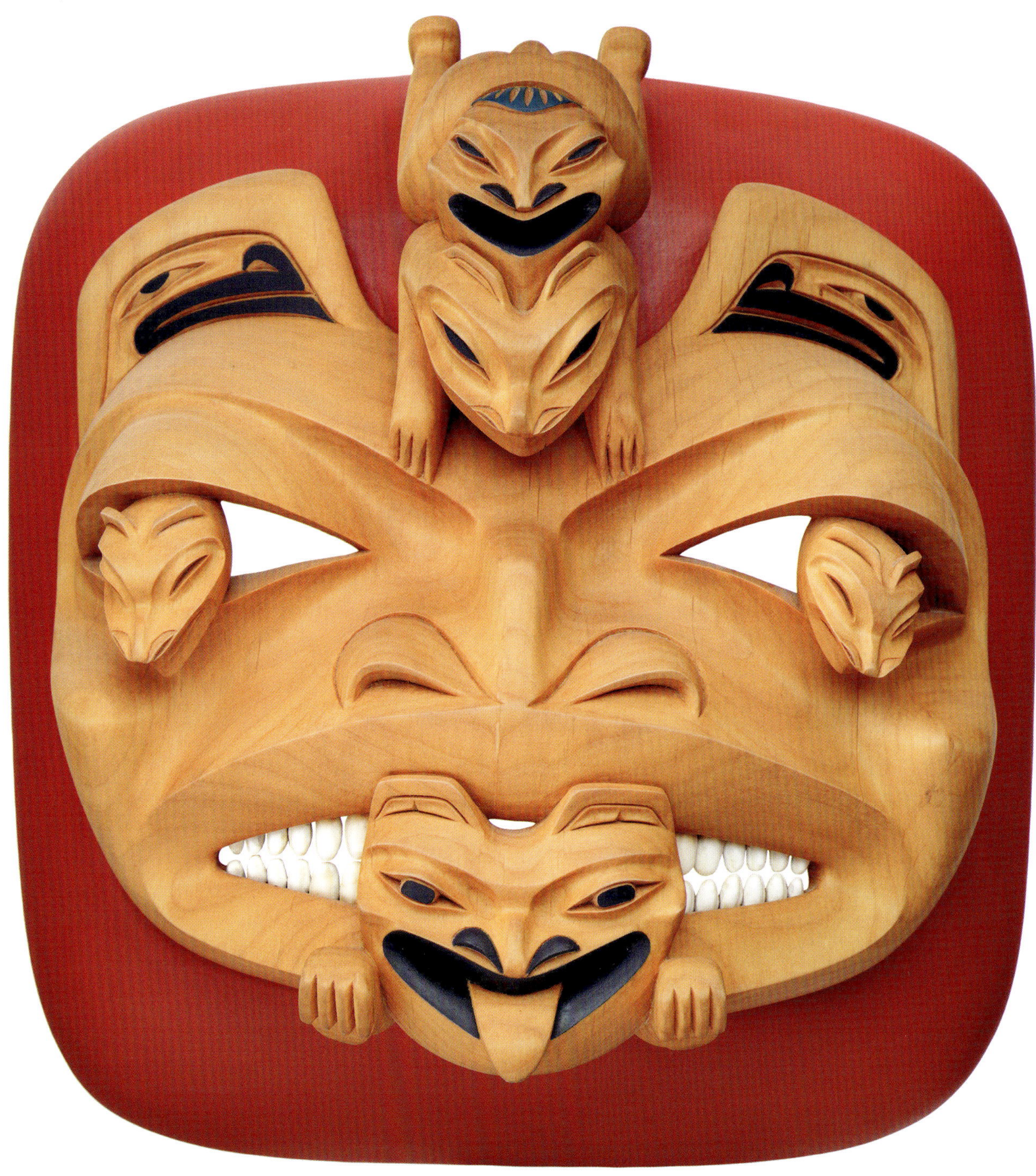

Bears Mask, 2006

now. What I'm trying to do is to get back to the level of our ancestors, and then go beyond. All great art eventually goes into abstraction.

I went to Russia, too, to St. Petersburg, to the Kunstkamera,[90] and saw the old Tlingit warrior armour, the helmets, everything. What I realized was that the Russians came from an old culture, a strong culture. They brought people that knew art and they got the best stuff they could find and took it back to Russia. I also saw some masks there, and some Tlingit war knives and spears. What happened in Canada is that we just have the leftovers. And of course the missionaries burned our pieces too. Our culture was outlawed until 1951, when the potlatch ban was lifted.[91]

I also went to see the American Museum of Natural History in New York, in the 1980s. The first time I went to New York, I looked at that stuff, and when I came back here I was so intimidated that I couldn't carve for a month.

We went back to the hotel after visiting the museum. There was a big chandelier in the bedroom. I woke up in the middle of the night and I saw all those old masks looking at me. I went out for a walk, down to the East River, and I looked at the river for a while, and as I was walking back I just started to cry. I realized what they took from us, what they did. Those pieces were calling me. They wanted to go home. They haven't heard our songs for over a hundred years.

I went to Washington, too, to the Smithsonian, and saw totem poles and bowls and masks there. Here in BC, I go to the UBC Museum of Anthropology in Vancouver and to the Royal BC Museum in Victoria. Every time I go back, I see more in these pieces. As you learn you see more and learn more about art.

In my travelling, I have also seen paintings by Vincent van Gogh—I like what he says about art. Where he's going, it's a powerful place, a spiritual place, and it can turn your brain inside out. You could go there but you've got to have lots of arrows; otherwise, you can't come back. It's so powerful and strong. He forgot to come back. When you go there, the whole sky is moving and it's in his colours, in his feelings and the light and it gets bigger the further you go and you're just this small. Knowledge is there, and the power is there. What my grandfather told me about it is to be careful because there are some things that you should never really know about.

Frog Raven Forehead Mask, 2007

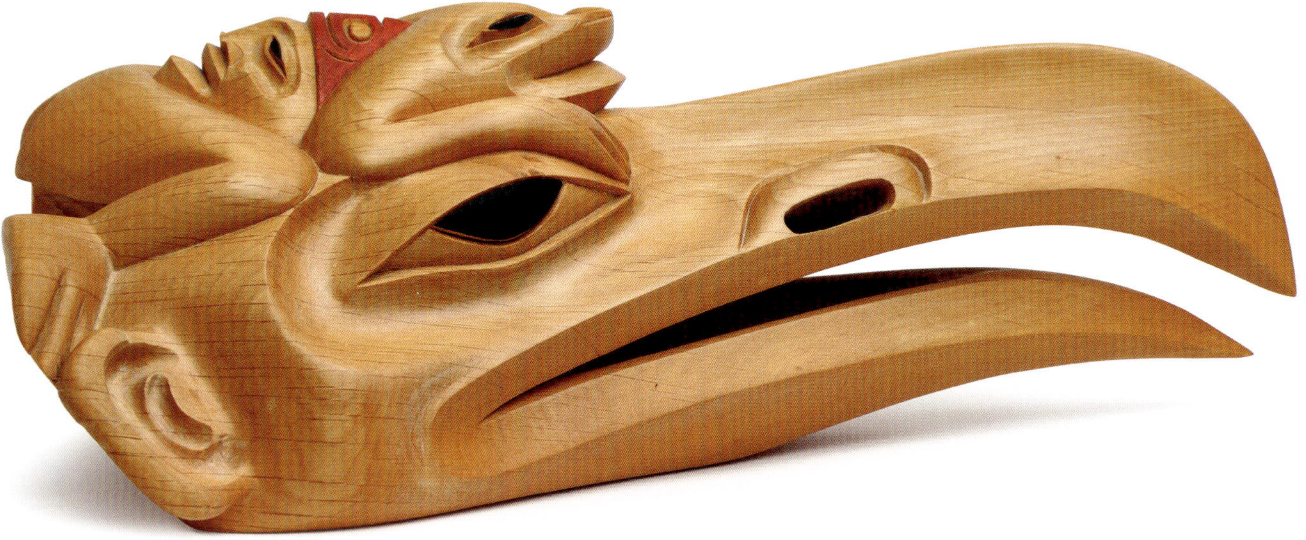

RAVENS

The ravens up there in Alaska are really big. They are really smart too. We used to look for the ravens because they know where the moose are. If one comes by, we are really quiet. Sometimes they will show us; they know they will eat too. The old timers used to watch them.

Those guys would know when the moose were lying down, when they're feeding, sleeping, where to look for them at a certain time of day. Early in the morning they're feeding around the water's edge. They like these certain willows, these kinds of poplars. The ravens follow the wolves too. They let the wolves rip up the meat, then they take their turn.

Eagle, Hawk, and Humans Mask, 2011

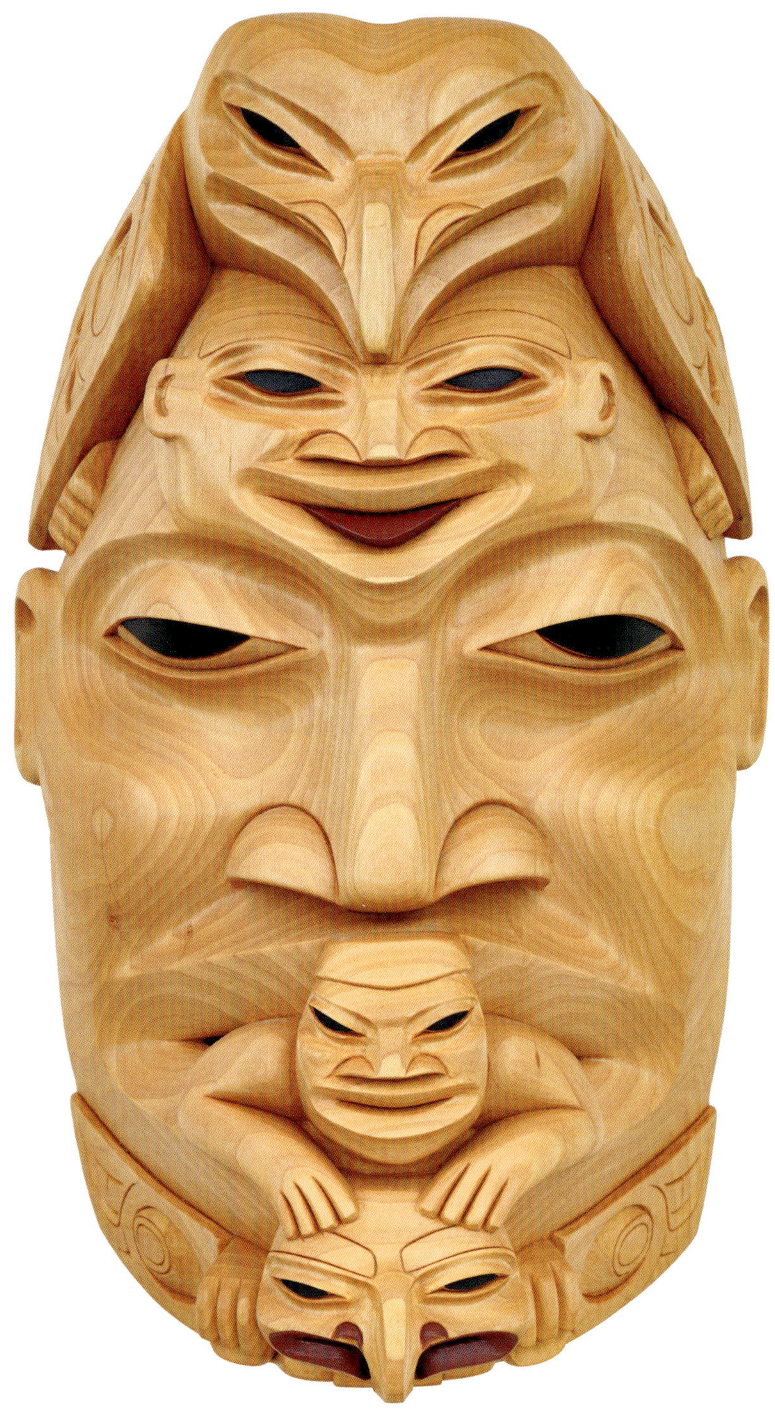

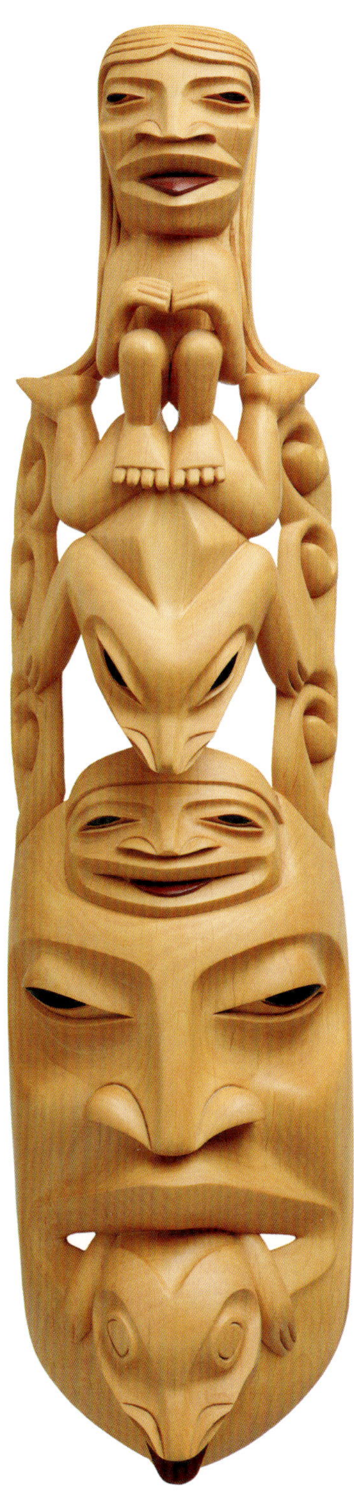

Frog's World, c. 2006

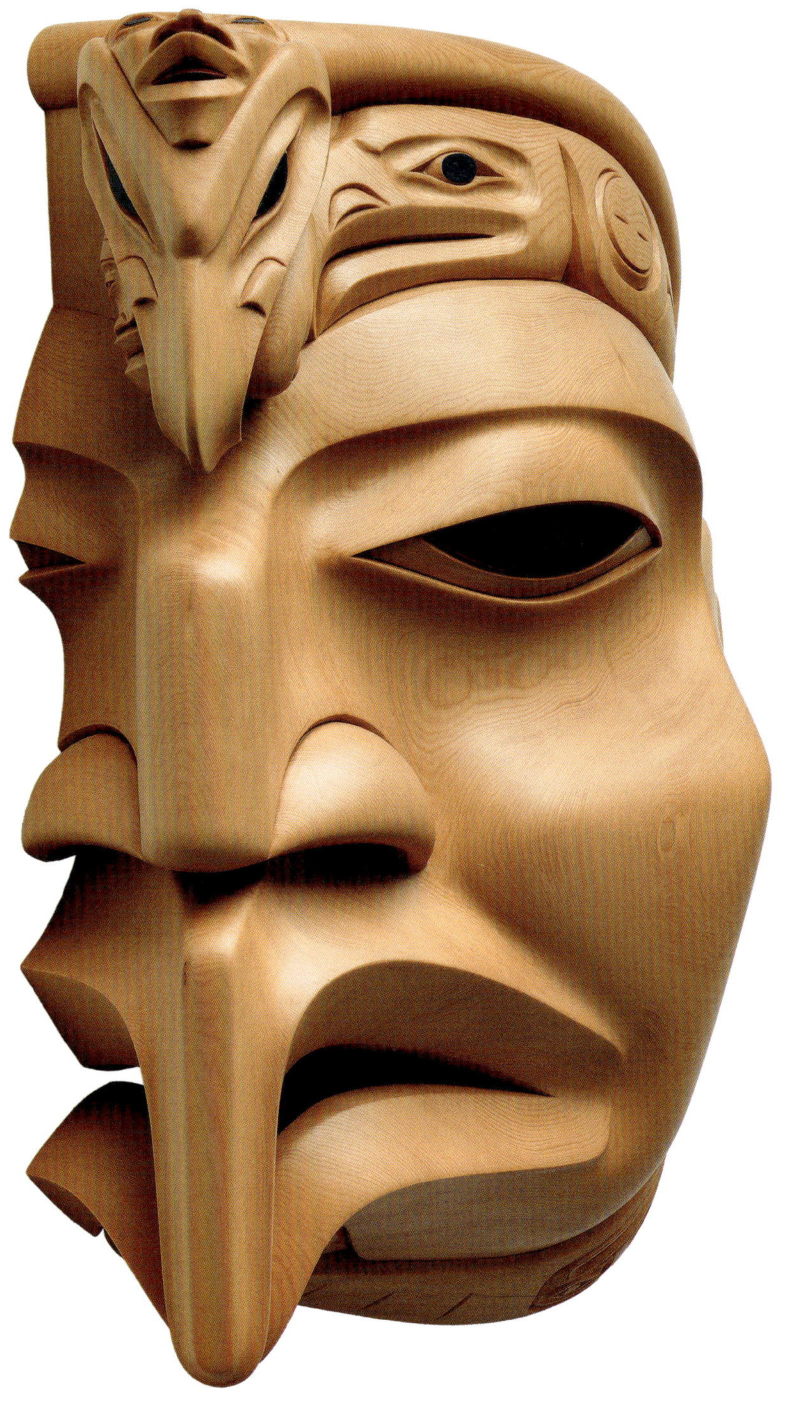

154

We use the feathers for protection. We hang them in our children's bedrooms—in the four corners of our houses.

I have always loved watching eagles. When I was teaching up in Hoonah, I met an Elder who made blankets. She showed me how to draw an eagle's beak with four lines. She said, "Just look at that eagle, study that beak, and practise. Just keep drawing." I got some newspaper and I kept drawing over and over and over, and then with the children I was teaching, to get that right curve of where it turns down—a nice strong curve there, the proper curve. Otherwise, it's weak; it doesn't look right.

One time I was up in Hoonah visiting with my friend Ernestine Glessing—she's a basket weaver up there—and we were looking out and we saw this eagle flying up above, circling around. She had some plastic ducks in the pond outside her house, and suddenly that eagle came swooping down and he grabbed a plastic duck and it slipped right out of his claws and flipped off to the side. Well, the eagle sort of wheeled over to look at it, like, "What the hell?" He looked back really hard, like he couldn't believe what happened. And we started to laugh.

Transformation, 2011

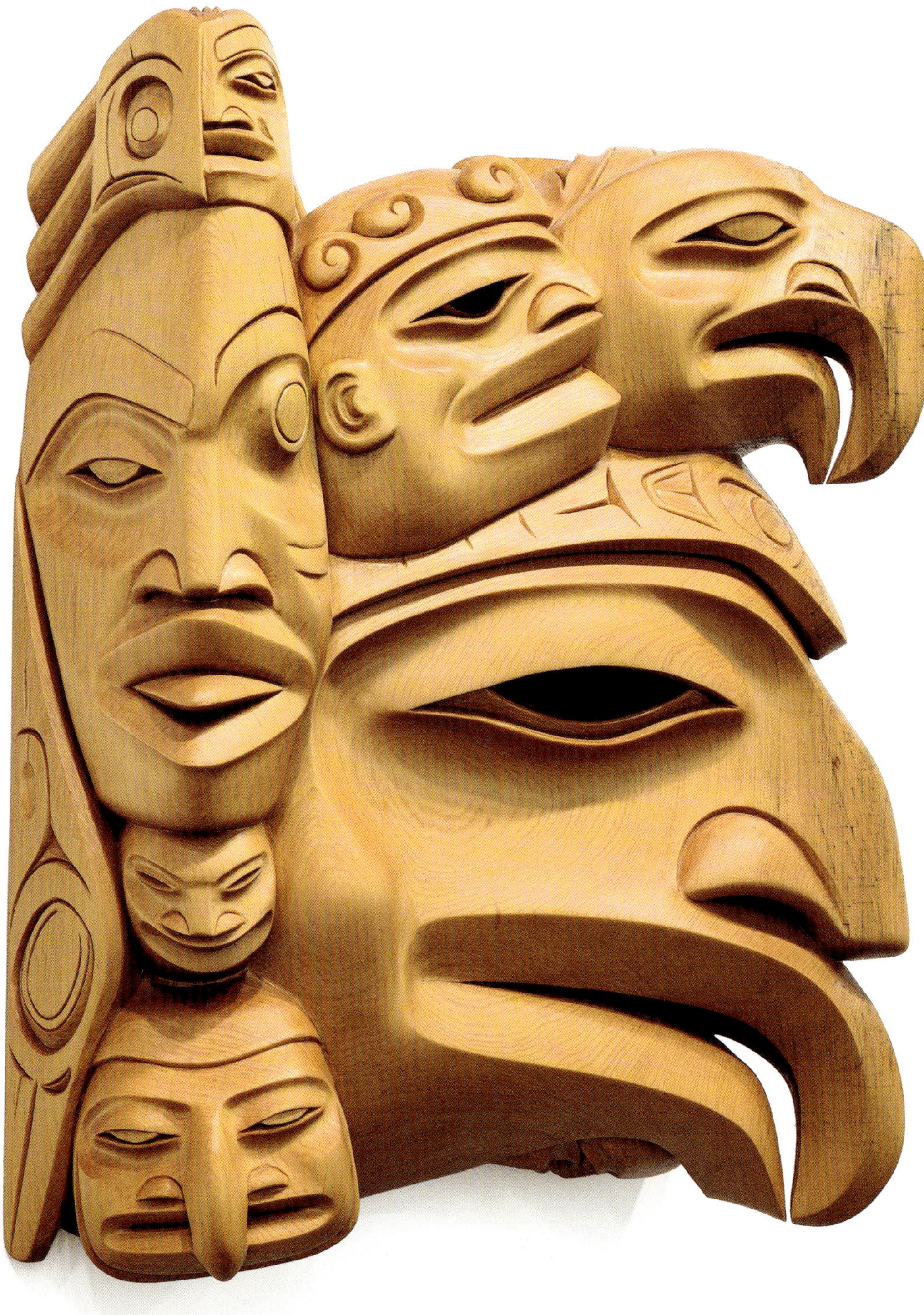

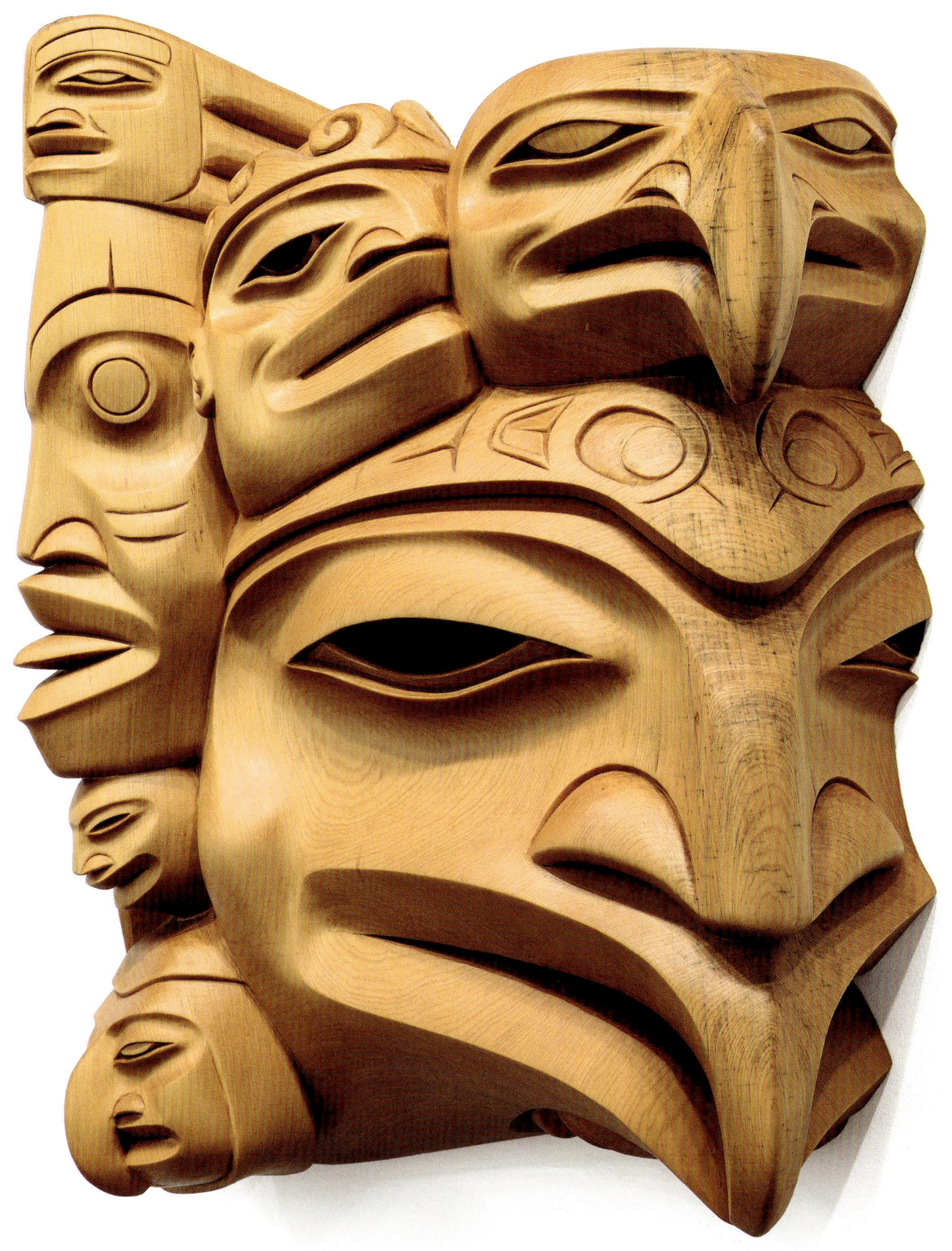

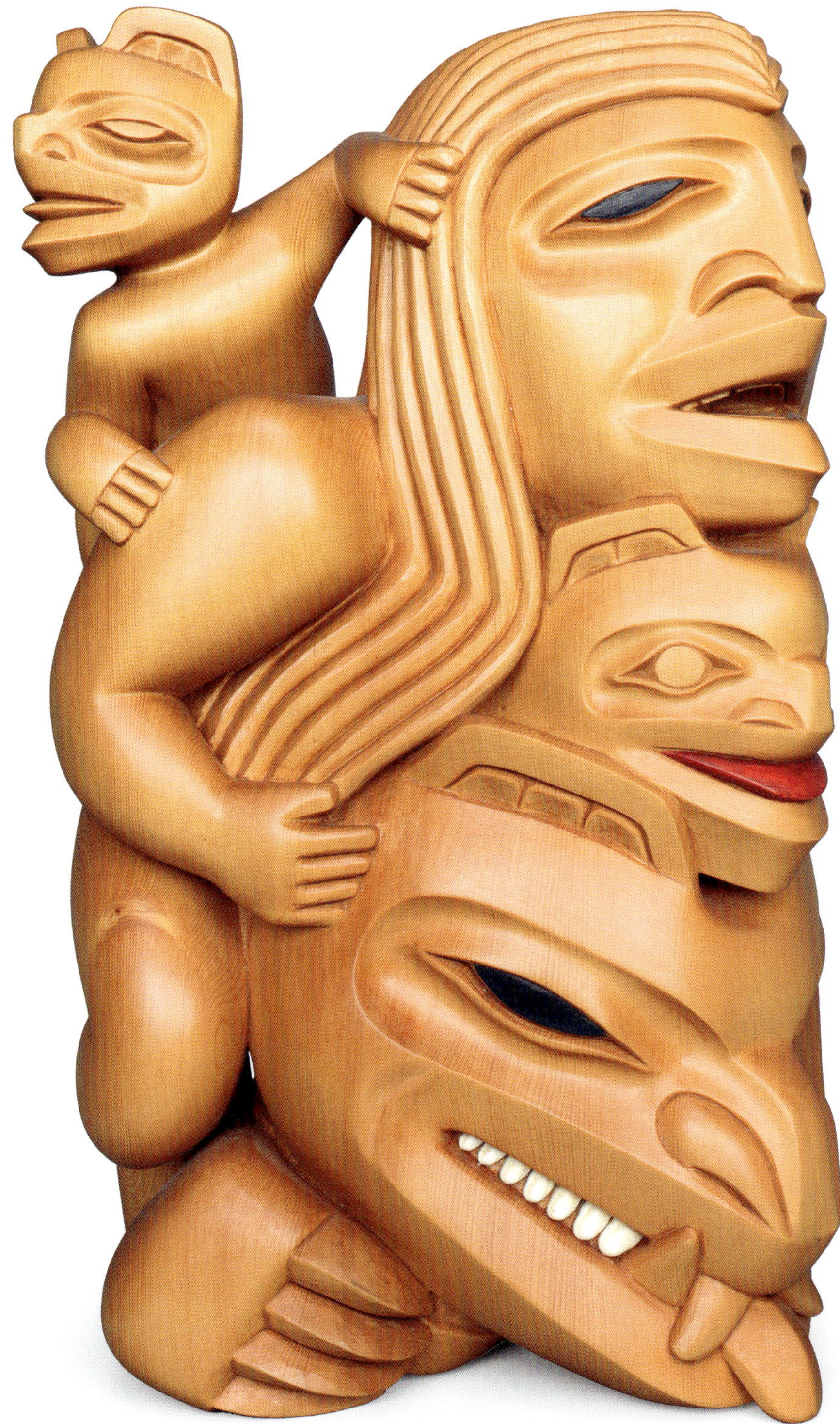

Bear Mother, 2012

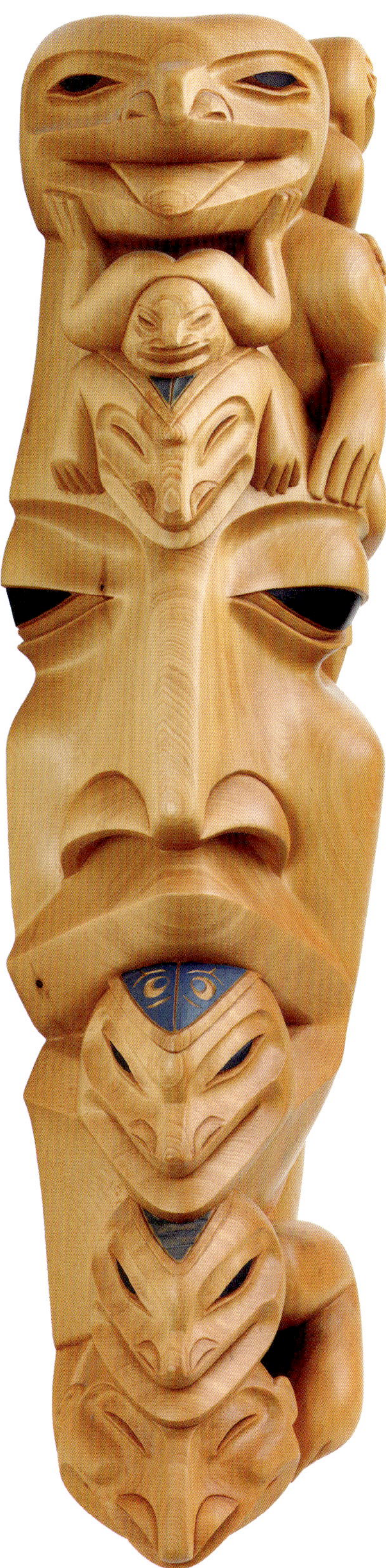

Rain Frogs, 2012

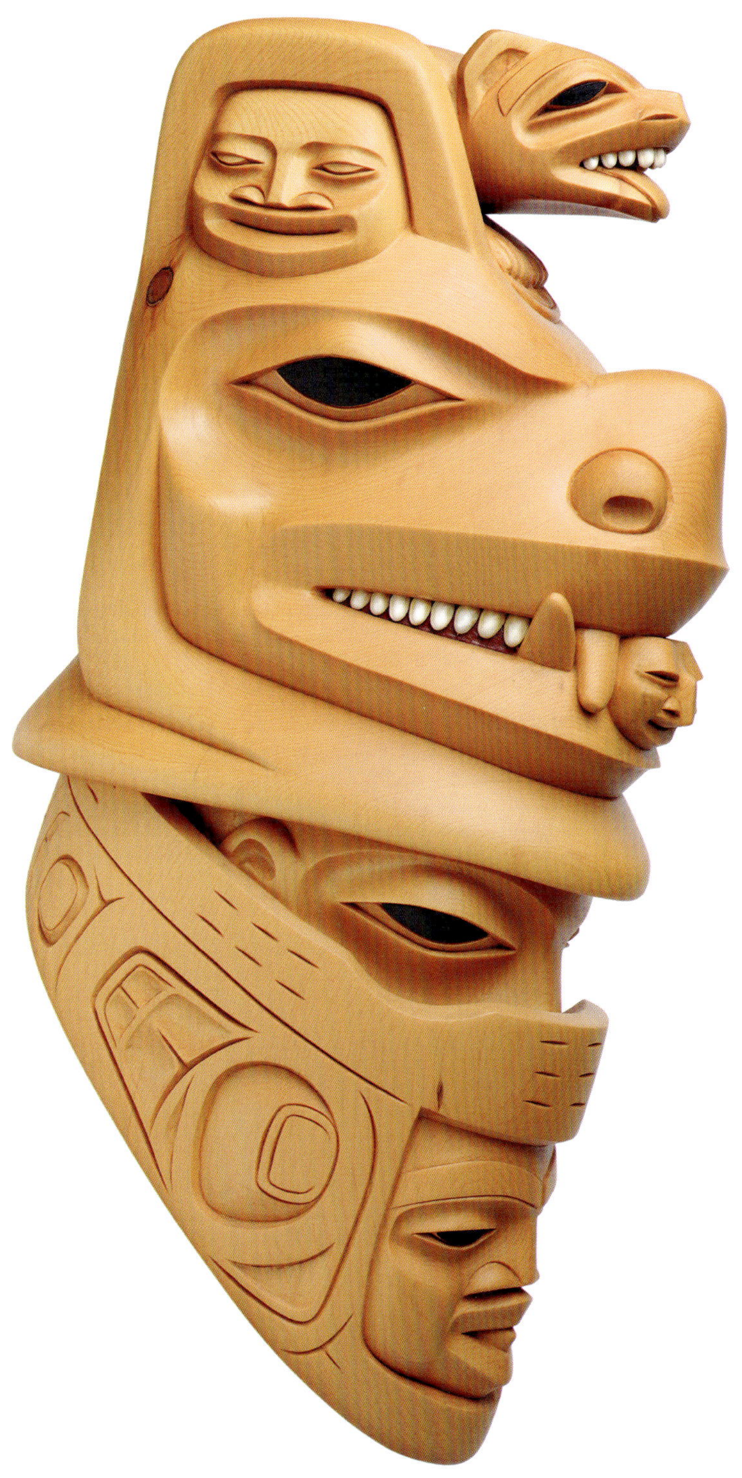

War Boss, 2011

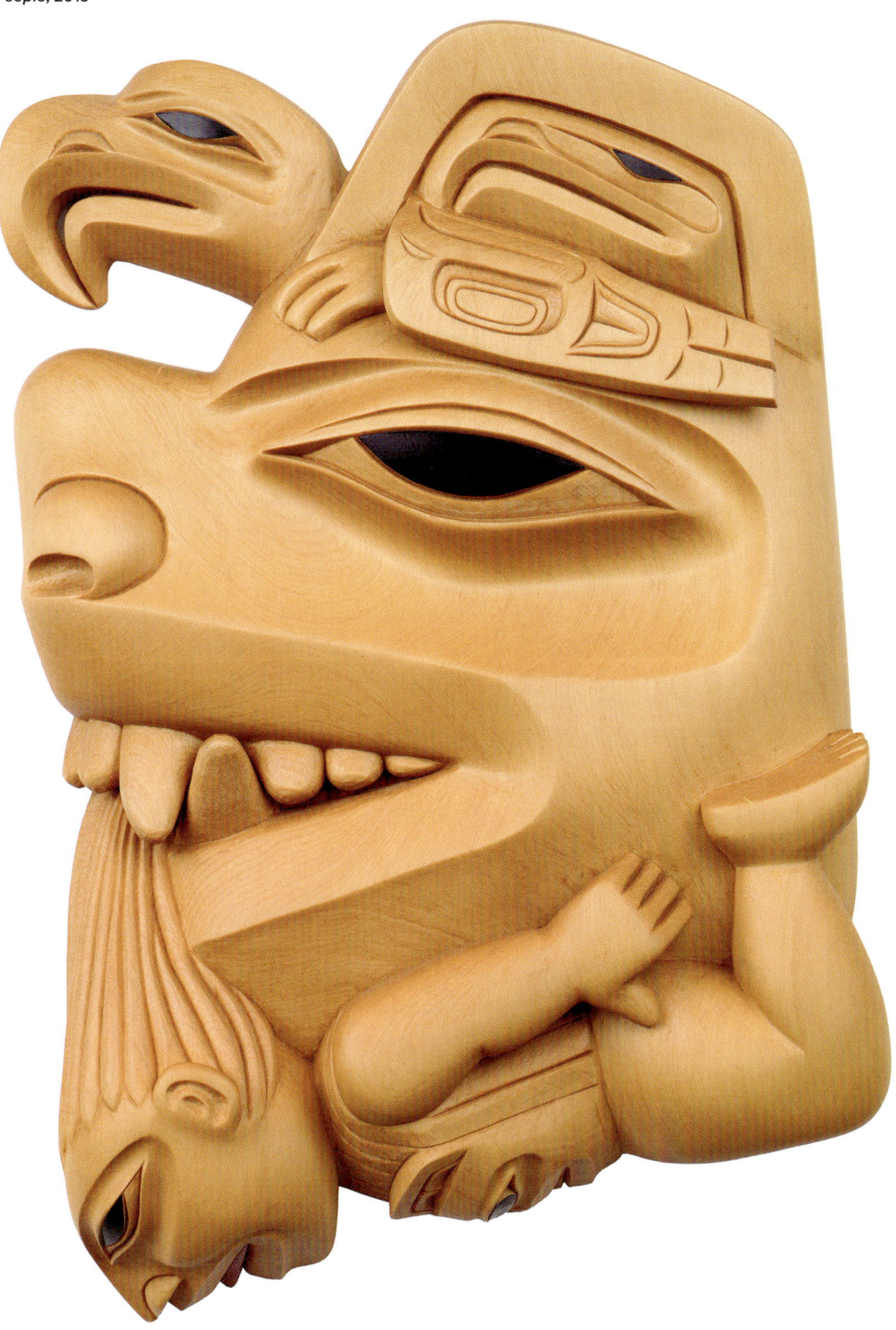

Eagle and the Bear People, 2013

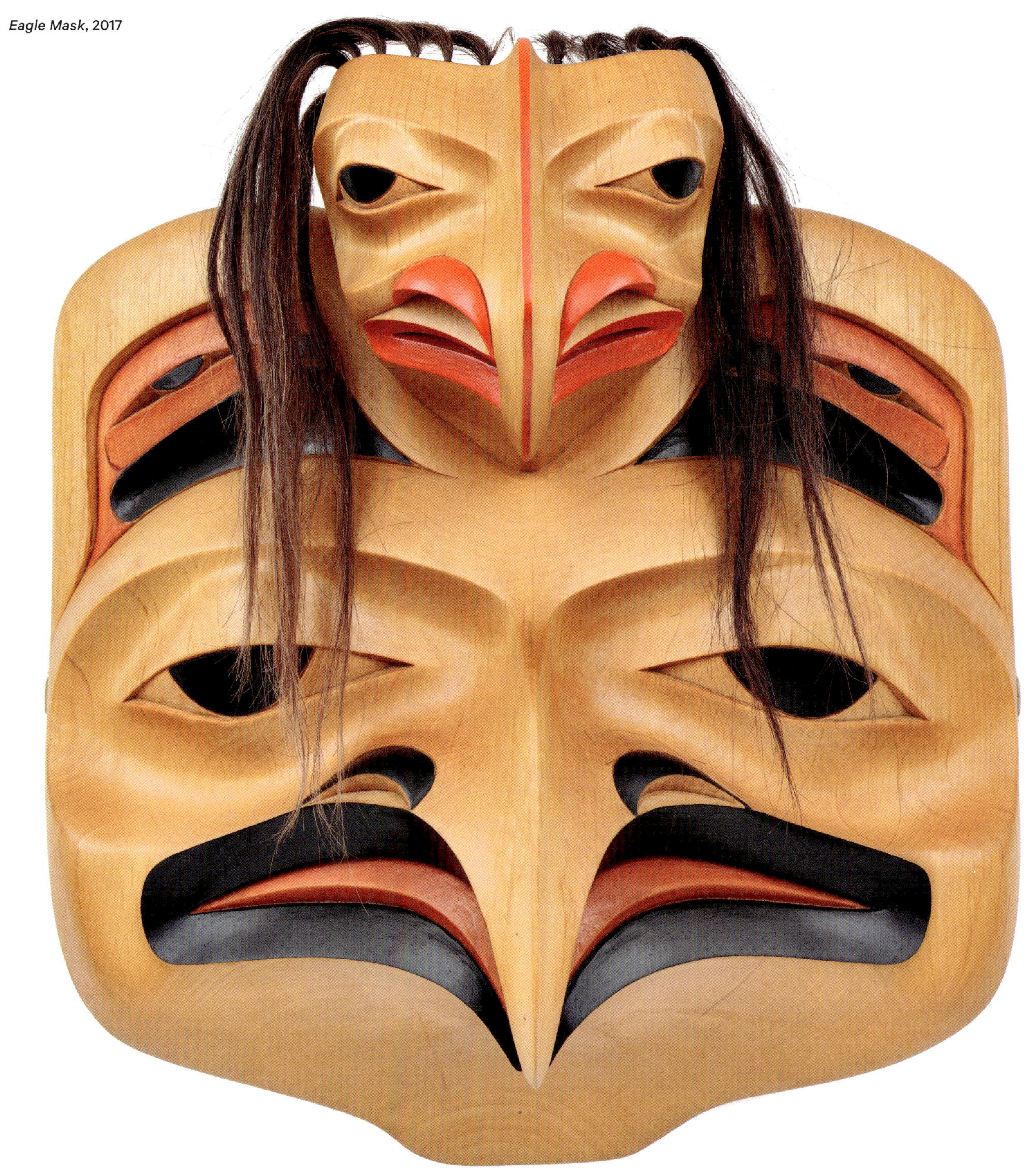

Eagle Mask, 2017

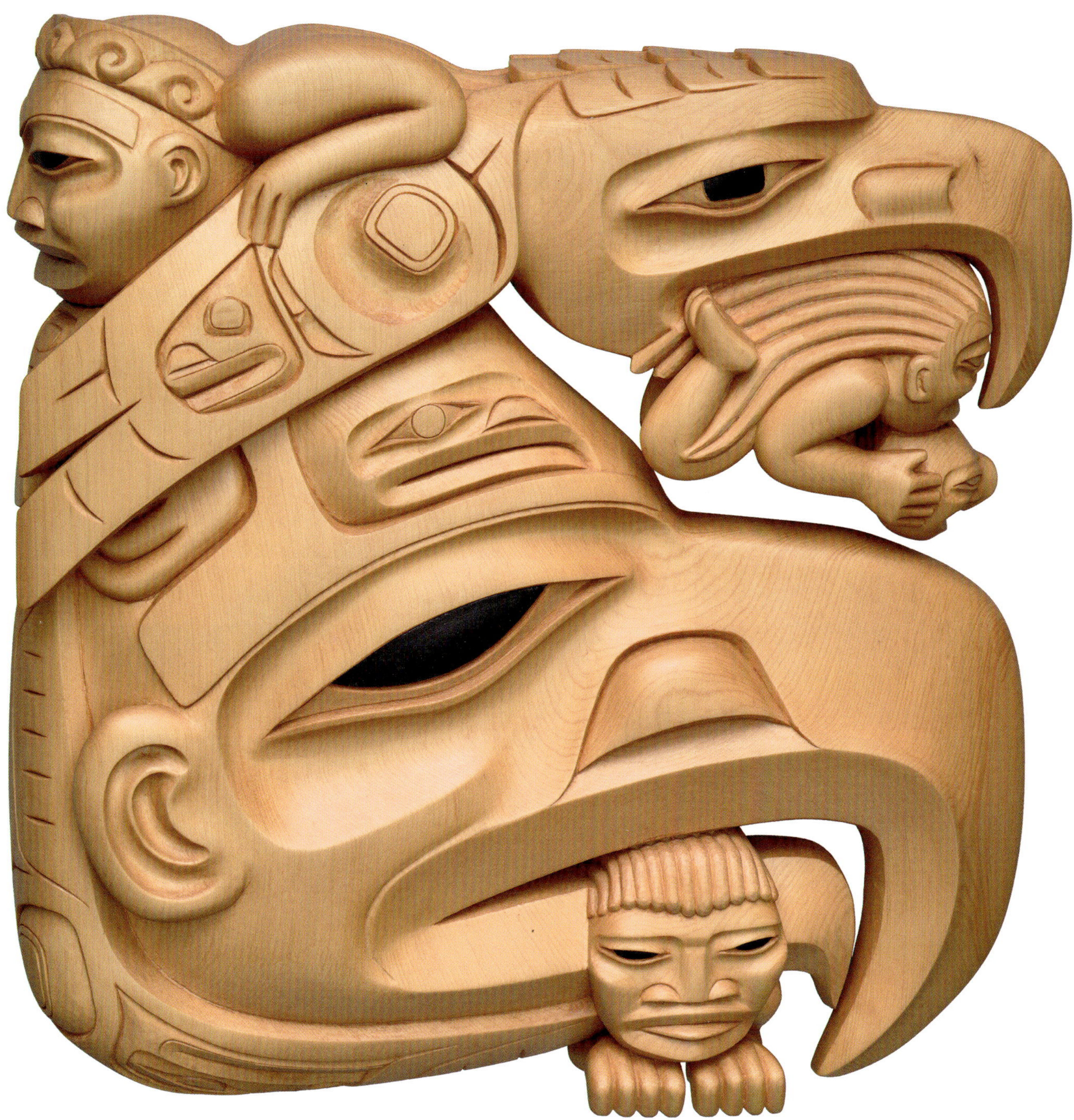

Eagles North, 2013

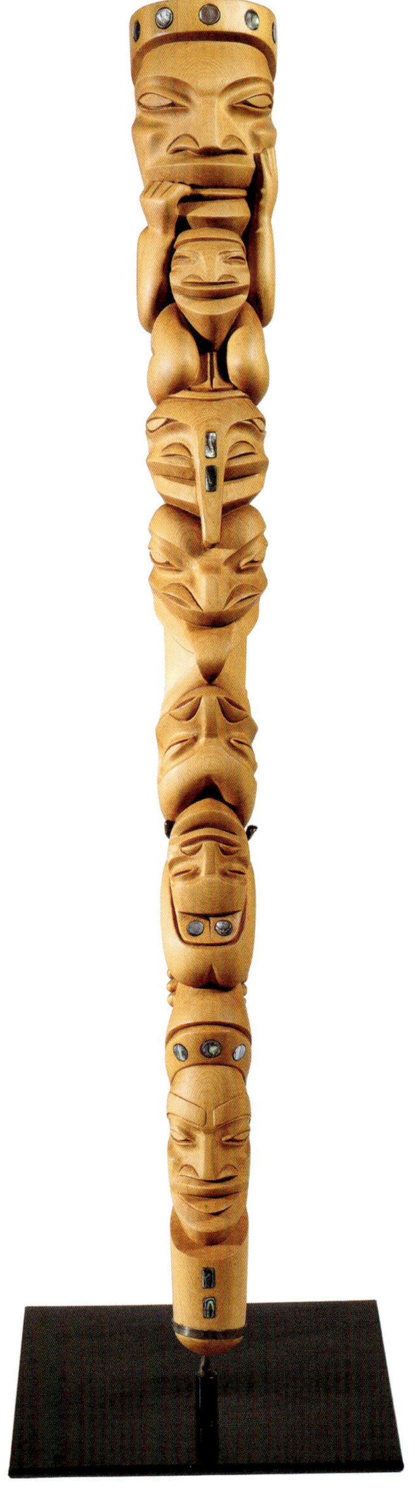

Frog Dance Staff, 2013

164

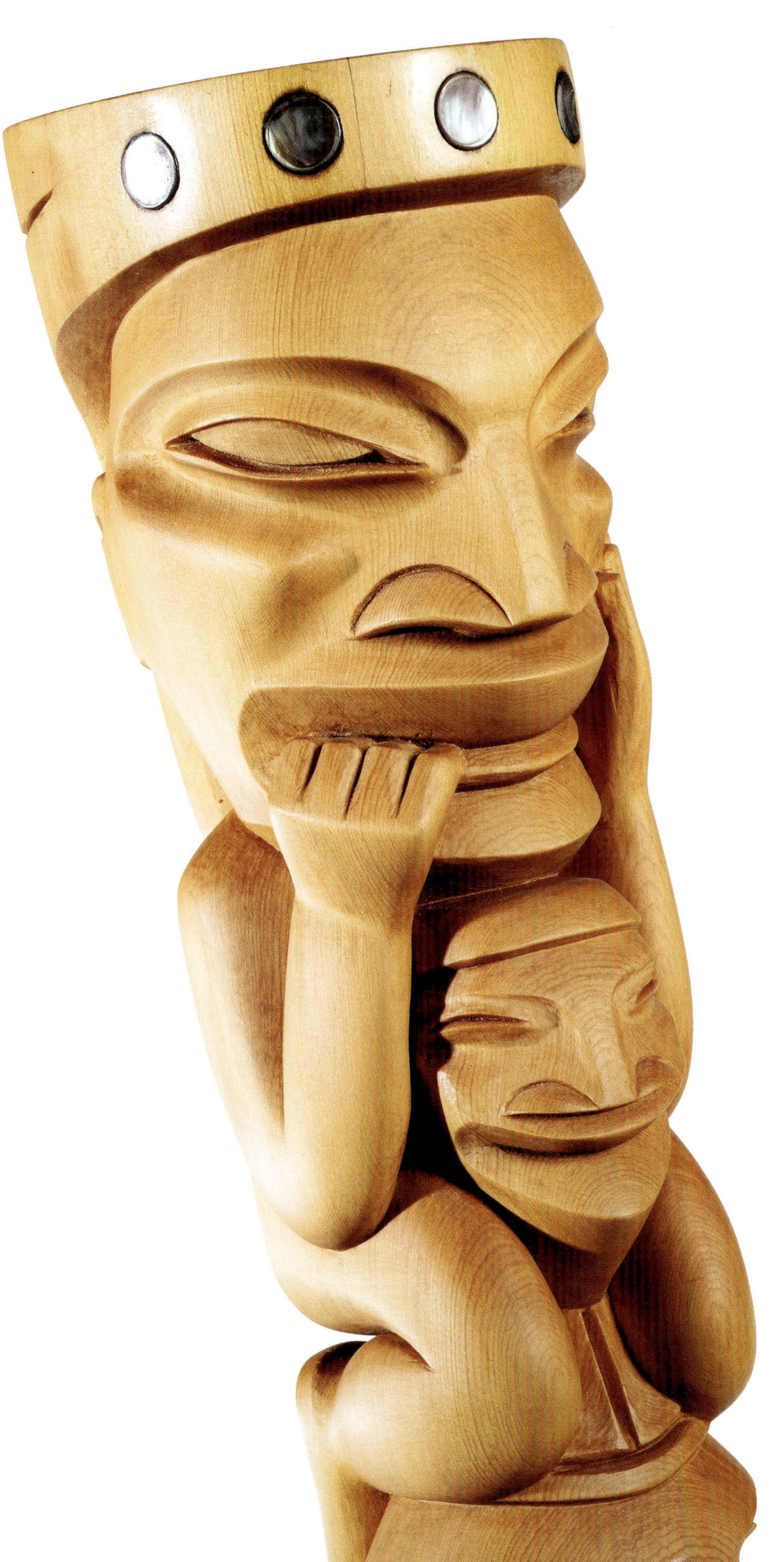

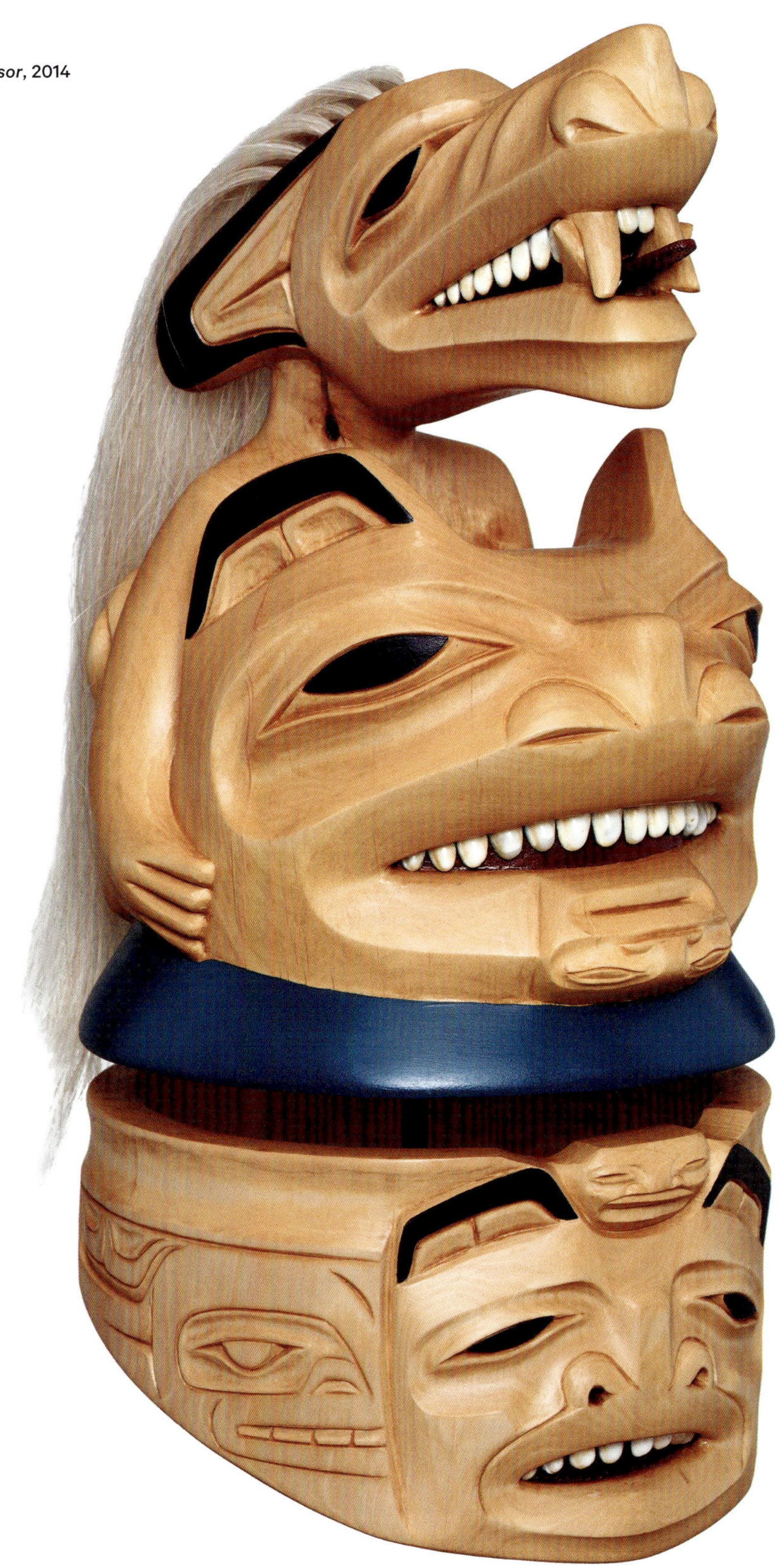
Wolf Warrior Helmet and Visor, 2014

166

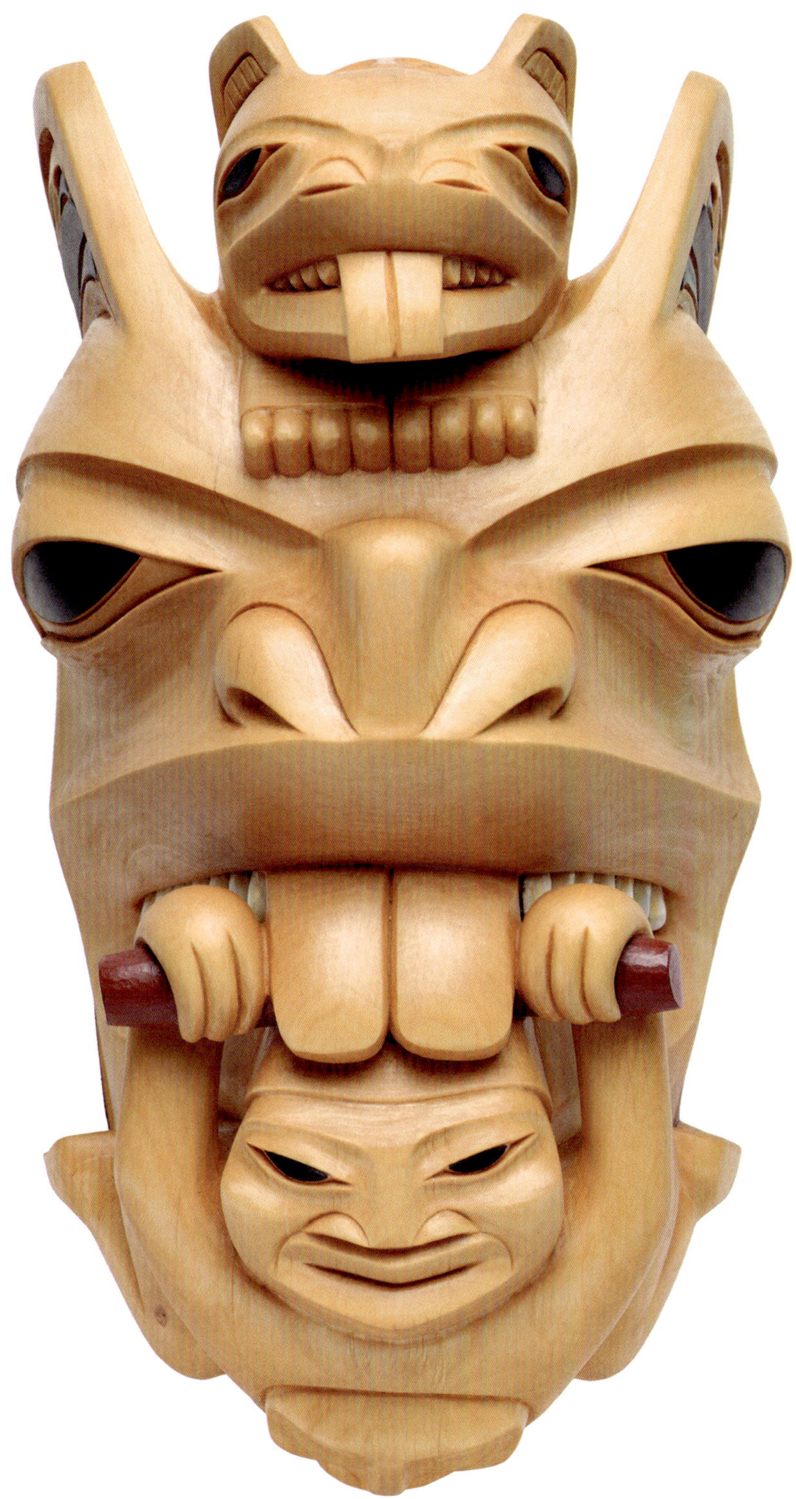

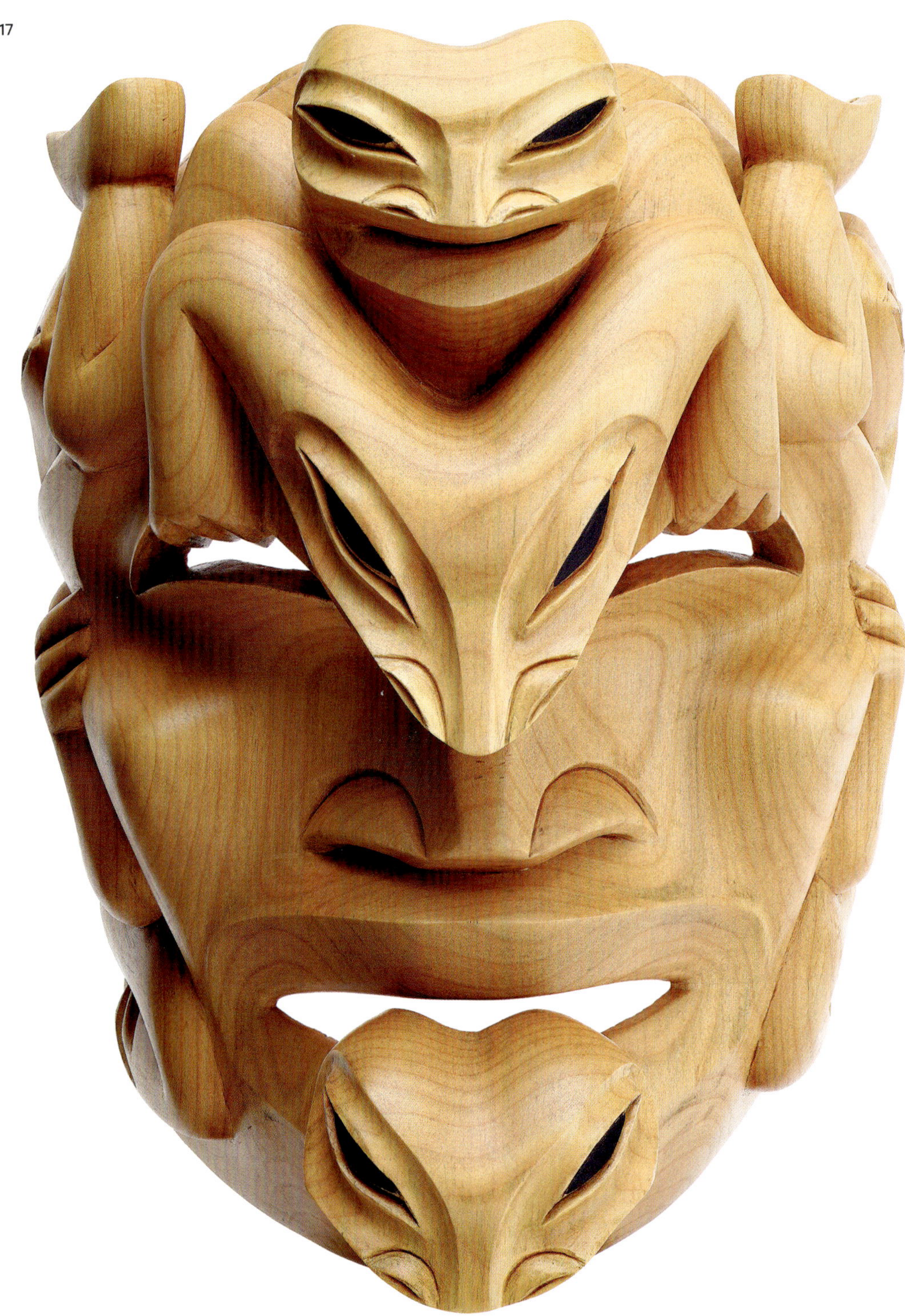
Frog Stories, 2017

168

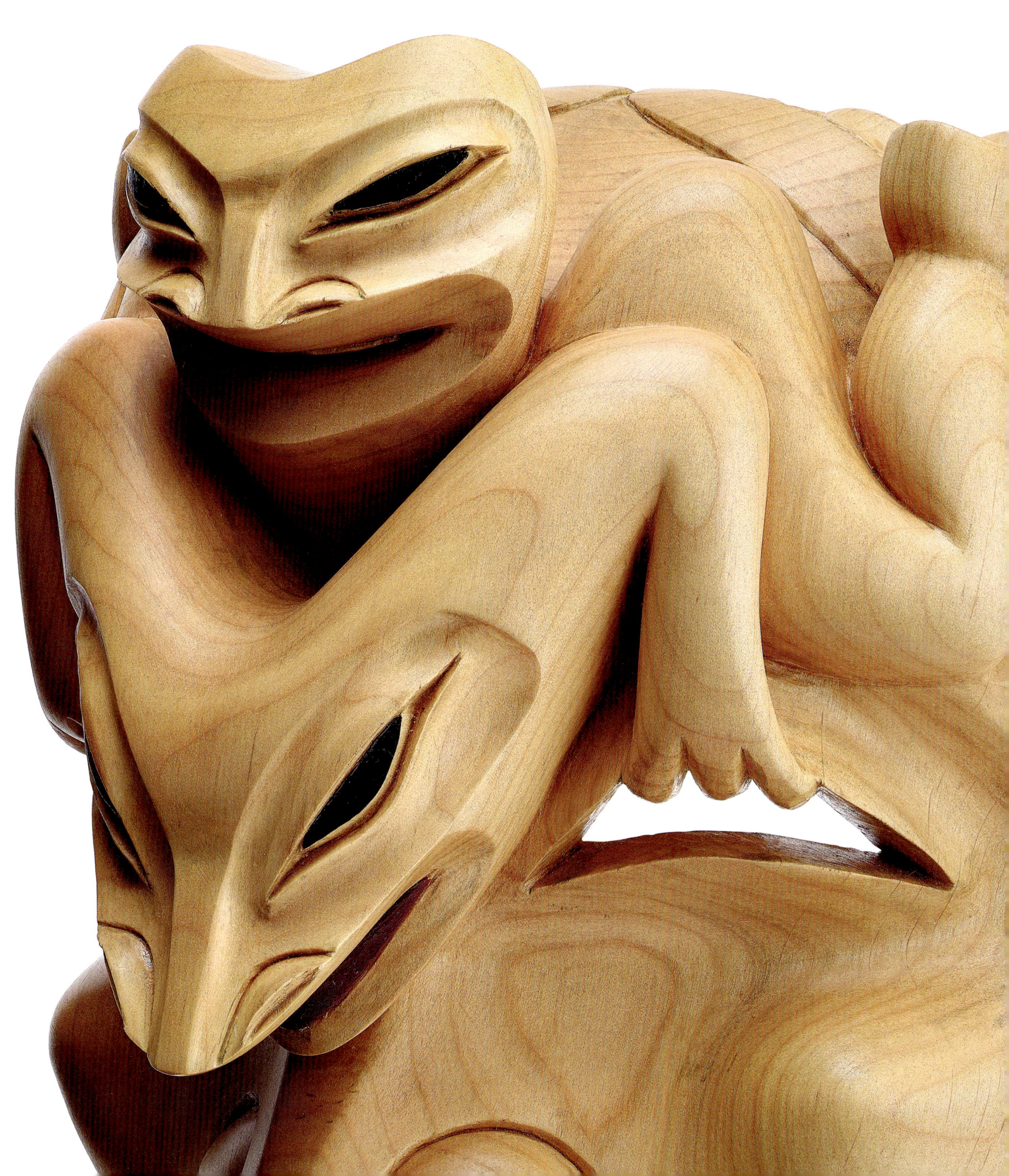

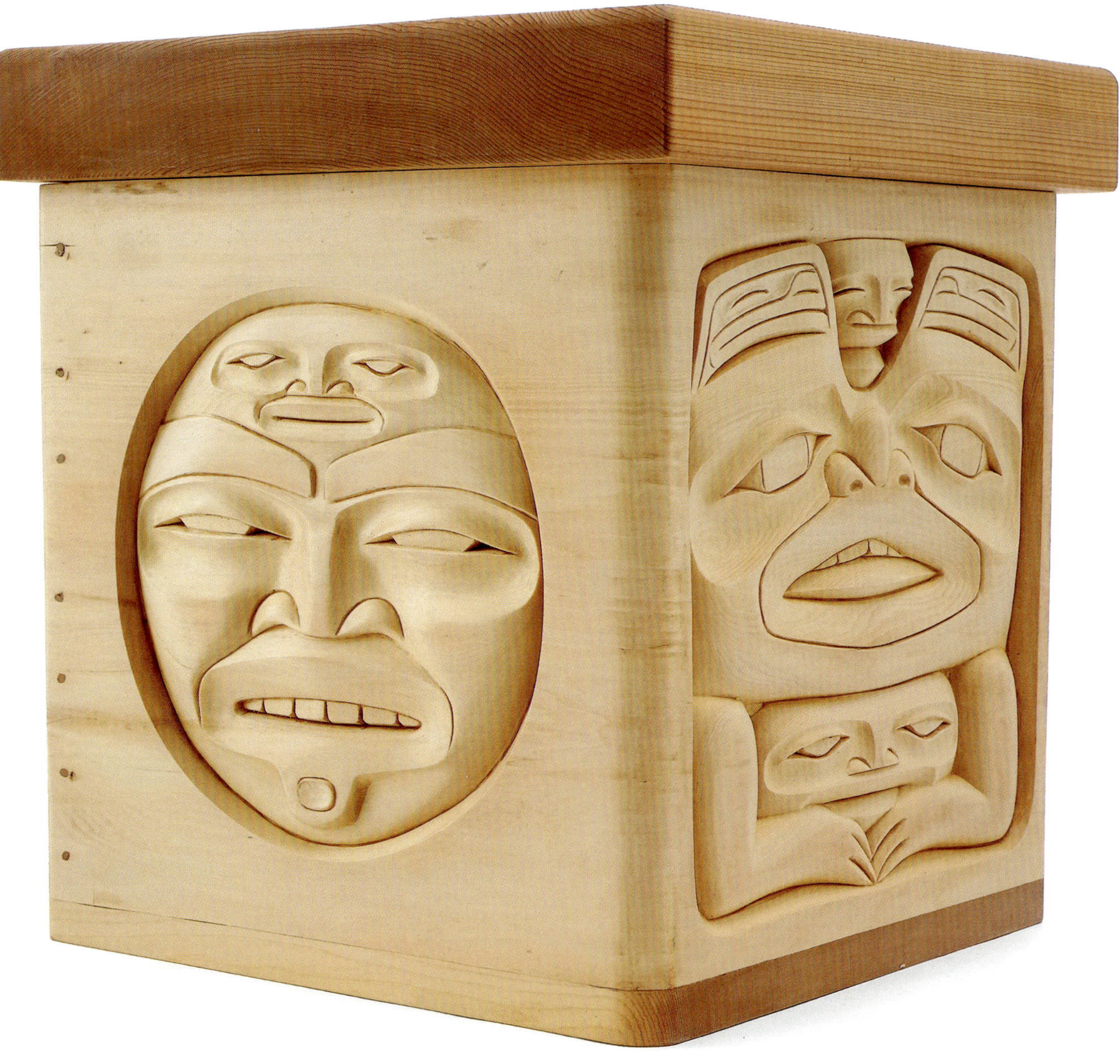

Bear Chief's Box, 2017

170

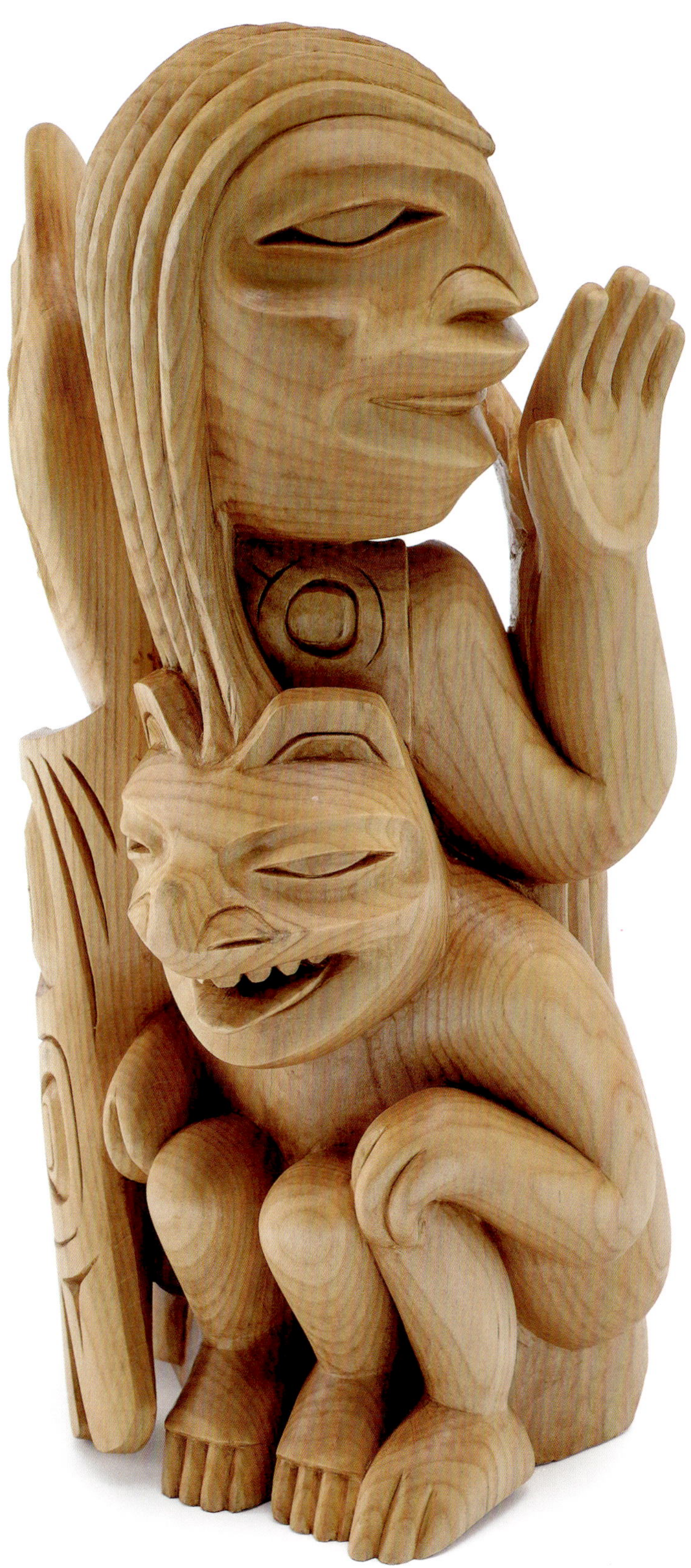

Eagles and Bears, 2017

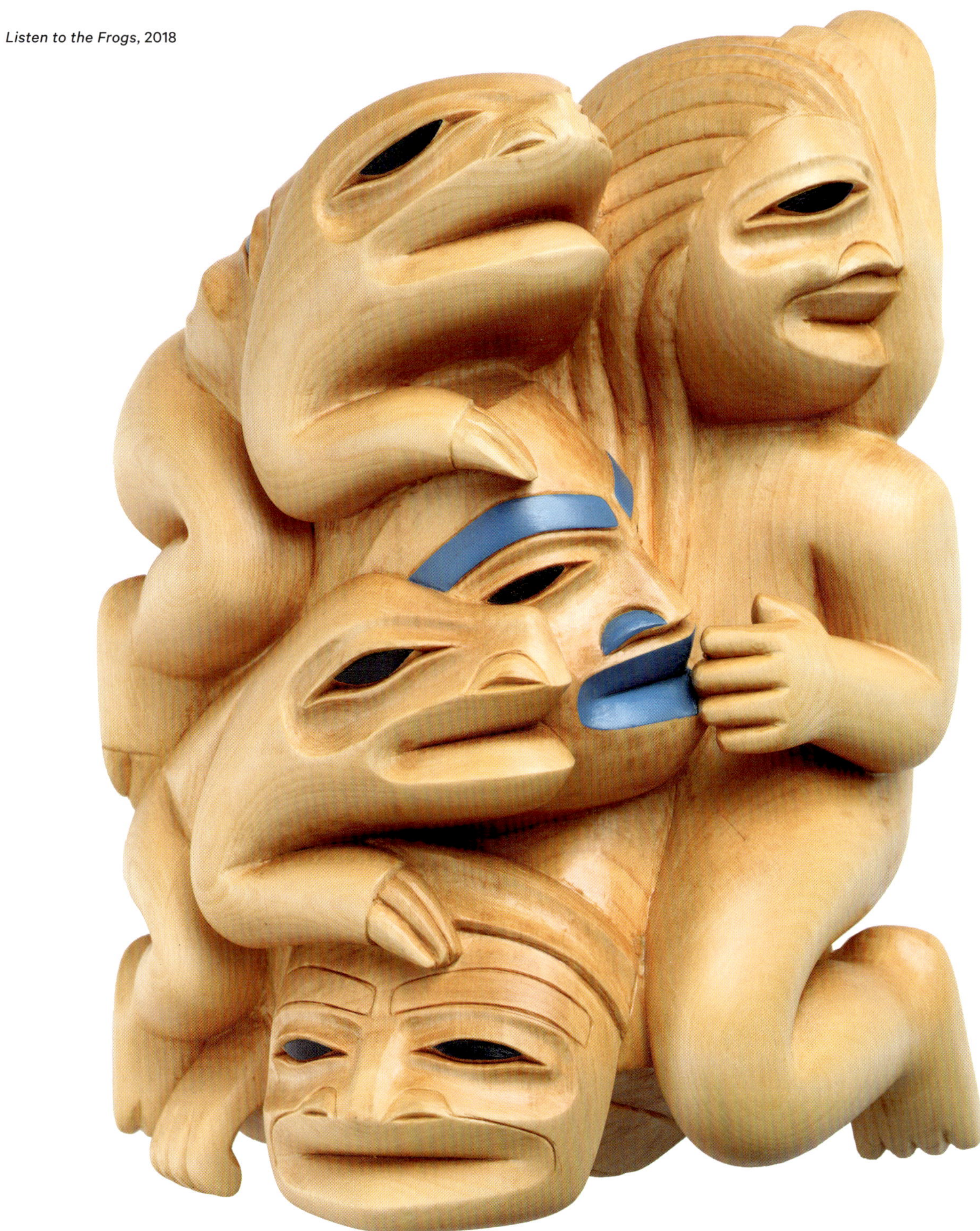

Listen to the Frogs, 2018

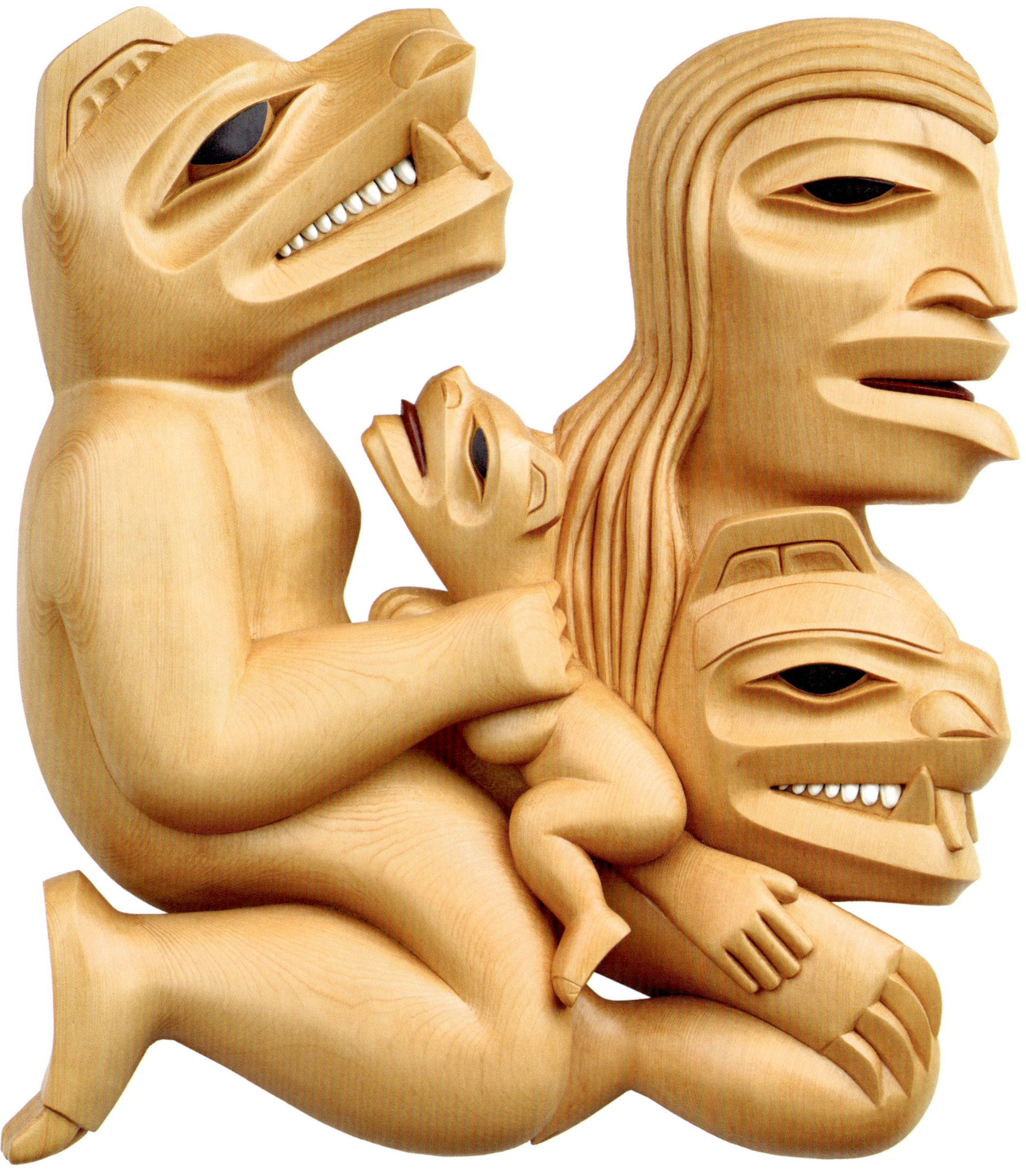

Khoh Dene, 2018

173

We started the school about fifteen years ago. We were talking about it for a while—I did a lot of teaching with Freda, so did my nephews Stan Bevan and Ken McNeil. We started talking to Rocque Berthiaume; he was teaching at the Northwest Community College here in Terrace at the time. We wanted to do something to honour Freda so she would not be forgotten. I felt that because she was female she didn't get the recognition. Those old man and old woman masks—she only got $2,000 or $3,000 for her masks, sometimes just $800. Now they sell for $30,000, $40,000.[92]

Rocque knew about the college system, how to structure the administrative side, how to set it up academically, and we knew the design process, how to carve, to develop the curriculum, the toolmaking—everything. Rocque's in Australia now; he retired early from the college and moved down there. But he was able to get money from the province. Stephanie Forsyth was the director of the Northwest Community College at the time—it's called Coast Mountain College now. She helped to make it happen too.

In our school now, we give them all brand-new chisels and gouges, and sometimes they don't look after them! When I started, we dreamed of those things. We had to make our own out of files. In those days we knew that if you don't work, you're going to starve. Everybody worked hard. Now everything is given.

They have talent, but you have to know art too. Not just about the knowledge of the techniques, the design, but about experience, truth, our culture, and our values. The young people now—they're so smart in some ways, but it's in pieces. I think it's from technology. The brain has changed somehow. They can only read so much and they're bored again. In our days the Elders were willing to share the stories. Our Christmas was for good food and for sharing. When we got oolichan, herring eggs, salmon, everybody got it. Potatoes for deer meat. That was our culture: respect for each other; helping each other out, sharing food.

92. In 2020 Diesing's *Old Woman with Labret,* 1973, sold for $33,600 and her *Old Woman with Lip Ornament,* 1976, sold for $40,800.

My grandson Nate—I'm trying to get him going. When he was twelve I told him, "You'd better carve something." I got him some tools. I asked him, "What do you want to carve?" He said, "I want to carve a penguin totem pole." "Well," I said, "we don't carve penguins." He looked at me and said, "I thought you were a master carver. A master carver can carve anything!" I thought, Uh-oh, I guess I'd better carve a penguin! (See p. 195.)

I'm teaching Keely, my granddaughter, our traditional designs too. Our way is, we don't push it on them. If they don't want to, we can't make them. But I try to get them just hanging around me and telling the stories and such. If they're not exposed to it now, when will they be? But to us, your free will is sacred. My grandparents didn't push me, but they told me stuff. Eventually I knew I had to do something.

What I realize, too, is that if you don't learn things when you're a kid, you're not going to learn it later. It's too late. I took my grandkids to the British Museum, and I showed them stuff. When we were in New Zealand last time, I took them to the museum. You have to expose them or they're not going to know. They won't even know what art is.

I did so much teaching and travelling when I was younger. One time I looked out the window of this hotel and I didn't know where I was. Now it feels good to be home. I've been mentoring for a long time, and I love it. But these days, my time feels more precious.

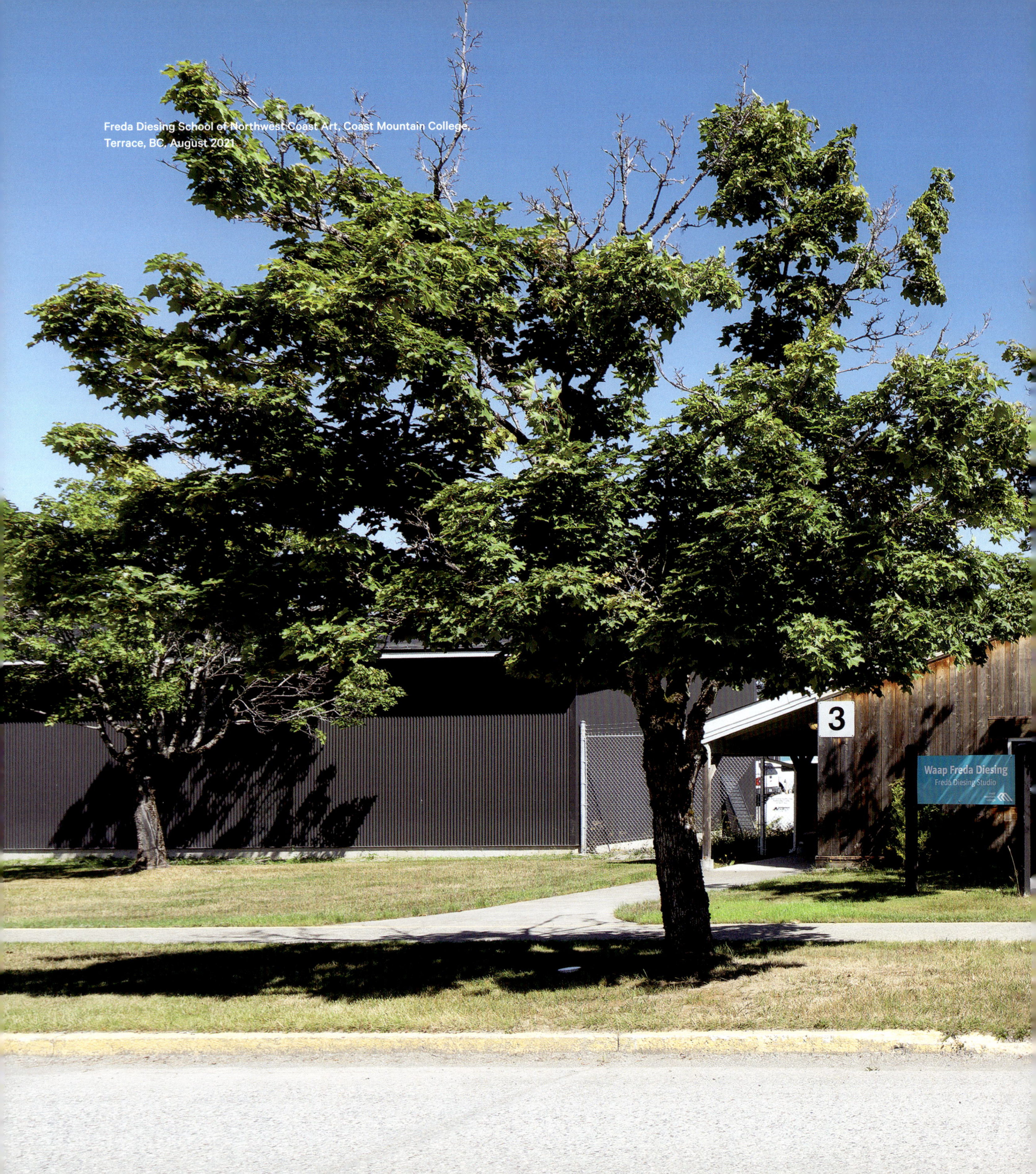

Freda Diesing School of Northwest Coast Art, Coast Mountain College,
Terrace, BC, August 2021
Waap Freda Diesing
Freda Diesing Studio

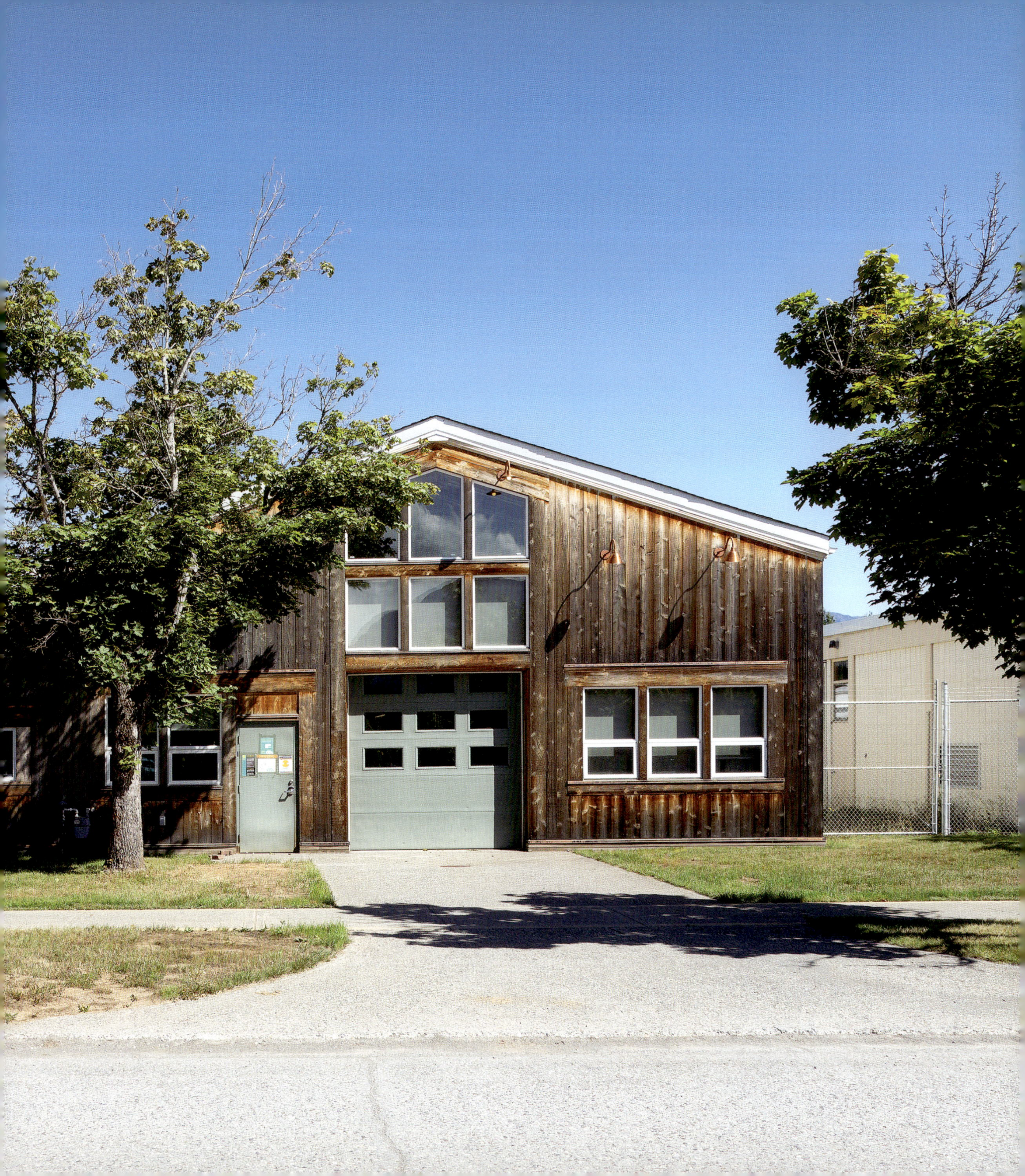

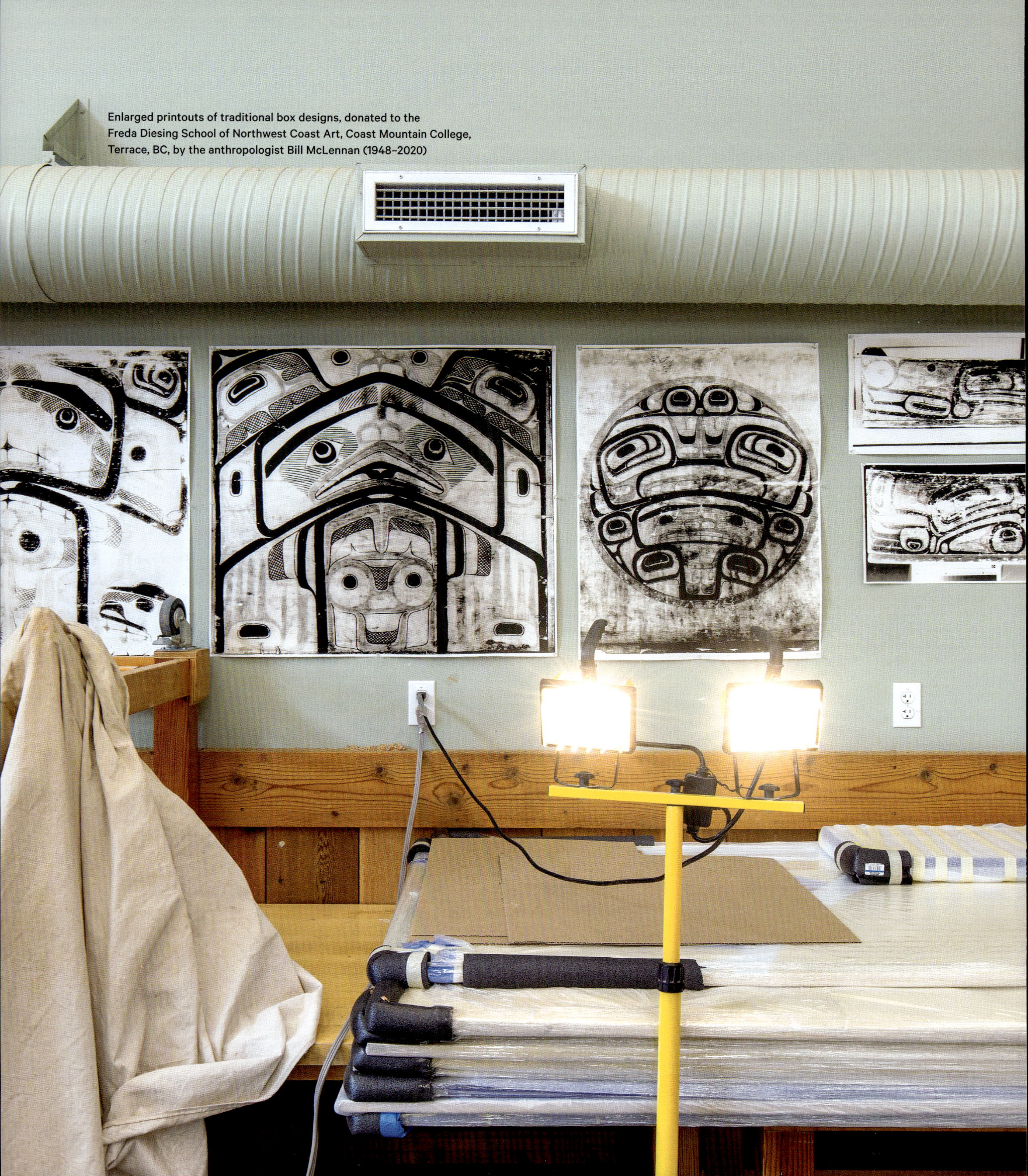

Enlarged printouts of traditional box designs, donated to the
Freda Diesing School of Northwest Coast Art, Coast Mountain College,
Terrace, BC, by the anthropologist Bill McLennan (1948–2020)

With Nathan Wilson and Nakkita Trimble Wilson, two of my fellow instructors at the Freda Diesing School of Northwest Coast Art, Coast Mountain College, in their home studio with their children, Maya and Kwin, Terrace, BC, August 2021

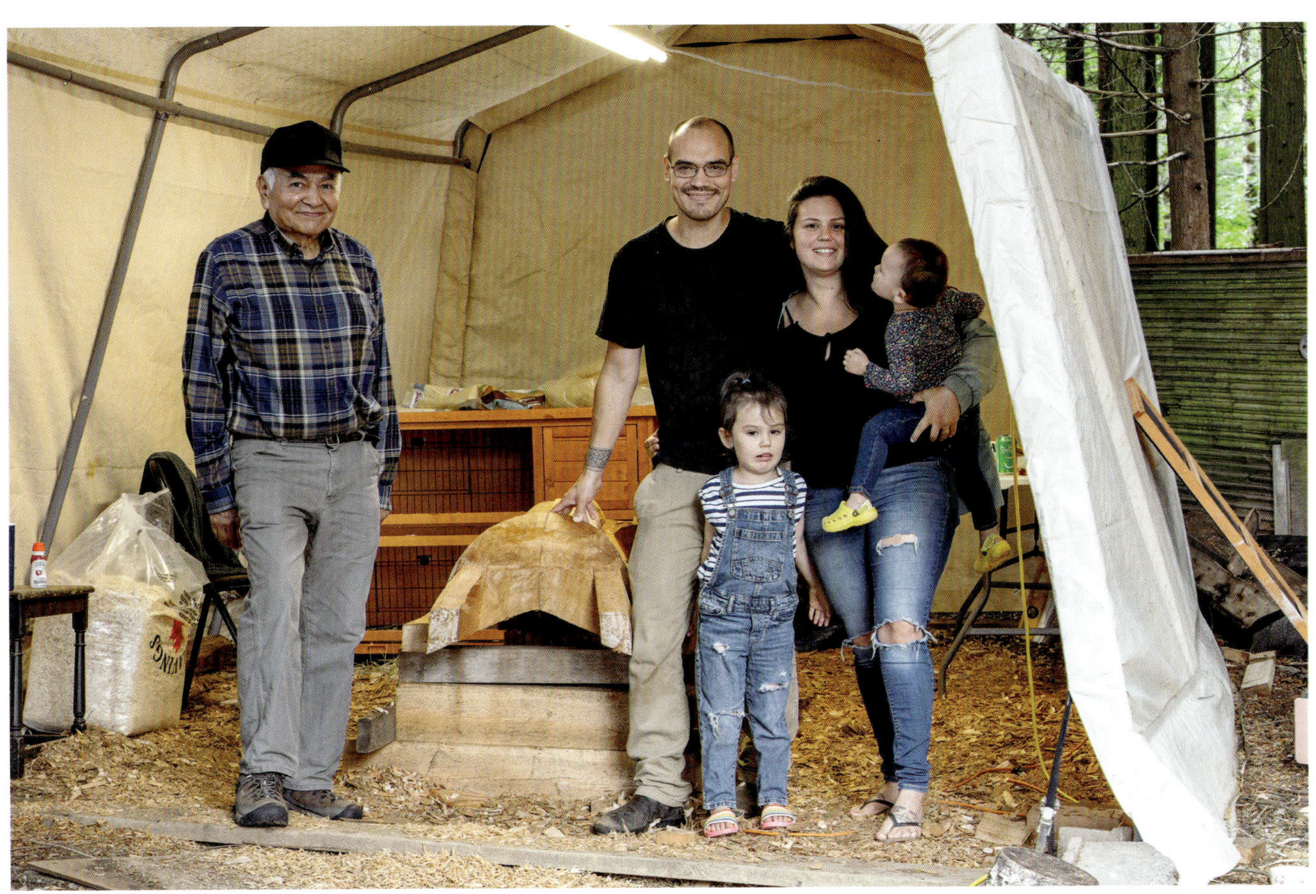

179

With Nakkita Trimble Wilson in her home studio, Terrace, BC, August 2021

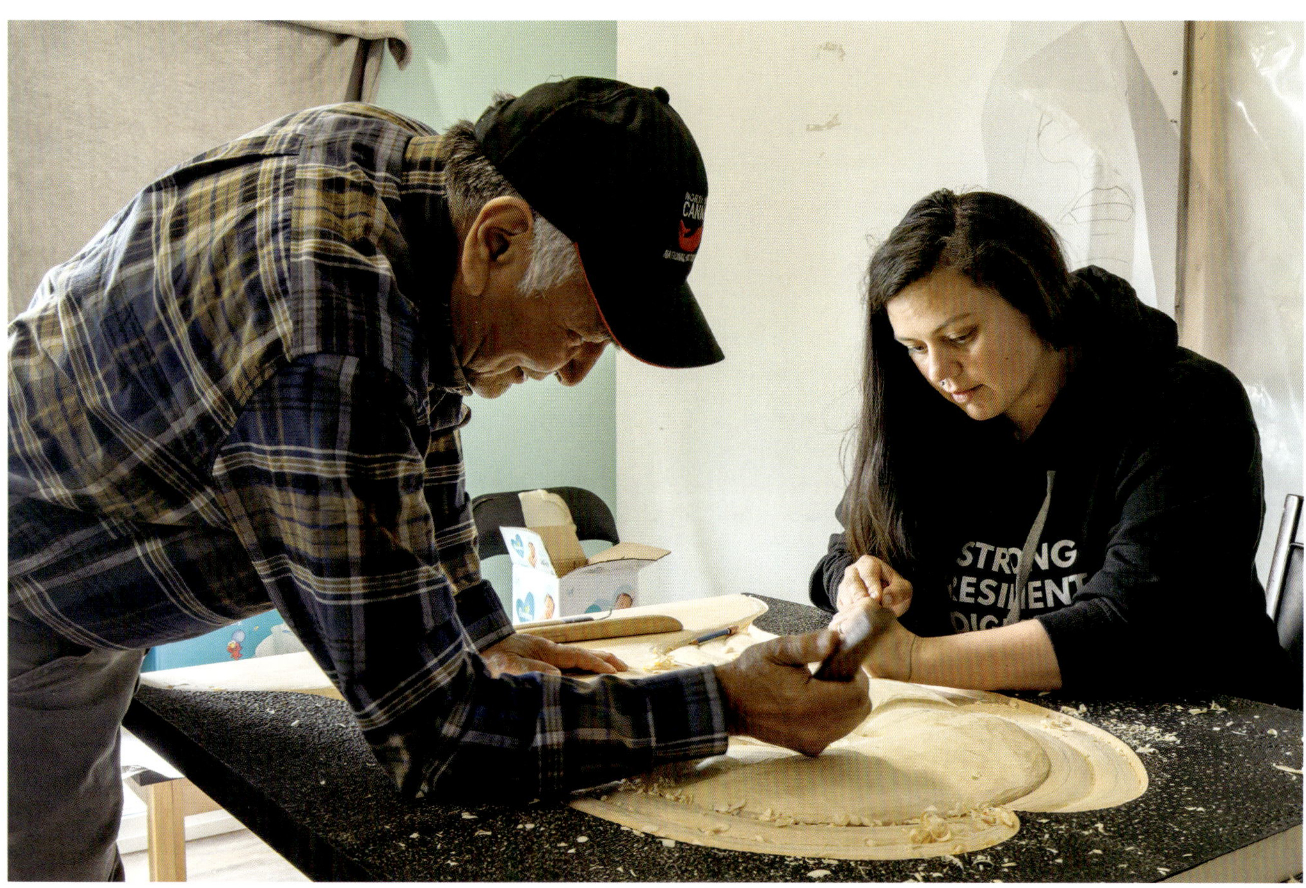

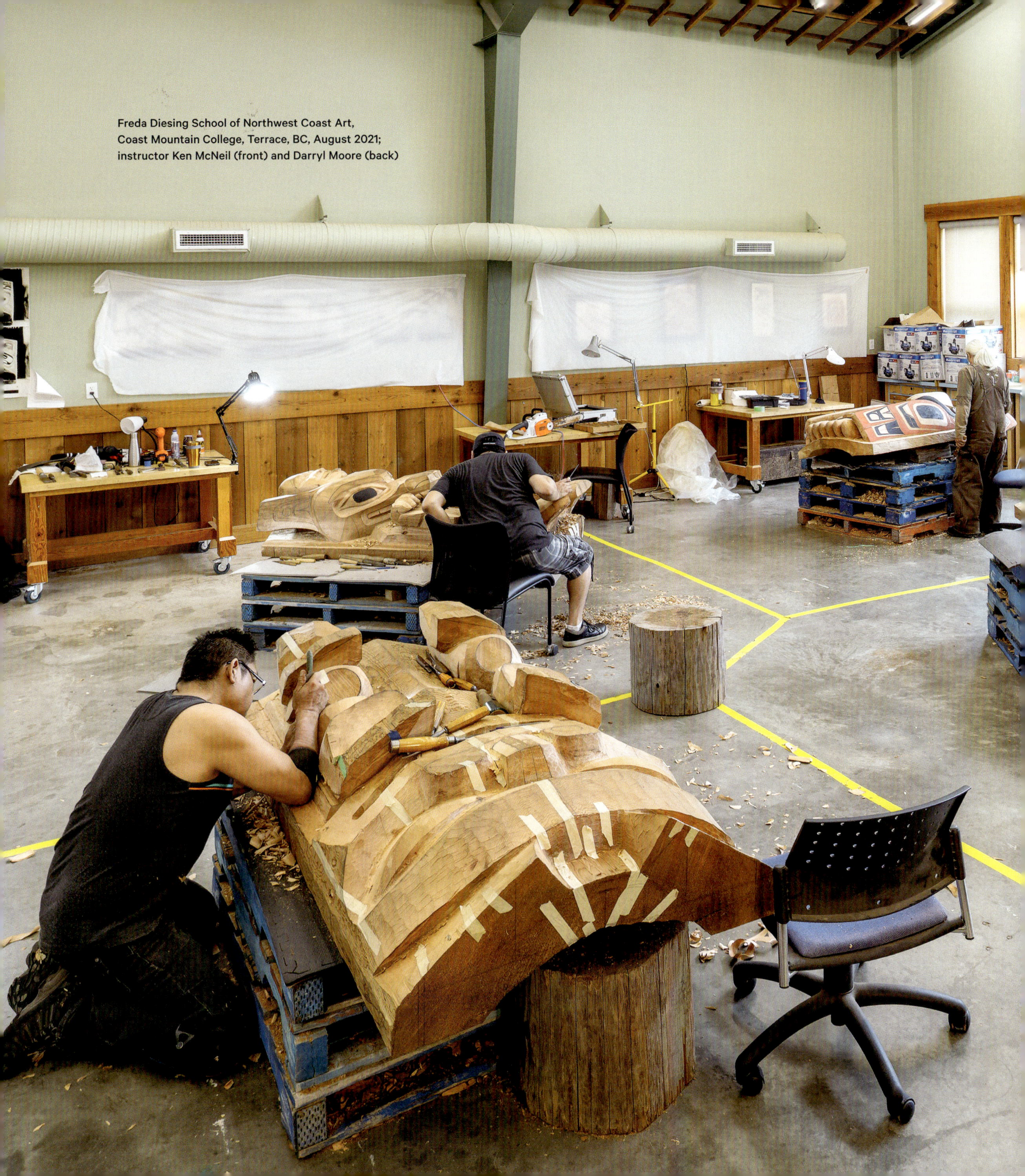

Freda Diesing School of Northwest Coast Art,
Coast Mountain College, Terrace, BC, August 2021;
instructor Ken McNeil (front) and Darryl Moore (back)

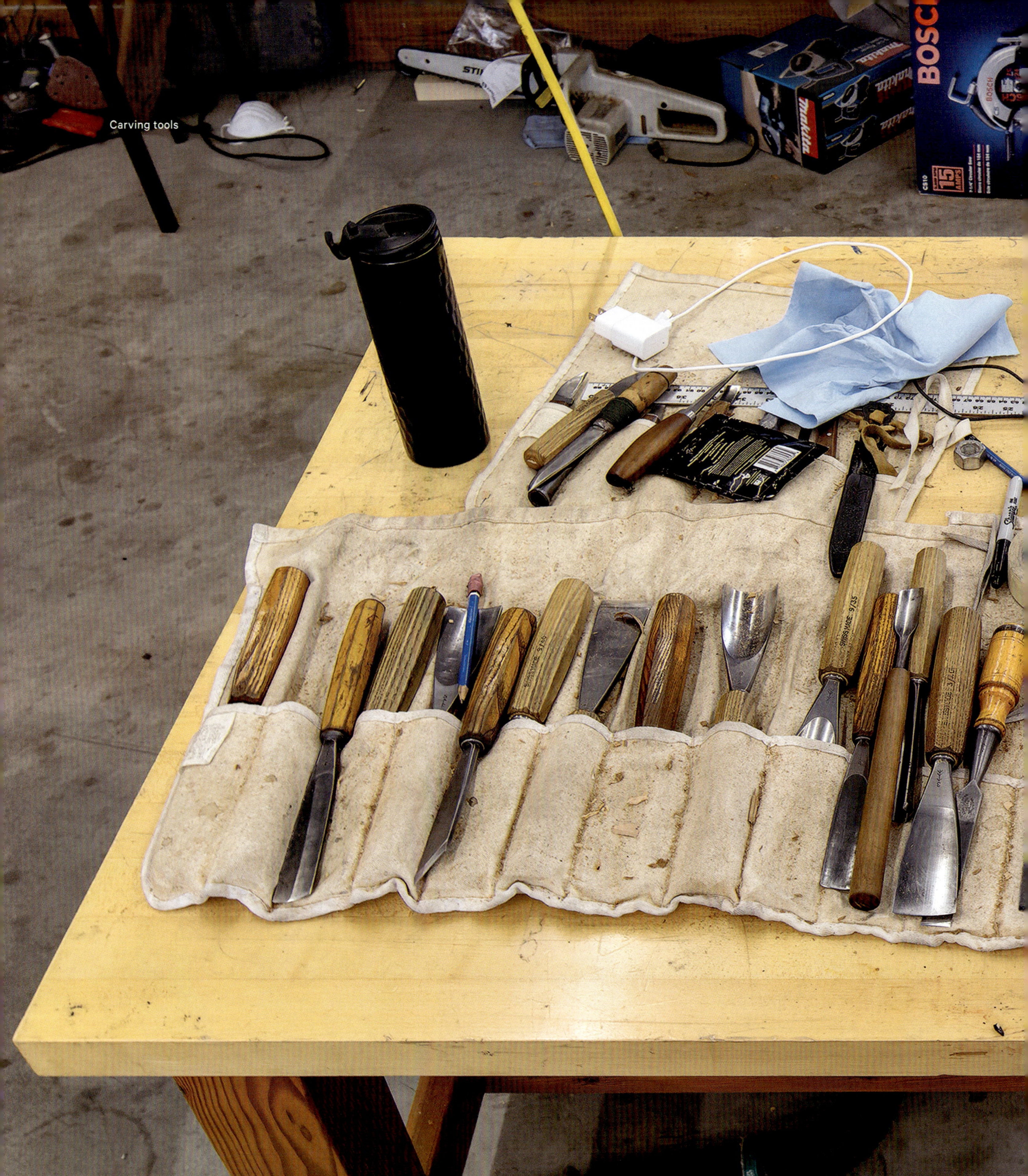
Carving tools

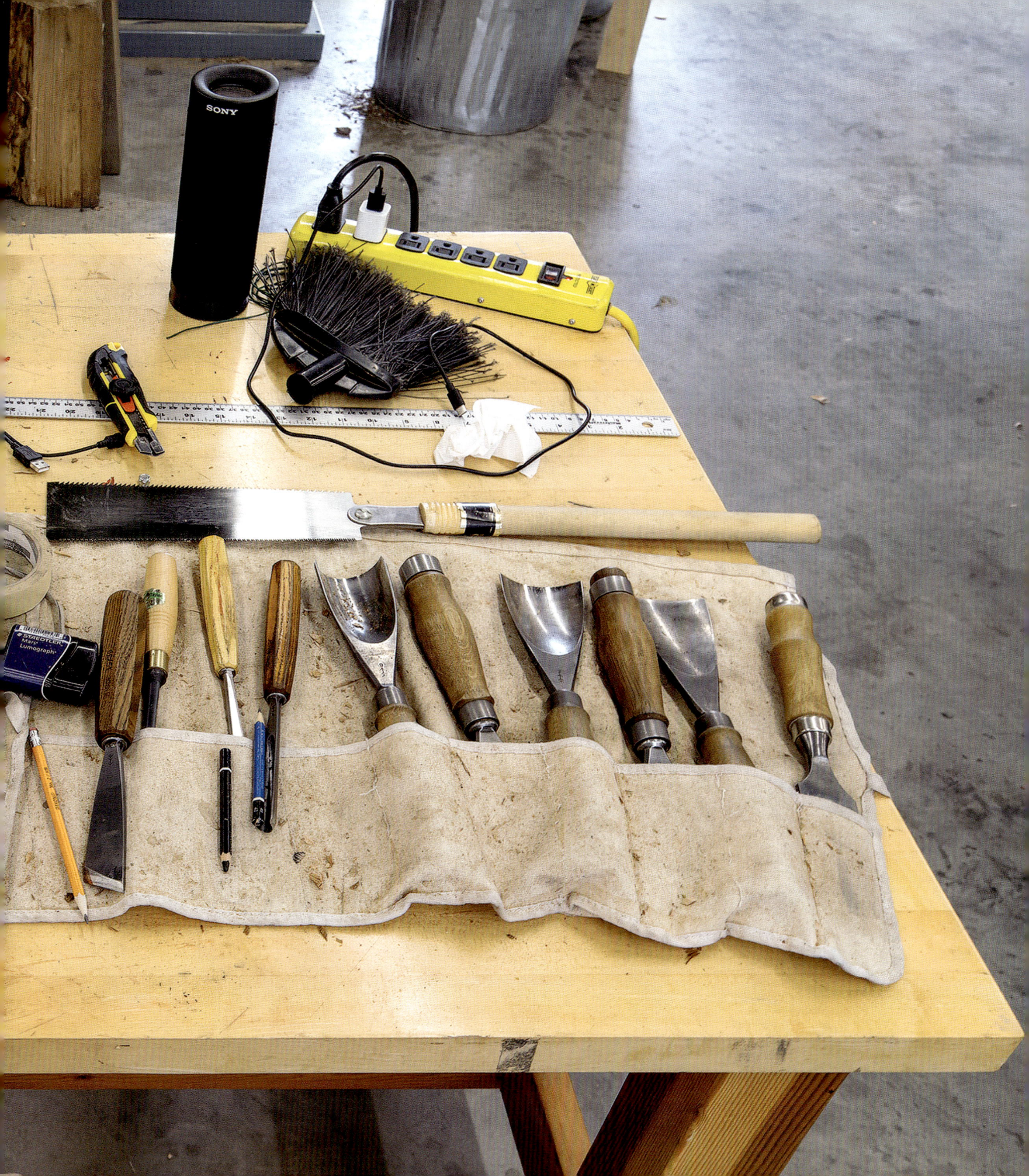

In the wintertime we used to get minus-thirty weather for weeks, even for a month at a time. Now we don't even get minus twenty. Maybe with wind chill. And in the summer it's so much hotter and dryer.

To get the fish in the rivers now, you have to wait for an opening in the weather. The streams are so low. The stocks are so low. The salmon—they know when the water is high enough to get up to the spawning grounds, and they know when the water is cool enough not to kill the eggs. If there's a cold rain, they know they have to get there before it warms up again. When the cottonwood blows off the trees—when that starts falling, that's when the salmon are coming. It's happening earlier and earlier and the salmon are not coming.

I know back home, up in Telegraph, there's not so many moose anymore. They've been hunted quite a bit, but these big forest fires have really been affecting them. But it does create new growth as well.

What I heard, too, is that the big forest fires have pushed the elk up into our Tahltan country. We never had them before, but the forest fires have been killing off their habitat farther south.

We worry about the snow pack because the salmon need the cold water to get up the creeks to spawn. Salmon have always been our supply in the winter—we smoked them and now we jar them. We used to eat salmon all summer long. Breakfast, lunch, and supper.

There are getting to be less and less salmon; they're losing their own habitat. There are lots of bears up in the mountains, but there's now building right up to the bear's house. It's their environment.

Some of the rivers up in Alaska have no more salmon because of the mining. Now there are just a few really good rivers and streams that are still clean, and the bears are all gathering there because it's the only place they can get salmon.

That's why the bears are coming into town. They need the salmon. If they don't get fat from eating the salmon they're not going to make it through the winter. And some years, if it's too hot, or if there's not enough rain, the berries don't ripen, and the bears suffer from that too. They need those berries to survive.

The eagle depends on the salmon, like the ravens and the bears. We are all connected. The salmon even fertilize the trees growing along the riverbanks. The bears carry the salmon into the forest and leave parts of it there.

Our generation has seen how important the salmon was to us in our livelihood. We used to preserve it and dry and smoke it for the winter. It was central to our culture. It gave us time in the winter to carve and make art. We had enough to last us for a year. When I was younger, we couldn't leave our nets in overnight. They would be too heavy to pull in.

I remember we used to catch about a hundred of them over the course of a few days, using a net—at 6 Mile, our family's spot on the river near Telegraph Creek. We grew up there fishing. The Stikine—that's our river, for the Tahltan people. I go there to fish still. For our kids, my brothers Willie and Lorgan—they still smoke them up there. We work together as families. We will jar ten, fifteen cases of salmon at a time.

One of the things I have been hearing about is that people are finding seals and even sea lions up in the rivers. They are making their way up there, looking for salmon. They are desperate for food, and they can't find enough salmon out in the ocean. That's a new thing.

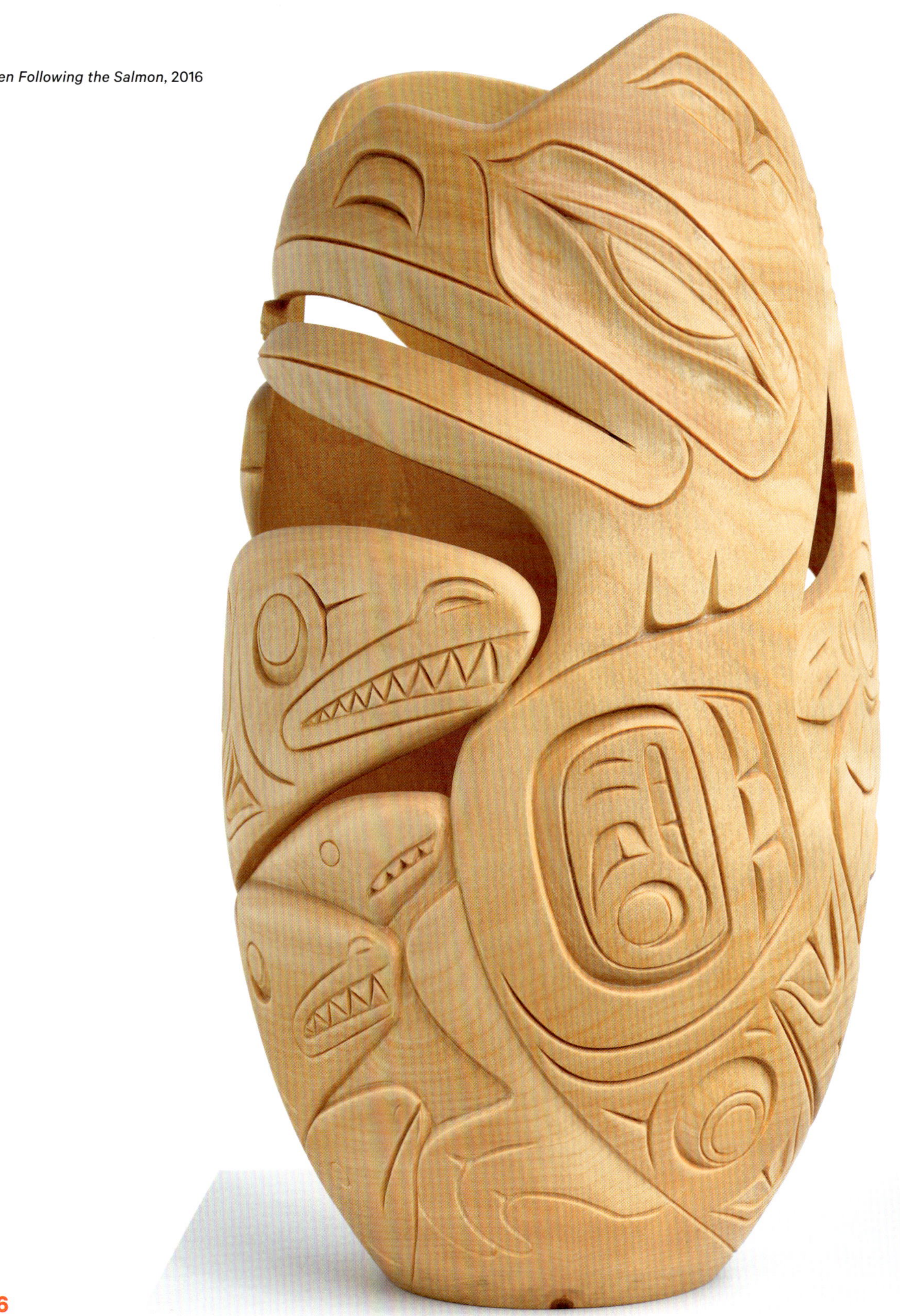

Raven Following the Salmon, 2016

186

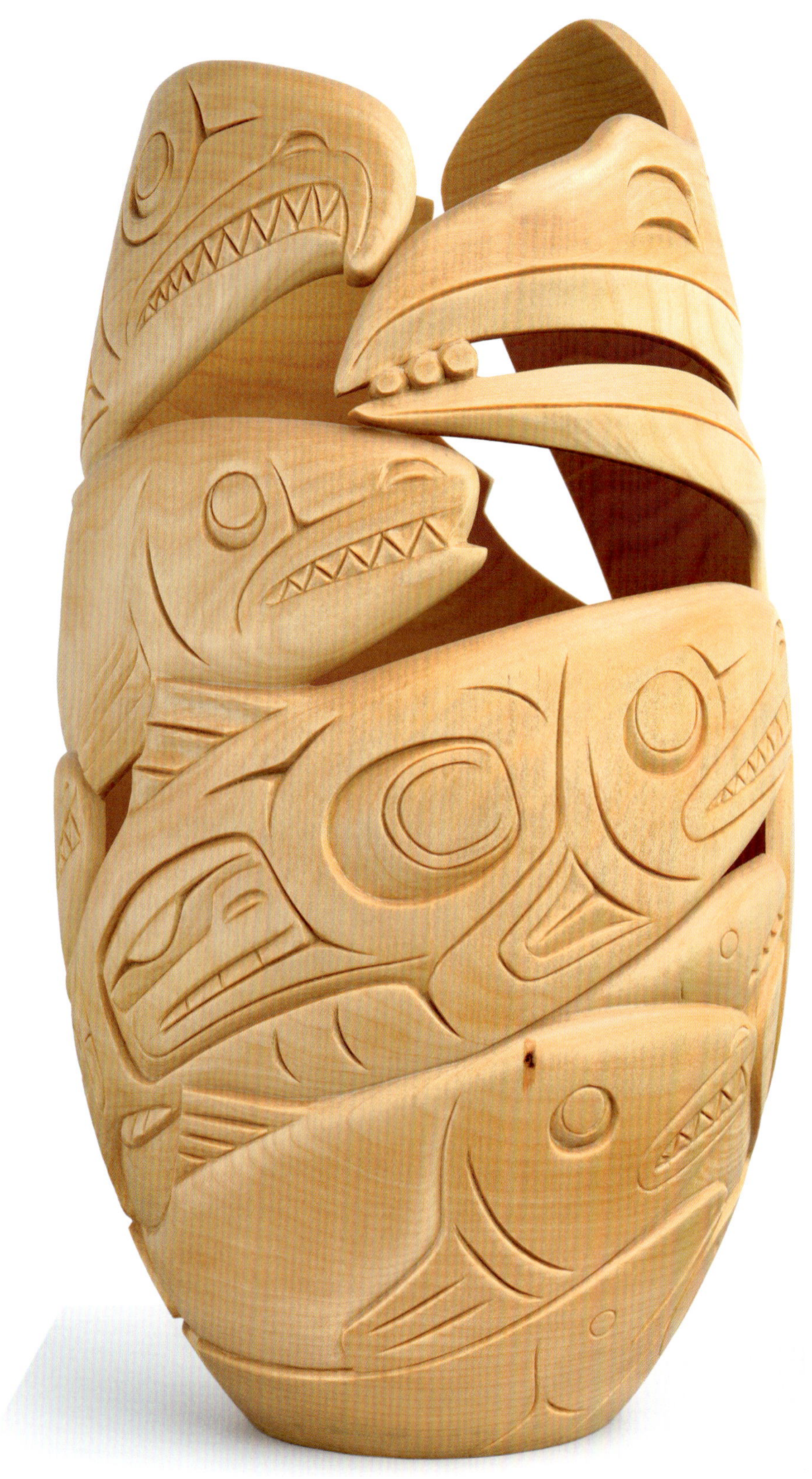

187

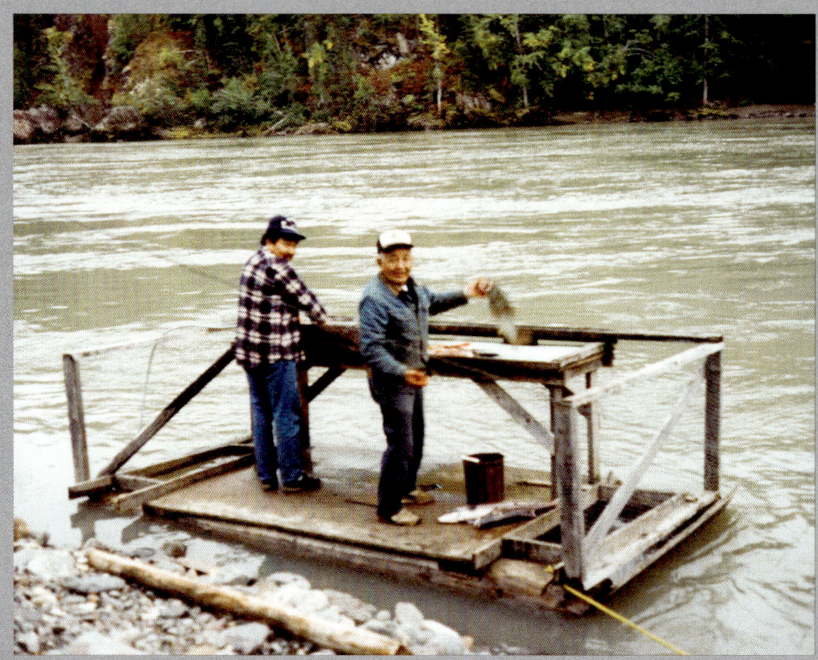

With Eddy Frank at Eddy's Cannery, Stikine River, 6 Mile, BC, 1980s,
near my family's traditional fishing spot

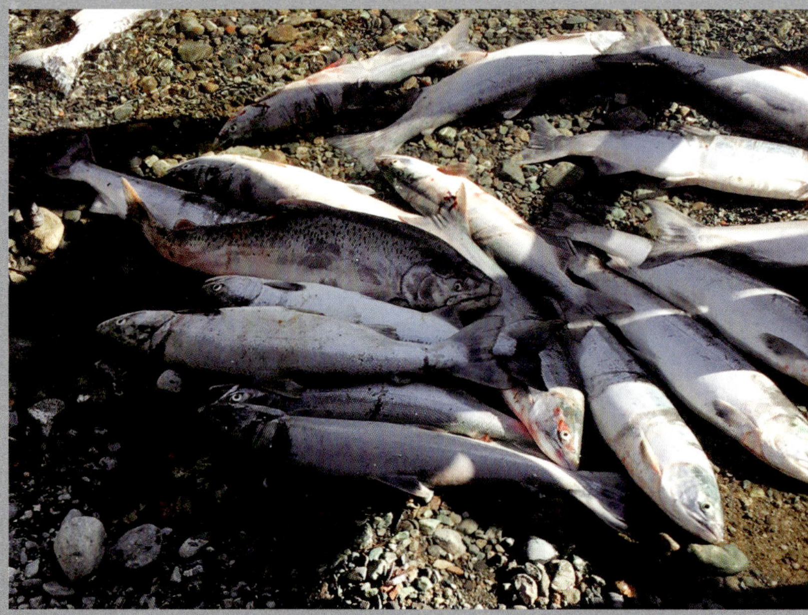

Stikine River, 6 Mile, Telegraph Creek, BC

As soon as the kids can understand, we start telling them stories. My grandpa Johnny Sinkoots said, "Don't swim in the creek because when the salmon dies you will go downstream in the salmon soul canoe, too, down to the ocean, and you won't come back to your people." You'd get scared! You'd stay away from the creeks. That story would keep you safe.

They'd say, "Don't swim in the sloughs, on the banks of the river, because at night there's a canoe full of salmon souls that goes down the river in the moonlight, and your soul will go in the salmon soul canoe, and you will never come back."

I think that story is about conservation, and keeping kids out of the creeks. If you're swimming in the creeks you're kicking up thousands of salmon eggs. The slough, in the sand— that's where the sockeye salmon spawn. Four years later there would be less salmon; you would have killed thousands just by playing around. That's how they taught children about respect for animals. All these stories have meaning.

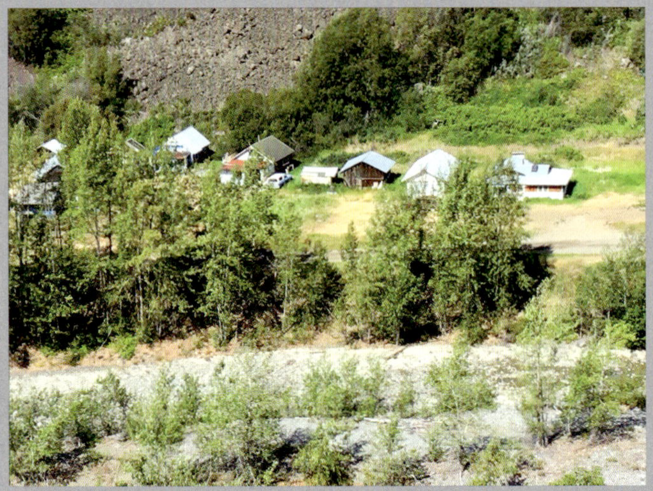

Tahltan village, BC, July 2018, one month before forest fire devastation

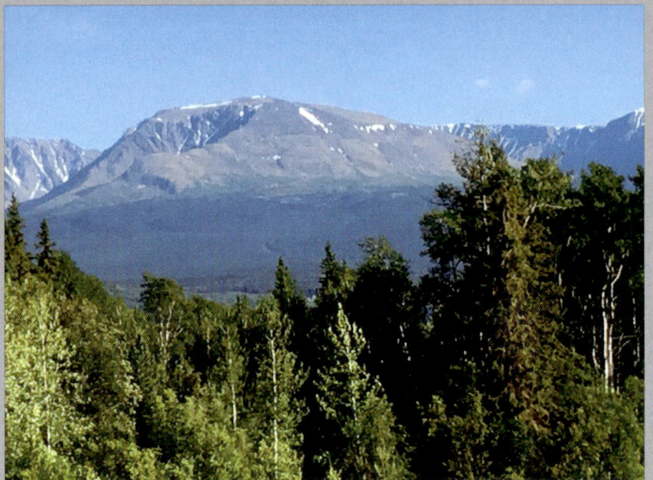

Stingy Mountains, Telegraph Creek, BC

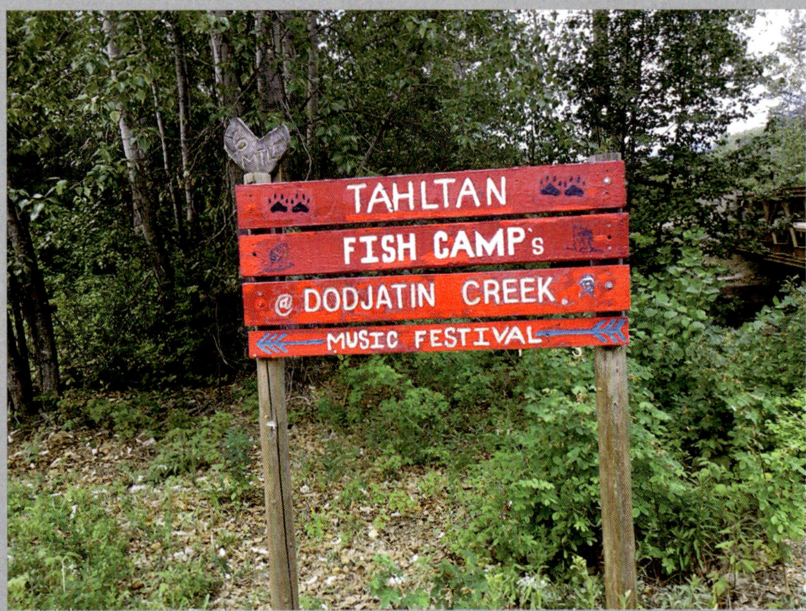

Stikine River, 6 Mile, Telegraph Creek, BC

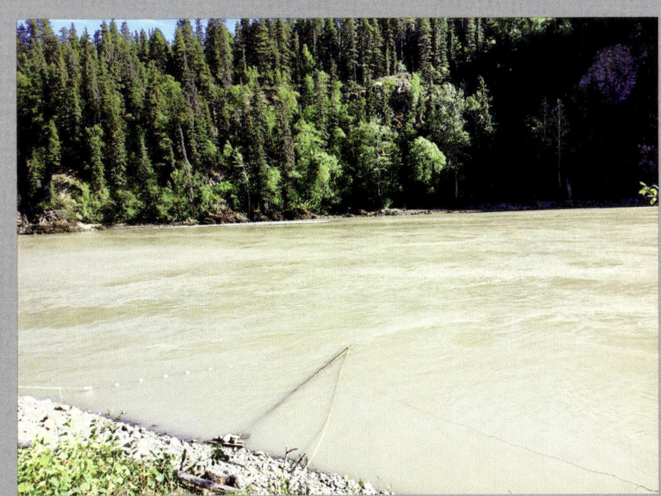

Stikine River, 6 Mile, Telegraph Creek, BC

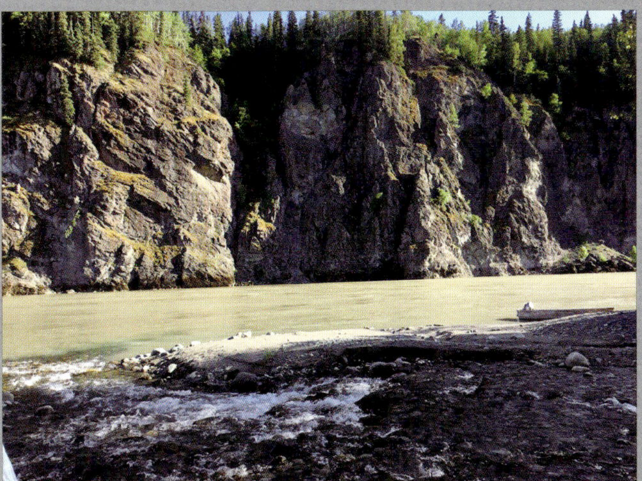

Stikine River, 6 Mile, Telegraph Creek, BC

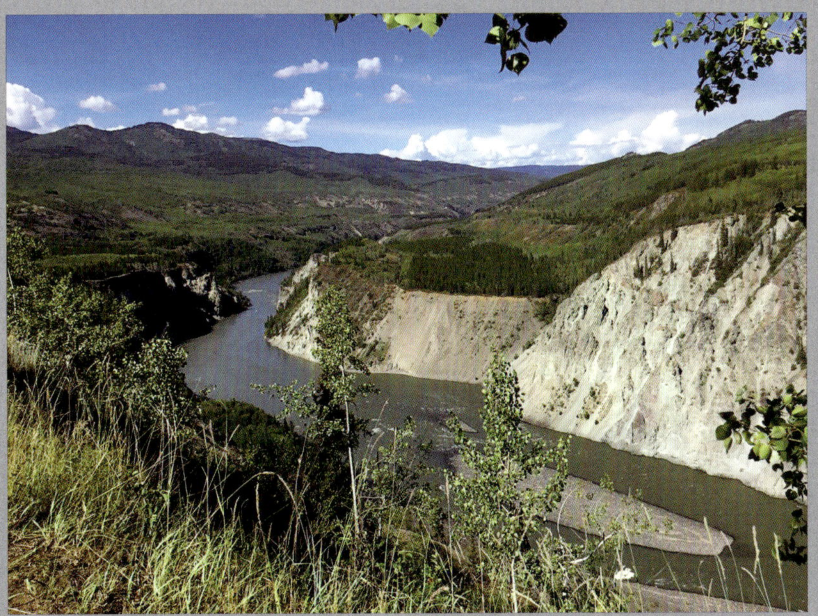

The mighty Stikine River, Tahltan country, BC

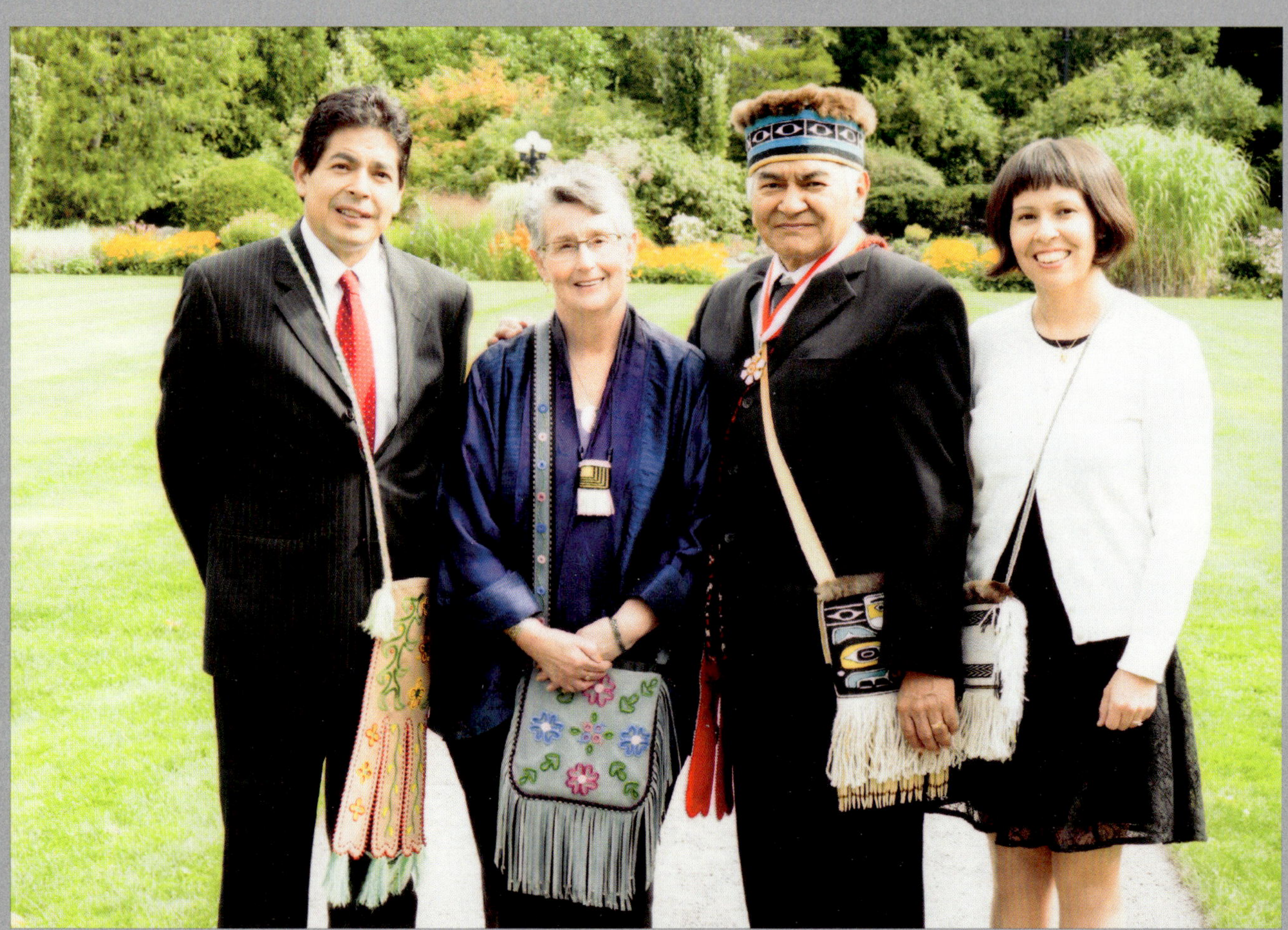

Pie and me with our son, David Nunn, and our daughter, Tanya Bob, in Ottawa when I was named an Officer of the Order of Canada, 2013. The beaded bags worn by David and Pie were made by Linda Bob. The chilkat bags worn by Tanya and me, and the headdress worn by me, were made by the Tsimshian weaver Willie White.

In May 1998 we were invited to go to Canada House in London. They were opening up the gallery there again, after some renovations, and we had a really good show—some of our old pieces and our contemporary pieces too.

We were presented to the Queen. You can't talk to her unless she talks to you; we were told that. I talked to her husband, though. He asked me about the ermine on our regalia. Phil Fontaine gave a speech that day. There was a whole group of us—Beau Dick, David Neel, Joe David, and David Reuben—we all went together.

Since the late '70s there have been two poles of mine in London at Canada House. They moved one of them to BC House in London, and then they sent it to Government House in Victoria. The other one is still at Canada House.

HONOURS AND AWARDS

I was named an Officer of the Order of Canada in 2013.[93] When I got that award, I thought about my mum and my people. At one time our art was outlawed. We would have been arrested for wearing a blanket or singing a song. It wasn't until 1951 that we could have our potlatches again. I was three years old. I was sad about our people who weren't allowed to practise their culture. This award, too, the Governor General's Award in 2021,[94] is for them. It's for my grandparents and my mum. That's what I thought about when they gave it to me.

93. In 2013 Dempsey Bob was invested as an Officer of the Order of Canada in recognition of his important contributions to the art and artists of British Columbia.

94. In 2021 Dempsey Bob received the Artistic Achievement Award at the Governor General's Awards in Visual and Media Arts.

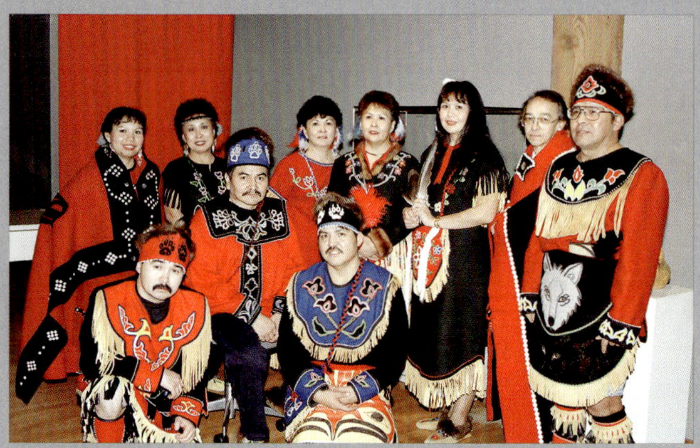

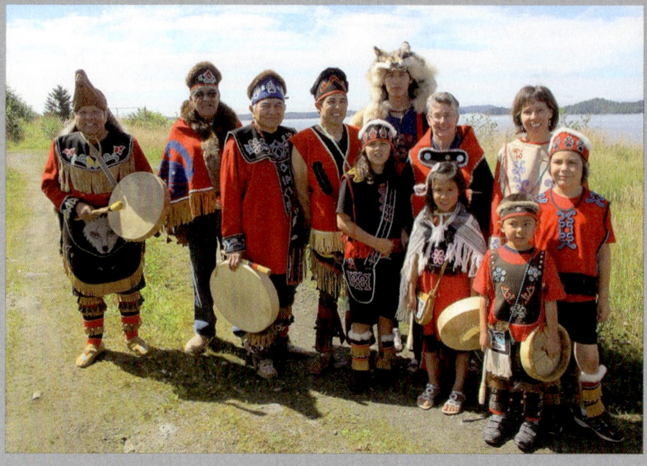

The Bob Family Reunion, Prince Rupert, 2013; (back row from left)
Tony Bob, Charlie Pete, me, David Nunn, Eric Bevan (behind), Pie, Tanya
Bob; (front row at right) my grandchildren: Grayson Nunn, Keely Chow,
Nate Bob, Roy Nunn. Most of the regalia had been designed and sewn
by Linda Bob. The Raven's tail robe (white), worn by Keely, and the chilkat
bag, worn by Nate, were made by the Tsimshian weaver Willie White.

Wolf and Bear Show, Inuit Gallery, Vancouver, 1995; (back row
from left) Donna McNeil Clark, Lovetta McNeil, Merle Bevan, Linda Bob,
Virginia Bob, Mel Bevan, Tony Bob; (front row at left) Stan Bevan,
me (centre), Ken McNeil (Photo: Harold Demetzer)

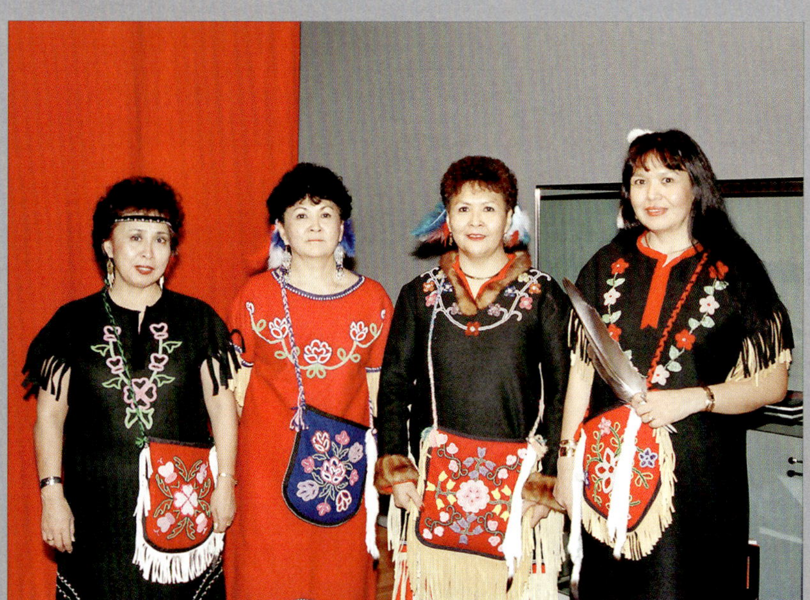

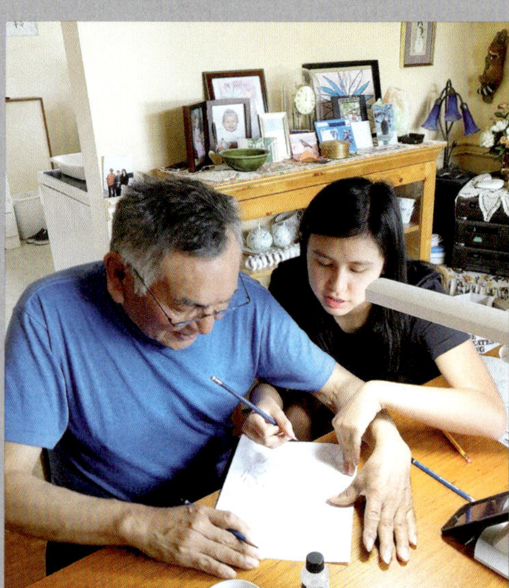

With my granddaughter, Keely Chow,
drawing together, 2021

My sisters at the *Wolf and Bear Show*, Inuit Gallery, Vancouver, 1995; (from left)
Lovetta McNeil, Merle Bevan, Linda Bob, Virginia Bob (Photo: Harold Demetzer)

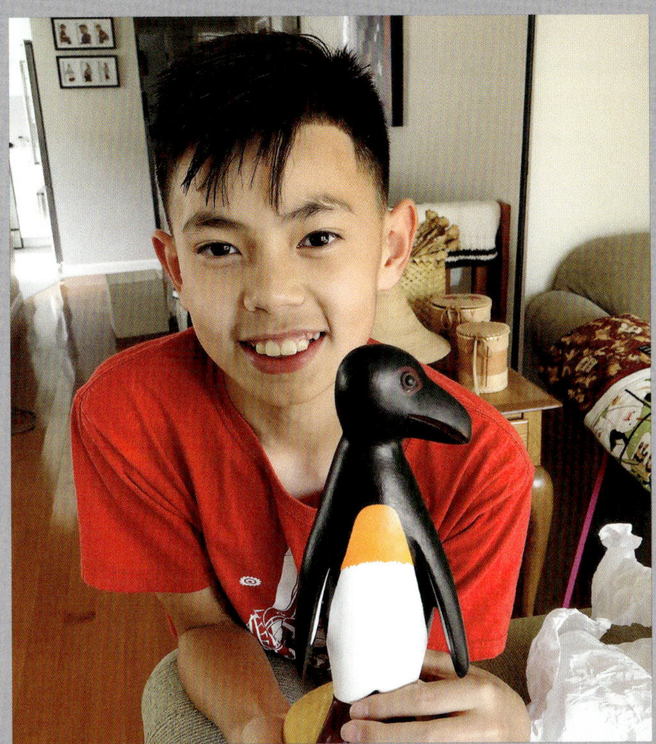

My grandson Nate Bob with his penguin, 2020

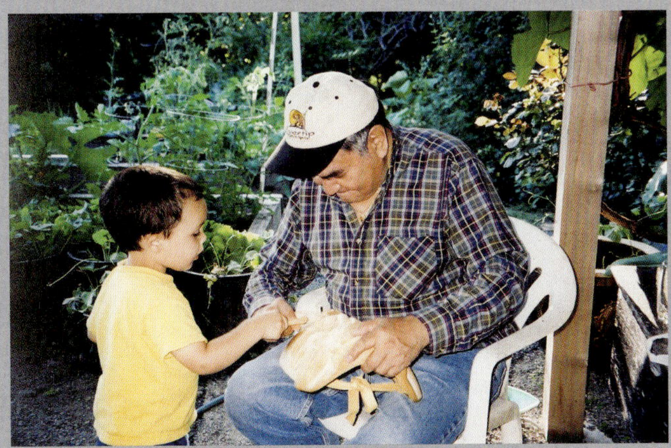

With my grandson Grayson Nunn, about 2005

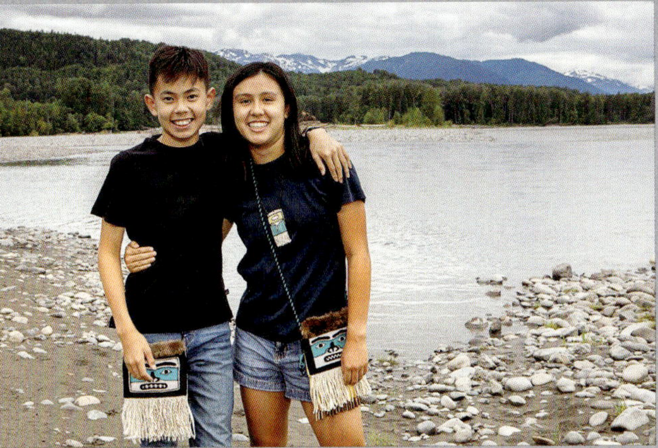

My grandchildren Nate Bob and Keely Chow (Crow Clan), Ferry Island, Skeena River, BC, 2021

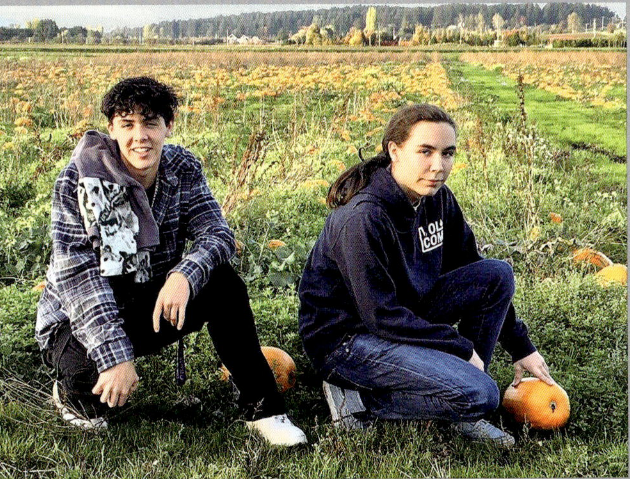

My grandchildren Grayson Nunn and Roy Nunn (Wolf Clan), Michell's Farm, Saanichton, BC, 2020

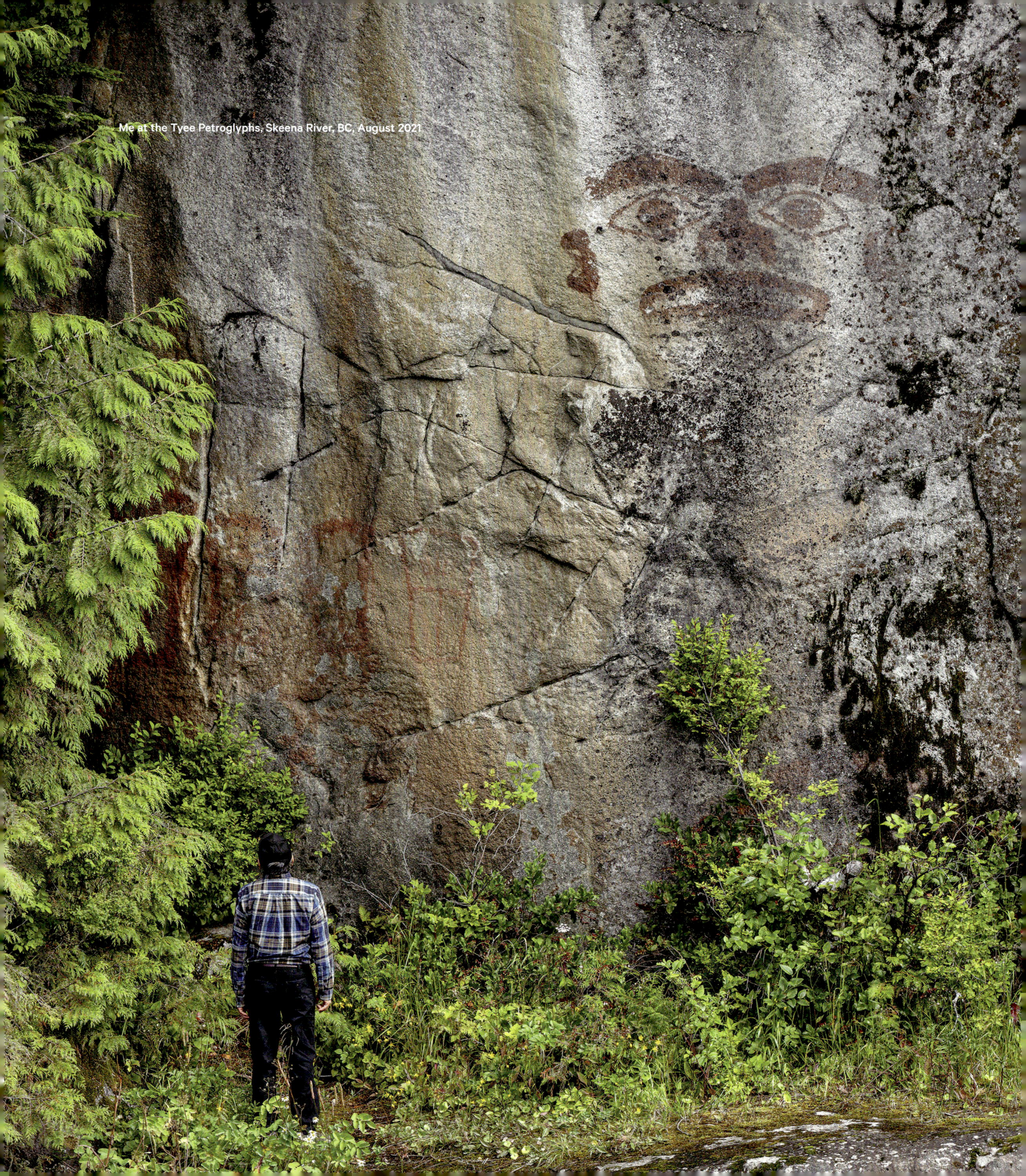
Me at the Tyee Petroglyphs, Skeena River, BC, August 2021

One time we were dancing up by Haines, Alaska, and afterward
we went down to the water and we were looking over the ocean,
and the whole sky was northern lights and they were moving
and the colours were changing. One of our Elders said, "That's
our ancestors dancing."

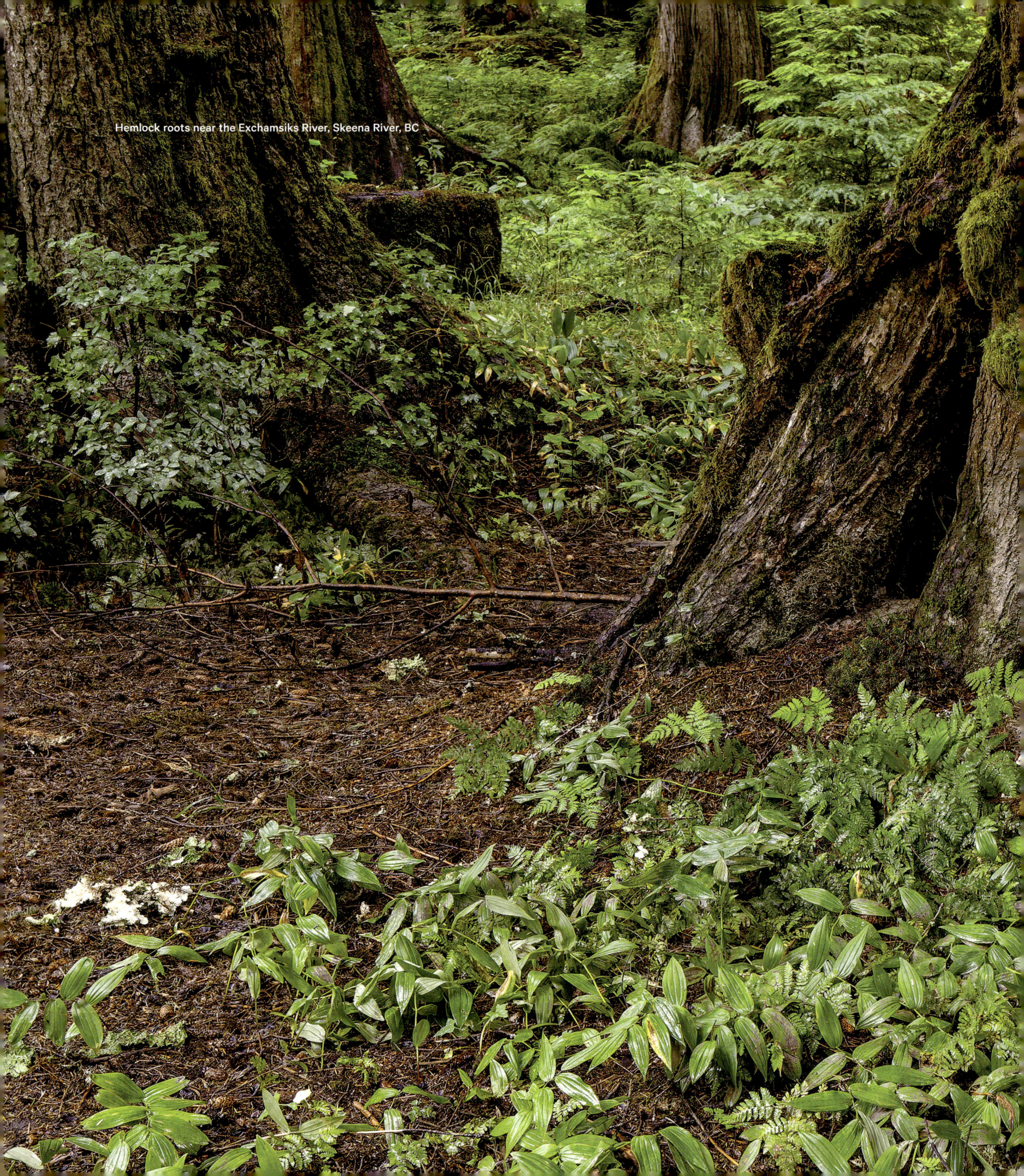

Hemlock roots near the Exchamsiks River, Skeena River, BC

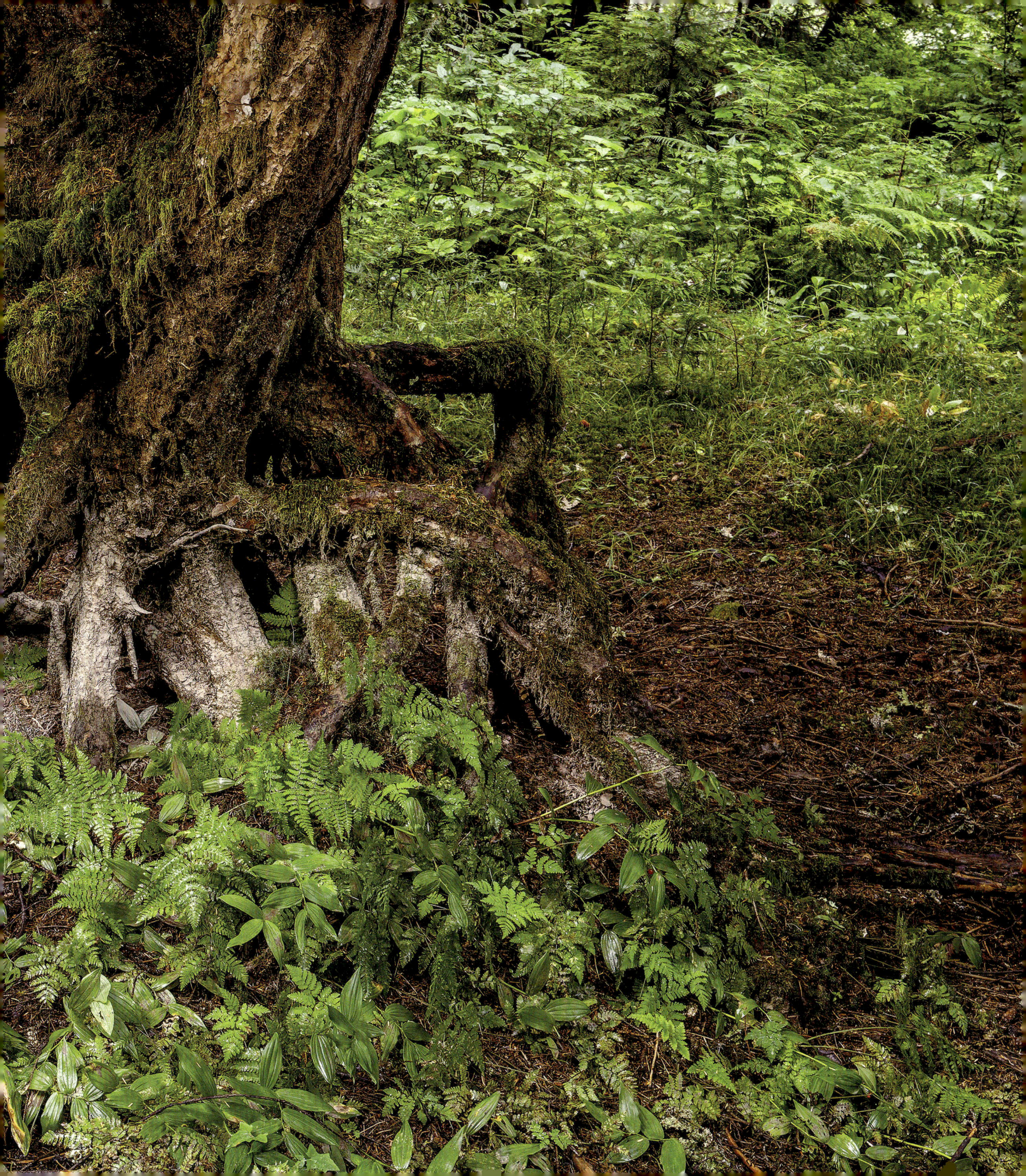

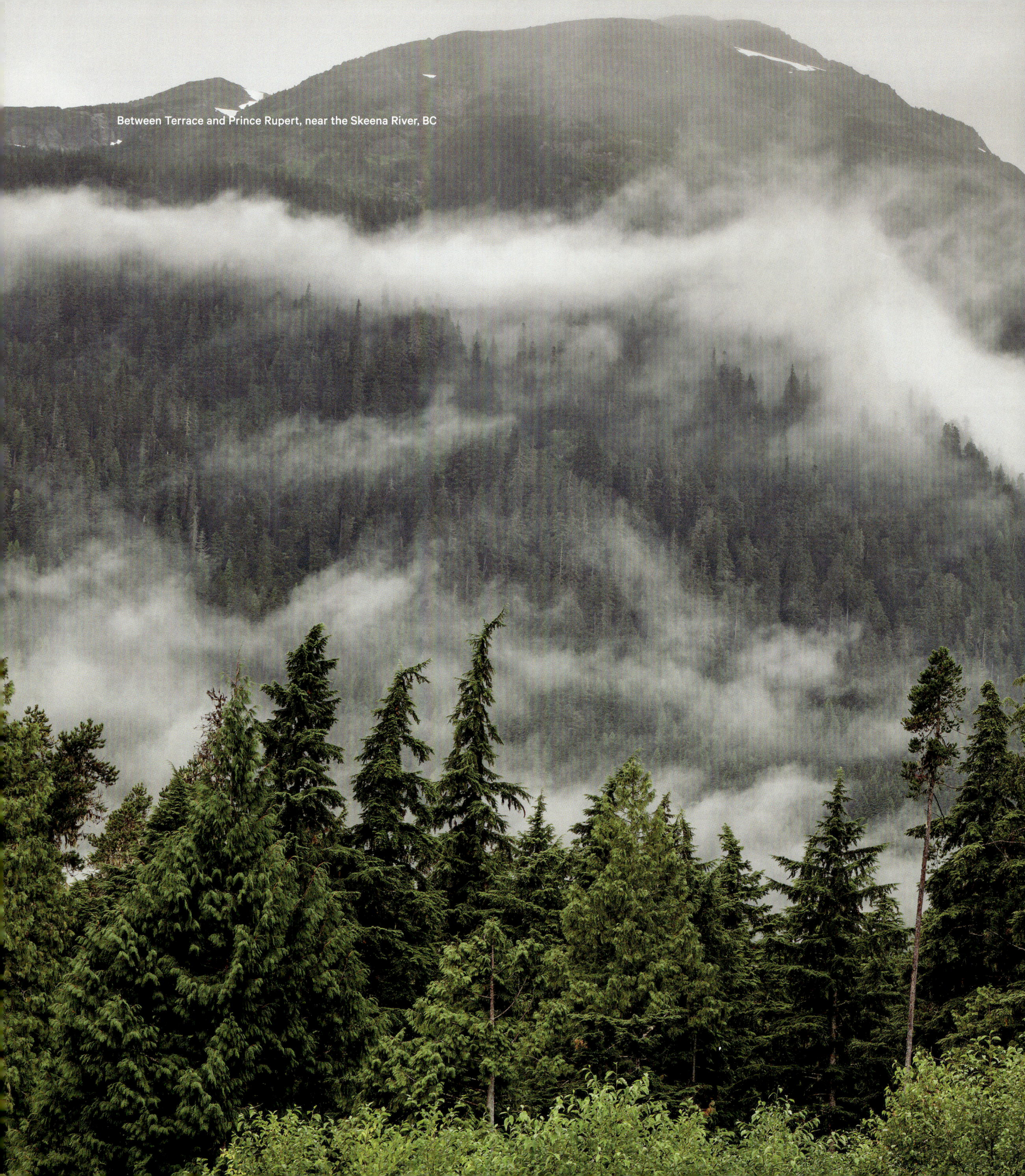
Between Terrace and Prince Rupert, near the Skeena River, BC

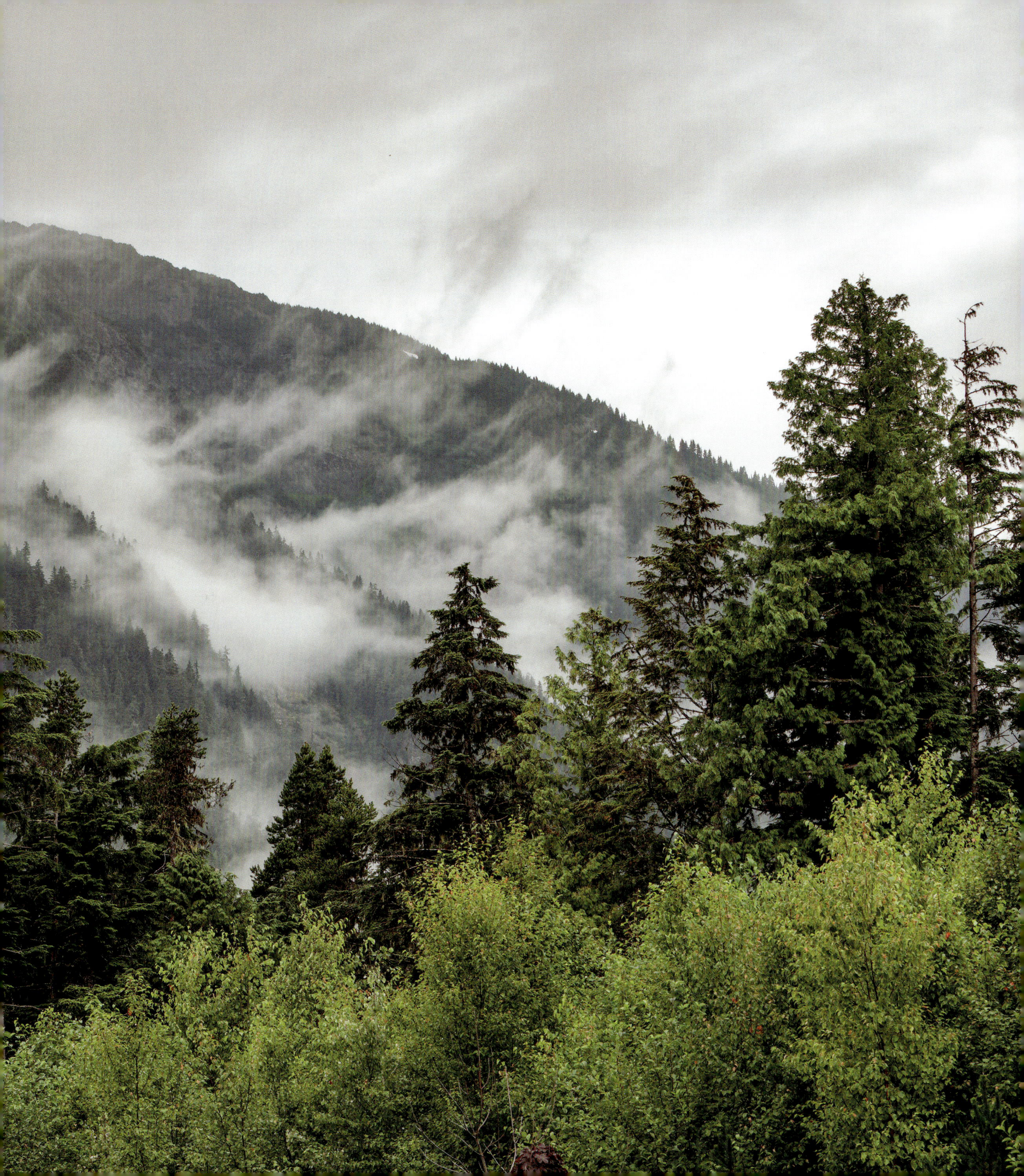

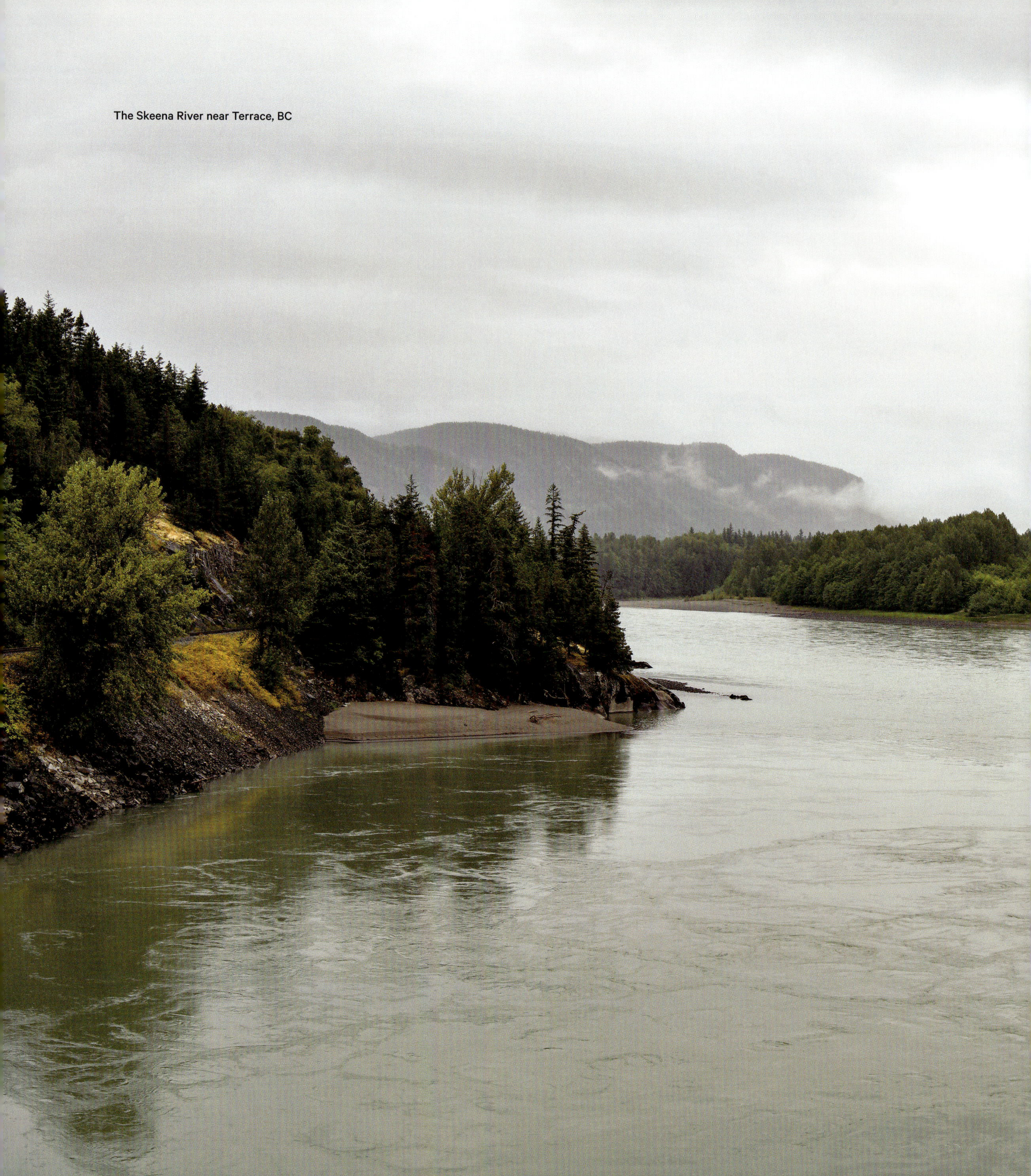

The Skeena River near Terrace, BC

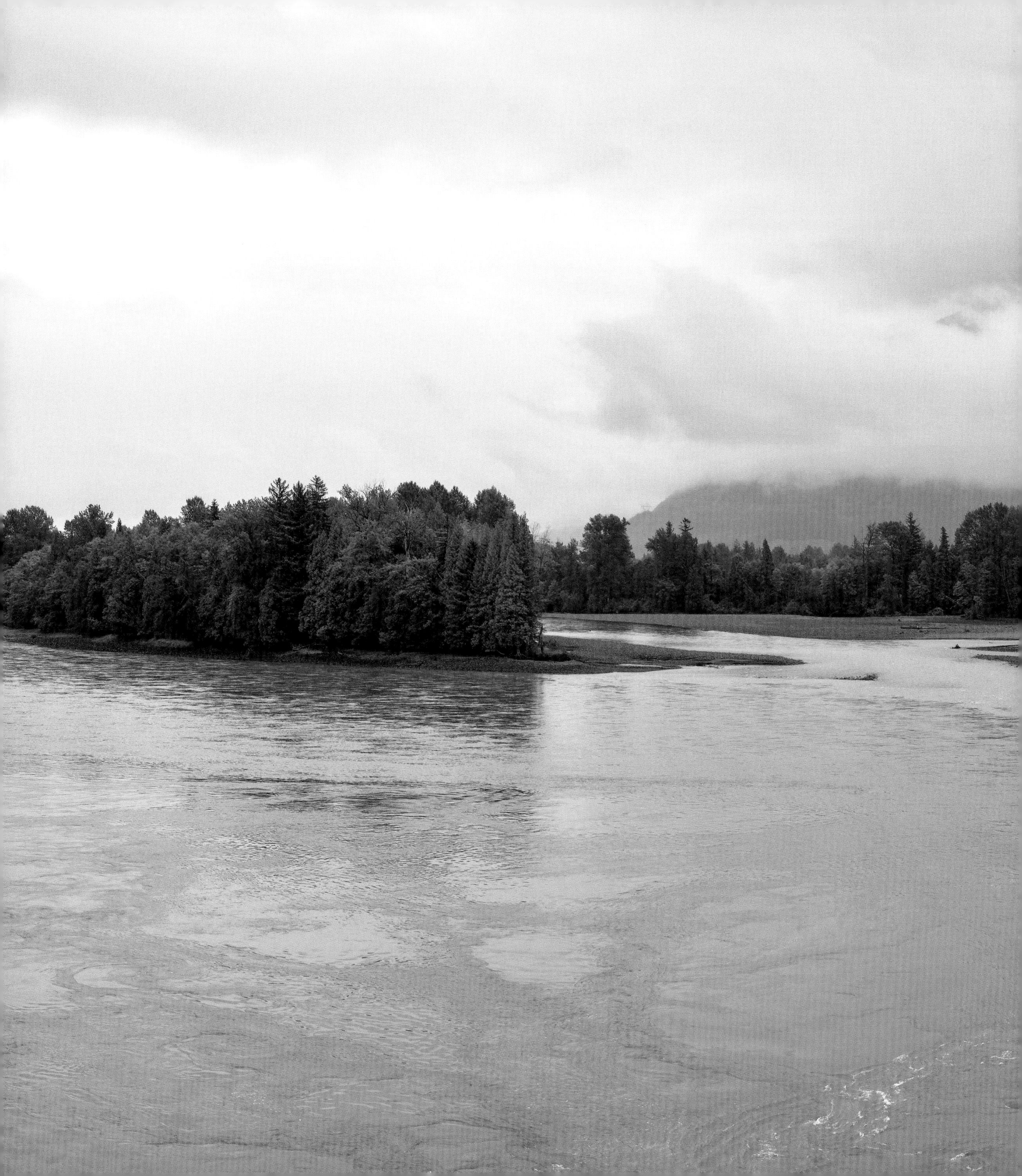

Bear Chief's Box, 2017
yellow cedar, red cedar
36.8 × 34.3 × 34.3 cm
Equinox Gallery, Vancouver
Photo: Byron Dauncy
p. 170

Bear Mother, 2012
yellow cedar, operculum
shell, acrylic paint
46 × 25 × 14 cm
University of British
Columbia, Museum of
Anthropology, Vancouver
Donated 2017
3260 / 122
Photo: Alina Ilyasova /
Courtesy of UBC Museum
of Anthropology
p. 158

Bears Mask, 2006
alder, acrylic paint,
operculum shell
33 × 33 × 14.6 cm
Collection of Eric Savics
Photo: Rachel Topham
Photography
p. 148

Beaver Eagle Mask, 1989
alder, acrylic paint, fur
27.9 × 21.6 × 15.2 cm
Christopher Bredt and
Jamie Cameron Collection
Photo: Craig Boyko
pp. 88, 89

Beavers Travelling, 2014
alder, operculum shells,
acrylic paint
50.8 × 27.9 × 25.4 cm
Equinox Gallery, Vancouver
Photo: Rachel Topham
Photography
p. 167

Chief's Headdress—Human,
1993
alder, ermine fur, melton cloth,
abalone shell, acrylic paint
114.3 × 25.4 × 25.4 cm
Collection of Eric Savics
Photo: Rachel Topham
Photography
p. 126

Eagle and the Bear People, 2013
yellow cedar, acrylic paint
55.9 × 34.3 × 10.2 cm
Collection of Michael Audain
and Yoshiko Karasawa
Photo: Rachel Topham
Photography
p. 161

Eagle Bear Mask, 1987
alder, acrylic paint,
black bear fur
28.5 × 26 × 18.5 cm
University of British
Columbia, Museum of
Anthropology, Vancouver
Purchased 1987
Nb22.76
Photo: Rachel Topham
Photography
p. 83

Eagle Chief's Frontlet,
c. 1992
alder, ermine fur, sea
lion whiskers, abalone
shell, acrylic paint
114.3 × 25.4 × 25.4 cm
Collection of Eric Savics
Photo: Rachel Topham
Photography
p. 127

Eagle Chief's Hat, 1982
cedar, acrylic paint, hair,
leather, metal, adhesive
30 × 38.5 cm
University of British
Columbia, Museum of
Anthropology, Vancouver
Purchased 1983
Nb22.75
Photo: Derek Tan / Courtesy of
UBC Museum of Anthropology
p. 77

Eagle Chief's Robe, c. 1992
(Designed by Dempsey
Bob; made by Linda Bob)
melton cloth, leather, abalone
shell buttons, acrylic paint,
deer hooves
106.7 × 152.4 × 5 cm
Collection of Eric Savics
Photo: Rachel Topham
Photography
pp. 128–29

*Eagle, Hawk, and
Humans Mask*, 2011
yellow cedar, acrylic paint
45.7 × 26.7 × 15.2 cm
Collection of Michael Audain
and Yoshiko Karasawa
Photo: Rachel Topham
Photography
p. 152

Eagle Human Mask, 1987
alder, yellow cedar, paint,
hair, leather, wax, fibre,
metal, adhesive, glass
26 × 17 × 16.5 cm
University of British
Columbia, Museum of
Anthropology, Vancouver
Purchased 1987
Nb22.77
Photo: Jessica Bushey /
Courtesy of UBC Museum
of Anthropology
p. 79

Eagle Human Vessel, 2009
birch
35.56 × 25.4 × 25.4 cm
Collection of Eric Savics

Eagle Mask, 2000
alder, acrylic paint
46.5 × 21.5 × 17 cm
Collection of the
Vancouver Art Gallery
Acquisition Fund
VAG 2000.27
Photo: Vancouver
Art Gallery
p. 144

Eagle Mask, 2001
bronze, edition 4 of 6
45.7 × 22.8 × 17.7 cm
Equinox Gallery, Vancouver
Photo: Rachel Topham
Photography
p. 145

Eagle Mask, 2017
alder, acrylic paint, horsehair
35.6 × 33 × 15.2 cm
Collection of Michael Audain
and Yoshiko Karasawa
Photo: Rachel Topham
Photography
p. 162

Eagles and Bears, 2017
alder
40.6 × 20.3 × 17.8 cm
Equinox Gallery, Vancouver
Photo: Byron Dauncy
p. 171

The Eagles Forehead Mask,
1996
alder, acrylic paint, horsehair
35.6 × 20.3 × 40.6 cm
Collection of Eric Savics
Photo: Rachel Topham
Photography
pp. 130, 131

Eagles North, 2013
yellow cedar, acrylic paint
63 × 60 × 10 cm
National Gallery
of Canada, Ottawa
Purchased 2016
46710
Photo: NGC
p. 163

Frog Dance Staff, 2013
yellow cedar
78.7 × 8.9 × 8.9 cm
Private collection
Photo: Denis Farley
pp. 164, 165

Frog Raven Forehead Mask,
2007
alder, acrylic paint
50.8 × 38.1 × 20.2 cm
Private collection, Vancouver
Photo: Rachel Topham
Photography
p. 150

Frog Stories, 2017
alder, acrylic paint
32.4 × 23.5 × 19 cm
Private collection
Photo: Craig Boyko
pp. 168, 169

Frog's World, c. 2006
alder, acrylic paint
76.2 × 17.8 × 15.2 cm
Collection of Eric Savics
Photo: Rachel Topham
Photography
p. 153

Hawk Human Portrait Mask,
2003
totara wood, acrylic paint
33 × 20 × 12.7 cm
Collection of Eric Savics
Photo: Rachel Topham
Photography
p. 138

Hawk Portrait Mask,
1974 or earlier
alder, synthetic fibre,
acrylic paint
32 × 17.9 cm
Canadian Museum
of History, Gatineau
VII-A-364
Photo: Steven Darby
p. 71

Human Shark Mask, 1997
alder, acrylic paint
30.1 × 21.7 × 11 cm
McMichael Canadian Art
Collection, Kleinburg
Gift from the Christopher
Bredt and Jamie Cameron
Collection
2014.6.2
Photo: Craig Boyko
p. 134

Khoh Dene, 2018
yellow cedar, acrylic paint
66 × 60 × 10.2 cm
Collection of Michael Audain
and Yoshiko Karasawa
Photo: Rachel Topham
Photography
p. 173

Killer Whale Forehead Mask,
c. 1997
alder
25.4 × 20 × 15.2 cm
Collection of Eric Savics
Photo: Rachel Topham
Photography
p. 137

Killer Whale Headdress, 1987
alder, abalone shell, acrylic
paint, hair, metal, adhesive, oil
31 × 22 × 43 cm
University of British
Columbia, Museum of
Anthropology, Vancouver
Purchased 1987
Nb22.79
Photo: Derek Tan / Courtesy of
UBC Museum of Anthropology
p. 81

Killer Whale Helmet,
1977 or earlier
alder, acrylic paint, hair
29 × 25 × 42 cm
Canadian Museum
of History, Gatineau
VII-A-363
Photo: Steven Darby
pp. 72, 73

Killer Whale Portrait Mask, n.d.
alder, acrylic paint
35.6 × 22.9 × 15.2 cm
Collection of Eric Savics
Photo: Rachel Topham
Photography
p. 132

Listen to the Frogs, 2018
alder, acrylic paint
38.1 × 30.5 × 17.8 cm
Equinox Gallery, Vancouver
Photo: Rachel Topham
Photography
p. 172

Little Frog Sculpture, 1989
alder, acrylic paint, horsehair
48 × 25.4 × 11.5 cm
Private collection
Photo: Harold Demetzer
p. 116

Mosquito Mask, 1989
alder, acrylic paint
30.5 × 22.9 × 15.2
Private collection,
White Rock, BC
Photo: Rachel Topham
Photography
p. 112

*Northern Eagles
Transformation Mask*, 2011
yellow cedar, acrylic paint
58.4 × 40.6 × 15.2 cm
Audain Art Museum
Collection, Whistler, BC
Gift of Michael Audain
and Yoshiko Karasawa
2018.058
Photo courtesy of Trevor Mills
p. 154

Old Woman Mask, 1974
alder, moose antler, copper,
abalone shell, human hair,
moose hide
22.2 × 15.4 × 11.9 cm
Private collection
Photo: Rachel Topham
Photography
p. 68

People's Moon Mask, 1980
maple, abalone shell, hair,
acrylic paint
59 × 31 × 12 cm
University of British
Columbia, Museum of
Anthropology, Vancouver
Donated 2016 by
Robert and Karen Gale
3194 / 24
Photo: Alina Ilyasova /
Courtesy of UBC Museum
of Anthropology
p. 70

Rain Frogs, 2012
yellow cedar, acrylic paint
88.9 × 24.1 × 15.2 cm
Private collection,
White Rock, BC
Photo: Rachel Topham
Photography
p. 159

Raven and Frog Headdress,
1988–89
alder, acrylic, abalone shell,
horsehair
58.4 × 58.4 × 33 cm
Private collection
Photo: Rachel Topham
Photography
pp. 86–87

Raven and Frog Mask, 1997
alder, acrylic paint
35.2 × 26.7 × 11.4 cm
Collection of Eric Savics
Photo: Rachel Topham
Photography
p. 135

Raven and the Box of Daylight,
2013
red cedar, yellow cedar,
acrylic paint
29 × 30.5 × 15 cm
University of British
Columbia, Museum of
Anthropology, Vancouver
Donated 2017
3260 / 118a-b

Raven Following the Salmon,
2016
birch
43.2 × 22.9 cm
Private collection, Vancouver
Photo: Rachel Topham
Photography
pp. 186, 187

Raven Forehead Mask,
1982 or earlier
alder, abalone shell, copper,
synthetic fibre, textile,
ermine skin, ermine fur
13 × 16 × 40.7 cm
Canadian Museum
of History, Gatineau
VII-A-365
Photo: Steven Darby
pp. 74, 75

Raven Frog Chief's Hat, 1989
alder with ermine fur
17.8 × 27.9 cm
Private collection,
White Rock, BC
Photo: Rachel Topham
Photography
p. 114

Sculpin Bowl, 1980
alder, acrylic paint
15.8 × 19.1 × 23.5 cm
Glenbow Museum, Calgary
AA.2157

The Smart One, 1989
alder, fur, acrylic paint
35.6 × 25.4 cm
Private collection
Photo: Harold Demetzer
p. 108

Transformation, 2011
yellow cedar
51.5 × 38.5 × 12.9 cm
Collection of Cheryl
Gottselig QC and Yves
Trépanier, Calgary
Photo: Kevin Baer
pp. 156, 157

War Boss, 2011
yellow cedar, operculum
shell, acrylic paint
71 × 15.2 × 35.6 cm
Collection of Eric Savics
Photo: Rachel Topham
Photography
p. 160

Wolf Chief's Hat, c. 1993
red cedar, acrylic paint,
operculum shell, horsehair,
leather, ermine fur
38 × 45.7 × 45.7 cm
Collection of Eric Savics
Photo: Rachel Topham
Photography
p. 102

Wolf, Eagle, and Human Mask,
1997
alder, acrylic paint
50.8 × 20.3 × 15.2 cm
Collection of Eric Savics
Photo: Rachel Topham
Photography
p. 133

Wolf Eagle Frontlet, 1996
alder, acrylic paint, abalone
shell, sea lion whiskers
45.7 × 15.2 × 10.2 cm
Collection of Eric Savics
Photo: Rachel Topham
Photography
p. 8

Wolf Headdress, 1988–89
alder, acrylic paint, fur,
operculum shell
40.6 × 20.3 cm
Private collection
Photo: Rachel Topham
Photography
p. 90

Wolf Human Mask, 1992
alder, acrylic paint
40.6 × 40.6 × 22.9 cm
Collection of Eric Savics
Photo: Rachel Topham
Photography
p. 208

*Wolf Warrior Helmet
and Visor*, 2014
alder, operculum shells,
horsehair, acrylic paint
53.3 × 25.2 × 29.9 cm
National Gallery
of Canada, Ottawa
Purchased 2016
46711
Photo: NGC
p. 166

Wolves in the Snow Blanket,
1999–2002
(Blanket made by Linda
Bob; mask clasp made by
Dempsey Bob)
blanket: felt, wolf fur, buttons,
thread; mask clasp: alder,
acrylic paint, leather fastening
blanket: 141.5 × 155.4 cm; mask
clasp: 20.3 × 15.6 × 6.7 cm
McMichael Canadian Art
Collection, Kleinburg
Gift from the Christopher
Bredt and Jamie Cameron
Collection
2014.6.3.A-.B
Photo: Craig Boyko
pp. 92, 94, 95

Young Killer Whale Mask, 1986
yellow cedar and alder, acrylic
paint, human hair, moose hide
47 × 25.5 × 11 cm
Indigenous Art Collection,
Crown–Indigenous Relations
and Northern Affairs Canada
306209.a.b.
Photo: Lawrence Cook
p. 78

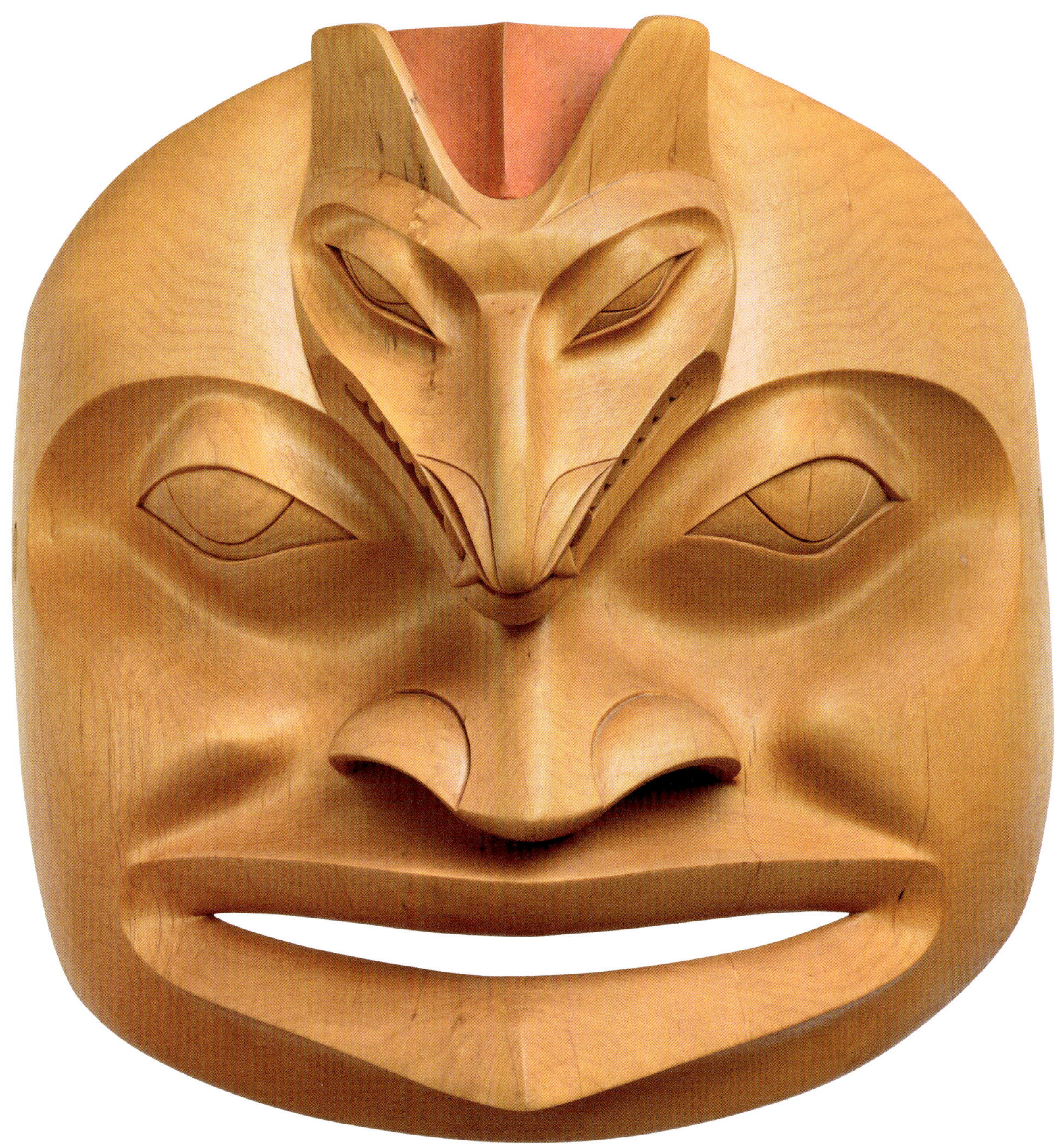

208

FIGURES

p. 18
Unidentified Tlingit /
Tahltan Maker
Dance Apron, late 19th century
leather, goat hair, cedar bark,
cotton, wool, deer hoof
116.8 × 60 cm
National Museum of Natural
History, Washington, DC
E224417, Department of
Anthropology, Smithsonian
Institution

p. 22
Telegraph Creek and
the Stikine River, 1971
Royal BC Museum and Archives,
Victoria
91-9578 / I-11387

p. 29
A Northern BC fish-packing
operation, c. 1930s
Royal BC Museum and Archives,
Victoria
193501-001 / D-08907

p. 29
A Northern BC fish-packing
operation, c. 1930s
Royal BC Museum and Archives,
Victoria
193501-001 / D-08908

p. 29
The North Pacific Cannery
buildings and docks, 1947
Royal BC Museum
and Archives, Victoria
I-28903

p. 64
Ulli Steltzer
Freda Diesing with the
totem pole she and
Josiah Tait carved for the
city of Prince Rupert, 1975
silver gelatin print
27.3 × 32.4 cm
McMichael Canadian Art
Collection Archives, Kleinburg
Gift of Carol A. Heppenstall
ARC-1999.1.2.6
© Estate of Ulli Steltzer

p. 64
Freda Diesing
Old Woman with Labret, 1973
alder, cedar bark, hair,
abalone, paint
20.3 × 22.9 × 15.2 cm,
excluding hair
Audain Art Museum
Collection, Whistler, BC
Purchased with funds
from the Audain Foundation
2020.005
© Estate of Freda Diesing

p. 101
Book cover of *The Legacy:
Tradition and Innovation
in Northwest Coast Indian
Art,* by Peter L. MacNair,
Alan L. Hoover, and Kevin Neary
(Vancouver: Douglas
and McIntyre, 1984)

p. 101
Book cover of *Indian Artists
at Work,* by Ulli Steltzer
(Vancouver: Douglas and
McIntyre, 1977)

p. 110
Dempsey Bob
Human Bear Mask, 1999
red cedar, horsehair,
acrylic paint
152 × 76 × 61 cm
Vancouver International Airport
Photo: Blaine Campbell

p. 110
Dempsey Bob
Bear Human Mask, 1999
red cedar, horsehair,
acrylic paint
213 × 91 × 61 cm
Vancouver International Airport
Photo: Blaine Campbell

p. 124
Dempsey Bob and Linda Bob
Raven and Salmon Blanket,
1985
cloth, wool, button, beads
129 × 135 cm
Royal Ontario Museum, Toronto
987.196.1
Photo © Royal Ontario Museum

APPRECIATION

I would like to acknowledge the traditional lands of the Tsimshian people of Kitselas and Kitsumkalum, BC, and the Tahltan people of Telegraph Creek, BC, Dease Lake, BC, and Iskut, BC. Also, thank you to the Taku River Tlingit of Atlin, BC.

I would like to gratefully acknowledge my parents, Flossie Bob and Johnnie Bob, my grandparents Julia Carlick and Johnny Sinkoots Carlick, and my great-aunts Helen Carlick and Eva Carlick. They believed in my work when I started to carve. Their support and traditional teachings came at a time when I really needed it.

I thank my wife, Margaret (Pie), for all her work and her support of my career. I thank my sister Linda Bob for her help with our dances and especially her work on our regalia. I owe thanks also to my sisters Virginia and Lovetta and my late sister, Merle, and to my brothers Charlie Pete, Tony, Lorgan, and my late brother, Willie, who have been part of our dance group; to my children, David and Tanya; to my grandchildren, Grayson, Roy, Keely, and Nate, and my many nieces and nephews. I would like to thank Mel Bevan for all his support. In particular, I would like to thank my nephews Stan Bevan and Ken McNeil for their help not only in our dance group but also in making large totem poles and panels.

I would like to acknowledge the kindness of my in-laws, Ed and Iris Clark. Ed used to help me to get my wood and supplies. He often told me that his car was not a truck when I filled it with alder wood for carving. He would always drive me to my work sites.

I thank Harold Demetzer for all he has done for me, for the support he has given to our art, for all the pictures he has taken, and for the advice he has given me over the past thirty-nine years. I also want to thank Brenda Crabtree of Emily Carr University of Art and Design and to acknowledge the help I received from the late Bill McLennan of the UBC Museum of Anthropology.

I thank my friends in Aotearoa (New Zealand): Ben and Hine Mamaku and family, Joe Harawira, Darcy Nicholas, Gary Nicholas, Lyonel Grant, June Grant, Sandy Adsett, Rangi Kipa, Tamahou Temara, Alex and Manos Nathan, Derek and Rose Lardelli, Tina Wirihana, and Te Hau o Te Rangi Tutua (Ching Tutua), to name a few.

I am grateful for the guidance of my teachers: Auntie Rosie Dennis, Esther Shea, Walter Harris, Earl Muldon, Victor Mowatt, Vernon Stephens, Kenny Mowatt, Sam Wesley, Phil Janze, Joe Fafard, and Phil Tremblay.

Finally, I want to give a special acknowledgement to the artist Freda Diesing. She was a great teacher and artist, and a good person. She gave me encouragement when I was down, showed me what good art is, and gave me the tools to learn. I think now, What would I have done if I hadn't met her? I was lucky that I was ready to learn when we met. She taught me to work hard and to study our culture and other artists. You have to really do your homework to mature as an artist.

Dempsey Bob

Dempsey Bob: In His Own Voice was developed as a companion volume to the touring exhibition *Wolves: The Art of Dempsey Bob* (2022–24), a partnership between our kindred museums: Audain Art Museum in Whistler, British Columbia, and the McMichael Canadian Art Collection in Kleinburg, Ontario. We have been honoured to share the task of presenting Bob's remarkable career in this exhibition, a collaborative undertaking of the artist, the Audain Art Museum Director and Chief Curator Curtis Collins, and Sarah Milroy, Chief Curator of the McMichael Canadian Art Collection.

This book has its origin in interviews conducted by Milroy over the course of the COVID-19 winter of 2021. Bob's engaging and enlightening stories kept us warm, and we feel privileged now to be able to share them with the public. Both of us are deeply grateful to the artist and to his wife, Margaret (affectionately known as Pie), for their trust, for the countless hours of help they offered as we ironed out the many details of exhibition organization and publication production, and for their boundless hospitality as we made our several journeys north to visit them in their world.

Equinox Gallery in Vancouver provided every kind of encouragement and assistance as we reached out to lenders, helping us to make the most of this opportunity. As well, they guided us to Blaine Campbell, who undertook the exceptional location shooting for this publication in August 2021. Rachel Topham provided the bulk of the documentation of Dempsey Bob's works. We thank both photographers for their unstinting high standards. Our thanks, finally, to the Canada Council for the Arts for their support in seeing this unique project through to fruition.

Sarah Milroy Curtis Collins
Chief Curator Director and Chief Curator
McMichael Canadian Audain Art Museum
Art Collection

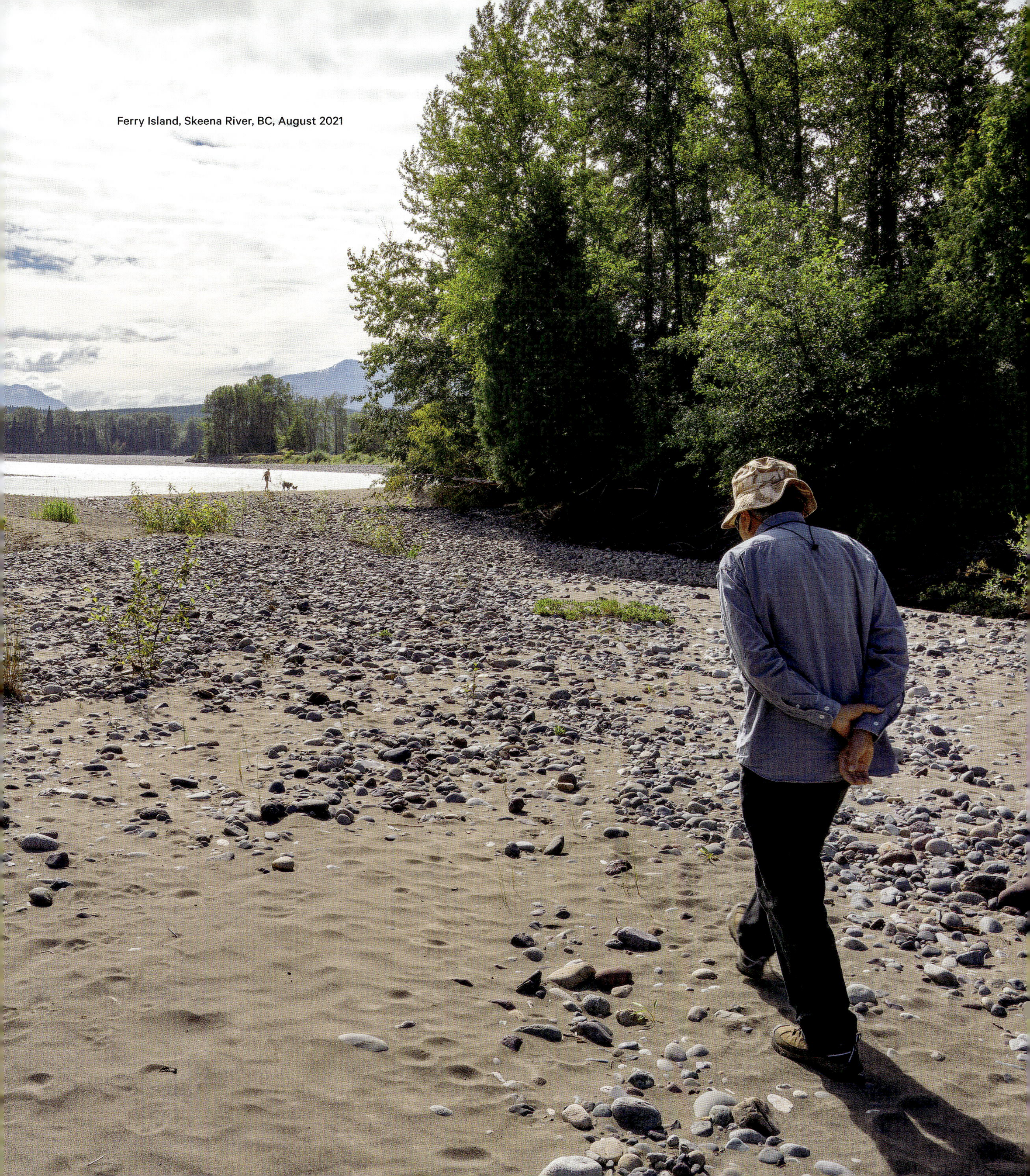

Ferry Island, Skeena River, BC, August 2021

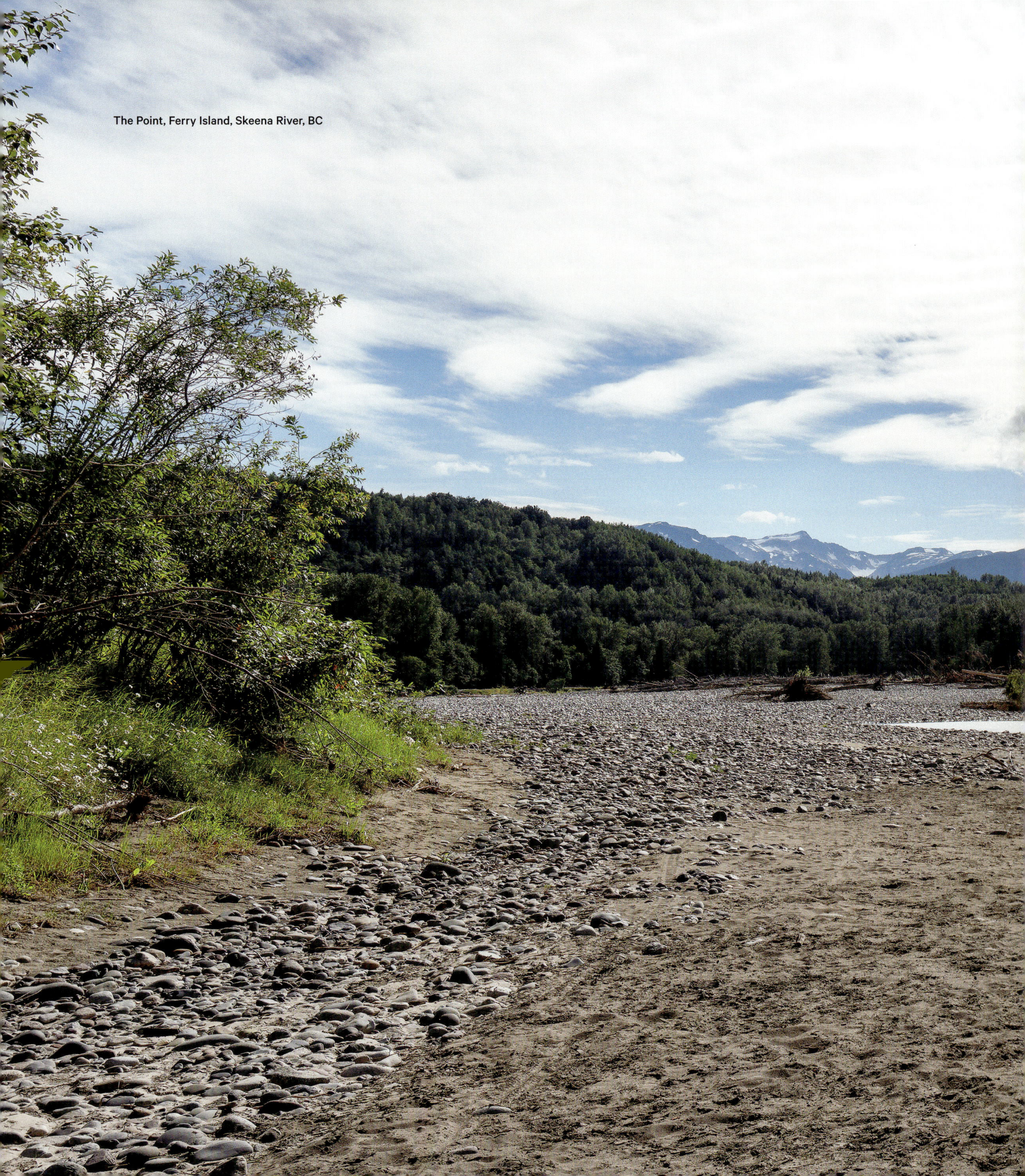

The Point, Ferry Island, Skeena River, BC

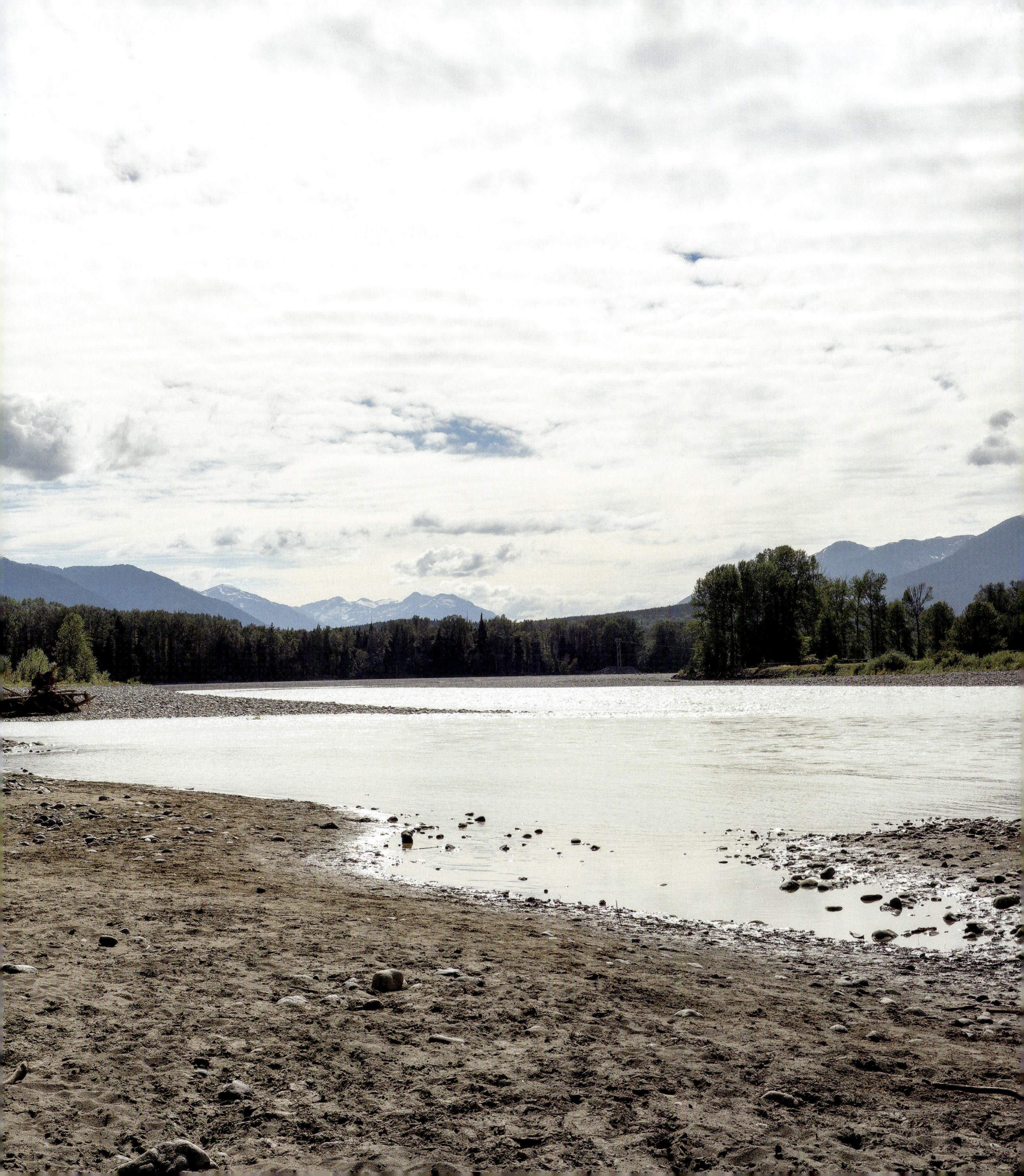

Published on the occasion
of the exhibition *Wolves:
The Art of Dempsey Bob*

Audain Art Museum, Whistler,
BC: April 2–August 14, 2022

McMichael Canadian Art
Collection, Kleinburg, Ontario:
November 19, 2022–April 17,
2023

Montreal Museum of Fine
Arts, Montreal, Quebec:
May 19–September 10, 2023

Kelowna Art Gallery,
Kelowna, BC: October 14, 2023–
February 18, 2024

Curated by Curtis Collins
and Sarah Milroy

Every effort has been made to
credit the copyright holders
and sources. If there are errors
or omissions, please contact
the McMichael Canadian Art
Collection so that corrections
can be made to any subsequent
editions.

All 2021 location photography
by Blaine Campbell

Archival photographs courtesy
of Dempsey and Margaret Bob
unless otherwise indicated

22 23 24 25 26   5 4 3 2 1

Figure 1 Publishing is located
in the traditional and unceded
territory of the xʷməθkʷəy̓əm
(Musqueam), Sḵwx̱wú7mesh
(Squamish), and səl̓ilw̓ətaʔɬ
(Tsleil-Waututh) Peoples.

Cataloguing in Publication
data available from Library
and Archives Canada

ISBN 978-1-77327-161-3 (hbk.)

Printed and bound
in Canada by Friesens

Distributed internationally
by Publishers Group West

Audain Art Museum
Whistler BC Canada
audainartmuseum.com

McMichael Canadian
Art Collection
Kleinburg ON Canada
mcmichael.com

Figure 1 Publishing Inc.
Vancouver BC Canada
figure1publishing.com

We acknowledge the support
of the Canada Council for
the Arts.

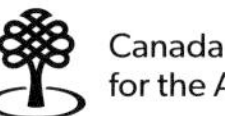

Canada Council   Conseil des arts
for the Arts   du Canada

Executive Editor
Sarah Milroy

Editor
Alison Reid

Publication Coordinator
Teija Smith

Proofreader
Jane Broderick

Researcher / Side Notes
John Geoghegan

Designer
Lauren Wickware

Colour and Retouching
Paul Jerinkitsch

Cover image
Eagle Bear Mask (detail), 1987